Same-Sex Affairs

The publisher gratefully acknowledges the generous contribution to this book provided by the General Endowment Fund of the University of California Press Associates.

Same-Sex Affairs

Constructing and Controlling
Homosexuality in
the Pacific Northwest

Peter Boag

UNIVERSITY OF CALIFORNIA PRESS
Berkeley / Los Angeles / London

University of California Press
Berkeley and Los Angeles, California

University of California Press, Ltd.
London, England

© 2003 by Peter Boag

Library of Congress Cataloging-in-Publication Data

Boag, Peter.
    Same-sex affairs : constructing and controlling homosexuality in the
Pacific Northwest / Peter Boag.
        p.   cm.
    Includes bibliographical references and index.
    ISBN 0-520-23604-1 (alk. paper)
        1. Homosexuality, Male—Northwest, Pacific—History.   2. Migrant
labor—Northwest, Pacific—Sexual behavior—History.   3. Gay men—
Northwest, Pacific—History.   4. Gay men—Oregon—Portland—
History.   I. Title.

HQ76.2.N67 B63   2003

306.76'62'09795—dc21   2002155794

Manufactured in the United States of America

13   12   11   10   09   08   07   06   05   04

10   9   8   7   6   5   4   3   2   1

To my parents

Contents

List of Illustrations   ix

Acknowledgments   xi

Introduction   1

PART ONE: WORKING-CLASS SAME-SEX AFFAIRS

1. Sex on the Road: Migratory Men and Youths in the Pacific
   Northwest's Hinterlands   15

2. Sex in the City: Transient and Working-Class Men and Youths
   in the Urban Northwest   45

PART TWO: MIDDLE-CLASS SAME-SEX AFFAIRS

3. Gay Identity and Community in Early Portland   89

4. From Oscar Wilde to Portland's 1912 Scandal:
   Socially Constructing the Homosexual   125

PART THREE: PROGRESSIVISM AND SAME-SEX AFFAIRS

5. Personality, Politics, and Sex in Portland and the Northwest 157

6. Reforming Homosexuality in the Northwest   185

Epilogue. Same-Sex Affairs in the Pacific Northwest:
1912 and After   217

Notes   223

Bibliography   283

Index   309

Illustrations

Figures

1. Ted Gladden, 1912   16
2. Men and boys at a logging camp in the Pacific Northwest, ca. 1900   23
3. Andrew Dillige, 1913   47
4. Bram Sing, 1915   56
5. Burnside Street in Portland's North End, ca. 1907   64
6. Claude Bronner, 1913   101
7. Portland's YMCA in the early twentieth century   102
8. Corner of Portland's Broadway and Washington Streets, ca. 1910s   113
9. Portland's Lownsdale Park, ca. 1910   114
10. Frank T. Collier, 1910   140
11. Dana Sleeth, ca. 1912   160
12. E. S. J. McAllister, 1910   169
13. A. W. Lafferty, ca. 1910   187
14. Oswald West, 1910   209
15. James Riley (aka Herbert Merithew), 1916   214

Maps

1. The Pacific Northwest   7
2. Portland's North End and central business district, ca. 1912   46

Tables

1. Nativity or race of males, fifteen years of age and older,
   arrested for same-sex sexual activities, Portland, 1870–1921   49
2. Occupations and ages of some white-collar workers
   caught up in Portland's 1912 scandal   99
3. Rates of oral sex among homosexual working-class
   and middle-class men born 1860–1924   120

Acknowledgments

This project has been one of the most challenging and rewarding of my professional career. The challenges came not only from what people might automatically assume are the difficulties facing a scholar studying the history of homosexuality—that is, first uncovering the source material and then using it to make sense of complex human desires and motivations. Surprisingly, some of the greatest obstacles I encountered came from the most unexpected places: individuals and institutions actually charged with the task of promoting intellectual inquiry. During the early years of my research, for example, a very prominent historian tried to dissuade me from my work. Confiding his support of gay people, nonetheless he warned me against pursuing a history of gays and homosexuality. During my research I also came across a librarian at a well-known liberal arts college in Portland who, upon learning the nature of my research, turned downright rude and unhelpful. But the greatest challenge I faced came from the Idaho Board of Education, which attempted to censor my work. I dealt with each of these annoyances in ways that turned out to be successful. In the first case, I simply ignored the advice. In the second case, I ended up staying longer at the library than the uncomfortable librarian would have liked. In the last case, I steadfastly refused to give up my project.

During the course of my work I discovered, however, that far more individuals, institutions, and organizations were willing and even excited to support and help me in my pursuits. Thus, I wish to acknowledge them here. Without the help of the Lesbian and Gay Rights Project of the ACLU and especially Jennifer Middleton, the Idaho Civil Liberties Union and its director Jack Van Valkenburgh, and John Hummel of Boise, this project would have taken many more years to complete than it did. Organizations who lent their moral support during some of my politically trying times include the American Historical Association, the Organization of American Historians, the American Association of University Professors, the Western History Association, the University of Nebraska's Center for Great Plains Studies, and the Gay and Lesbian Archives of the Pacific Northwest. Also supportive were many courageous faculty members, faculty organizations, and students at Idaho State University (ISU), Boise State University, the University of Idaho, and Lewis-Clark State College. In the wake of my difficulties with the state of Idaho, Edwin House, Victor Hjelm, and Karen Skinner, all at ISU, made it possible for me to receive additional time and financial assistance to research and write. I also acknowledge ISU for a sabbatical leave during the spring of 1998 and the ISU Humanities/Social Science Research Committee, which partially funded some of my research through grant FY98–04.

A number of valued colleagues shared resources, time, tips, and thoughts. They include Judith Austin, Hope Benedict, Richard Maxwell Brown, Rita Bybee, Nick Casner, George Chauncey, Tom Cook, Gail Dubrow, John M. Findlay, Jonathan Ned Katz, Matthew Klingle, Larry Knopp, Regina Kunzel, Heather Lee Miller, George Painter, Bill Parmenter, Peggy Pascoe, Martin Ridge, Marcus Robbins, Wilhelm von Rosen, Sandy Schackel, Virginia Scharff, H. Wayne Schow, Alan Virta, and Walter L. Williams. In particular, Robert D. Johnston provided me with a wealth of information on Portland's early-twentieth-century reform history and especially on E. S. J. McAllister (an early Portland resident, reformer, and participant in the city's homosexual subculture). Robert also read portions of my manuscript. Chris Friday not only generously shared with me some of his own research on the Northwest, but he also allowed me to draw on his knowledge about the history of race. Peter D. Sleeth made available to me some very important materials from his grandfather's private papers. I also thank my sponsoring editor at the University of California Press, Monica McCormick, as well as others at the press for their support and help in bringing this book to publication.

Librarians and archivists proved essential to my work. The staff of ISU's interlibrary loan office kept materials streaming in at my request. Diana Banning and Brian Johnson of the wonderfully rich Stanley Parr Archives and Records Center in Portland made me feel more than welcome and afforded me a great deal of research time. My good friend from graduate school M. C. Cuthill at the Oregon Historical Society arranged for me to come in at special times to do research and also helped me track down various sources, references, and photographs. Others at OHS also gave generously of their time, offered encouragement, uncovered valuable tidbits, and opened the reference and manuscript areas to me at special times. They include John Mead, Johnyne M. Wascavage, Chris White, Todd Welch, and Rick Harmon. At the Idaho State Historical Society, Troy Reeves and Gary Bettis helped me uncover obscure sources. Karyl Winn and Linda Long, manuscript librarians at the University of Washington and the University of Oregon respectively, also assisted me during stays at their institutions. The staffs at the Oregon State Archives, the Washington State Archives in Olympia and Ellensburg, and the Multnomah County Archives and Records Center often made their collections accessible in ways beyond the everyday routine. Kath Pennavaria and the staff at the Kinsey Institute for Research in Sex, Gender, and Reproduction at Indiana University were particularly helpful to me during my stay in Bloomington. Carol Elliott of the Provincial Archives of British Columbia made my visit to Victoria one of the most productive periods of my research.

I am especially grateful to Bob Swanson and Ron Hatzenbuehler of the History Department at ISU. They both read my manuscript more than once and helped me clarify thoughts and express better what I wanted to say. Bob also rendered much encouragement and provided a helpful and critical ear when I encountered particular difficulties with my writing. Clayton Koppes and Marianne Keddington-Lang read parts of my manuscript and made valuable suggestions. I am also grateful to various readers that the University of California Press provided. Collectively they helped strengthen my interpretations and writing. Kevin Leonard gave valuable comments on race issues. John Howard took a great deal of time to comb through a later draft of my manuscript. He made extremely important and generous suggestions that have had a vital impact on this book's final form. I also acknowledge my new colleagues who have welcomed me into the History Department at the University of Colorado at Boulder.

Friends and family—indistinguishable from each other—gave me the daily sustenance a scholar needs when involved in a project that seems overwhelming at times. Brent Owens took care of house, garden, and pets while I was away from home for months at a time. Brent also afforded me moral support through the difficulties of research, writing, and political struggles. Pam and Richard LaMar and Ross Bunnell provided me places to stay in the Seattle area while I conducted research there. Ann and Dave Johnson offered me a room in their home in San Francisco while I researched in Berkeley. Paul Rohde and Carroll Noel housed me while I worked in Eugene, and Paul also gave me invaluable assistance when I had questions regarding psychology.

Finally, I am very fortunate to have the parents I do. On the everyday level they provided me with a place to stay, laughter, and companionship while I spent months in Portland. My mother made space in her cramped office for my computer and ever-increasing number of note-filled boxes. But not only did Mom and Dad give me a great deal of support during my research, they have done so in various ways through my life. Going home again to work on this book, then, fulfilled me in ways that words cannot express. I love my parents and it is to them that I dedicate this work.

Introduction

At the turn of the twentieth century, Portland, Oregon—nicknamed the Rose City—was among the most dynamic midsize urban centers in North America. From a population of roughly 46,000 in 1890, Portland blossomed to more than 300,000 inhabitants by 1930. As it grew and matured, the Rose City grappled with problems similar to those that plagued other American urban centers during this remarkable era: municipal corruption, uncertainty over utilities, political discord, urban planning, moral dilemmas, racism, economic turmoil, and so on.[1]

The issue of homosexuality also forcefully came to the attention of Portland's citizenry during these years. In 1912 an indigenous same-sex vice "scandal" exploded on the scene, unlike anything the city had witnessed before. It began precisely at 7:10 in the evening of November 8 when the Rose City's finest booked Benjamin Trout, a nineteen-year-old American-born white male, for a petty crime. During his interrogation, the youthful Trout became so frightened that he not only admitted to the transgression for which he had been apprehended but also made a more "troubling" confession. Trout nervously detailed to authorities the contours of a local homosexual subculture and connected it to others that apparently were flourishing in major cities up and down the West Coast.[2]

After Trout's revelations became front-page news, dozens of men, some of them prominent in local society, fled Portland to escape being implicated in the scandal. Authorities from as far north as Vancouver, British Columbia, and as far south as Los Angeles cooperated in hunting them down. A few of those apprehended resided at Portland's

Young Men's Christian Association. This information ignited a citywide controversy over untoward goings-on at the Y and the possibility of institutional mismanagement. In time it became clear that the association's direct role in the sexual affairs that rocked the Rose City was limited. But initially, salacious accusations and the organization's local prominence—among other things, it was the beneficiary of the largess of Portland's better families—combined to make the Y the lightening rod of the scandal.

Attention soon focused beyond the YMCA. As even more sensational stories unfolded in 1913, so-called Progressive reformers across the Pacific Northwest reacted fiercely. They began efforts, which continued into the 1920s, to strengthen existing laws and to promote new legislation designed to punish more severely those who participated in same-sex affairs. They also worked to channel public discussion of homosexuality and even heterosexuality in ways that they hoped might cause the former phenomenon to disappear. All of the reform activities resulting from the 1912 scandal shaped the region's juridical and cultural responses to same-sex affairs for at least the next half century.

This reformist reaction grew directly out of one of the most significant of the scandal's disclosures: in 1912 the broader Northwest citizenry first learned that a thriving male homosexual community existed in their midst. To be sure, historians have debunked the fallacy of the perpetual newness of homosexuality as "revealed" in early scandals such as the one that occurred in Portland in 1912. They have cautioned that past news and other accounts which imply by the hyperbolic tone of their reports that "homosexuality" had only now appeared should be viewed with great skepticism. Indeed, already in the 1890s newspapers had educated people across the Northwest about the homosexual affairs of Alice Mitchell and Oscar Wilde,[3] and at least since the 1880s the local print media had submitted to readers occasional items about same-sex sexual transgressions in the region.

Still, what the 1912 scandal revealed *was* new in many ways. This was the first general disclosure anywhere in the Northwest of a local multifaceted homosexual underworld. Newspapers and various official publications reported more than just (the usual) names and crimes. Numerous lists of suspects along with spicy details about drag parties, men with female names, secret codes of communication, male brothels, nationwide networks of perverts, and local sites where men met for sex enlivened the region's dailies for weeks. Although similar information had been made available in the tabloidlike coverage of Oscar Wilde in 1895, never before had it been connected to *local* conditions in such a public forum. The particulars uncovered in 1912 were also the first regarding indigenous Northwest same-sex sexual conditions to be reported and commented on regionwide. Moreover, the harsh response to the reports—fierce public, legal, and reformist outrage—suggests that these events were perceived as somehow different. Most of all, the 1912 disclosures were new because of the type of men suspected of same-sex affairs: white and middle-class. In previous years, local news items had occasionally mentioned the same-sex affairs of men who were working class, racial minorities, and immigrants. For this reason, as well as a host of others, the general public seemed blind to the possibility that middle-class white men might also be involved in and even develop an elaborate subculture around homosexuality. The 1912 news of an indigenous homosexual community that middle-class white men created was indeed a revelation, and it helped precipitate a full-blown scandal.

Although it was the greatest of the era's and region's same-sex vice scandals, the 1912 affair was not alone. In the spring of 1913, just weeks after the 1912 scandal erupted, Portland police nabbed several working-class men and youths who had been carrying on relations with each other in the city's North End "vice district." Dubbed the "Greek scandal" because of the national origins of the men involved, it never approached the scale of the middle-class YMCA affair. Whereas the latter received front-page attention for weeks on end, the former was dealt with quietly by the authorities and subsequently buried in legal documents. But the Greek scandal is significant, for it reveals that middle-class anxieties over the sexuality of racial minorities and its threat to social stability boiled beneath the surface of the Progressive-era Northwest.

From the 1880s until the 1912 scandal, the most visible same-sex sexual subculture in the Northwest was one that the region's predominantly transient labor force had forged. Its visibility was due in part to middle-class white society's concerted surveillance of the racially diverse working class for a number of reasons, including the sexual. In fact, by 1900 middle-class Americans generally associated sexual deviancy with the lower classes, new immigrants, and various racial minority groups.[4] In the Northwest, legal authorities and reformers blamed them for "spreading" same-sex sexual "habits," expressed concern over them for transgressing racial boundaries in their sexual practices, and accused them specifically of imperiling white youths and therefore the middle-class family. Portland's Greek scandal involved all these issues and erupted at a time of virulent anti-immigrant and particularly anti-Greek sentiment in the Northwest.

In recent years historians have argued that America's twentieth-century concepts of race and homosexuality emerged in close association with each other.[5] Thus when we study the history of homosexuality, we must also discuss race, as the "Greek" scandal might suggest. But the Northwest and its history make possible a more subtle reading of the racial and sexual connection. In what follows, I argue that while dominant Northwest society harbored appreciable concerns about the sexual practices of working-class, racial minority, and immigrant males, for many years it did not confer upon these men a "sexuality" per se; more precisely, it did not associate them with "*homo*sexuality." Rather, it considered them transgressors of, and serious threats to, behaviors that the white middle and upper classes deemed acceptable.

The construction of the "homosexual" in the Northwest followed a Foucauldian model of the dominant class's deployment of sexuality.[6] That is, only after the white middle and upper classes realized that some of their own men engaged regularly in same-sex sexual activities did the "respectable" classes conceive of "homosexuality" and its existence in their midst. At that point law enforcers and social reformers added "being" homosexual to the reasons they already had for harassing working-class men. This is not to say that earlier public representations in the Northwest of working-class sexuality had no influence on the emergent notion of homosexuality. On the contrary, as homosexuality became located within the middle classes, the dominant social groups also universalized the transient working class's (apparent) penchant for pairing the adult male with the youth. Thus, in the second decade of the twentieth century when white middle-class homosexuality emerged as the broader public representation, it also became identified with what the socially dominant classes viewed as the most outrageous aspect of working-class practices: sexual relations with "children."

Medical, legal, religious, and popular discourses had all played a role for years in socially constructing the "homosexual" in Portland, just as they had elsewhere across North America.[7] But the 1912 scandal and the white middle-class characteristics of those it enveloped proved decisive in the Northwest. It spread from Portland through the region and even across the nation, both along old fault lines and especially along newly forming fissures of class, race, gender, and sexuality. The seismic shift occurring in 1912 helped demolish the old and begin crystallizing in its place a modern public understanding of homosexuality and the homosexual. The surviving documents from Portland's 1912 YMCA and 1913 Greek scandals clearly demonstrate the varied and mutating social concerns over, and perceptions of, homosexuality during the Progressive era. Just as important, they also reveal much about the separate middle-class and working-class male same-sex sexual subcultures that existed in the region at the time. Examined in greater detail in the pages that follow, these are briefly outlined here in the stories of E. S. J. McAllister and Andrew Dillige, two of the dozens of men whom these scandals brought before the Oregon court system.

At the time of his entanglement in the events of 1912, McAllister, who was American-born and white, was forty-three years old, an attorney and social reformer, and a rising personage in the state's Democratic Party. He had recently been living at the posh Alexandria Court on West 20th Street, in one of the most desirable neighborhoods in the city. Dillige, whom authorities apprehended in connection with the Greek scandal, was thirty-five, a Greek immigrant, and a casual laborer.[8] He periodically inhabited the "vice district," Portland's North End. In fact his arrest occurred there at the Fairmount Hotel, a relatively inexpensive establishment known for the prostitutes—male and female—who frequented it. Dillige's Fairmount stood only fourteen blocks from McAllister's Alexandria.

Although the physical space separating McAllister and Dillige was only a few city blocks, their sexual subcultures remained worlds apart. One was decidedly middle-class in nature, the other working-class. The former grew out of complex changes sweeping America at the turn of the century, such as the rapid growth of the city and the emergence of the corporate capitalist system. This same-sex sexual subculture had much in common with the gay subcultures of white and middle-class male homosexuals typically identified with other large North American cities of the time and closely resembled those generally associated with the later twentieth century. In McAllister's world, relations between adult males were common; those between adults and youths were less frequent. Additionally, for these men, including McAllister, the favored sexual practice was oral eroticism.

Andrew Dillige, on the other hand, represented the vast numbers of transient working-class men in turn-of-the-century North America who seasonally divided their time between temporary employment in the countryside and jobless tenancy in larger cities.[9] Within the rural transient culture, participants created same-sex relationships that were based only partly on sexual acts. Typically, and for a variety of reasons, these relationships paired an adult male with a youth or boy. When seeking refuge in the region's cities during industrial downtimes and economic downturns, this couple brought its sexual system to the urban center; there it flourished, although in somewhat altered form. Whether in the city or the countryside, the working class's dominant sexual practices were anal and interfemoral intercourse. In fact, these were the crimes for which authorities arrested Dillige.

In recognizing at least two distinct male homosexual subcultures in the early-twentieth-century Northwest, this study accepts the historiographical principle that both pluralizes sexuality and argues that the heterosexual/homosexual binarism that many people in the Western world today take for granted is in fact a construct of the twentieth century.[10] The general scholarly acknowledgment of plural sexualities has arisen in part from postmodern theories that maintain that race, ethnicity, gender, class, sexuality, and place continuously interact with each other and mark people as bearing multiple identities. Many scholars today prefer to use the term *queer* to encompass the broad range of "transgressive" sexualities that actually exist in addition to just *gay, lesbian,* or *homosexual.* In fact, the term *gay* has today fallen on hard times as it tends to naturalize a single and exclusive identity, that of the twentieth-century urban white gay male.[11] Nonetheless, I do argue in the pages that follow that Portland's modern "gay" male subculture did first emerge within a middle-class and white racial framework, largely separate from the working classes and the racial and ethnic minority communities. I even assert that the gay male subculture of Portland traces its roots to sources that are considerably less socially diverse than those that other scholars have identified for the subculture that developed in North America's megalopolises, notably New York, at this time.[12] In this study I also gravitate toward the tradition that holds that modern "gay" and "lesbian" communities emerged first in cities.[13] But I also consider the dynamics of same-sex desire and activities in the rural setting, investigating how these have significantly influenced sexuality in the city.[14]

It seems appropriate here to let readers know that I identify myself as gay. I come from a middle-/lower-middle-class background and I trace my genealogy to northern and western Europe; my ancestors migrated to North America between 1620 and 1920. I do not, however, claim an association with any gay urban ghetto, either now or in the past, having spent most of my adult life in small-town southeastern Idaho.

In this study I examine the various social and sexual issues outlined above by concentrating on Portland yet drawing on material from other Northwest cities, towns, and rural areas to give a more regional perspective (see map 1). Although such a regional approach to exploring sexuality might seem unconventional, the history of the early-twentieth-century

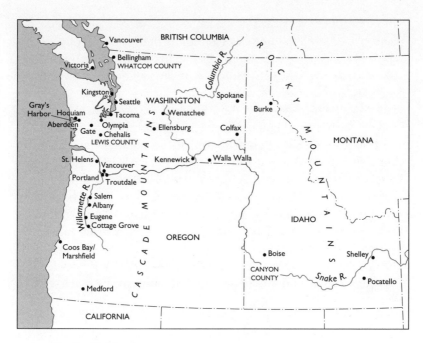

MAP I. The Pacific Northwest

Northwest suggests why it is appropriate.[15] First, the transient laborer culture in which Andrew Dillige participated pervaded the Northwest: the region's economy was rooted in extractive, natural resource–based industries (e.g., logging, fishing, mining, and agriculture), shipping, and construction, all of which encourage a mobile labor force. In fact, this region—composed of Washington, Idaho, Oregon, northern California, western Montana, British Columbia, and southern Alaska—at the time had the highest percentage of transient laborers of any area in North America. Among themselves, the men of this world developed a complex culture that included a system of sex and sexuality revolving around male participants. The men and youths of this world moved seasonally between the region's hinterlands, where they found employment, and the major urban centers, where they wintered over. Thus, to understand urban male-male sexuality in the Northwest more fully, it is imperative to examine events and developments occurring in the region's hinterlands and on its rural byways.

Second, some of the participants in the Northwest's urban, middle-class, gay male world migrated to the city from the region's smaller towns. Many readily moved between urban areas and communicated with others like themselves in the larger cities of Portland, Seattle, and Vancouver. As will become clear, a number of those caught up in Portland's 1912 affair lived in Seattle and Vancouver or had recently migrated from them to the Rose City. Moreover, many sought to escape detection by Portland authorities by fleeing to their former haunts as soon as the crackdown on them began. A third and final reason to pursue a regional study of the history of homosexuality is to make clear that events and social responses to events occurring in the economically and culturally dominant city of Portland had effects that pervaded Oregon and ultimately spread to neighboring states, notably Washington and Idaho, that shared strong historical ties. Although the 1912 scandal briefly took on national dimensions, its impact was far greater locally and regionally. It helped push forward new understandings of sexuality across the Northwest and it significantly influenced legal responses to homosexuality throughout the region. Thus, Portland's story of varied male same-sex sexual systems and social responses to homosexuality is in a sense regional.

These factors help explain why this book focuses on Portland. Another reason is that the Rose City affords more available historical sources regarding same-sex sexuality than do some other major cities of the region, in part because of the 1912 scandal itself. Also, among Northwest cities only Portland sponsored a municipal vice commission during the Progressive era. Although its extant reports provide limited information on homosexuality, they nonetheless offer invaluable insights into early-twentieth-century local views on sexuality in general. And the considerable records of a chapter of the American Social Hygiene Society, very active in Portland at this time, reveal much about period reactions to same-sex sexuality. But most important, Portland has more extensive legal materials than most other cities of the region. For example, detective day books and daily police arrest ledgers still survive; the latter stretch almost uninterrupted from 1870 to 1921.

Obviously this study, like all historical investigations, is necessarily shaped by the sources available, which are always incomplete, inaccurate, and biased, and a reliance on legal records presents particular difficulties. American legal records have historically been prejudiced against the working class, the transient laboring world, and racial minorities. For one thing, those who wrote these documents were not the men they pertain to. Thus what we have are the interpretations of law enforcement officials, court recorders, lawyers, and judges, imparting primarily middle- and upper-class and white perspectives and biases. In addition, sometimes arresting officers and prosecutors lied outright and manufactured incidents and evidence to make a case. Also, such materials usually draw on the testimony of people who would rather not be appearing before the legal system. Reacting to fear, inexperience, personal need, and pressure, those involved in same-sex sexual relationships might well provide conflicting or inaccurate information, which was in turn recorded by officials who filtered it through their own prejudices. An example of a witness's unreliability comes from 1910 when the lawyers of a forty-nine-year-old man appealed their client's conviction for sodomy with a youth to the Washington State Supreme Court. They petitioned for a reversal, on the grounds that the juvenile supplied "uncertain and contradictory" testimony. Even the justices agreed that the witness had made "exaggerated" statements, which he later admitted were untrue.[16]

The problems with legal documents do not end here. This study deals with a variety of same-sex affairs, including those between adults and juveniles. In the early twentieth century, especially among the working classes, such relationships were commonplace and not necessarily coercive.[17] Certainly force was sometimes employed, but also true is that working-class youths and boys regularly sought out men for economic, emotional, and sexual fulfillment. For a variety of reasons, during this period such relations came under closer scrutiny from the legal system and moral reformers. The official records generated in this process necessarily convey the biases of those whom such affairs horrified and who little considered the feelings of the youthful participants. Difficult to distinguish in the sources, then, are the differences between those cases involving coercion and those involving free will: inevitably this study draws from both types in making its conclusions.

A drawback to legal documents from the early twentieth century that has very much shaped this study is their limited purview. When I began this project I had intended to consider women as well as men. Not long after delving into the extant records, however, I realized the impossibility of that plan, as legal documents and newspapers for the era are almost mute on the issue of female same-sex sexuality. Although I did uncover some provocative material on lesbianism and female-to-male transgenderism, its fragmentary nature precluded its equitable treatment here, given the much greater quantity and quality of information that I found pertaining to males. The history of female homosexuality in the Northwest still waits to be told.

Finally, court and police records are problematic in that they make public the very acts that people usually have good reason to conduct in private. Thus, the legal system necessarily subverts the meanings people ascribe to their own sexual activities. Perhaps the truth behind such actions, desires, and emotions will forever elude the historian. Nonetheless, faulty as legal documents might be, they sometimes provide most of the material available to us for reconstructing history. Without them, this book could not have been written.

I have divided *Same-Sex Affairs* into three parts. Part 1, "Working-Class Same-Sex Affairs," considers working-class male-male sexuality as manifest both in the Northwest's hinterlands and in major urban centers. Chapter 1 investigates various types of same-sex affairs that the region's transient workforce participated in, concentrating on the adult-juvenile relationship that seemed to dominate this group's homosexual system. Chapter 2 investigates the adult-juvenile working-class relationship within the city. It also considers the urban middle-class responses to the sexuality of the transient laborer and, more specifically, of the racial minority and immigrant males who largely made up this workforce. It thus explains the era's concerted official attacks on them and on the city spaces that they inhabited and frequented.

Part 2, "Middle-Class Same-Sex Affairs," also comprises two chapters. Chapter 3 investigates the nature of Portland's middle-class gay community as revealed in the documentary evidence of the 1912 affair and of a smaller scandal that occurred in 1928. It also examines the formation of white middle-class gay subculture in the context of the national and even international development of corporate capitalism. That economic system, unlike the entrepreneurial capitalism of an earlier day, enabled young men of the city to earn decent wages from white-collar work and generally to live independently from their biological families. It is around this group, as the 1912 scandal demonstrates, that the first modern and urban gay subculture emerged in Portland and, likely, in other similar midsize North American cities. Chapter 3 concludes by discussing the sexual practices of these gay men and makes the argument, largely ignored in earlier scholarship, that middle-class sexual forms contributed a great deal to America's first sexual revolution. By analyzing various forms of public discourse, chapter 4 examines the emergence of the modern male homosexual and his location within the middle classes. Specifically, it traces changing public representations of homosexuality in the Northwest from the time of the sensationalized coverage of the Oscar Wilde scandal in 1895 through Portland's 1912

scandal. The chapter ends with a brief consideration of the dominant social group's deployment of the homosexual identity among working-
class men.

Part 3, "Progressivism and Same-Sex Affairs," investigates the 1912
scandal's impact on local and regional legal systems, on reformers' activities, and on broader cultural responses to homosexuality. Chapter 5
considers the various ways in which local forces in Oregon and Washington used the news of Portland's 1912 scandal to advance their own
political agendas, focusing on their reactions to certain high-profile local
figures accused of homosexual practices. Chapter 6 looks at the history
of regionwide reform activities regarding homosexuality, arguing that
the greatest efforts to confront and control it were a result of the 1912
scandal. Although earlier crusades specifically attacked the working-
class, racial minority, and immigrant male, the involvement in this case
of middle-class men elicited a far more harsh response from society in
general. Indeed, Portland's 1912 homosexual scandal finally made forced
sterilization—the most radical demand of the early-twentieth-century
eugenics movement, which had been debated for years—more acceptable to a majority in Oregon.

As for E. S. J. McAllister and Andrew Dillige, both were convicted in
1913 for their "crimes." McAllister was sentenced to one to five years in
the state penitentiary, but only after a lengthy trial and the jury's request
that the court treat him leniently. His lawyers successfully appealed his
conviction; the state supreme court overturned it by year's end. Dillige,
with fewer resources available to him, pled guilty to the charge of attempting to commit sodomy, was perfunctorily declared guilty, and
went to prison to serve a sentence of from one to two and a half years.
He earned his parole nearly fifteen months after his arrest. McAllister's
and Dillige's stories, along with the stories of hundreds of other men
who shared similar sexual passions and similar retribution for them in
the early-twentieth-century Pacific Northwest, are recounted in greater
detail in the pages that follow.

PART ONE

Working-Class
Same-Sex Affairs

Sex on the Road

*Migratory Men and Youths in the Pacific
Northwest's Hinterlands*

Ted Gladden (figure 1) was born into a large Minnesota Methodist
family on an early spring day in 1880. His father made a modest living
as a wainwright while his mother stayed home to care for their nine
children. Despite the large family and their limited means, Ted later re-
membered his parents' marriage as a happy one. Tragedy struck in 1897,
however, when Ted's father died. Ted, who had completed seven years
of schooling, remained at home just one more year; apparently after
leaving he found work nearby and helped support his mother until her
death in 1908. She may have succumbed to typhoid, an illness that Ted
himself suffered in that same year. At no time, during his young adult-
hood or later, did Ted show interest in marrying. He seems to have
desired a solitary existence: in the first years of the new century not
only did he leave his mother's home, but he slowly estranged himself
from his siblings and cast aside his family's religion. As an adult, the
midwesterner had a medium frame, stood little more than 5' 5" tall,
weighed about 145 pounds, and had a dark complexion, gray eyes, and
dark brown hair.[1]

Following the demise of his mother, and like so many thousands of
his peers in North America who were able-bodied but had little education, no particular skills, and no strong family ties, Gladden took to the
road. He headed to the Pacific Northwest, where over the next decade
or so he alternated between periods of unemployment in the region's
larger cities and seasonal jobs in the hinterlands. Gladden occasionally
worked as an agricultural laborer and sometimes toiled in paper mills.

FIGURE 1. Ted Gladden, 1912. Gladden's life as a migrant laborer in the Pacific Northwest between 1910 and 1921 was punctuated by stays in prison in both Idaho and Oregon for sexual relations with youths. Idaho State Historical Society, Inmate 1916, Penitentiary Collection.

He quickly entered hobo culture and the life of the transient laborer, which included activities that got him into serious trouble with the law: he engaged in a number of sexual relationships with teenage males. In the spring of 1912, while southwestern Idaho residents were expressing their usual concern over the seasonal migration of "tramps" through their district, authorities arrested Gladden near the small town of Caldwell for sexual relations with a youth. Convicted of sodomy, Gladden spent nearly five years in Boise's penitentiary. After earning his parole, he headed to Oregon. In the fall of 1917 outside Albany, a tiny community eighty miles south of Portland, he had another brush with the law. This time he faced three more charges for sexual activities with youths. Convicted once again of sodomy, Gladden ended up at the state prison in Salem. He served exactly two years, but only a few months after his release, and for unknown reasons, he returned to the penitentiary. One late spring day in 1921 as he toiled away in the prison commissary, Gladden's heart failed him. At the time of his death, he was forty-one.

In a number of respects, Gladden's life and activities typified those of many men living in the Northwest in the late nineteenth and early twentieth centuries. Thus his biography provides a fitting introduction to this chapter and the next, which investigate the region's transient working-class men, their lives, their sexual activities, and the difficulties they faced in a society that held same-sex affairs in contempt. Chapter 1 sketches the causes and pervasiveness of transience in the Northwest and describes the varied attributes of the region's young male population. It then examines the distinctive culture that migrant laborers forged, concentrating on the same-sex sexual system they developed and that so dominated the rural work camps and byways. As Gladden's life attests, the most typical on-the-road same-sex relationship paired an adult with a youth. Those who entered into such couplings did so for a variety of reasons beyond simply a desire for sex; factors tied to gender, emotion, isolation, and survival also played significant roles. While adult-youth relationships dominated the physical expression of sexuality, other same-sex configurations did exist. Indeed, as we will see, the insular and transient nature of the region's work culture seems to have facilitated a variety of sexual relations between adult males as well. The chapter closes with a brief consideration of the physical geography of transients' same-sex sexual desires and activities in the rural Northwest, pointing out the need for increased historical attention to the conditions affecting homosexuality in nonurban settings.

The Pacific Northwest and the Migrant Laborer, 1880s–1930s

The last couple of decades of the nineteenth century and the first two or three of the twentieth are sometimes called the "golden years" or "heyday" of the casual worker. The economy at the time afforded an abundance of low-skill, seasonal, and labor-intensive jobs that still had not felt the full effects of mechanization.[2] In the West generally and the Northwest specifically, precisely because their economies were rooted in natural resources and agriculture, the demand was particularly high for seasonal workers with strong arms and sturdy backs.

The transformation of the Northwest from sleepy frontier into a center of extractive industries and a mecca for transient laborers largely occurred after 1880, caused primarily by the extension of transcontinental railroads to the region. Some railroads soon inaugurated their own shipping lines that linked Northwest ports more systematically to Asia, supplementing an already-existing, though hitherto limited, maritime trade. The steel road and international shipping stimulated exploitation of the region's natural and agricultural resources, many of which reached the pinnacle of their importance in the Northwest's overall economy between 1880 and 1930. But one industry dominated all others. Between 1889 and 1929, except when shipbuilding briefly surged during World War I, the lumber industry provided more than 50 percent of the manufacturing jobs in the region.[3]

This great economic expansion necessarily induced phenomenal population growth. In 1880 the combined population of Oregon, Washington, Idaho, and British Columbia neared 332,000. Fifty years later the population was more than ten times that. Because the region's labor-intensive jobs attracted men, they greatly outnumbered women. In 1890 there were 15.5 males for every female in the Northwest. Twenty years later the disparity remained high, at 14.1 to 1.[4] With males more numerous than females, proportionally more bachelors could be found in the Northwest than elsewhere in the country. In 1890, 41 percent of males above the age of fifteen in the Northwest were married, whereas the figure in the country as a whole was 54 percent. In the same year, more than 74 percent of Northwest laborers were bachelors, but in longer-settled East Coast locations far fewer were single—in Massachusetts, for example, only about 44 percent.[5]

The Northwest's adult male population was also youthful, as the work available demanded strength and agility. In 1890 close to 57 percent of the region's males fell between the ages of fifteen and forty-four, while for the country as a whole the figure stood at about 47 percent. Twenty years later the disparity, though smaller, still remained: about 53 percent in that age range in the Northwest, compared with 49 percent for the United States as a whole.[6]

Moreover, the men of the Northwest with whom Ted Gladden traveled and labored were ethnically and racially diverse. American-born white males like Gladden made up the largest group of transient laborers, but African Americans, Native Americans, Latin Americans, Pacific Islanders, and men who hailed from a wide variety of Asian and European countries also found work in the Northwest. In 1910 the residents of Portland's Third Ward, the neighborhood in the city most dominated by transients, were 79 percent male. The population was 44 percent Asian, African American, Native American, and, to use the census's designation, "foreign-born white."[7]

Migration patterns, gender expectations, work availability, Old World expectations, and U.S. immigration restrictions favored males in the late nineteenth century, and as their numbers vastly increased, the preponderance of single men in the Northwest grew. In Washington State in 1910, bachelors accounted for nearly two-thirds of the 118,211 Native American, African American, Chinese, Japanese, and "foreign-born white" males. The Chinese provide the classic case of bachelor society in the American West during the era, but other migrant groups, such as South Asians and Greeks, were also primarily male and single.

The California gold rush of 1849 first drew large numbers of male Chinese laborers to the West; South Asians and Greeks began arriving somewhat later in the century. The Chinese dispersed as successive gold rushes took them across the western territories. Greek men, too, labored throughout the West, especially in mining, fishing, and railroad construction, but South Asians were generally confined to logging and agriculture on the Pacific Coast. Job potential, culture, and American laws limited the number of female migrants in these groups. For example, between 1863 and 1910 women never represented more than 5 percent of the total Chinese population in Idaho's Boise Basin mining district. The lack of Asian women and racial animosities and miscegenation laws prevented many Chinese and Indian men from marrying in the Northwest. By 1910, of the 5,369 Chinese males ages fifteen and older residing in Portland, 75 percent were single. Although Asian Indian men in California often married Mexican American women, the absence of the latter in the Northwest, as well as the same barriers that the Chinese faced, contributed to the creation of a South Asian bachelor society on the shores of the North Pacific.[8]

Perhaps 95 percent of all Greek migrants to America between 1899 and 1910 were male. As with the South Asians and Chinese, racist sentiments thwarted Greek men from mixing with American-born white women. But certain features of their own culture also discouraged them from developing permanent relationships with women in the United States. Because marriage to a woman outside of the Greek community might sever or restrict connections with that community, some immigrant men were dissuaded from taking such a step. In addition, sons in Greek families generally did not marry until after their sisters. The burden fell in part on the boys to ensure that the girls had an adequate dowry to attract a husband. Many Greek men migrated to America in order to earn the trousseau that their sisters needed. Therefore, marriage for them was out of the question, at least until their family had been provided for. Such traditions affected Greek men in the Northwest. For example, Haralambous (Harry) Kambouris, who worked throughout the region, ignored Greek custom when he married before his sisters did so in Greece. This action, which according to his son demonstrated "unusual independence," enraged Harry's mother back home.[9]

Regardless of where they came from, the workers in the turn-of-the-century Northwest were habituated to mobility. The very act of migrating to the region, repeated individually thousands of times, endowed the young men with a common experience of transience before they had even arrived in the Northwest. Moreover, many had long pursued a peripatetic life, following certain natural resource–based industries from one part of the country (or, sometimes, the world) to the next as local supplies repeatedly ran out. Stewart Holbrook, a chronicler of the Northwest, depicted this scenario as he outlined the history of the American logging industry. He described how men left the cut-over Great Lakes region in the latter 1800s and made "the ghastly trip across [the Great] plains where there weren't even stumps to look at, and struck for the Pacific Northwest and California; many of them moved direct to British Columbia. The others went to the Deep South [pineries], from whence they would have to move again, and move West, too[.]"[10]

Economic conditions also contributed to worker transience. Although the Northwest economy enjoyed an overall robustness throughout this era, external and sometimes random forces produced instability. Outside control of transportation and resources, regional dependence on nonindigenous sources for investment capital, periodic overproduction as a result of competition and abundance, and especially the Northwest's reliance on distant rather than local markets all contributed to extreme volatility in the region's economy. Between the 1880s and the 1930s, recessions and depressions descended on the Northwest with a regularity paralleled only by the region's rains. During such times unemployment skyrocketed, increasing the number of men on the road.[11]

The seasonal character of the natural resource–based trades also caused transience among workers. On the one hand, planting, harvesting, logging, mining, fishing, and railroad construction all slowed or ceased operations in the wet, cool, and stormy winter months, only to start up again in the spring and summer. On the other hand, the period extending from early autumn until early spring coincided with the peak of international shipping. Oceangoing vessels usually anchored for a couple of months at a time in North Pacific harbors while waiting for their loading to be completed. To avoid the expense of feeding and caring for sailors, shipping companies dumped their men and boys into the region to mix and mingle with the unemployed seasonal workers, thereby periodically increasing the number of unattached males in coastal portions of the Northwest.[12] Other factors contributing to the workforce's mobile nature included easy accessibility to transportation—notably the expanding network of railroads, enabling one to hitch a ride on a freight train for nothing. Because extractive industries dominated, the jobs they provided required strong backs and arms and not a great deal of technical skill. Therefore, especially during boom times, a laborer found it relatively easy when dissatisfied with one job to quickly find work in another.[13]

Between the 1880s and 1930s, transience typified labor in the Northwest.[14] Popular opinion, largely shaped by prejudice, has generally held the transient life to be lonely and dissipated. In reality, transients created a complex society among themselves replete with rules, an etiquette, a distinct language, a number of codes, a compendium of songs and ballads, an informal news network, a host of social and political organizations, and relationships that endured in various ways. Their migratory society also maintained a social hierarchy. At the top stood the "hobo," who saw himself as the true migratory worker. Below him perched the "tramp," an itinerant nonworker. On the periphery of this world operated the "yegg" and the "bum," both of whose reputations among other transients were less than acceptable. The yegg lived by means of thievery. He alternately traveled or stayed put in larger cities' transient-occupied neighborhoods, which were known as "main stems." Nels Anderson, an observer of and participant in migratory life in the 1910s and 1920s, claimed that this character's "laziness" precluded his inclusion in the good "tramp" category. Further below the yegg came the "bum," a one-time worker who because of age, injury, or other forms of displacement generally took up residence on the main stem and there sustained existence through begging.[15] The men and the youths of this transient culture also developed a multilayered sexual and gender system and integrated it into other aspects of migratory life.

A Sexual Geography of the Road

When twenty-nine-year-old Ted Gladden left his Minnesota home for a life on the roads of the Pacific Northwest in 1909, he entered into a largely male social world that traced its roots deep into history. At various times and places this transient world has countenanced and even promoted sexual relations between its participants. The historian B. R. Burg found that for the bands of male vagrants roving about England in the seventeenth and eighteenth centuries, a lack of access to women led to increased same-sex sexual activity.[16] So common did homosexual practices become that the migrants considered such intimacies to be ordinary, while the broader society viewed them as exotic transgressions. A similar situation existed in the turn-of-the-twentieth-century Northwest, though it is impossible to determine how many migrants engaged in such sexual relations. One transient queried in 1923 asserted that "all" men and boys on the road "do it." In contrast, Josiah Flynt, an observer of and participant in migratory life in the 1880s and 1890s, estimated that about one in ten men practiced "unnatural intercourse."[17]

There is evidence that some groups of migratory workers at specific times and in particular locations entered into homosexual relationships at relatively high rates. In his monumental 1948 survey of sexual behavior in the human male, Alfred Kinsey reported that the highest frequency of homosexual activity in the United States occurred in the most remote locations, such as logging, mining, and ranching communities. Donald Roy undertook a more modest investigation of Seattle's Hooverville in 1934. Most of its six hundred male inhabitants, Roy discovered, had backgrounds in the extractive industries such as those mentioned in Kinsey's study. Roy claimed from his various experiences with these men that among them "homosexuality is undoubtedly rampant."[18]

Early-twentieth-century studies and anecdotal evidence confirm that homosexual activities were common in and around logging districts on the North Pacific coast. A 1914 investigation of a northern California camp determined that "sex perversion within the entire group is as developed and recognized as the well known similar practices in prisons and reformatories."[19] Various regional sources attest that, as in the case of Ted Gladden, same-sex relationships in logging and milling areas often paired an adult with a youth or even a boy (figure 2). For example, Ernest Seavy, a thirty-three-year-old lumber mill worker originally from Wisconsin but working in Whatcom County, Washington, landed in prison in 1911 on charges of sodomizing an eleven-year-old boy. According to legal documents, this was only one of a series of such affairs that Seavy had engaged in. Similarly, in 1919 in the forested district east of Portland, the forty-three-year-old logger Charles Brown hired teenage boys to help him clear land and then "after a few days would insist that they have sodomist relations with him."[20] In mining camps and in bustling seaports as well, the typical scenario was an adult having sex with a youth. In 1916, witnesses "caught in the act" a forty-one-year-old Oregon miner with a fourteen-year-old youth. In Victoria in 1907, a forty-five-year-old Scottish seaman faced charges of gross indecency with a thirteen-year-old whom records described as "incorrigible"; the boy previously had affairs with several other men in the port.[21]

Observers were in no more agreement about the sexualities that one could find on the road than about the number of peripatetic laborers involved in same-sex acts. Josiah Flynt and Nels Anderson, the two most

FIGURE 2. Men and boys at a logging camp in the Pacific Northwest, ca. 1900. Logging and other extractive industries provided thousands of jobs for men and youths at the close of the nineteenth and beginning of the twentieth centuries. At work camps, sexual contacts between male workers of all ages were common. Oregon Historical Society, #OrHi 66880.

prominent and prolific turn-of-the-century investigators of transient men, maintained that the migrants who had relations with each other could be divided into three categories. One consisted of transients who temporarily substituted males for females simply because the latter were scarce, although Flynt believed that few such individuals existed. In another grouping, Flynt included "sexual inverts." Anderson proposed a third category, "congenital" homosexuals.[22] Moreover, Flynt and Anderson were not always precise about whom they would include in or exclude from these groups. This uncertainly in part reflected the tremendous changes that notions about sexuality were undergoing when Anderson and Flynt were making their judgments. It also arose because the men Flynt and Anderson studied in fact harbored an assortment of desires.

By 1900, when Flynt came to write that some migrants were "sexual inverts," the larger society and particularly the medical profession had defined the invert as a female in a male's body or a male in a female's body. Sexual desire was not then distinguished from gender—the latter, as Judith Butler has so eloquently explained, being "the repeated stylization of the body, a set of repeated acts within a highly rigid regulatory frame that congeal over time to produce the appearance of substance, of a natural sort of being."[23] At the time Flynt labored to understand migrant sexuality, only a "female," it was believed, could desire a "male," and vice versa. If a biological male somehow sexually desired a man, then he was really innately a female. A male sexual invert was thus understood as necessarily evincing a variety of particularly "effeminate" gender characteristics. It was taken for granted that a male invert would be sexually attracted to noninverts of his own sex, but that was only one of many of his "feminine" traits. The working class also felt that a male who appeared and acted like a "man" and performed traditionally "male" social and cultural roles, even if he did have sex with another male, was not a sexual invert (although he would undoubtedly be considered a criminal).[24]

During this same period, however, interrelated cultural and scientific developments were leading to the belief that the biological sex was more important than the gender of one's preferred sexual partner in "determining" one's sexuality. That is, a "homosexual" was now increasingly defined by his sex acts and not by his gender stylization. The British sexologist Henry Havelock Ellis and the Austrian psychoanalyst Sigmund Freud helped lead the way in this new sexual formulation.[25] Although the term *homosexual* had been around since 1869, from its inception medical experts had typically associated it with sexual inversion. For example, G. Frank Lydston, a Chicago physician, wrote in 1904 that inverts are "characterized by effeminacy of voice, dress, and manner. In a general way, their physique is apt to be inferior...although exceptions to this rule are numerous. Sexual perversion, and more particularly inversion—i.e., homosexuality, or sexual predilection for the same sex, is more frequent in the male[.]"[26]

Paradoxically, Flynt's use of "sexual inversion" in the 1890s when identifying tramps who engaged in "unnatural intercourse" was prescient, in that he also claimed that these tramps were "abnormally masculine" (i.e., especially masculine). In reporting what he saw on the road, Flynt took the definition of sexual inversion out of its traditional context and aligned it with the emerging understanding of homosexuality as a sexual phenomenon separate from gender. Flynt also differentiated such particularly masculine "inverts" from the hoboes on the road who chose to have sex with other males only because of an absence of females. Unfortunately, Flynt did not explain exactly how he made such a distinction. He simply related one interviewee's response when asked why he had sex with other males: "Cause there ain't women enough. If I can't get them I've got to have the other."[27]

As this notion took form at the turn of the twentieth century, homosexuality also became a fixed identity. It is thus not surprising that when Nels Anderson wrote of transient laborers in the 1920s, he drew on the work of Havelock Ellis and declared some migrants to be "congenital" homosexuals. Yet Anderson did not completely jettison the older conception of sexual inversion, for he stated that most of the congenital homosexuals on the road were "men who had developed from childhood feminine traits and tastes, and they may be regarded as predisposed to homosexuality."[28] It is true that Anderson may have been speaking here of individuals who in a later era might have identified themselves as transgendered or transsexual, for one of the problems with the notions of homosexuality then emerging is that they collapsed these varied identities.[29] As we will see, however, transgendered and transsexual males had a limited presence on the road—as Anderson himself indicates (though he also contradictorily asserts that effeminate males made up "most" of the homosexuals he discovered). A further complication is that Anderson, like Flynt, fails to make clear how he differentiated the masculine homosexuals from the apparently heterosexual males who turned to same-sex acts only because no women were available. In addition, it is hard to understand why Anderson's congenital homosexuals tended to be effeminate while Flynt's sexual inverts inclined toward masculinity. These variations and apparent discrepancies in the historical record do not just demonstrate past difficulties in categorizing sexualities; they also caution against such an endeavor today.[30] Certainly, the writings of Flynt and Anderson evince such fluctuating conceptions of and meanings for same-sex sexuality that great care must be exercised when using these men's descriptions to analyze the sexuality of the men on the road.

Further complicating this picture are the perspectives of the transient men and youths themselves. Of all the sexual relationships that occurred on the road, observers of the late 1800s and early 1900s commented almost exclusively on the very type for which Ted Gladden had been jailed: the coupling between an older and a younger male. Male migrants often referred to the adult as a "wolf" or a "jocker." Although the origins of these terms are uncertain, the juxtaposition of wolf and "lamb" (the boy in the relationship) suggests a certain level of intimidation—and descriptions of the wolf in the early twentieth century did indeed paint him as a rather coercive figure (as discussed in more detail below). *Jocker*, on the other hand, derives from a term for penis; and in the relationship between the transient adult male and youth, the former used his penis in sexual relations while the latter generally did not. The wolf and jocker could be men who substituted boys for women because of their circumstances. Or they could be men who, according to Josiah Flynt, truly had a "passion" for boys. For many years, those in this migratory society did not differentiate between the two. By the early 1920s, however, members of the working class and in particular of the penitentiary population increasingly applied the term *wolf* specifically to the otherwise masculine man who performed traditionally masculine roles but apparently preferred to have sex with males rather than females.[31] The wolf differed categorically from transgendered males. According to the 1920s reformer Thomas Mott Osborne, wolves "by nature or practice prefer unnatural to...natural vice." Osborne was somewhat vague on the difference between "unnatural" and "natural" vice, implying that there might have existed a hierarchy of deviance with the wolf at its lowest rung. He also pointed out that the wolf should be seen as different from the effeminate male who submitted to sex with other men. This suggested, furthermore, that the "effeminate male," because of his gender and therefore identity, was somewhat better than the wolf because his effeminacy coincided with his inclinations, thereby rendering his vice "natural." At the same time, Osborne distinguished the wolf from the "ordinary men" who will avail themselves of other males only when deprived of women.[32]

The younger male in sexual relationships on the road also was variously labeled, most commonly "punk," "prushun," and "lamb." In the turn-of-the-century West, *punk* typically referred to any young male. Thus in the logging culture laboring youths and boys were called punks without any particular sexual connotation being conveyed. One of the jobs in logging camps, for instance, entailed operating whistles that marked time for a variety of social and work activities; the boy with that task was called a "whistle punk." On the road, however, a punk was a boy who submitted to the receptive role in sex with men. The origins of *prushun* is even less clear. Gershon Legman, who collected a glossary of such terms in 1941, claimed that it was a corruption of "prussian," which in a slightly earlier time referred to the inserter rather than the receptive partner in male sex. Exact definitions aside, accounts of the late nineteenth and early twentieth centuries lead us to conclude that the adult-youth configuration was the dominant sexual relationship in transient society. Such an intergenerational pairing, with a mixture of "homosexuals" and "heterosexuals" as represented in the jocker-punk and wolf-lamb relationships, further undermines a neat categorization of male sexuality on the road by either the historian or the eyewitness.[33] Because the sexuality of the adult-youth relationship remains obscure, but also because it influenced the dynamics of other male homosexual systems in the Northwest at the beginning of the twentieth century, it is imperative that we examine it more thoroughly.

At the beginning of the jocker-punk relationship, the younger male was commonly in the middle of adolescence.[34] The adult male, if we take at face value contemporary reports, preferred sexual relations with teenage boys to those with men. Observers of the time believed that men who might under other social circumstances be attracted to females found that boys became desirable because they lacked certain masculine characteristics of older males. Apparently the "maleness" of the adult and the "femaleness" of the boy played such a critical role in some of these relationships that the former called the latter by feminine names or endearments. Nels Anderson asserted that jockers might sometimes dub their boys "Mabel," "Dollie," "Susan," "sweetie," or "the old lady," and even apply the prefix "Miss" to their names. Donald Roy discovered one inhabitant of Seattle's 1930s Hooverville who referred to a youthful sex partner as his "wife."[35]

Sometimes transient society used the term *fairy* to refer to punks. But the punk should not be confused with the fairy more typical of the era's larger urban centers. The historian George Chauncey, who has extensively studied the fairy in his history of gay New York, points out that the fairy stood at the center of the male sexual system of the period and "influenced the culture and self-understanding of *all* sexually active men."[36] He argues that the fairy served as the dominant public representation of the homosexual in the late 1800s and early 1900s. Consequently, many boys and men, especially those of the working classes, who had vague feelings of sexual and gender difference modeled themselves on this figure—embracing the fairy's carriage, demeanor, physical appearance, and clothing. Furthermore, the fairy adopted the traditionally "female" role (i.e., the receptive or insertee position) in sexual encounters (both oral and anal) with men. At the same time, because broader working-class society interpreted the fairy as more female than male (i.e., as a sexual invert), he did not pose much of a threat to other "normal" men. It was possible, then, for "normal" men to have sex with fairies—and perhaps even with other men—as long as they took the traditionally "masculine" sexual role of inserter. Because the role of inserter was so imperative to maintaining a reputation as a "normal" man, many observers in the first part of the twentieth century concluded that "homosexuals" (by which they meant effeminate males) did not take on this role in sexual encounters. As late as 1941, Gershon Legman wrote that the inserter role in anal intercourse "is only infrequently practiced by male homosexuals, and is more often a matter of heterosexual vice or convenience, as in prisons or on ships or among tramps and hoboes. On the other hand, passive pedication [anal sex in the receptive role] is, after fellation, the most common practice of homosexual men[.]" In any case, the centrality of the fairy to the male sexual world leads Chauncey to conclude that this figure "offers a key to the cultural archaeology of all male sexual practices and mentalities in this era and the configuration of sex, gender, and sexuality in the early twentieth century."[37]

This fairy and the punk differed in a number of ways. In sexual relations the punk did take the receptive role, but seldom performed fellation. The vast majority of legal documents pertaining to the transient world report anal and interfemoral coitus (rubbing the penis between one's partner's thighs), with the older man performing the inserter role. This was the case in the example of Ted Gladden. When he was arrested in Albany, Oregon, officials charged him with having "attempted copulation between thighs and buttocks" of a number of adolescent boys.[38]

Both jockers and punks seemed averse to oral eroticism, perhaps reflecting their class background in their preferences. For the first half of the twentieth century, Alfred Kinsey found that males of the working class were considerably less likely than males of the upper classes to engage in petting, foreplay, and oral stimulation in their sexual encounters. Because in their own experience oral sex played a limited role, the adult in the sex couple of the road probably preferred anal or interfemoral intercourse to fellation with youths. Moreover, the same class-related factors probably made the youth less inclined to performing oral sex on the adult even if he were pressured to do so. Kinsey's data do reveal that young males from the lower social strata engaged in fellation less frequently than did youths from the middle class.[39]

These class-related factors might at first glance seem to explain why anal and interfemoral intercourse dominated the jocker-punk sexual relationship. But the working-class fairy, whom the same class-related factors also undoubtedly influenced, more willingly performed oral sex than did the punk. This contradiction may be more apparent than real. Because the fairy had vague feelings of (trans)gender difference, he might very well have been more open to, and even desirous of, performing the more taboo receptive sex role in fellation. The punk, however, did not necessarily enter into sexual relations with men because of same-sex desire nor because of feelings of gender difference. The punk and the fairy were distinct characters in the working-class world. Desire, background, and other social factors considered below shaped their sexuality differently and also seem to have influenced the type of sexual intercourse that adult working-class males engaged in.

We must also take into account that the punk, though he performed a receptive role in sexual relations with men, did not necessarily act effeminately, as did the fairy. While Josiah Flynt asserted that some of the punks he came across seemed to him "uncommonly feminine," this was by no means the rule. Furthermore, Maury Graham, a hobo who spent time on the road in Idaho, related in his autobiography a story about a man in a boxcar who grabbed his crotch and demanded, "Boy, you wanna have some fun?" At the time, Graham was fifteen, about the average age of a punk, but somewhat more than 125 pounds and a champion wrestler. His size, strength, and skill hardly marked him as "effeminate." Nonetheless, Graham found that a number of men approached him for sexual relations.[40] Moreover, unlike the fairy who performed a specified role and faced permanent stigmatization in the working-class urban environment, the punk could change his role in sexual relations within a relatively short span of time. Both Flynt and Anderson explained that punks commonly became jockers one day, sometimes when still relatively youthful. Young males taking the inserter role with those even younger than themselves did indeed exist on the road. Take, for example, the story of the drifter Heber DeLong, whom authorities arrested on a mid-December day in 1906 in the small eastern Idaho community of Shelley. A "bunch of boys," according to a local newspaper, divulged to the sheriff that DeLong, who had been in town for a short time, committed sodomy on them a number of times. According to prison records, DeLong was only nineteen, stood 5' $\frac{1}{2}$" tall, and weighed 120 pounds. Although we do not know if DeLong's previous sexual history included a period as a punk, nonetheless his example demonstrates that relatively youthful males also performed the jocker role.[41]

With all this in mind, we should not be surprised to discover that transient males distinguished between the punk and the fairy. Moreover, they favored the former over the latter. Anderson commented that the city's transgendered youths, whom he described as "lithe, lean youths with rouged lips," only occasionally wandered onto the main stem and sometimes tried "their fortunes at being hobos for a while." Some members of the broader transient society, notably the "yegg" and the "bum," did like to see the fairy come around. But the rank and file of the transient world did not necessarily share the opinion of the bum and yegg, two characters who occupied the very outskirts of migratory society. Transient laborers, Anderson suggests, did not generally care for the fairy. In fact, the sociologist claimed that transgendered males "do not belong" in the migratory world at all. By definition, however, the punk did.[42]

In addition, when transgendered males did take to the road, they seemed generally to have stuck to themselves. One man, known only by the name "Vilma," described himself and a few of those he ran with in 1930s Seattle as "queens." In his colorful depiction of an occasional life on the road during the Great Depression, he suggested a certain clannishness that separated him and his cohorts from other migratory men. Vilma recalled,

Some of the Seattle queens would bunch up and travel to San Francisco in boxcars and stay for three or four months. Then the queens in San Francisco would come up and stay in Seattle for three or four months. . . . Sometimes we'd meet each other in between the cities on the rails. That was a wild time, lots of hot stories and carrying on and we shared our food over a campfire along the tracks. We covered ourselves with newspapers at night. We traveled the rails as males but I heard about queens who traveled the rails in drag.[43]

A separation between the typical transient laborer and transgendered males like Vilma is also depicted in our scant documentation from the 1920s of a male sex trade on the West Coast.[44] Various salmon-canning companies operating in the North Pacific annually recruited laborers from the West Coast for seasonal work. Apparently understanding the sexual appetites of these workers who lacked access to women, as well as having an eye on the money to be earned, some transgendered male sex workers also migrated to northern shores. A report from 1923 claimed that men "dressed in silks and women's clothes" passed from one cannery to the next "for the sole purpose" of prostitution. More typically, cannery foremen enlisted sex workers. Aboard ship en route to the north and in Alaska, company foremen might hire them out for mock marriages and sexual relations with other men, usually splitting the profits with the sex workers. Foremen also realized that to win these sex workers' affections, cannery employees would spend additional money on candy, cigarettes, and liquor at company-owned stores. Because the Alaskan canning industry was isolated and because the sex workers apparently hired on or traveled together specifically to make money, they can be seen as somewhat outside the mainstream of transient society. But it should also be noted, as the same reports cited here relate, that other male sex workers who were not transgendered made their way to northern shores as well.[45]

The punk and the fairy were distinct characters, who performed slightly different sexual roles. If on the road, the transgendered male generally remained apart from other transients. Most significantly, he was not directly linked to on-the-road culture except in unusual cases, such as being hired for sex in the Alaska salmon cannery trade. Not surprisingly, because the transgendered male was not a regular and integral part of that world, transients generally derided him, although they might take advantage of him in certain circumstances. In contrast, transient society embraced the punk. The punk also differed from the fairy because as part of the transient culture he had many roles to play beyond the sexual. A brief investigation of these roles enlightens us even more as to the culture, gender system, and sexuality of working-class men (transient and otherwise) in the Northwest and North America more generally at this time.

Part of the jocker-punk relationship grew out of domestic considerations. Among the tasks required of the youth were building fires, doing laundry, sewing, running errands, and even shaving the jocker. It makes sense that a boy away from home for the first time and fresh to life on the road would more willingly accede to perform these duties than would an older, more self-assured individual. As long as the youth carried out his chores, the relationship progressed smoothly. Anderson noted that a partnership between man and boy generally ended when the latter attained a level of "confidence in his own ability"—a scenario illustrated dramatically in a story Donald Roy uncovered while surveying men in Seattle's Hooverville in 1934. In one instance, a punk refused to perform certain "household duties." After a number of months of being nagged, while the shack accumulated all sorts of "dirt and rubbish," the "boy turned upon his . . . 'husband' with a revolver and shot him." Although the adult survived, the shooting effectively put a stop to the affair.[46] The adult's control over the youth spilled over into certain economic aspects of the migratory world. The tramp and the yegg often required their punks to beg and steal. One hobo reported that a wolf he met in eastern Washington maintained that his boy "was the best little bum y'ever saw" as he successfully mooched sandwiches and other food as well as clothes and even shoes. Sometimes the jocker purposely maimed the punk, realizing that an injured youth could garner more sympathy from those likely to offer a handout.[47]

The jocker-punk alliance had other explanations as well. Many of the participants drew on such relationships for emotional fulfillment, which

could come in a variety of forms. "The fiercest fight" Flynt ever witnessed came about when two hoboes battled over a boy whom they
both claimed to love. Love could also act as a lure into such relationships. For instance, in Walla Walla, Washington, in 1917 a sometime itinerant laborer, thirty-two-year-old George McElroy, invited seventeen-
year-old Roy Church, who had just arrived in town from northern
Idaho, to his room at the inexpensive Tango lodging house. There, according to Church, McElroy attempted to coax him into a sexual relationship, claiming that "warm friendships...had been known to exist
between men who indulged in that sort of intercourse."[48] Although the
youth did not respond in the way McElroy had hoped—he fled the
Tango in his bedclothes for the police station and McElroy landed in
the state penitentiary—eyewitnesses to jocker-punk relationships reported it not unusual for the boy to reciprocate the adult male's feelings.
Thomas Minehan studied hoboes in the early 1930s and discovered that
wolf-lamb relationships "seemed to be one of mutual satisfaction." Similarly, Nels Anderson remarked that while affairs between men and
youths he knew were generally brief, the attachments were nonetheless
"very intense and sentimental." Sometimes such partnerships could last
for years and even become conjugal in nature. Furthermore, Anderson
claimed that he had twice made the mistake of stepping in between a
man and his boy. On one occasion "his interference was resented by
both." In the other, he found that the "lamb" would not be separated
from his "wolf." Likewise, Minehan reported of a case in which he found
that "the boy did not want to be separated from his friend. He resented
and refused all efforts at his 'rescue.'"[49]

For a variety of reasons, then, the jocker-punk relationship was based
on more than sex, which by definition it included.[50] It is thus safe to assume that factors such as the demographics of the road, the remoteness
of some work locations, and generally poor relations between transients
and urban fairies all contributed to migratory male culture distinguish-
ing between punks and fairies. Even though they appeared to perform a
similar sexual role, punks were held in much higher esteem. To be sure,
the jocker-punk relationship could have harsh and coercive aspects. An
account of a 1925 incident claimed that "the tramp always ruled the
'punk' by fear, the same crude brutal psychology that the pimp practiced
over the weak woman of the underworld." Josiah Flynt reported in 1896
that the punk had to do exactly what the jocker commanded, or the latter might kick, slap, and generally maltreat him. Other investigations
have argued the same, insisting that punks became a virtual slave to their

"masters." Nels Anderson, however, tried to dispel the belief that all such relationships were exploitive. Whether his efforts reflected reality or his wish to win sympathy for transient men is difficult to know with certainty.[51]

The context in which these reports were written also makes it difficult to separate fact from fiction in their depiction of such relationships. As the century progressed, two broad social changes led jocker-punk associations to be cast in increasingly pejorative terms: social disapproval of "homosexuality" intensified, and tolerance of transients decreased. Mechanization, unionization, public relief, federal regulation, and the development of the automobile all transformed western agriculture and extractive industries in the 1920s and '30s, undercutting the need for casual laborers and undermining more traditional forms of transience. The hangers-on increasingly became the "drunken bums" intolerable to society. Associated with debauchery, perversion, and industrial displacement, these men faced additional social castigation. In the 1890s, when Josiah Flynt described what he saw as negative in the jocker-punk relationship, he also reported on positive aspects, finding "some jockers to be almost as kind as fathers to their boys[.]" By the 1930s, observers were commenting only on the negative. One transient in Wenatchee, Washington, described the first "wolf" he came across as "a horrible-looking individual with red hair, bent nose, and repulsive lips." And Maury Graham claimed that the punks he encountered "were a ragged, seedy-looking bunch with sad, frightened eyes embedded in hard, unhappy faces."[52]

Moreover, the jocker's coercion of and control over his punk stressed by outsiders were in no way universal. In studying working-class statutory rape "victims" and "criminals" in 1910s California, Mary Odem has found that about three-quarters of the teenage girls in these sexual encounters described themselves as willing partners. Many actually encouraged their unions with older men. And like youths in relationships with men, teenage working-class girls entered into these sexual relationships for a wide variety of reasons, including economic rewards, romance, love, and sexual pleasure.[53] Like Odem's female subjects, youths benefited from their relationships with jockers. Boys received much-needed advice and information about life on the road. They also gained warmth and compassion—something particularly needed, as a broken home was the leading cause of boys' transience. Additionally, observers remarked that jockers guarded their punks jealously. Traveling alone, without a jocker's protection, could be far more dangerous for a boy. For example, while in company with eight hoboes on a slowly moving train, Flynt witnessed a young lad scramble into the freight car, where he was then "tripped up and 'seduced'... by each of the tramps."[54]

Although some of these examples bespeak child molestation and an unwillingness on the part of boys to engage in some sexual relations with men, many youths sought out men for sexual pleasure. Flynt reported that some of the punks he encountered in the 1890s told him that "they get as much pleasure out of the affair as the jocker does....[L]ittle fellows under ten...describe it as a delightful tickling sensation in the parts involved....Those who have passed the age of puberty seem to be satisfied pretty much the same way that the men are." Alfred Kinsey's research for roughly the same period corroborates Flynt's observations. The sexologist found that homosexual play was an essential part of boy culture and that the children of the lower levels of American society were the least restrained, usually becoming involved in such activities at an early age.[55]

Flynt even encountered punks whom he described as "willfully tempt[ing] their jockers to intercourse." The motive of some was undoubtedly their own sexual satisfaction; of others, more basic needs of daily survival; and of yet others, a complex blend of the two. In the transient-labor world, compliant boys could make money and receive food, clothing, and shelter.[56] Donald Roy, a university student at the time he surveyed Seattle's Hooverville, was offered "chickens, pork chops, oranges" as well as money, a job, and "a happy home life" if he would submit to the passions of the men who propositioned him. Nels Anderson noted that boys often became sexually active in their relationships on the road and "even commercialize[d] themselves." Such was the case of a boy who, on the outskirts of the western railroad town of Ogden, Utah, in 1921, promised transient men that "he would 'do business' with anyone in the crowd for fifty cents." The young entrepreneur furthermore claimed this as "his method of 'getting by,'" rendering other work unnecessary. Many boys on the road probably found that having sex with men enabled them to make the best of an unfortunate situation. For example, legal documents describe how while riding on a boxcar through Kennewick, Washington, in 1911, Charles Smith "was practically caught in the act" of committing sodomy on a sixteen-year-old youth "with the consent of the boy, for the price of a meal."[57]

Historical evidence and past studies of sexual practices demonstrate that the jocker-punk relationship was not necessarily one-sided. The adolescent boy could and often did have his own emotional and sexual as well as economic reasons for forming relationships with men. Such evidence also supports Nels Anderson's theory that in the jocker-punk relationship, force might not have been "so extensively employed as sometimes believed."[58]

A variety of factors beyond the sexual affected the adult-adolescent male relationships so prevalent in the transient world of the Northwest. The youthfulness of the punk proved imperative for certain domestic and economic aspects of the partnership to operate smoothly. The emotional rewards of the teacher-apprentice relationship or even basic warmth and compassion could also be gained by both jocker and punk. Such relationships provided safety and protection as well, giving boys themselves significant reasons unrelated to sex to submit to or even initiate these alliances. While the jocker might expect the boy to play a specific sexual role, the punk's background and sexual desires also seem to have shaped the sexuality of the adult. Such considerations help distinguish the punk from the urban fairy. The punk thus adds a significant dimension to our understanding of past working-class sexualities.

Variations in Migratory Male Sex and Gender Patterns on the Road

Turn-of-the-century "Hobohemia" literature commented more on the adult-adolescent male pairing than on any other sexual relationship found on the road. It may be that observers focused on it because society generally considered adult-juvenile couplings the most abhorrent. Moreover, that disapproval undoubtedly brought these relationships before the law more often than those in which two (or more) adult males mutually consented to sex with each other. Consequently, adult male–teenage boy pairings appear in the record most often.

Another possible reason why chroniclers of transient life focused on the sexual relationships between youths and men is their difficulty in accepting that men might actually be attracted to men. As long as men had relations with boys, a certain imbalance in power and possibly gender existed.[59] But hobohemia literature and other source material verifies that a variety of male-male relationships, whose participants had different age configurations and performed a variety of sex roles, also existed on the road.

As remarked on earlier, homosexual relationships regularly occurred in and around logging camps—but not all these paired an adult with a youth. The 1914 northern California investigation asserted that sexual relationships occurred between "men." Also, one individual later recalled of his time spent in a small western logging camp in the early 1900s that seven of the nine adult male employees there engaged in sex with each other.[60] Consensual sexual relations between adult males were found among other western migratory and casual worker populations as well. The same man who reported on the homosexual activities of loggers in the early twentieth century also claimed to have labored in a western mining camp where fully half the fifty-five adult male employees got "relief from one another." And according to the early-twentieth-century cowboy Manuel Boyfrank, men on the western ranges commonly had sex together. Furthermore, federal officials who investigated Alaska's salmon canning industry in the 1910s and 1920s intimated that the men they found on transport ships had relations not only with boys.[61] In the late nineteenth and early twentieth centuries, a diversity of male-male sexual relations occurred in the Alaskan canneries. As noted above, transgendered sex workers, either on their own or as subcontractors, sold sex and sometimes entered into "marriages" with cannery employees. In addition, underage boys who worked illegally in the canneries engaged in sexual relations with older laborers. There is also evidence that nontransgendered adult males hailing from a variety of ethnic and national backgrounds sold sex in the canneries.[62]

The practices that both men and youths engaged in varied widely. Although the 1914 investigation of northern California loggers gives no details, it does stress that "sex perversion" in lumber camps was as "developed and recognized as...in prisons and reformatories" in part because the "men sent out from the employment agencies are without blankets or even sufficient clothing, and they are forced to sleep packed together for the sake of warmth."[63] This sleeping arrangement might lead to anal or interfemoral coitus, as it did in an industrial work camp in northern California in October 1894. There Thomas Hickey and Harry Blair shared the same bunk for several weeks while others in the camp either witnessed or heard about the former anally sodomizing the latter on a number of occasions. Similarly, the anonymous informant who reported on his western logging and mining experiences, admittedly in a dramatizing tone, claimed that the men he knew in those occupations preferred anal sex. In all these cases, some adult, working-class men had to play the receptive role. Nels Anderson described a male sex triangle in northern California: one "wolf" lived "with two men in a room....serving both of them and one of them was 'going 50–50' with him. That is, they would take turns playing the female role."[64]

Cramped sleeping arrangements might also result in other forms of intimacy. For example, investigations of the ships that delivered male workers to Alaska's canneries reveal that some individuals on board these vessels had contracted venereal diseases in the throat.[65] Oral sex took place among other migratory laborers as well. Gus LaMere, a forty-three-year-old shingle weaver originally from Maine but working at Clear Lake, Washington, went to prison in 1909 for voluntarily submitting himself to oral coitus performed by Reuben Boyd, who seems to have been younger than LaMere. In 1912 in the restroom of a barbershop located in the eastern Washington mill and agricultural town of Colfax, twenty-eight-year-old John Mustard, a migrant, fellated thirty-seven-year-old David Gunreth, a worker traveling with the 101 Ranch Real Wild West Show.[66]

In these latter instances, it appears that the younger male took the receptive role in the same-sex sexual encounter, but he used his mouth. And the Mustard-Gunreth case makes clear that the younger male was hardly a boy, being close to thirty years old (although records did question his mental condition). There are also cases in which older men performed fellation on youths. In August 1915, Charles Altwater, a forty-eight-year-old itinerant shoemaker, stopped in the small Northern Pacific spur-line community of Burke, Idaho, and there encountered seventeen-year-old Joseph McCarthy. According to McCarthy, Altwater told him a story of a man down the tracks in the mining town of Wallace who became acquainted with a boy at the Sweets Hotel. Within a short time, according to the tale Altwater supposedly spun, the older fellow "got some pop beer and sand-wiches and they went up the track a ways...and went in the bushes layed [sic] in the shade and had a good time, drank the beer and ate the sand-wiches, and...took down his pants and had a good time." After recounting this titillating tale, Altwater was said to have asked if McCarthy might meet him the next day, pledging to supply soft drinks if McCarthy would bring some sandwiches. McCarthy kept the date and also brought along his sixteen-year-old friend Harold Warner. The boys claimed that Altwater coaxed them into a nearby warehouse, which the older man asserted would be "a good place for some hoboes to sleep" and a "boss place to get a couple of girls." After a few minutes, McCarthy and Warner sat down on some bales of hay. According to the two boys, Altwater first opened Harold's pants and then went over to McCarthy and took out his penis. It "got hard and he sucked it off."[67]

If we are to put much faith in hobohemia literature, later recollections, and contemporary legal documents, transient laborers engaged in a variety of sexual and generational partnerings, transgressing the expected gender norms that apparently regulated same-sex relationships in other settings. In 1941 "Donald H.," who spent time on the road in California and Oregon, provided a possible explanation for this phenomenon. He asserted, "It isn't really the old man who buggers the young man. Very often a man past forty gets his pleasure being buggered by a young man." Donald claimed that the man with the "most vitality" played the "active part."[68] Gus LaMere from Clear Lake gave another rationale; he claimed that he permitted Reuben Boyd to perform fellation on him because he had "heard of this party being of such charicter [*sic*]" that he would submit himself to such a role.[69] Was LaMere implying that Boyd was transgendered, or was he an otherwise masculine male who just liked performing oral sex on other men? Unfortunately, the records tell us nothing more about Boyd and his "charicter." Nor do our records reveal anything notable about the character and demeanor of Charles Altwater, who was past forty and fellated a teenage boy. Was he a "homosexual" who more willingly would engage in these sorts of relationships? Or was he simply Donald H.'s "less vital" older man? Yet Gus LaMere, also in his forties, took the opposite part in oral sexual relations. The records are simply too fragmentary for us to draw any more precise conclusions.

There may, of course, be other reasons why sexual relationships between men, in a variety of forms, could be found on the road, especially in the Northwest. The region's great imbalance in numbers of men and women and the isolation of various work locations probably helped make it easier for some men to turn to other men for sex as well as to fulfill emotional needs. Such circumstances also apparently made it easier for some men to cast aside considerations of gender role. That a number of individuals had same-sex sexual relations undoubtedly had a "normalizing" effect, making it possible for yet other men also to participate in them. Moreover, the high mobility of workers in the Northwest, where faces in work camps or hobo jungles or main stems constantly changed, might also have diminished the peer pressure that forced men in other settings—such as urban areas back East or even in prisons—to stick more closely to prescribed roles. Nels Anderson commented on this particular circumstance of transient culture and its relationship to sexual "perversion" in the early 1920s when he stated that "so long as one is in the tramp class" there is little worry about social ostracism:

The tramp is not identified with any community or any social group. He is ever surrounded with the cloak of anonymity. Not even arrest reveals his identity. It is not easy to get this class of men into a position where they fear any stigma, for they only need to pass on and start anew elsewhere without reference to their past. Each lives in his own world, and this promise of security is often taken advantage of.[70]

The Physical Geography of Sex on the Road

Nels Anderson remains one of the most informative observers of early-twentieth-century transient workers, but his conclusions about them are contradictory. Such contradictions are due in part to a discrepancy between reality and what Anderson really wanted his society—which had a negative view of migrant laborers—to know about his subjects. In the passage quoted above, for example, Anderson suggested that their lack of "community" accounted for the ability of some "tramps" to engage in "perversion." Yet at other times Anderson wrote eloquently about the complexities and cohesiveness of the transient community. Transient homosexuality caused Anderson discomfort. To explain it as aberrant, he called on the very stereotypes that he otherwise worked so hard to dispel.

In maintaining that transients' sexuality resulted from "the cloak of anonymity" (rootlessness, ability to change identities, and thus relative insularity from the watchful eye of society), Anderson resorted to what sounds suspiciously like the modern metaphor of the closet. Eve Kosofsky Sedgwick has explained that "[t]he closet is the defining structure for gay oppression";[71] indeed, it applies more broadly to all people with nonheteronormative sexualities. The closet both permits and at the same time enforces denial, isolation, concealment, and ignorance. In summoning the closet, Anderson attempted to erase the pervasiveness of migratory laborers' same-sex sexual activities and confine them to the most specific and unusual set of circumstances. But in fact, homosexual practices pervaded transient society. Migrating men and youths constructed an elaborate same-sex sexual culture that was anything but anonymous and furtive. They also applied a variety of identities to those among them who participated in it. Indeed, their *community* provided for and reinforced same-sex sexual activities. Thus openness, acceptance, and common practice rather than obscurity, disdain, and infrequency were responsible for transient same-sex sexuality. Anderson's closet is rooted in the sociologist's own homophobic society.

In recent years, geographers have pointed out that the closet is more than just a metaphor. It is physical space, too. As such, it is also something positive—often a refuge from a disapproving broader milieu. Historically, people who share "transgressive" sexualities have carved out their own places that support, reinforce, conceal, and even permit their activities.[72] Most scholarly attention to this so-called queer space has focused on the city, because of the overall urban bias in gay studies—the long tradition that poses the city as the location of the first communities of people who had same-sex sexual desires and engaged in homosexual activities. This tradition holds that the city historically acted as a magnet. Over the years it drew to it rural men and women with same-sex desires who wished to find others like themselves and enjoy an overall atmosphere that was relatively more permissive, though there, too, they had to carve out their own protected spaces.[73]

Did the heavily transient nonurban settings like those found in the turn-of-the-century Northwest hinterlands also attract men who already had same-sex desires? Responding to this question is difficult for at least two reasons. First, as already noted, the available documents are sketchy and inherently biased. Second, unlike urban gay community, which grew and flourished over the course of the twentieth century, the transient worker world largely dissipated by the mid-1900s. Because it was not renewed and sustained, it lacked a continuous influx of new people with stories to tell. Nevertheless, there is evidence that suggests we should answer "yes." Male-male sexuality abounded on the road and was no secret. Although not always clear in their definitions, both Flynt and Anderson avowed that "homosexuals" did appear on the road. Moreover, the pervasiveness of same-sex sexuality among transient laborers enabled men with some form of homosexual interests to act on them. And without downplaying the exploitive control over transient labor that the capitalist system exerted, we do know that the seasonal nature of the Northwest's employment and the relative ease of finding successive jobs in different industries did entice to the region some men who preferred periodic rather than constant work.[74] By analogy, it seems likely that men and youths with homoerotic interests found the road attractive because of its sexual system.

Donald H. offered suggestive material on this point. Since his youth, Donald had engaged in both same- and opposite-sex activities. Having formed intimate relationships with peripatetic men on the West Coast when in his twenties, Donald nonetheless later chose to marry. Conjugal bliss never materialized, so he resumed a life on the road, intermittently playing the role of a hitchhiker and pickup and engaging in same-sex affairs as he did so. Ultimately he hit the road with one of his closer male friends, and they traveled to Oregon and worked as miners. Donald already knew at the time he fled his failed marriage for the road that "there is a tremendous amount of homosexuality among hobos and generally a great deal of affection."[75] Such snippets speak to the likelihood that in the early twentieth century the urban center was not alone in attracting men with homoerotic desires; rural transient culture seems to have acted as a magnet for working-class men with such passions. It appears that some men sought transient society as a refuge and did not merely perceive it as a closet. These conclusions refute the traditional "wisdom" that rural America is a place averse to homoeroticism and lacking in attractiveness to a community of individuals with same-sex sexual interests.[76]

Throughout the twentieth century most large cities, despite drawing in gay men, remained hostile to them in a number of ways. That hostility made it necessary for urban gays to establish their own spaces for socializing and for sex, such as restrooms, parks, rooming houses, YMCAs, bathhouses, bars, and so on. In the urban setting, men moved between these "closeted" sites and the more open and public spaces of their families and jobs. Travel—whether by foot, in streetcars, or later by automobiles—was essential for many to realize their sexual and social interests in the city. Tim Retzloff has written that the automobile was the greatest force in "nurturing community and identity formation" among gay males in post–World War II Flint, Michigan. The car facilitated travel to gay spaces within Flint and to nearby and larger Detroit. The auto itself was a gay place; men used it for socializing and sex. Travel was also important to men with homosexual interests in other mid-twentieth-century settings. John Howard has noted that in this era the increasing availability of the automobile, the concomitant expansion of the highway system, and the establishment of roadside rest areas enhanced the possibilities for social and sexual encounters among men in the rural South.[77]

For the Northwest in an earlier era, mobility was the defining characteristic of a large segment of the male populace. Natural resource–based industries throughout the region's hinterlands depended on a multitude of men and youths migrating to them for work. The seasonal nature of these industries and the tendency of work camps to move after quickly depleting the raw material on which they relied intensified itinerancy. By 1914 West Coast laborers could expect in a single season for work in a lumber camp to last for fifteen to thirty days, in a mining camp for sixty days, at a railroad construction site for ten days, and in harvesting for seven days.[78] The constant movement of males to such locations where they concentrated in large numbers did more than make sexual contact likely: it provided the milieu in which sexual contacts regularly occurred. Thus rather than having to travel from one site to the next for sexual relations, men found that the hinterland itself was a sexual space. Moreover, there were specific rural sites where sexual contacts were most likely: the work camps, the so-called hobo jungles, and on board the means of transportation. With regard to the first, Alfred Kinsey reported for the early twentieth century that "the highest frequencies of the homosexual which we have ever secured anywhere have been in particular rural communities in some of the more remote sections of the country. . . . [I]t is found among ranchmen, cattle men, prospectors, lumbermen, and farming groups in general[.]"[79] As this chapter has demonstrated, homosexual relations regularly occurred among men such as these and in these very places.

"Jungle" was what migrating men called their campgrounds on the outskirts of cities or along rural rail lines. Jungles could be permanent or temporary. Transients laid them out to maximize cover from legal authorities, taking advantage of a variety of natural amenities such as shade and water as well as proximity to transportation. In the jungles transients exchanged stories and information, socialized, did their laundry, read newspapers, and so on. Jungles also acted as sites for sexual relations; indeed, as already noted, transient youths could make a living as sex workers in them. Because the jungle's sexual potential was so great, Josiah Flynt found in the 1890s that some jockers withdrew from them entirely, "simply to be sure that their prushuns were not touched by other tramps."[80] In the 1930s—possibly because the dynamics of the road by then had changed, or possibly because he wished to ameliorate society's views of the hobo—Maury Graham reported that jungles had become segregated between those who engaged in same-sex relations and those who steadfastly refused them. So well-known had jungles become as sites of sexual activity that during the first part of the twentieth century some urban homosexuals frequented them. Those who "cruised" the jungles became known as "railroad queens."[81] As later chapters suggest, railroad queens were likely few in number in the Northwest at this time; but the point here is that male-male sex commonly occurred in these locations and they had a decided reputation for it.

The mode of transportation used by transients also provided opportunity for sexual encounters, whether invited or not. Between the 1880s and 1917 more than 16,000 miles of railroad were laid in Oregon, Washington, Idaho, and Montana. Transients used the iron road as their primary means of travel. They might cling to the undersides of railcars; for safety and comfort, many preferred the boxcar, which some dubbed the "side-door Pullman." As noted earlier, it was in a boxcar where some-time Northwest hobo Maury Graham was first approached for sexual re-lations. It was also in a boxcar in eastern Washington where the twenty-eight-year-old laborer Charles Smith "was practically caught in the act" of having sexual relations with a sixteen-year-old fellow traveler. And a boxcar was where Josiah Flynt witnessed eight hoboes "seduce" a youth only moments after he had jumped on board.[82]

Railway construction eased in the Northwest in the 1920s, just as au-tomobiles were becoming more affordable. In 1916, Washington, Ore-gon, Idaho, and Montana together had registered 132,755 motor vehi-cles. Only four years later, the number of licensed cars had nearly tripled. Road construction progressed slowly, however. By 1918 Idaho had only five miles of highway outside its urban centers. But as automobile travel became more common, migrants turned increasingly to hitching. As Donald H. found in the 1920s and '30s, both thumbing for rides and providing rides to transient men increased his chances for sexual en-counters.[83]

During this period, male workers who left West Coast ports for the canneries of Alaska traveled by ship. Before the mid-1920s, they boarded sailing vessels; later, they increasingly took steamers. But whatever their means of propulsion, transports offered a place wherein sexual contacts abounded. By the 1920s, federal investigators complained that the ships provided only cramped bunks that two men shared without the benefit of an intervening partition to protect their "privacy." Authorities also noted the spread of venereal diseases on board, where they found a vari-ety of male sex workers and others with same-sex sexual interests.[84]

Because of the large numbers of unattached men and because the transient community approved of and encouraged same-sex affairs, mi-grant workers did not necessarily have to travel for sexual encounters as did (and do) some men in other settings. Within the transient world both fixed and moving sites served as locations for sex. But as men and youths of the transient culture engaged in any of their possibly socially unacceptable behaviors, they ran the greatest risk of discovery in the small towns that also sprinkled the Northwest's hinterlands. These com-munities, though their economies in some ways relied on transient la-borers, consistently lamented their presence, blaming them for all sorts of local problems and accusing them of creating a general menace. As early as 1889, Oregon officials reporting to the National Conference of Charities and Corrections on the social dangers that confronted the re-gion's youth claimed that "prior to the advent of railroads, the communities were almost entirely free from the inroads of tramps, gypsies and other vagrants." In southwestern Idaho in the spring of 1912, anxieties about transients were heightened. Day after day, local papers ran unfavorable headlines about the large numbers of laborers passing through. "The hobo harvest keeps up," one reported, "and if there was ever a bumper crop of the product it has been this spring." Another charged that the local police have "their hands full these days, the tramps and hobos going through the city in droves." At the same time a front-page story appeared accusing hoboes of attacking and injuring a local brakeman.[85] It was within this very atmosphere, at this very time, and in this very place that Ted Gladden, with whom this chapter began, first encountered his troubles. On the one hand, then, the late-nineteenth- and early-twentieth-century North American hinterlands helped create the conditions in which a particular working-class same-sex sexual subculture formed and flourished. Yet on the other hand, certain attributes of those hinterlands also presented dangers for the transient laborers who participated in same-sex affairs there.

In 1909, after leaving behind surviving family members and his Minnesota home, Gladden headed to the Pacific Northwest; there he entered into and readily participated in a thriving transient culture. For a variety of reasons this culture countenanced sexual relationships between its male participants. The relationship that made Gladden a historical figure was the one that epitomized the transient experience: the adult and adolescent male partnering. Typically the younger males who engaged in sex with men on the road were referred to as *punks*. As this chapter has outlined, the punk differed markedly from the urban fairy, another prominent figure in North America's working-class world at this time, though considerably less common in the Northwest because of the nature of its economy and workforce. On rural byways and in rural work camps the punk shaped working-class sexuality, and working-class sexuality in turn shaped him. But he also made his appearance in the region's major urban centers, as did the men who had sex with him. Ted Gladden, we know, spent some of his time in Portland. Together, the transient youth and the migratory adult male influenced male same-sex sexuality in the city, too. This is a subject that the following chapter examines more thoroughly.

CHAPTER 2

Sex in the City

*Transient and Working-Class Men
and Youths in the Urban Northwest*

In early April 1913, Portland authorities received a tip that the Monte Carlo pool hall, located in the very heart of the city's transient working-class North End (see map 2), was acting as "a clearing house for immoral boys who pander to the passions of vicious Greeks who hang around the place." The police chief promptly assigned the detectives R. H. Craddock and John Goltz to monitor the Monte Carlo. During their ten-day investigation, the two hauled into the district attorney's office five teenage boys and exacted "some sensational statements" from them. The detectives' biggest break came on April 18 when they shadowed Andrew Dillige (figure 3), a thirty-five-year-old transient laborer and immigrant from Greece, and Grover King, a nineteen-year-old white American-born laborer, as together they made their way to the Fairmount Hotel. Located a block or two from the Monte Carlo on North Sixth between Burnside and Couch Streets, the Fairmount long had a reputation as one of a number of "houses of ill fame" in the area. Shortly after Dillige and King disappeared into room 29, the two detectives burst in, apprehending the former as he placed his "private parts . . . against [King's] rectum." Convicted of attempting to commit sodomy, Dillige spent fifteen months behind bars. King faced charges of vagrancy, but after Dillige's trial, the court released him without further penalty.[1]

Although limited, the scraps of information we have on what the Portland police referred to as the "Greek *scandall*" [*sic*] are a rich source for understanding both working-class male homosexuality in the North-

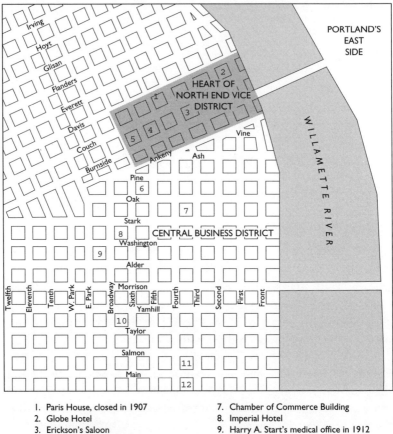

1. Paris House, closed in 1907
2. Globe Hotel
3. Erickson's Saloon
4. Monte Carlo Pool Hall
5. Fairmount Hotel
6. E.S.J. McAllister law offfices in 1912
7. Chamber of Commerce Building
8. Imperial Hotel
9. Harry A. Start's medical office in 1912
10. YMCA Building
11. Lownsdale Park
12. Chapman Park

MAP 2. Portland's North End/Whitechapel Vice District and Central Business District, ca. 1912

west city and class, racial, and sexual prejudices of the dominant social groups at the turn of the last century. In this chapter, I first investigate the latter phenomenon, arguing that the Dillige-King and other similar relationships did not come to official attention as the result of objective application of the era's laws: instead, urban police forces in the Northwest purposely concentrated their surveillance of male-male sexual activities in the transient working-class neighborhoods. In doing so, the local authorities clearly utilized laws against same-sex sexual activities as only one part of a larger middle-class campaign to persecute working-class

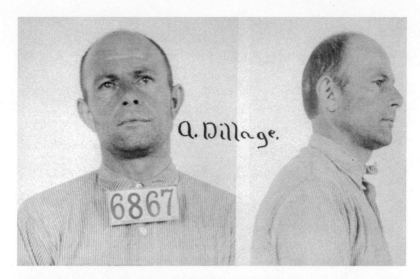

FIGURE 3. Andrew Dillige, 1913. Portland police detectives arrested the Greek migrant laborer Andrew Dillige at the working-class Fairmount Hotel, located in the heart of the city's vice district, for sexual relations with a young American-born male sex worker. Oregon State Archives, Oregon State Penitentiary, Inmate Files, Photograph 6867.

men of racial and ethnic minority backgrounds, particularly the foreign-born. The urban middle class perceived these men as sexual threats to society generally and specifically to the white American boy, and thus to the middle-class American family. At the same time, the dominant social classes conflated the working-class neighborhood—what they referred to as the "vice district"—with the sexual dangers that the men who occupied them presumably posed. Thus not only did authorities and reformers in the Northwest pursue the men of this urban space, but they also attacked the space itself.

I then consider urban working-class male-male sexuality. As the Dillige-King relationship suggests, sexual relations between transient men and youths were as common in the Northwest's large cities as in the region's hinterlands. Such relationships concentrated in the "vice" districts, which doubled as the seasonal residence of migratory laborers. Also, the jocker-punk relationship was transmuted by the large city, where the youth experienced greater independence than he did on the road. He therefore often resorted to soliciting sex around working-class establishments such as poolrooms and saloons, as did Grover King. Furthermore, King typified the youthful working-class same-sex sex partner in the city; authorities referred to him as a "punk." Indeed, the work camp–like atmosphere of the Northwest's vice districts encouraged the presence of the punk and limited that of the fairy. Finally, the typical sex act engaged in by working-class men and youths, again fashioned especially by on-the-road culture, was anal and interfemoral intercourse with the adult, like Dillige, taking the penetrative role.

Race, Class, and City Space: Middle-Class
Responses to Working-Class Same-Sex Affairs

Between 1870 and 1921 Portland police charged thousands of men with "disorderly conduct," "vagrancy," "indecent exposure," "indecent and immoral acts," and being "lewd and dissolute persons." Each of these crimes might entail some sort of same-sex sexual "transgression." For example, Grover King faced charges of "vagrancy" even though his crime involved an act of sodomy. From detective day books, which go into considerable detail, we know more about King's offense than we could have learned from arrest ledgers, which list only the official charge. Regrettably, because of the terseness of arrest records, the most accessible and comprehensive documents for surveying crime in early Portland, the great majority of those apprehended for same-sex sexual acts have slipped through the historical cracks. Of the thousands arrested in the Rose City between 1870 and 1921 for the various vaguely worded crimes listed above, only 123, ages fifteen and older, can verifiably be linked to some type of homosexual act.[2]

Like Dillige and King, most of those arrested were from the working class. For the eighty-two males whose occupations we know, some 62 percent came from the most transient of backgrounds: laborer, fisherman, sailor, soldier, railroad worker, logger, ship worker, bootblack, and teamster. Taken together, males who held occupations as either skilled or unskilled manual laborers made up a total of 78 percent of those arrested for same-sex sexual offenses; only 7.3 percent came from what we might call "white-collar" occupations. The arrest and other legal records reported the nativity and "race" of 97 of the 123 men and youths considered here. As table 1 indicates, roughly 42 percent of those apprehended were American-born whites, like King. The remaining were, like Dillige, men of foreign birth or of a minority racial group.

As was true of the Northwest's male workforce in general, the men arrested for homosexual acts were relatively young. Of the ninety-six for

TABLE I. *Nativity or Race of Males, Fifteen Years of Age and Older, Arrested for Same-Sex Sexual Activities, Portland, 1870–1921*

Nativity	Total Number	Percentage of Total (n=97)*
United States: white (41), African American (3), American Indian (1)	45	46.4 (*white=42.3*)
Southern Europe: Italy (4), Greece (11)	15	15.5
Ireland	15	15.5
Australia, north/west Europe: Holland, England, Germany, Scandinavia	11	11.3
Asia	6	6.2
Latin America	3	3.1
Eastern Europe: Bulgaria, Russia	2	2.1

*Because of rounding, this column does not total 100.

whom we have records, the oldest was seventy-three. Dillige, at age thirty-five, was only slightly older than the average, thirty-two. The median age was twenty-nine, and twenty-eight-year-olds showed up in arrest records in larger numbers than men of any other cohort.

Portland's legal records are not always explicit about their partners in crime, particularly when the accomplices were juveniles. (The definition of *juvenile* changed over the years, ranging from below twenty-one to below eighteen.) Nonetheless, many of the cases involving same-sex sex crimes did include a "juvenile," such as King at age nineteen in 1913. That juvenile-male same-sex activities often came to the attention of the authorities is confirmed by an investigation launched in 1912; it expressed considerable anxiety that during a twelve-month period ending October 1 of that year, more than thirty cases of same-sex crimes involving males between nine and fifteen years old had come before the legal system.[3] I have been able to verify the same-sex sexual nature of sixty-two cases (other than the few associated with the 1912 YMCA scandal) involving adults and juvenile males that occurred in Portland between 1890 and 1921. In many of these the charge leveled against the adult was "contributing to the delinquency of a minor."

Available legal records thus suggest the following: The typical male same-sex sexual offender was working class and likely had a transient background. He might be of foreign birth or come from a racial minority group, but had almost as good a chance of being American-born and white. He was also a young man, and his partner was just as likely to have been a juvenile as not. In all these various ways, then, Andrew Dillige and Grover King typified those in early Portland who engaged in same-sex sexual activities—or, more precisely, they exemplified those who were brought before the law for such crimes. For although Portland authorities apprehended American-born white males for same-sex sexual offenses in numbers almost as large as for males of all other races and national backgrounds, men from the latter group were in fact vastly overrepresented in arrest records. While foreign-born white males were less than 20 percent of the male population of Portland through the years 1900–1920, they made up more than 44 percent of those arrested for same-sex crimes between 1870 and 1921. Similarly, African Americans and men of Chinese, Japanese, and "other" origins constituted about 4 percent of the Portland male population during this era, but they represented about 13.5 percent of these arrests.[4]

The Rose City police department's purposeful targeting of males of foreign origin and of racial and ethnic minorities for same-sex sex crimes was part of a larger, regionwide and even national campaign then under way. Between the 1880s and World War I, millions of southern and eastern Europeans, Latin Americans, and Asians migrated to the United States. They were dubbed the "new immigrants," and their backgrounds were quite different from those of earlier immigrants from northern and western Europe to whom most American-born whites in 1900 could trace their ancestry. In the last years of the nineteenth century these longer-established Americans, who also held the country's economic, social, and political power, grew uneasy over the increasing number of new arrivals. Clinging to Social Darwinist ideas and the era's assumptions regarding biological differences between races, some believed that the recent immigrants were inferior, would infect the so-called American race, and would act as a drag on society. Others concluded, especially in light of the growth in labor unrest and, in particular, the emergence of the communist Industrial Workers of the World (IWW), that the new arrivals who came largely to work in America's industrial order brought with them radical ideas designed to overthrow capitalism and democracy. Adding to the prejudice of the day was the fear that many Catholic arrivals had a greater allegiance to Rome than to the United States. Many members of the native-born middle classes also believed that the new immigrants, who tended to concentrate in the burgeoning urban centers, were taking over some municipal governments and operating corrupt regimes, and various spokesmen for "American" labor claimed that immigrants stole their jobs.[5]

For these and other reasons, the late nineteenth century had witnessed a strong nativist reaction that resulted in immigration restrictions and biased laws. For example, the Exclusion Act of 1882 prohibited most Chinese from entering the country. Through the era, legislators on both the national and local levels enacted various codes and statutes that prohibited some noncitizens from being employed on public works projects and also from owning land. By the end of the century, America had some of the strictest naturalization regulations in the world. Despite the growing number of immigrants and the strong undercurrent of xenophobia, the country's thriving economy between 1897 and 1906 kept racist sentiment in relative abeyance. But in the years after 1906, when economic crisis hit, "nativism" grew sharply. On top of this, American involvement in World War I and the accompanying federal propaganda also heightened suspicions of foreigners. Capping off the era, in the early 1920s Congress adopted some of its most restrictive immigration legislation, specifically targeting the new immigrants.[6]

The Northwest witnessed its share of racism and nativist and antilabor sentiment during this era. Although the provision was never enforced, in 1859 the Oregon constitution forbade African Americans from entering the state. In the 1880s, race riots drove many Chinese from the region. Early in the twentieth century, Northwest states enacted laws discriminating against Japanese in the fishing industry and in the ownership of land. The growth and success of the IWW in the region caused considerable consternation in the 1910s and early 1920s. The Northwest served as one of the nation's centers for radical labor activity because the IWW was almost the only union that paid attention to the plight of loggers, miners, and farmhands. In the struggle against labor, middle-class society did not lose sight of the fact that many of the workers were foreign-born. The Northwest even became a stronghold for the Ku Klux Klan, which had revived in the 1910s and which by the 1920s counted several million members nationwide.[7]

The experiences of African Americans, Greeks, and Asian Indians in Portland and in Vancouver, British Columbia, exemplify how general race prejudice and nativist sentiment combined with disapproval of same-sex sexual activities to lead to the persecution of immigrant men. During these years, the reporting on same-sex sex crimes by law enforcement officials and news writers made clear their racist and ethnocentric concerns. Portland newspapers in the 1880s and 1890s limited their comments to rather bland pronouncements when such sex stories involved white American men. Thus in 1890 the *Evening Telegram* matter-of-factly stated that two white men, "Jack Stafford and Robert Wilkinson, charged with a crime against nature, waived examination and were held in default of $1000 each." Yet when an African American man was arrested for a similar transgression less than a year later, the reports had a strikingly different tenor. The very same paper featured a story about Mark Weeks, whom courts "found guilty of trying to dissect the innermost anatomy of a shipmate named John Goodock." The reporter could not resist the temptation to describe Weeks as "a 'gemman' of color."[8]

Prejudicial treatment of racial minority males went well beyond simply the words chosen in news accounts. In Portland, authorities arrested men of Greek origins, such as Andrew Dillige, for same-sex sexual offenses at rates far above their representation in the overall population. Between 1890 and 1920 men born in Greece never exceeded 1 percent of the total male population in the Rose City, yet they accounted for more than 11 percent of the arrests for same-sex sexual transgressions. During a five-month period stretching from November 17, 1912, to April 18, 1913, more Greek men were arrested for such crimes than at any other time in Portland history. Within this span occurred the "Greek scandal" at the Monte Carlo.

That period coincided with some of the most virulent expressions of racist and nativist sentiment that the city and the region had witnessed since the attacks on the Chinese in the 1880s. On November 29, 1912, for instance, officials from various regional and national social work organizations assembled in Portland. They announced cooperative plans to deal with the flood of immigrants expected to follow the impending completion of the Panama Canal. A newspaper evoked the anxiety articulated in and outside the conference with the headline "PREPARE FOR INFLUX OF ALIENS IN 1913." About a month later the police department asserted in its year-end accounting that "many of the law offenders" in the city "have been of the foreign element." Out of 16,311 arrests that year, "foreigners" accounted for 6,557. The report then singled out for specific mention only "Greeks" for giving particular "trouble."[9] Tensions between the native-born white and the Greek immigrant communities in Portland reached a boiling point in early 1913. In January, County Sheriff Tom Word arrested B. H. Baruh, a bootblack, for supplying Nellie Beulieu's house of prostitution with both customers and, apparently, "girls." Word assumed that because Baruh was "foreign" and a bootblack, he was also Greek. The sheriff then broadly asserted to the press that Greeks in the city aided the white slave trade, "acting as agents for immoral purposes of girls ranging in age from 16 years up."[10] Even after learning that Baruh was not Greek, Word refused to print a retraction. This decision outraged the local Greek community. Members drafted resolutions denouncing Word and sent copies to local newspapers, the Oregon governor, and the Greek ambassador in Washington, D.C. They also implored the Greek consul in Tacoma to assist them in their struggle against the city of Portland. Over the next few years, Rose City officials continued to wage a racially charged battle against the Greek community, but the greatest expression of prejudice surfaced during the winter of 1912–13, the period corresponding to the increase in arrests of Greek men charged with same-sex sex crimes and the period that saw Andrew Dillige dragged before the justice system.[11]

In a similar case of same-sex affairs in Vancouver that involved men from India, the records capture even more brazen bias. Native-born society on the West Coast contemptuously referred to Indians as "Hindoos"—more in reference to Hindustan than to the Hindu religion, which in fact few immigrants espoused. Being British subjects, many South Asians first migrated to British Columbia before crossing the border to the south. By 1913 about three times as many Indians lived in the United States as in Canada.[12] In both Canada and the States, the growing numbers of Indians met with stepped-up harassment. In September 1907 white working-class mob violence in Bellingham, Washington, drove several hundred Indians across the international border. In July 1913 the *Portland News* charged in bold letters that Indians "breed like rats, live in squalor and die by the millions of the plague, yet Uncle Sam is allowing them to overrun the Pacific Coast States." Anthony Caminetti, U.S. commissioner-general of immigration, spoke in Portland a few months later and further inflamed resentment: he accused the Indian immigrants of posing a danger even greater than the "yellow peril," a familiar racist reference to both the Chinese and Japanese presence in the region. Caminetti asserted that Indians menaced the Pacific Coast in two ways. First, their supposed low standard of living led them willingly to take jobs for less pay than the "white man" would. And second, Caminetti charged that they suffered from hookworm, a parasite that they would, as agricultural laborers, spread to North Americans.[13]

In Canada officials suspected Indians of agitating for their homeland's independence from the British Empire. Because American and Canadian authorities felt a common cause, they worked together for years to halt or at least partially curtail South Asian migration—a difficult task for Canadian officials, as within the British Empire all subjects could theoretically travel freely.[14] The situation came to a head in 1914.

In that year, 376 Indians hired a Japanese ship, the *Komagata Maru,* to sail from Asia to Vancouver in an attempt to break restrictions placed on South Asian British subjects trying to enter Canada. The *Komagata Maru* arrived at Vancouver on May 23. For two months officials refused to permit its passengers to disembark as their attempt became the focus of a battle in the courts, and some minor scuffling occurred shipside when immigration officers and police tried to board. Finally, on July 23, a Canadian cruiser escorted the Japanese vessel to sea. It returned to Asia with its passenger list intact.[15]

The historian Indiana Matters has discovered that within this context of growing animosity between whites and Indians in British Columbia, local authorities (representing the Anglo-Canadian community) brought an unusually large number of charges of same-sex transgression against Indians in Vancouver. An examination of a few of these incidents clearly demonstrates that police, sometimes acting alone and sometimes working with local white residents, purposely entrapped Indian men in sex crimes. In a 1910 case, the principal witness for the prosecution admitted to being a regularly paid informant. In his testimony he also confessed his uncertainty over what the accused Indian man had initially wanted from him during the incident in question. Finally the witness claimed he had leadingly asked the defendant, "'What do you mean do you want to fuck me?' And [the Indian] nodded his head [yes.]" In another case that year, the prosecution's main witness allegedly received several propositions from an Indian man who declared he would show him what "Hindoo fucking" was. The witness proceeded to the police and worked with them to successfully manufacture yet another incident that resulted in the Indian's arrest.[16]

Another example comes from December 12, 1912, when two police officers, N. McDonald and David Scott, became suspicious of Nar Singh, whom they reportedly observed for four or five nights in succession hanging about the corner of Pender Street and Columbia Avenue. At two in the morning, Scott claimed, "we saw the accused walking up and down the street. The first we saw of him there was a man apparently to me under the influence of liquor came out of the Great Northern Hotel and went east on Pender Street.... The accused went a few doors up and stopped him and spoke to him." Once Singh and the other man went their separate ways, the policemen chose to pursue the former. McDonald followed him to a back-alley stable. There, he claimed, Singh took down his suspenders and pants and "went on his knees in front of me[.]" After this encounter, Scott followed Singh to his lodgings. And there, according to Scott, Singh attempted the same maneuver allegedly made at the stable.[17]

Perhaps the most infamous of these incidents occurred in 1915. A white Canadian chauffeur having a drink at Vancouver's Panama Hotel bar encountered an Indian man who allegedly expressed interest in having sex with him. According to the chauffeur, the accused agreed to pay him and a friend seventy-five cents "for the two and two dollars every Sunday and pay car-fare both ways to Central Park" to continue the sexual relations. The two men, each of whom would bring a friend, made an appointment for later that day on the railroad tracks. Immediately after working out the tryst's details, the chauffeur headed to the police. One detective eagerly agreed to pose as the prostitute friend, while another assented to hide in trees that lined the tracks where the rendezvous was to take place. Shortly after arriving, the chauffeur and the undercover detective took down their trousers and turned their backsides to the Indian men. Within minutes, but only after a scuffle and attempted escape, the latter were securely under arrest. In this case, one of the defendants and one of the detectives, who had carefully hidden his face in the encounter so as not to be recognized, had previously been involved in a murder trial connected to the *Komagata Maru* incident.[18]

These Vancouver incidents demonstrate how local authorities, working with white civilians, purposely ensnared South Asians by manufacturing compromising situations (if not evidence itself). Elsewhere in the region and even outside the urban center, "race" also influenced juries that convicted South Asians for same-sex sex crimes. In February 1912, authorities in the small logging community of Gate, Washington, arrested Don Sing, Bram Sing (figure 4), and Jago Sing, employees of a local lumber company, for anally sodomizing Clarence Murray, a seventeen-year-old white youth. The story told was that on February 11, Murray and a few cousins and friends went into Gate, met the Indians, and enjoyed a few drinks. The other boys left the scene, but Murray accompanied the men to their segregated quarters. There Murray drank more liquor and passed out. From all reports, only Bram and Jago stripped the boy of his trousers, laid him face down on a couch, and then alternately performed anal intercourse on him. Nonetheless, all three Indian men faced charges of sodomy, Don apparently because of guilt by association.

A few months after a local jury found all three guilty and shipped them off to the state penitentiary, the interpreter in the case, P. L. Verma,

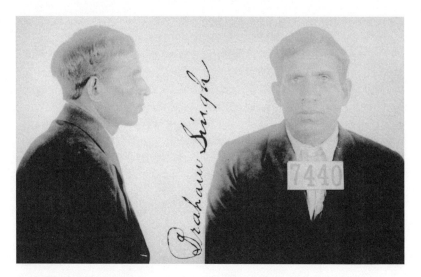

FIGURE 4. Bram Sing, 1915. While working for a logging company in Gate, Washington, in 1912, Sing and two other Asian Indian immigrants faced charges of sodomy with a seventeen-year-old American youth. Oregon State Archives, Oregon State Penitentiary, Inmate Files, Photograph 7440.

a member of Portland's Indian community, fought to overturn Don's conviction. In a well-argued letter to the prison secretary, Verma outlined Don's excellent past behavior, his good work record at Gate, his family's dependence on him, his contributions to charities, and his importance to the Indian community in Portland. Verma also produced supporting documents, including testimonials from Don's previous employers in Washington and Oregon; an appeal from Don's wife in India, who was likely to starve because of her husband's incarceration; and a petition signed by many members of Portland's Indian community. Pointing out that during the trial none of the witnesses ever testified to seeing Don sodomize Murray, Verma concluded that in the rush to convict the other two men, Don became the victim of prejudiced prosecutors and jury members. He noted that the latter, mostly farmers, undoubtedly knew of the recent troubles on the coast that pitted Indian against North American labor and were likely to take sides against the former. Moreover, Verma outlined a long history of racism and its sad effects on immigrants:

When there is a question between American and the Hindoos, it is natural that the Americans may be in some cases disposed to American side. Still more this inclination is manifest when a wrong has been done to an American by some other nationality. Much more is manifest in the case of those who have not been in touch with other nationalities and do not know what their thoughts may be. This case may be seen among the farmers especially, as they generally do not come in connection with other nations and live generally absorbed in their own affairs.

Verma's entreaty ultimately worked. In the face of grave doubts about his guilt, officials released Don in 1913, some months before Jago and Bram. Bram would come before the Oregon legal system a few years later for a similar crime and would meet with a chillingly different fate — a story recounted later in this volume.[19]

It is clear from our latter-day perspective that these authorities in the Northwest unfairly singled out men from India and Greece for allegedly breaking laws against same-sex sex. Some early-twentieth-century inhabitants of the region arrived at the very same conclusion. In November 1912, a Portland resident wrote a letter to the editor of a local newspaper decrying the apparent failure of the police to apprehend some middle- and upper-class white men in connection with the city's growing YMCA homosexual scandal. "If these degenerating practices were committed by Greeks or Hindus," he charged, "these lily whites ... would be in favor of drowning them in the Willamette [River]."[20] Though the threatened punishment is rhetorical hyperbole, it suggests that the region's judicial systems utilized immigrants' actual or alleged same-sex sexual activities to get rid of them in other ways. The evidence for such efforts is clear. In Spokane, Washington, in 1911 the county deputy prosecuting attorney, C. C. Dill, wrote to the secretary of the penitentiary outlining for him the case of Christ Vlassis, a Greek immigrant, who had been sent up on a sodomy conviction. Dill concluded his letter, "I have taken up the matter of his deportation with the immigration people."[21]

These cases involving Greek and South Asian immigrants also demonstrate that such laws were more than a tool in a campaign against men of racial and ethnic minorities: they were tied to dominant society's fears of these men's sexuality. That concern, however, seemed to be expressed not over *homo*sexuality per se but rather over the general sexual threat that these men presumably posed, which might include homosexual practices. This perceived threat is pointedly demonstrated in one of P. L. Verma's complaints. He explained to authorities that the white jurors' suspicions of deviant sexuality were undoubtedly heightened when they learned that Don Sing was arrested in his bunk while wearing nothing at all — because they did not know that sleeping nude, which seemed aberrant to them, was the Indian custom. Also contributing to the rising tide of race prejudice and nativist sentiment throughout America was the white middle-class American belief that the working classes and poor generally, and the "lower races" more specifically, were by nature lustful and sexually degenerate. Thus they were apt to engage in a variety of "deviant" activities, including relations with both the same and opposite sexes.[22]

We know that white middle-class America at the turn of the twentieth century feared racial minority and immigrant male sexuality generally, not just because of a potential to participate in same-sex acts. But that they specifically feared the latter was certainly true. Popular writers and sexologists bolstered the era's conviction that men from the Mediterranean region as well as from India readily had same-sex sexual intercourse. For example, in 1885 Sir Richard Burton, translator of the *Arabian Nights,* commented at length on the perceived commonness and acceptability of male-male sexual relationships in what he called the "Sotadic Zone." According to Burton, this area encompassed southern France, the Iberian Peninsula, Italy, Greece, and the coastal regions of North Africa from Morocco to Egypt, stretching to India. Burton claimed that here such practices are "popular and endemic, held at the worst to be a mere peccadillo." The British sexologist Henry Havelock Ellis relied on Burton's reportings in arguing that southern Italian men were more likely to engage in such relationships than were their northern compatriots. He rationalized this tendency as the influence of "Greek blood" in southern Italy.[23]

Such feelings prejudiced views of men from the Mediterranean in the Northwest. In 1917 the Seattle physician W. Ray Jones expressed concern about a "Turk" who apparently paid a fifteen-year-old Seattle youth twenty-five cents to submit to sodomy. "Because of the pain caused him," Jones surmised, "the boy cried for help and the officers who responded to the call witnessed the act through a crack in the door before arresting the man." The following day the immigrant supposedly "admitted all, but did not consider it an offence, as intercourse with a male was perfectly legitimate in Muhammadan countries." The "Turk" was convicted, but Jones was vexed because the "boy who manifestly had practiced sodomy before[,]...who willingly submitted to passive pederasty for money," and who suffered from gonorrhea (left untreated by the authorities) was set free. At the same time "[t]he man who had always been taught that he could have intercourse with no woman other than a wife or legal concubine, goes to prison for a term of years for a

crime which according to the custom of his native country was not considered a crime."[24] While in this case the Seattle physician spoke up on
behalf of a man from the Mediterranean region—or at least used his
story to draw attention to an inadequate response to a Seattle youth—he
did so from the deep-seated belief that same-sex sexual relations commonly occurred in the immigrant man's homeland.

During the years from 1907 to 1916, mainstream society blamed immigrant men for the apparent general decline in American morals, the
spread of venereal diseases, and increasing rates of prostitution. White
middle-class Americans assumed all these to be endemic to the working
class, the poor, and especially minority racial groups, thus socially constructing them as carriers of sexual diseases and perpetrators of general
moral ruin while at the same time casting themselves in the role of hap-
less victim. Attention particularly focused on the immigrant in the
"white slave" panic that gripped the country, as the foreign-born were
accused of operating an international traffic in white women.[25] Not surprisingly, given the view that the "lower races" had a predilection for
same-sex sexual activities as well, the dominant society also blamed immigrants for the apparent spread of such practices in the United States.
Alfred J. Zobel, a San Francisco physician who in 1909 treated three
teenage "American boys" for gonorrhea of the rectum, claimed that the
condition "has been rather rare in this country, but since the influx of
foreigners from those countries where unnatural practices are common,
more cases are now seen." Two years later, the Immigration Commission
presented the U.S. Senate with its lengthy findings regarding white slavery, claiming in passing that "it is clear that there is a beginning...of a
traffic in boys and men for immoral purposes. The same measures employed for the restriction of the traffic in women should be applied with
even greater rigidity...in the case of men."[26]

Immigrant males' sexual links to white "American" men and *especially*
to white "American" youths, suggested in these and other sources cited
above, deepened white middle-class racial and sexual fears.[27] The late
nineteenth and early twentieth centuries witnessed increasing concern
on the part of the socially dominant classes over youths and boys generally. A variety of factors—including industrialization, the growth of the
impersonal city, population expansion, and the increasing independence
of women—all combined to transform the middle-class American family and its internal relations. Many reformers saw evidence that the "traditional" family was now breaking down in a perceived reduction of
parental supervision and an intensification of juvenile delinquency,

crime, truancy, and even gang activity. Ameliorating the problems of the middle-class youth, and thereby saving the family, became a particular focus of the era's reforms. That concern is demonstrated in the Boy Scout movement, the proliferation of YMCA youth-centered projects, the founding of boys' and girls' aid societies, the development of juvenile departments in the nation's court system, and the movement to separate youths from adults when incarcerated.[28]

An emphasis on the difficulties facing youths and on the connection between them and the health of society is apparent in Portland during these years. Between the 1890s and 1910s, Rose City newspapers ran innumerable articles with such titles as "Who Is Responsible for the Boy?," "Bad Boys on Parole," "Reform for the Boys," "A Plea for the Boys," "Homeless Boys," "Boy Values," "Habits of American Youth," "A Lesson for Boys and Parents," "Helping the Boys," and "Child Education Is Urged as a Remedy for Social Condition." Furthermore, Portland also served as home to a very active YMCA movement, and the Girls' and Boys' Aid Society of Oregon was founded in the city in 1885. In 1905 the Oregon legislature created in Portland the first juvenile department in the state's court system. A 1913 mayoral committee strongly advocated the establishment of a house of detention and an industrial home for youths, in part as a result of discovering in one of the city's jails a nineteen-year-old "boy" who was "shut up in one room...with fifty other prisoners....Thieves, drug fiends and vagrants, with the occasional sex perverts, were this boy's intimate daily and nightly companions for some months."[29]

As the committee's report evinces, reformers expressed grave concern over the possibility that youths might participate, willingly or otherwise, in any type of sexual activity. The historian Jeffrey P. Moran has pointed out the centrality of sexuality to changing social views of children at this time. Before 1900, society perceived children and teenagers simply as incompletely developed adults and not, as Moran explained, as "a separate class unto themselves." Only in the waning years of the nineteenth century did broader society begin to recognize the existence of an intermediate phase in life. With the publication of the psychologist G. Stanley Hall's two-volume 1904 work titled *Adolescence,* the idea of the adolescent finally crystallized. As it did, sexuality became "critical to the new, scientific concept of adolescence," according to Moran.[30] Social attention increasingly focused on chastity for youth, as adolescence was seen as both a period of sexual maturity and a phase wherein youths had not yet matured socially. Middle-class reformers accepted that the sublimation of sexual energies was necessary for the adolescent's successful socialization and development. Exposure to sexual corruption and immorality not only threatened the youngster with ruin; it spelled doom for society as a whole.[31]

The circumstances in which adolescence emerged as an idea and a reality for the middle classes, and the concomitant perception that the family was collapsing, exacerbated fears about the vulnerability of the boy and thus also the family to the sexual dangers posed by the immigrant male. Indeed, we can see those fears in the 1909 lament of the San Francisco physician Zobel, who declared that the "American" teenagers had contracted gonorrhea of the rectum from "foreigners." A few years later the Portland judge J. P. Kavanaugh echoed the same sentiments in his assessment for the state's parole board of Tony Lagallo, whom the magistrate had sent to prison for sodomy on a young white boy. Lagallo "is an Italian laborer," Kavanaugh claimed, and therefore "prison officials should keep in mind that [in] turning him loose upon the community other persons maybe [*sic*] corrupted into the practice of this unnatural crime."[32]

A particularly telling example of heightened concern over male-male sexual relations between white youths and racial minorities comes from the pages of Portland's *Evening Telegram*. An article of 1894 indignantly broadcast to readers, "One of the most atrocious crimes ever committed in this city came to light early last evening, and the perpetrator of the crime—a big stalwart negro named Fred Jones, a scowdweller in the north part of the city—was placed under arrest.... The victim of this brute is an English lad 17 years of age[.]"[33] It did not matter that the "victim," Thomas Mosey, actually appeared to have been a willing participant in the relationship. Taken together, the age of Mosey and the interracial nature of the affair motivated the newspaper's dramatic vocabulary, including such words as "atrocious," "perpetrator," "stalwart," "victim," and "brute." In the Stafford-Wilkinson case mentioned earlier in this chapter, which the *Evening Telegram* had covered rather more prosaically a few years before, arrest records reveal that the individuals concerned were both white. They also gave Stafford's age as somewhere between forty and forty-five and listed Wilkinson's in the neighborhood of fifteen to eighteen—precisely the age of Mosey. Although the Stafford-Wilkinson affair did garner notice, the *Evening Telegram* cast no particular (let alone racial) aspersions on Stafford.

It should be stressed, however, that regardless of the racial or ethnic background or even the age of a working-class, immigrant, or racial minority man and his male sex partner, they likely ended up before the legal system. Once again, this suggests that the feelings against such men were related to a variety of white middle-class anxieties and not just to a concern over "foreigners" mixing with white American boys. Even two adult immigrant males who had sex with each other demanded attention. For example, in 1914 Vancouver authorities apprehended an Asian and a Greek immigrant who were having sex in a rooming house on the corner of Main and Powell Streets, a locale within that city's transient working-class neighborhood. Accompanied to the room by the proprietor, the policeman

rapped at the door and got no answer.... I stood on the table and looked over the transom and both the accused were at it right there. The Greek was stripped up to his shoulders, with his hands on the bed.... And the other man, the Hindoo had his pants open.... The Hindoo was running his penis into the rectum of the Greek, and we rapped several times, and they kept us there five minutes.... This Greek... he turned round, before they stopped at this business, he turned round to the Hindoo and he pointed to the door and never said a word, and they kept on doing this business.[34]

Continual popular and official concentration on and reference to "foreigners," "aliens," and racial minority men for their supposed sexual threat, along with other forms of stereotyping and prejudice, worked to construct a stark division in the urban Northwest between "insiders"—the respectable and white middle-class families—and "outsiders"—working-class, immigrant, and racial minority males. The urban visibility of the outsiders necessarily demanded that authorities and reformers also focus their attention on the areas and establishments within the city frequented and inhabited by these men. Various factors caused working-class, transient, immigrant, and racial minority males to be drawn to, or segregated in, what the middle classes dubbed the "vice districts" of the Northwest's larger cities. In Portland it was the Whitechapel or North End; in Seattle, Skid Road; in Vancouver, Hastings Street. The middle classes then conflated these districts and their patrons. While certainly various "vices" such as prostitution, gambling, drinking, drug use, crime, and same-sex sexual activities were found and probably (but not always) concentrated in these areas, the official attention only worked to magnify ever more the dangers that they and their inhabitants seemed to pose.[35]

From the beginning, the dominant classes associated Portland's vice district with the sexual, the dangerous, and the foreign, as its earliest name, the "Whitechapel," indicates. In the late summer and fall of 1888, a killer known as Jack the Ripper savagely murdered at least five female sex workers in London's Whitechapel neighborhood, an area regarded as a haven for prostitutes, immigrants, and the poor. Even as contemporary news services trumpeted these horrific crimes to the Western world, Portland's then-inchoate vice district was experiencing a wave of violent murders of female sex workers that lasted for several years. It began in 1885 with the exceptionally brutal killing of Emma Merlotin, whose identity as a "French courtesan" intensified thoughts of the exotic. Shortly before eleven o'clock on the wintry night of December 22, a policeman discovered Merlotin's body in her cottage on Third Street, lying face down in a three-foot-wide pool of blood. Clothed only in a chemise, boots, and stockings, Merlotin had suffered gruesome bludgeoning and slashing that the papers reported in graphic detail.[36]

Within a couple of days authorities arrested the "Finnish" sailor William Sundstrom, whom they found lurking around the murder scene. He had blood stains on his clothing and a hatchet in his possession. Yet the police charged neither Sundstrom nor anyone else with this vicious crime. During the next four years other brutal murders occurred in what was developing into the red-light district. Offenses ranging from slaying to picking pockets beset this area for years, leading the police to characterize it as "the scene of some of the most terrible crimes. Murders and robberies were of frequent occurrence."[37] Thus, for a number of reasons—Merlotin's murder was unusually sinister, the victim had an exotic background, an immigrant sailor was implicated, the crime went unsolved, Jack the Ripper undertook a similar killing spree in London's Whitechapel at about the same time, and the area was notorious for its violent activities—Portlanders latched onto "Whitechapel" as an appropriate name for their city's tenderloin.[38]

By about 1905 the Whitechapel was better known as the "North End," a label that corresponded to its geographic location relative to the central business district.[39] The boundaries of the Whitechapel/ North End shifted over the years. Roughly speaking, the district moved slowly north several blocks from a somewhat ambiguous downtown axis in the early 1880s at about Stark Street to a more cohesive area during the first years of the twentieth century, bounded by Ankeny on the south, Irving on the north, perhaps Eighth on the west, and the Willamette River on the east. Although this seventy-block area included any number of properties completely unrelated to "vice," at its very heart lay what the authorities felt was the most inglorious area of all: the three east-west running streets of Burnside, Couch, and Davis and the area from the river west to about Fifth (figure 5).

As the Whitechapel migrated northward, it collided with one of the most desirable residential neighborhoods in the city. Beginning in the

FIGURE 5. Burnside Street in Portland's North End, ca. 1907. Burnside was the axis of the transient working-class district in Portland from the 1890s to well into the twentieth century. On the left of the photograph is a sign for Erickson's saloon, which boasted the longest bar in the world. The arch over the street reads THEATRE on both sides. Oregon Historical Society, #OrHi PGE 130–37.

1860s, Portland's leading families constructed expensive homes on North Third and Fourth Streets. But as the neighborhood began changing in the early 1880s, they fled west to Nineteenth Street and southwest to Portland Heights. By 1884, Third and Fourth had been transformed. That year the *Portland City Directory* reported that the Whitechapel was decidedly not a middle-class space and intimated that the new habitués and the altered atmosphere were of a piece: "our most elegant residences have been abandoned ... and the denizens of that portion of the city have as completely changed in character as their surroundings."[40] Well before the turn of the century, Portlanders mapped the physical boundaries of the North End by what they viewed as the less-than-savory activities that occurred there. Thus in 1903 when the Rose City's chief of police devoted entire sections in his annual report to such subjects as the police manual and salaries, the mounted police, the city jail, fire escapes, dance halls, the rock pile, opium smoking, streetwalking prostitutes, and various other aspects of law and (dis)order in Portland, probably no one was surprised that one segment of his summary was given over to the "Whitechapel District." He singled it out from all other neighborhoods in the city as an area with its own distinct criminal and moral problems.[41]

The Whitechapel was, most notably, racially diverse. Initially bordering it, Chinatown eventually became part of the North End. By 1900, 62 percent of the Rose City's African Americans lived there. In 1910 individuals who were foreign-born, who were black, or who had one or both parents of foreign origin composed almost 60 percent of the population of the three wards that took in parts of the North End. Although Portland is noteworthy during this era for the wide distribution of its residents of foreign birth and parentage, the highest concentrations of them could be found in the wards of the Whitechapel.[42] The dominant social classes thus necessarily perceived the North End as a racialized space, further helping to construct it as a district of dangerous outsiders. White Americans at this time believed there to be a multiplicity of races, with Africans, Chinese, Indians, and Japanese, as well as Greeks, Italians, Slavs, and other Europeans, each being distinct. The so-called Anglo-Saxon stood at the top of the racial hierarchy. Individuals from this group then projected their fears onto those "beneath" them and, using circular logic, embraced the belief that, according to Michael Omi and Howard Winant, "differences in intelligence, temperament, and sexuality (among other traits) were . . . racial in character."[43]

From the 1880s through the early 1900s, Portland's middle classes therefore unremittingly blamed the North End's racial minorities for the moral and criminal problems of the area. For example, they focused on the Chinese for encouraging opium smoking and gambling. By the early 1900s they had turned their attention to Greek immigrants, whom one official report from 1913 described as "laboring men of a very low class and degraded character." At the same time the police identified the Greeks with the "rapidly growing ghetto district" and accused them of causing the most "trouble" in the city. Only a few years earlier local officials had singled out "colored" female sex workers of the North End as responsible for an upsurge in the city's cases of larceny. Whereas "a very few reports of robberies have been made in connection with the white women [prostitutes,] . . . [t]his cannot be truthfully said in relation to the colored women. . . . They were bold in their operations and defiant in their attitude."[44]

While immigrants and racial minority groups concentrated in the North End, the district also attracted a broad range of transient working-class males, a large number of whom seasonally migrated to the city. Harvey Scott, an influential newsman, wrote in 1890 that "with the increase of foreign commerce, in 1868, and onward the foreign sailor class became much larger. With the rise and growth of the salmon fishing business, the fishermen of the Columbia River...made periodical trips to Portland,... as did also the miners, and to some extent the ranchers, from east of the mountains."[45] By the late 1870s city officials already noted a seasonal pattern of transient laborers "drift[ing] here from the interior and from California in the Fall." Well into the twentieth century, Mayor A. E. Rushlight would note in his annual messages that "[d]uring the winter months thousands of unemployed men come to Portland from logging camps and lumber mills adjacent to the city." It is difficult to know with precision how many filtered into the Rose City on a seasonal basis; some officials asserted that their number reached twenty thousand. The urban historian Chris Sawyer has conservatively calculated that anywhere between three and twelve thousand transients seasonally came to Portland.[46]

The North End thus became a decidedly male space. In the late nineteenth and early twentieth centuries men outnumbered women in all major Northwest cities, but in neighborhoods such as the North End the imbalance was the greatest. In 1910 Portland's Third Ward, which included most of the North End, was 79 percent male while the rest of the city was only 57 percent male. The Second and Fourth Wards, each of which took in slivers of the North End, also had high concentrations of men (61 and 66 percent of their population respectively) in 1910.[47] Local authorities, news editors, and middle-class reformers responded just as they had to racial minority groups, attributing to the North End's men an unsavory reputation. "The comparative absence of women [there]," charged Harvey Scott, "stimulated grossness and coarseness of speech and manners, and the temptation toward immorality intensified." Scott described the Whitechapel in his 1890 *History of Portland* with particular indignation. He also used the past tense, hoping to assure readers who did not know any better that middle-class propriety had won the day: "They were a class of hard drinkers, stimulating themselves from successive nights of indulgence in their games.... Gambling and other indulgences were carried to the same violent excess[.]" Then, "with the building of the railways a large floating population of men...not on their best behavior, came on pleasure excursions..., crowding the low hotels, and saloons, the theatres, and places of popular amusements."[48]

Scott's biased rantings hold a certain grain of truth: for various reasons, the North End did draw to it working-class transients. By the

1890s Portland was a bustling seaport with several major railway lines. Also, although the continuing paucity of manufacturing limited the jobs available in the Rose City in the winter months, over the years a number of employment agencies opened in the North End. Portland thereby became a base in the spring months for men searching for work to carry them through until the autumn, when once again they would be laid off. The city also offered the transient trade inexpensive eateries. For many years the police department provided any number of peripatetic men free room and board in the nearby city jail, while in the North End Erickson's saloon offered complimentary lunches (see map 2). The transient Andrew McGraw claimed in 1895 that he paid only five cents for a meal in the Whitechapel. He supplemented his fare with fish caught in the Willamette River.[49]

In addition, the North End abounded in inexpensive lodgings. One historian has determined that if a survey had been conducted in 1898 to determine numbers of lodging houses, Portland would have ranked fourth nationally, behind New York, Chicago, and San Francisco. North End denizens occupied lodging houses and hotels at greater rates than residents of any other part of the city, as can be inferred from the 1910 census. In that year, the city of Portland counted an average of one dwelling for every 5.5 residents. Certain eastside neighborhoods experienced rates as low as 4.3 residents per dwelling. The Third Ward, however, averaged 14.8 inhabitants per dwelling—the most in the city.[50]

Reformers, police, and news writers in all cities of the Northwest pointed to such housing in the vice district to underscore the differences between this area of town with its residents and the respectable middle classes and their neighborhoods. First, they associated the former with the exotic. In case after case in which local authorities investigated sexual transgressions in working-class hotels, they identified the accommodations with the "race" of their proprietor. "Japanese"-owned establishments received particular notice. When a Vancouver policeman went to a lodging on March 21, 1914, to investigate the report that Greek and Indian males were having sex there, he described the place as "a Jap rooming house." In Walla Walla, Washington, in 1918, authorities characterized the hotel where the African American George McElroy attempted to seduce the American-born white Roy Church as "a Japanese lodging house."[51] Moreover, reformers claimed that the atmosphere of the working-class lodging houses threatened the broader urban citizenry. In 1910 the Portland Woman's Club undertook an investigation of North End accommodations. It bitterly complained that more than three hundred men crowded into some of the district's "cheap lodging houses." "These places," the Woman's Club charged, "are breeding grounds of crime." Showing little interest in the welfare of those who lived in such conditions, club representatives concentrated on the ways in which these places supposedly menaced the better classes. The lodging house "air was foul to an unspeakable degree," the report accused, "the bedding was filthy...infested with vermin if not with the germs of infectious and epidemic diseases, which though started in the poorer quarters of the city may spread to the prosperous portions and endanger the lives of its residents."[52]

Where middle-class respectability perceived danger, transient men found inexpensive hospitality. But the North End attracted them with more than just its lodgings; the neighborhood's various diversions also acted as a lure—and the middle class looked askance at these, too. In a series of articles relating the unfortunate local effects of the nationwide economic downturn in 1907, the *Oregonian* maintained that transient men "so densely...pack the sidewalks at Second and Burnside streets and in that vicinity, that one could hardly elbow his way through the throng....Poolrooms and saloons are crowded until closing time, 1 A.M., and are quickly filled again at the opening of the morning." Later in the month the same paper remarked, "The amusement halls of Erickson's and Blazier's are packed with the idle humanity, for each performance, and at the end of the entertainment in the one place the throng flocks across the street to attend that in the other."[53] From 1885 until the onset of citywide prohibition in 1916, Portland's saloons were concentrated in the North End. Among the best-known was Erickson's, which boasted the "longest bar in the world," running 684 linear feet. Other establishments combined a variety of amusements. Fritz's included a bar, grill, vaudeville show, and movie theater. Other entertainments and vice-related businesses—opium dens, gaming resorts, shooting galleries, prize-fighting rings, massage parlors, pool halls, and obscene picture shows—could also be found in the North End at various times between the 1880s and the 1920s. Through the early twentieth century, moral reformers and local authorities variously investigated and raided such establishments in direct response to their supposed threat to the broader Portland citizenry.[54]

As the Whitechapel/North End formed in Portland during the last decades of the nineteenth century, the city's middle classes defined it along the lines of race and class and all the hazards that its immigrant, racial minority, and transient working-class inhabitants were thought to pose to urban respectability. It should come as little surprise that 89 percent of arrests of men and youths for same-sex sex crimes in Portland occurred within the North End or other areas where single, working-class, immigrant, and primarily male populations resided (in this regard, too, the case of Andrew Dillige and Grover King was typical). Part of the social construction of the North End, then, was the middle-class designation of this place as a space of sexual transgressions. Certainly such activities did occur there. However, the middle class's own fears led its officials to scrutinize ever more closely the men and the establishments of the North End, focusing their vision as they did so on what most seemed to imperil the boy.

Throughout the period, Portlanders expressed general concern over youths who frequented the North End. As early as 1888, one investigator complained of young males traipsing in and out of opium dens, gambling parlors, saloons, and burlesque shows and expressed particular shock at finding them scattered throughout the notorious Tivoli Theater. This sleuth also discovered to his horror an underground gambling den where there operated "four games in full blast.... Two of these were conducted by Chinese, one by an ancient negro. The bar was kept by a white man. While the majority were Chinamen, a considerable number of white men and beardless youths were actively engaged in the games."[55] The presence of such underage males in the Whitechapel continued for years. Although the mayor's report boasted in 1903 that the "energetic action on the part of the police in looking after minors" had led to the absence of both boys and girls from "pool-rooms, saloons, or resorts unsuitable for minors to visit," arrest figures belie his claim. In 1901 and 1902 respectively, the police apprehended 376 and 329 minors in these and other places. In the year in which the police congratulated themselves for a job well done, they apprehended 1,045.[56] Such an increase in the number of arrests might demonstrate the "energetic action" of authorities, but it also indicates that very large numbers of minors were still frequenting the North End.

Poolrooms, saloons, and other resorts came under surveillance because same-sex sexual liaisons might occur there between "vulnerable" youths and working-class, immigrant, and racial minority men.[57] The saloon acted as the central institution of male working-class America during the years before Prohibition. The historian Roy Rosenzweig has called it "the axis" of the working-class world, providing at various times check-cashing services, free newspapers, entertainment, free food, public toilets, gaming and gambling opportunities, homes for fraternal organizations, and employment information; more specifically it served as a place where men could meet other men for political debate, sports talk, storytelling, and treating. Especially for men who inhabited the cramped, dorm-style lodging houses, the saloon provided a pleasant atmosphere, one in which they could while away the months before the work season started up again.[58] News editors, reformers, and authorities were obsessed by its dangers.

In 1889 a reporter for the sensational *Sunday Mercury* told a disturbing story of an incident at a Portland saloon. This establishment apparently had long been a place of trouble, where "the shrill whistle for the police can be heard on almost every evening." On one Sunday in mid-June, the reporter happened by when "the usual crash and rattle was heard at the corner." He elbowed his way through a large crowd that had assembled to observe what was taking place. On entering the saloon, the curious investigator

found an old man coming out of the back room, which is a very dingy looking place, with a large gash cut over his left eye, and the blood running down the side of his cheek, clogging up his whiskers, while near by stood a young man whose appearance would indicate that he was about 25 years of age. As he came out of the back room also he looked as if he was some worse the wear, for the scuffle which he had just taken part in almost disrobed him. As he proceeded to replace his clothing...he stated that he was jumped upon, and simply protected himself from being completely "done up;" however this caused a great many remarks, wondering how he could have ever gotten into that condition while in a common scuffle. To say the least he was in a very compromising condition when he made his appearance. These low places should not be granted a license to sell liquor.[59]

Officials and reformers in various Northwest cities for years focused on the dangers lurking in the working-class saloon. In late 1912 Rose City police arrested the twenty-five-year-old Greek immigrant railroad worker George Stfe for "persuading" Dorman Rice—seventeen years old, American-born, and white—to enter a saloon. Stfe allegedly supplied Rice with liquor, took him to his room, "undressed and exposed...his naked body, and then and there endeavor[ed] to have the said Dorman Rice to go to bed with him...for an immoral purpose." In Seattle at the same time, Juvenile Court Judge Archibald Frater reported that one of his officers had informed him that he frequently observed at midnight groups of twelve- to fifteen-year-old boys in the Skid Road area "being solicited by drunks." "[H]e has seen ten-year-old boys," Frater continued, "jostle past drunks through the front entrance of bar rooms. He has seen as many as six little fellows under fourteen years swarming about a swaying crowd of drunks at the very doors of the worst resorts on Washington Street." Frater commanded the police to take every youngster they see "by the ear and lead" them away from Skid Road. "Such method followed with eternal vigilance is the only means by which boys can be kept away from the dangers that will persist there so long as the character of the population is what it is." Frater expressed further hope that sometime in the future the "entire bar-room evil" would be modified and the "army of homeless men down there" will be provided "with better encouragement to live wholesomely."[60]

Among reformers, pool halls had a particularly wicked reputation for luring underage boys into a life of iniquity. A 1911–12 Portland survey found 232 such establishments. Although legally males younger than nineteen were prohibited from entering these businesses, boys regularly could be found there. Vice commission operatives observed that one downtown pool hall was "a rendezvous for young fellows between 16 and 21[.]" Many cases involving sex between men and youths revolved about the pool hall. That authorities and reformers focused their attention on such places is clear from the role played by the Monte Carlo poolroom during Portland's "Greek scandal" of 1913.[61]

Various other working-class entertainments, wherever they might be in the city, also were seen by the middle class as presenting a sexual menace. During this era amusements parks, dance halls, and movie theaters took the United States by storm. Already in the 1900s, Portland had its share of such places. Oaks Park south of town and Council Crest Observatory and Scenic Park in the hills above the central business district opened in the first decade of the century, with Council Crest sporting a dance hall as well. Some Portlanders decried their unsavory reputations. In 1905 a city council member described the Oaks as "an immoral place and that he had seen more drunkenness there than he had ever seen at any place in the City." In 1908 the proprietor of Council Crest wrote to city officials begging that a special police officer be appointed for duty at the park "[t]o maintain order....There is...an element who bring up liquor, and to break up this practice before it goes too far[.]"[62] By 1914 Portland had more than fifty movie theaters with a weekly seating capacity and attendance that exceeded the total population of the city. The 1913 Vice Commission report noted that the "number of attendances" at Portland's moving picture shows "is remarkable—far surpassing any other interest." A year later investigators lamented that 28.4 percent of juvenile males between the ages of six and eighteen attended motion pictures at least twice a week. More frightening was that 63.7 percent of these boys generally attended at night.[63]

The same-sex sexual dangers that amusement parks and movie theaters posed to local youth confounded local officials in the Northwest. In the early 1910s Portland's Juvenile Court Judge William Gatens despaired over a ten-year-old "truant" who met a man at a theater, accompanied him to his room for money, and subsequently engaged in sex with him on nine or ten occasions before authorities found out. In another case, a man approached a fifteen-year-old in front of a movie house, "talked to him awhile, took him to a theater, and later to his room." And in still another incident, "men" picked up two boys "at an amusement park...and later accompanied them to moving picture shows, the city park, and other places. The men gave them money. Things [i]nconceivably vile followed." In Seattle, the social worker Lilburn Merrill condemned five youths who regularly had sex with men and "voluntarily frequented low-grade amusement resorts and the water front to solicit men with whom they consorted for financial consideration."[64]

Legal records suggest that local authorities' efforts at saving boys were concentrated on the inexpensive lodging houses in working-class districts—the Fairmount Hotel in the Dillige-King affair, for instance. The examples are many. On February 4, 1909, Rose City detectives arrested in the North End "[C]laus Novig for taking boys to his room for immoral purposes." In 1915 they apprehended Harry Smith, a twenty-eight-year-old American Indian who worked as a longshoreman, for the crime of sodomy. According to authorities, the affair was "[j]ust an ordinary case of Sodomy," Smith taking a "young man to his room[.]" According to Smith, "I was drunk at the time. I was going over to the East-side. I went up into my room one evening and this kid was there. I went to bed and the kid took off his clothes and sat on the edge of the bed. Then two fellows came....They arrested me and indicted me for this crime[.]"[65] In the same year authorities also went to the North End's Globe Hotel "to investigate a man who was a sexual pervert & supposed to have a boy in his room[.]" The Globe, located on First between Couch and Davis (see map 2), had a particularly disreputable reputation among some Portlanders. One had complained in a letter to the city council about the "slums" of the North End and their denizens, "the inebriate and the buffoon," who patronized the Globe lodging house, a "Homely Old Place for the Habitues of desert Wilds [and] Hobo wanderings[.]"[66]

This complaint against the "hobo" well represents a certain reality in the urban Northwest during the late nineteenth and early twentieth centuries: the socially dominant group's various moral fears focused primarily on working-class and in particular transient men. Thus, in day-to-day arrest records and court proceedings, men from this class appeared far more often for same-sex sex crimes than did men of any other class background. This imbalance is explained in part by class, but factors of race and immigrant status also played a role: men of racial minority and immigrant background tended to be laborers. A broad range of class animosities, race prejudices, and nativist sentiments pervaded the Northwest at the turn of the twentieth century. In particular, it was widely accepted among the middle class that the "lower classes" and the "lower races" were by nature sexually degenerate and therefore posed a moral threat to the broader public. Such fears intensified in the city, where racial minority and immigrant men and others of the laboring classes concentrated in specific and highly visible urban spaces. In combination with class and race anxieties, urban space sharpened middle-class worries. Through class, race, and space, the dominant social group in the urban Northwest constructed outsiders and the sexual dangers that they seemingly presented. In an important way, then, the middle-class citizenry, local authorities, and reformers perceived same-sex sexual activities as a threat coming from without. One consequence, of course, was that working-class, racial minority, and immigrant men and their urban spaces would suffer retribution. Another was that the middle classes failed to recognize for some years that male-male sexual activities occurred among the members of their own class and in middle-class urban spaces—a subject, with fascinating implications for the emergence of a more modern notion of homosexuality, that will be addressed in the following two chapters.

The socially dominant group's concentration on racial minority and immigrant males, and thus on the working class, has provided us today with various records that make it possible to describe certain attributes of working-class and transient male-male sexuality in the urban center. The remainder of this chapter is dedicated to such a description. It must be kept in mind, however, that these records exist as a result of prejudice, which necessarily colors any attempt to draw "objective" conclusions from them. Indeed, to underscore the biased context in which the following cases are situated, I have chosen to include in my analyses many of the ethnic and racial identities of men, youths, and city spaces that appear in the records themselves.

Urban Youths and Transient Working-Class Men

Intent on issues of morality, early-twentieth-century Portland authorities and reformers regularly patrolled the working-class North End. As a result of this surveillance we know that male-male sexual activities commonly occurred there. Because authorities and reformers concentrated on the "imperiled" youth in the North End, documents pertaining to adult-juvenile male relations are the most abundant. Boys who had sex with men were common in other North American cities at the time. Typically, they maintained their relationships in working-class neighborhoods. Yet it should be stressed that in the cities of the Pacific Northwest, a preponderance of intergenerational same-sex relationships had links to the sexual culture of migratory workers. It is impossible to say just how many boys in Northwest urban centers who had sex with men were also transients themselves. Some seem to have had no direct links to life on the road, born and sometimes living with their families in the city where they were sexually active. For example, sixteen-year-old Dan Davis was one of the youths who hung about the Monte Carlo. Police arrested him at his mother's home, located on Portland's lower-middle-class eastside. In Seattle, Lilburn Merrill found that "Case H," a nine-year-old boy, "was involved with vagrant men," but resided with his mother in the city.[67]

It is likely, however, that many—perhaps even most—young males who came before the law in the Northwest for relations with working-class men had some transience in their backgrounds. Nels Anderson claimed that generally speaking, "Most boys found in the Hobohemian areas have had experience on the road."[68] Portland documents for the era contain little personal information about young males who had sex with men. But in those cases where they do, sources most often list the occupations of these youths as laborers or sailors, both lines of work strongly associated with transience. In Seattle, Lilburn Merrill reported in 1913 on "Case U," a boy of fifteen who consorted "with vagrant men whose relations he solicited." Case U had a history of running away from home and an arrest record that included apprehensions in Seattle and "another town." A few years later, Merrill found that a group of Seattle youths whose experiences "abounded in homosexualism" had "nomadic" backgrounds. Local police in Northwest cities also occasionally used labels associated with on-the-road culture when referring to some of these boys. In the Greek scandal, for instance, detectives stated that Grover King "is a Punk." A couple of years earlier, Portland police officers "[a]rrested one John McDonald…a yegg…with a punk-kid Andrew Stewart[.]" The police booked both for vagrancy, a charge typically used for same-sex offenses.[69]

Working-class adult-juvenile sexual contacts in "vice" districts of the Northwest had important links to the jocker-punk relationship. They were especially influenced by the transmutation of this relationship when it entered the city. Once in the urban setting, economic considerations typically led jockers to end their partnerships with boys. "Whereas, out of town the pair can travel as companions aiding each other," Nels Anderson noted, "in the city they can get along better alone. It is difficult for partners to remain together long in the city, especially if one has money and the other none. . . . Living in a metropolis is a problem the tramp can solve better alone." Indeed, migratory laborers found economic opportunities particularly limited in Northwest urban areas. Unlike the industrial cities of the East and Midwest, Portland had few year-round jobs in manufacturing; its economy relied principally on commerce, which in itself fluctuated with the seasons.[70] Thus when casual laborers looked to Portland, and even Seattle and Vancouver, as seasonal havens, they hoped that with their last paycheck in hand, these city's inexpensive lodgings, meals, and amusements would sustain them until the work season started up again in the spring. They likely found it difficult in this atmosphere to maintain their on-the-road relationships, and had less desire to do so. In these circumstances, according to Anderson, the punks became "promiscuous in their relations and many of them even commercialize themselves" when in the city.[71] Indeed, the punk, now on his own, had good reason to turn to sex work for survival. Still, not all jocker-punk alliances foundered in the city. Even Nels Anderson reported that in the urban setting transient men and youths sometimes sustained longer relationships. An example from Portland supports this claim. In April 1917, authorities arrested the Italian immigrant and transient worker Tony Lagallo at the St. Helens Hotel on Second Street. They charged him with attempting to commit sodomy on Albert Ambrose, an eleven-year-old boy. Reportedly the two had maintained a relationship in the city for "nearly a year."[72]

While cases similar to Lagallo and Ambrose's do appear in records, more often when authorities hauled working-class adult-juvenile couples into the police station, they discovered that some financial transaction had taken place. Selling sex was only part of the survival strategy for transient and other working-class boys in the urban setting. As already indicated, juvenile males who were "laborers" were apprehended in Portland for same-sex crimes more than were boys who had any other occupation. But we also know that in the city many found jobs in the various street trades, such as peddling newspapers and shining shoes. Others hired on as collectors, messengers, elevator operators, and even pin setters. For example, in late November 1912, seventeen-year-old

Raymond Enneking was arrested in Salem, Oregon. An interrogation revealed that he had found employment there as a bootblack, but previously had worked as a messenger boy in Portland. In the latter city, Enneking admitted, he "and a large number of others" had sexual affairs with men "for a money consideration." Just a year earlier, the Seattle judge Archibald Frater complained of the newsboys who in the Skid Road area "know there is plenty of easy money to be had" prostituting themselves among the men there. Whatever job the street boy might find, it was among the most meanly paid. This reinforced the necessity, if not desire, of boys to supplement their livelihoods with sex work.[73]

Occasionally, boys had sex with their working-class employers. In Spokane in 1911, thirty-two-year-old Christ Vlassis—a Greek fruit peddler—faced charges of sodomy. According to documents, Vlassis had taken "young boys" to his room in a downtown hotel on different occasions. The proprietresses of the hotel where Vlassis lodged grew "suspicious of him." On one occasion, "when he took a twelve-year old boy to his room, they arranged a ladder and looked through the transom over his door, and then opened the door and caught him in the act." According to Vlassis, in this particular instance the boy did work for him at his fruit stand.[74]

To be sure, not all boys in cities who willingly had sex with transient men did so for financial gain. Others sought men out for all the emotional and sexual reasons that pertained when they were on the road, as set forth in the previous chapter. But urban legal records tend to concentrate on the more mundane considerations of the adult-juvenile male sex exchange. For example, in Spokane in early 1912, a twelve-year-old newsboy became sexually involved with a forty-six-year-old Norwegian-born laborer in exchange for a trip to the theater and a meal at a restaurant.[75]

That many boys received admission to the show, or a meal at a restaurant, or even clothing in return for sex with their patrons suggests a certain parallel to the "charity girls" or female "chippies" of the early-twentieth-century American city who, in the words of the historian Kathy Peiss, traded "sexual favors of varying degrees for male attention, gifts, and a good time." Because such women did not accept money for their sexual encounters with men, street culture differentiated them from prostitutes. Nonetheless, according to Peiss, only a "thin line divided these women from 'occasional prostitutes,' women who slipped in and out of prostitution when unemployed or in need of extra income."[76] The "charity boys" of the Northwest also seemed opportunistic, having no qualms about accepting any gift, whether cash or other items. In fact,

Nels Anderson declared that "a great many boys...make it a business to exploit passing attachments" with men on the road; "they get all they can...and move on." In Boise in 1905, eighteen-year-old and white street-boy Ben Murray had sexual relations with African American Henry Bacon in the latter's room at the edge of that town's red-light district. Murray later testified that he was hoping to get clothes, money, and a place to sleep. In Vancouver, sixteen- or seventeen-year-old Louis Massi (the youth was uncertain of his own age) had about three or four encounters with the Greek immigrant Thomas Pappas; over that time, Pappas paid him irregularly. On February 21, 1914, the two met up again in a Cordova Street "Japanese" pool hall attached to Pappas's rooming house. "Papas [*sic*] happened to come in," Massi testified in court, and "asked me if I would do it for him...so I said 'all right.'" This time, however, Massi insisted on some sort of payment. "I said 'what are you going to give me?' He said 'twenty-five cents.' So I went up the stairs [to his room]."[77] Apparently, it mattered little to Massi what he received, just as long as he obtained something to "do it."

Money did tend to be the most common medium of exchange in such affairs. Case after case reads like that of Nick George, who in 1913, in Seattle, gave Ernest O'Grady "money for the purpose of inducing [him] to submit to...carnal knowledge." The motivations of each party are unclear—perhaps boys desired money most, or transient men found a cash transaction less expensive than a more formal date, or both. But consider the case of Thomas Tassus, a thirty-year-old Greek laborer who arrived in Seattle from Alaska in October 1912. On the 29th of that month, he became acquainted with two teenagers on Pioneer Square. Rather than lavishing much attention and resources on them, Tassus simply offered them twenty-five cents, instructing them to go to a show and then meet him later that evening at the same location. When the youths kept the appointment, Tassus took one to his room and gave the other an additional twenty-five cents and suggested that he see another "show."[78] Such transactions as these apparently simplified life for both the men and the boys involved.

While many street youths associated with men to earn extra money, others found that the city's transient districts provided distinct opportunities for stealing from customers. The migratory laborers who regularly passed through or seasonally resided in districts such as the North End provided a good target for young thieves. The men sometimes carried their entire savings on their persons or, more often, stashed it in their rooms in inexpensive lodging houses. Boys regularly haunted such locales waiting for an opportunity to strike. In November 1913, for example, Portland police twice arrested two "boys," Frank Smith and Isaac Forest, for "loafing around a pool room" and having several "pass keys and a skeleton key in their possession."[79] We do not know whether Smith and Forest also performed sex work at the pool hall that they had "been hanging around" for weeks, but there seems to have existed a link between robbery and juvenile male sex work. During the Monte Carlo scandal, detectives picked up sixteen-year-old Ira Tucker for his sexual relations with several men only after he had "held up a Greek named Tom Mawvais at the point of a large knife and took $75.00 from him."[80] Tucker's case suggests that a man who participated in sexual transactions with street boys might face life-threatening dangers, and another case confirms it. In early June of 1912, the police investigated a robbery at Portland's Third and Burnside Streets "where a Greek named Tom Kallas took a boy to sleep with him and the boy beat him over the head and robbed him of [his money] and two watches. We had his head dressed by the city Dr. and later was sent to St. Vincent Hospital in bad shape."[81]

Their ready cash was not all that made men of the transient districts good targets. Boy sex workers realized that an adult whom they robbed would avoid going to the police because of the particulars of the crime. That is, the man had broken the law himself by participating in a same-sex sexual relationship, a transgression that had its own stiff penalties. At various times in the region, the penalty for sodomy ranged from one year to life in prison. Typically, the legal system punished only the adult while boys would go scot-free, or at worst would be sent to reform school. Except in unusual circumstances, or when an older and younger boy were apprehended for relations with each other, the youth would not be held accountable for his sexual transgressions until he was twenty-one.[82] Youngsters in the Northwest evidently understood this, for they often used their relations with men to shield themselves. Obviously, the records contain little evidence of men choosing not to press charges of robbery against their youthful partner. More typical is the story of George Foot (yet another Greek immigrant). He took the risk and went to authorities, consequently finding himself in significant legal difficulty when the youth turned on him. In 1912 Foot filed a complaint with the Portland police against Ray Gibson for "larceny of some money and a watch." When authorities apprehended Gibson, he admitted to stealing, but then promptly "put a complaint against Foot for a crime against nature. Who we arrested."[83]

Youths also used their extralegal relationships to shield their other criminal activities. In 1911 Portland police were on the trail of Charles Ferris, a fifteen-year-old whom they suspected of pilfering "several watches and about $60.00 in cash." As they questioned Ferris, the teenager quickly deflected the investigation, volunteering "some damaging statements" concerning Fred Selkok and a man named Gile who had "been enticing this boy...and staying all night with him." These sex stories immediately took precedence, and the police dropped their investigation of Ferris.[84] Scholars and social workers who have studied young male sex workers active later in the twentieth century have found that like Ferris, many combined sexual activities with robbery, thievery, and blackmail.[85] Illustrating this pattern was the Portland newsboy Albert Bliss, who, after putting John Anderson to bed on July 1, 1909, then robbed him. Sometimes youths might deliberately lure a client into a vulnerable position by promising sex and then assault him, as did the boys in the Mawvais and Kallas cases recounted above. Males who combined sex work with assault were known later in the twentieth century as "hustlers" or "hoodlum hustlers." Such terms seem apt for the adolescent boys of the Monte Carlo in 1913, each of whom had various previous brushes with the law. The detectives R. H. Craddock and John Goltz, in fact, referred to them collectively as "the reform school boys."[86]

In 1918 Lilburn Merrill completed a two-year investigation of the relationship between "sexual pathology"—in his words, "habitual, pathological functioning of the sexual mechanism"—and various sorts of criminal behaviors among one hundred juvenile males in Seattle. Merrill found that any number of youths there also engaged in various crimes and had experiences that "abounded in homosexualism with older boys and homeless men." Merrill told the story, for example, of a fourteen-year-old who stole "from the hotel room of a man directly after they had mutually induced orgasms." Curiously, Merrill refused to concede that any of his youths was homosexual, even as the term was understood at that time. "It is gratifying to note that [the] subjects," Merrill declared, "in addition to their interest in homosexual acts, [have] normal amative desires and probably were limited in their heterosexual relations only by their environment. Likewise all of the homosexual behavior recorded was found to be directly due to environmental influences."[87] Interestingly, their criminal records suggest that these boys may indeed have not been "homosexuals." In 1982 Jennifer James concluded from her study of Seattle's juvenile male sex workers that "[h]eterosexual male prostitutes were involved in more serious crimes and arrested more frequently than homosexual prostitutes." Though one cannot simply project back onto the early twentieth century observations made in the 1980s, some early-twentieth-century evidence indicates that boy sex workers who also engaged in various other crimes were distinguishable from youthful sex workers who saw themselves as "gay." Vilma, who at age eighteen came to Seattle during the height of the Great Depression, identified the "queen" and the "hustler" as two types of boys who had sex with men for money on Seattle's Skid Road. The queens hung out at the Casino on Second and Washington, which sported billiard tables, card tables, and even "a picture of FDR[.]" Across the street stood another pool hall. There, a decidedly different type of boy gathered. According to Vilma, they were "boosters" (i.e., shoplifters) and "hustlers."[88] Of course, Vilma did not say that the "queens" never engaged in petty or serious crime; but by differentiating them from the "boosters" and "hustlers," whose labels directly associate them with crime and danger, he demonstrates that those in the latter group had an identity that necessarily included malfeasance beyond sexual transgression.

Vilma's use of the terms *hustler* and *queen* might also be taken as another way to distinguish between types of juvenile males who engaged in homosexual activities in the Northwest city by the 1930s. The hustler might have identified himself, as Lilburn Merrill would have agreed, as someone who had desires for women, but because of circumstances turned to men for sex. In his glossary of homosexual terms compiled in 1941, Gershon Legman maintained that the "hustler" was a "male prostitute...especially so called if he is himself heterosexual." Legman also claimed that only homosexuals used the term. According to Vilma, a "queen was anyone who was gay and didn't try to hide it."[89]

At first glance, then, there appeared to be several types of sex workers in the world of youthful male prostitution in Northwest cities: those who had sexual desires for men but who hid the fact, those who identified as "queens," and those who were neither but had sex with men because of the circumstances in which they found themselves. Those in the queen crowd might be identified by their mannerisms, clothing, and demeanor. Vilma related that they had female nicknames for themselves, were somewhat effeminate, and occasionally dressed in drag, but "most of us weren't drag queens." The pervasiveness of these sex workers—individuals we might term *transgendered*—on city streets of the Northwest before the end of the first third of the twentieth century cannot be determined, however. Vilma's account reveals that transgendered sex workers appeared in Seattle by 1930. He also recalled the story of Hanna

Banna, "a darling old queen who lived in and out of drag all her life....
She'd been around Seattle since the Alaska Gold Rush days.... She said
Seattle was always a hot town...because of all the single men that traveled through." Other records note the presence of male-to-female transgendered sex workers among the salmon canneries of Alaska by 1923, as
described in the previous chapter. And Lilburn Merrill reported from
Seattle in 1913 on "Case Y," a seventeen-year-old who burglarized four
houses, stealing "an assortment of female wearing apparel. A case of sexual inversion." Merrill did not comment on whether this youth also engaged in sex work.[90]

A number of sources besides Merrill's extensive study suggest that
transgendered sex workers may have had a limited presence in the urban
Northwest before 1920. During World War I the Portland policewoman
Lola Baldwin earned an appointment as supervisor for the Pacific Coast
and Arizona division of the Commission on Training Camp Activities,
which monitored morals. One of Baldwin's operatives in San Francisco
on the night of December 7, 1918, observed at Third and Market Streets
a youth whom Baldwin later described as an "American boy" of about
seventeen who "was powdered and rouged and perfumed." According
to Baldwin's informant, the youth worked the streets seeking to attract
Greek immigrants and charged them fifty cents. The observer also
learned from a San Francisco police officer that as many as fifteen boys
worked that very corner in an evening. Baldwin's unusual interest in this
case and her report that this practice "was not unusual" on the Barbary
Coast suggests a certain disbelief on her part. Given Baldwin's background—she had worked with the Portland police since 1907 and had
specifically monitored female sex work and moral conditions—her in-
credulity over the customs in San Francisco further suggests that in
Portland transgendered sex workers might have been relatively uncom-
mon before the 1920s.[91]

Furthermore, in Portland's legal documents during these years none
of the boys or men ensnared with the law for sex work are described in
ways that would lead one to conclude that they were transgendered.
There are two interesting hints: Nick Adon was arrested in 1911 "as a sexual pervert at 3d & Burnside" on the complaint of a man "whom he
[took] to his room at the Uncle Sam Hotel 5th & Couch and there as-
saulted him"; and precisely four years later, Portland police apprehended for vagrancy Ernest B. Carter, a pressman, and George H. Graham, a laborer, referring to both of them as "sexual perverts."[92] These
are the only instances I found in examining some fifty years of legal

records between the 1870s and 1920s in which the term *sexual pervert* appears in the context of same-sex sex crimes. It is possible that authorities used it to refer to transgendered males; but chapter 4 will offer a more likely explanation for its application to working-class men at this time.

The apparent lack of transgendered youths on the streets of pre-1920s Portland is also suggested by the alacrity of police in arresting a number of "females" clad in men's clothing. Nor did the local press fail to report on them, sometimes devoting considerable space to such stories. These arrests seem unlikely to demonstrate that females were receiving more attention because they were seen as posing a greater threat to the established order, as the evidence points to the contrary: the North End was under keen surveillance for its male-male sexual activities. But only one article pertaining to a male who dressed in traditionally women's clothing in Portland has come to light from the early twentieth century—a story that became front-page news. In this case, James Arthur "Alice" Baker, a biological male, was only a temporary visitor to the city. She had arrived in town in the spring of 1913 from California in men's clothes, switched to women's, and then found refuge at the women's Peniel Mission in Portland. Complaining to newfound female friends that she had lived life as a man so long that she had lost her feminine traits, Alice quickly acquired from those who took pity on her feminine attire and a "transformation" wig. So successful was the disguise that Baker even reportedly secured a marriage proposal from a local evangelical minister. After the wife of the Peniel Mission's superintendent became suspicious, Baker absconded from town on a ship sailing to California, only "minutes ahead of an investigating body." She was last seen in women's garb and on the arm of an unknown man.[93] That Baker should receive such attention, that more male-to-female cross-dressers did not make it into the news, and that female-to-male transvestites did grace the pages of the local papers—all these factors suggest that few transgendered "males" may actually have existed in the Northwest city at this time.

The limited presence of transgendered youths in the North End to 1920 was likely due to the dominance of transient culture there. As noted in the previous chapter, Nels Anderson asserted that his "lithe, lean youths with rouged lips" of the urban center did occasionally visit hobohemia, but they did not belong there. Additionally, a certain amount of animosity existed in the relationship between the hobo and transgendered males.[94] Sources considered later in this study do reveal that cross-dressing had a place in the "gay" community that middle-class men of Portland created by the first decade of the twentieth century. But there appear to have been relatively few effeminately attired boy sex workers in the urban Northwest before the 1920s, probably owing to conditions specific to the region's transient culture. Because of the sketchiness of evidence, such a conclusion can be only tentative at best.

Transient culture may have influenced the lack of transgendered youths among the juvenile male sex workers in Northwest cities, but it definitely conditioned the forms of sex that boys typically engaged in with men. Such sexual practices differentiated these early-twentieth-century youths of the Northwest from other boy sex workers, both those in later periods and even contemporaries in other North American settings. In various studies undertaken later in the century, researchers have commented on the tendency of certain young male sex workers, particularly those who had backgrounds in various sorts of criminal behavior and who also identified as heterosexual (the "hoodlum hustlers" or "rough trade"), to engage in sexual relationships with men solely on the condition that they themselves play the more "masculine" role. In such cases, the boys allowed the adult only to perform fellation on them—a sex act that also served to limit bodily contact, part of the juvenile male's strategy to preserve his self-definition as heterosexual. These studies also demonstrate that if a sex partner made unreasonable demands on the youth, such as insisting on other forms of sexual acts, the boys would turn to violence or simply make themselves unavailable for future encounters.[95]

Conditions specific to transient male culture, however, dictated a different sexual dynamic in the early-twentieth-century Northwest. In the city, the transients' sexual culture undermined whatever wish a "heterosexual" boy might have had to perform in the "masculine" role: the jocker-punk relationship almost always mandated that the adult act as the penetrator and the youth act as the receptor, regardless of the latter's "sexuality." This cultural script seems to have prevented the street boy from clinging to a "masculine" role in a sexual encounter. In other places in North America in the early twentieth century less affected by transient culture, or in later years in the Northwest when transient culture declined and a more cohesive gay community formed (a community in which the men would be more willing to play a different sex role), a boy might be able to make more exacting demands on his sex partner; boys among the transient men in Portland or Seattle before the mid-1920s did not seem to have that option. Consider Grover King, whom police referred to in 1913 as a "reform school" boy. One of his close friends was

Ira Tucker—the youth who held a knife to Tom Mawvais as he robbed him. King's background in crime is similar in many ways to that of the "hustler" of a later era. Yet he acted as the receptor, not the penetrator, in his encounter with Andrew Dillige. In Seattle between 1916 and 1918, Lilburn Merrill's subjects, who combined a wide array of criminal behaviors with acts of sex with men, also performed the receptive role, although Merrill claimed that these boys had "normal amative" or "heterosexual" desires. It is likely that the rules of the road, which dictated the type of sex that men and boys should have, influenced boy sex workers in the city. It deterred those like King, who from all evidence seemed to be the "hustler" type, and Merrill's delinquent and apparently "heterosexual" subjects from making particular sex-role demands on a client. Rather, they all seemed limited to the receptive role.

In most cases, sexual intercourse between the working-class adult and the youth in the city was anal and interfemoral and not oral in nature—mirroring the situation on the road. A few such cases have already been reported: for example, those of Andrew Dillige and Grover King, Nick George and Ernest O'Grady, Henry Bacon and Ben Murray in 1905, and Tony Lagallo and Albert Ambrose in 1917. Others include that of the twenty-one-year-old Australian immigrant laborer Tom Conley, arrested at Park and Burnside in Portland in 1908, who anally sodomized twelve-year-old Ernest Hollenbeck. In the same year, the twenty-eight-year-old South Asian S. G. Ahmed, arrested on Third Street, attempted to anally sodomize seven-year-old George Russell. Three years later the police apprehended the railroad traveler Albert Keller for vagrancy after they caught him underneath the North End's Couch Street dock, attempting to penetrate a youth.[96]

To be sure, records of the period also present evidence of some flexibility in the sexual roles taken by the men and boys of the urban working-class world. For example, Portland police arrested forty-five-year-old Ed Montgomery among the saloons and lodging houses at Second and Burnside on October 22, 1908. Court records claim that he both anally sodomized and performed oral sex on sixteen-year-old Narcisse Belanger. On August 4, 1920, Portland police apprehended the forty-four-year-old American laborer Michael Dixon at a lodging house on North Sixth and charged him with performing oral sex on the eighteen-year-old American laborer Richard Brooks. In Seattle on June 28, 1919, a Greek immigrant fish peddler, H. Demas, who had a wife and two boys in the Balkans, gave fourteen-year-old Milton Draper a ride in his truck up one of the steep hills north of Seattle. Although Demas denied it, the youth testified that the man first asked him, "You have got a pretty good prick, aint you?" And then, "I put my hands down and he started feeling and he said 'No, take your hands away; I wont hurt you,' and...he forced my hand away." According to Draper, Demas stopped the truck, took the boy across a fence and some shrubs. "Well, he took my trousers down, and then he took my—then he took it in his mouth, and while he did that he did it to himself—took his own trousers open and took it himself." We also know of some cases in which boys performed fellation on the adult, thus stepping outside the more typical anal and interfemoral relations of the jocker-punk relationship.[97] These cases are relatively few in number compared to those in which the adult and the youth in the city mirrored the typical roles taken by jocker and punk while on the road. Their scarcity suggests that boys in the urban setting, regardless of how they might have perceived their masculinity, yielded to men in ways characteristic of the transient culture of the region's rural roads, a culture that invaded the region's cities on a seasonal basis.

This chapter has demonstrated that working-class establishments as well as other places in the urban Northwest's transient neighborhoods afforded ample opportunity for males interested in same-sex sexual relations to find them. For New York City as early as the 1890s, the historian George Chauncey discovered, "The institutions and social forms of the [working-class] gay subculture were patterned in many respects on those of the working-class culture in which it took shape: the saloons, small social clubs, and large fancy-dress balls around which fairy life revolved were all typical elements of working-class life." By the 1930s in the Northwest's urban working-class neighborhoods, some conventionally modern gay institutions could be found. Vilma, for instance, recalled of Seattle that during the Great Depression a number of resorts such as pool halls and speakeasies in the traditional vice district "let the queens in." And the Casino, located near Pioneer Square, was designated a place exclusively for gays in Seattle by 1930.[98]

But during an earlier era in Northwest cities, a social-sexual dynamic apparently different from that in New York—or even in the Northwest at a later period—was at work. Beginning in the 1880s, districts such as the North End began to take shape. As they did so, they were filled by the men and boys connected to the transient, laboring life that so dominated the region's hinterlands. The work camp–like atmosphere of Portland's North End as well as Seattle's Skid Road and Vancouver's Hastings Street reinforced transients' rural social and sexual culture. This culture generally prescribed specific male-male sexual activities and age configurations of its participants. It also encouraged the presence of the punk and precluded that of the fairy. Additionally, as Vilma noted of the 1930s (when the era of the casual laborer in the Northwest was in decline), the punks and queens had separate resorts and a certain animosity existed between them. Furthermore, Nels Anderson wrote extensively in 1923 that the homosexual man was "not a popular person even among tramps." The feeling was apparently sometimes mutual, for homosexuals occasionally spoke "disparagingly of the 'wolves' and 'jockers'" as well as the punk.[99]

Evidence shows that some working-class men and youths who may have been homosexuals—perhaps even transgendered—did find their way into the urban Northwest's transient districts. However, the distinctive culture of those places, plus an established animosity between jockers and punks on the one side and homosexual men on the other, thwarted the formation of a gay subculture before the 1920s. As the next chapter argues, this and a variety of other reasons led the early "gay" community to form elsewhere within the Northwest's urban setting.

PART II

Middle-Class
Same-Sex Affairs

CHAPTER 3

Gay Identity and Community in Early Portland

The "Greek scandal" reveals much about working-class male sexuality as well as weighty middle-class Progressive-era anxieties regarding same-sex activities, race mixing, the supposed dangers of the immigrant male, and the vulnerability of the "American" boy. Yet another Portland male-male sex scandal, the one that occurred in 1912, is even more significant in shedding light on the history of homosexuality in the Northwest. It began by chance in early November when authorities apprehended nineteen-year-old Benjamin Trout for some petty crime.[1] Like so many other young frightened men who find themselves in custody, Trout probably began talking about more serious transgressions in order to divert authorities' attention from his own minor infraction. But unlike so many others who had previously come before the legal system and who had some sort of connection to same-sex sex crimes, Trout's confessions reached beyond the relatively small audience of the police, the courts, or even reformers. For one thing, Trout spoke of a complex homosexual underground existing in the city, in which some well-respected men were involved. One of the first collared in the aftermath of Trout's confession was H. L. Rowe, a thirty-eight-year-old credit man for a large hardware wholesaler in town. Rowe resided at the local Y.[2] The connection between that distinguished organization and homosexual affairs ignited a firestorm in the city, which quickly spread across the region. Although news regarding homosexuality had generated comment in the Northwest in earlier years—for example, the Oscar Wilde affair of 1895 and occasional items in papers regarding local same-sex sex crimes and criminals—the level of outrage was unprecedented.

As the so-called YMCA scandal ran its course over several months, it took on many dimensions, some of which part 2 of this study considers in detail. Chapter 4 examines how the largely middle-class attributes of Portland's gay subculture, along with the sensationalism of the 1912 scandal, helped alter some notions of male same-sex sexuality dominant in the Northwest since the internationally reported Oscar Wilde affair. But first, the present chapter considers the various characteristics of the early gay community that the scandal for the first time brought to broad public awareness. Along with the relatively abundant records generated from this affair, chapter 3 also employs more fragmentary sources available from the 1890s through the 1920s, including the documents resulting from a 1928 crackdown on homosexuals in Portland. Using all these sources, I first establish that the "modern" gay community in the Rose City originated in the middle classes. I then investigate why this was so, arguing for direct links between the emergence of corporate capitalism, the creation of white-collar work, and the formation of a gay subculture in turn-of-the-twentieth-century America. In the final section I scrutinize various contours of Portland's early gay community and identity, examining the nature of that community and identity, exploring the limited role of youths in this subculture, mapping the physical geography of this subculture, and analyzing the gay middle-class male's sexual activities. The underlying theme here, as throughout the chapter, is that significant social, racial, geographic, and sexual differences separated the middle-class gay subculture of the Northwest's urban center from the transient and working-class same-sex sexual subculture that could also be found there.

Class, Homosexuality, and the Men of Portland's 1912 Scandal

One newspaper declared that at least one hundred men were involved in Portland's 1912 scandal, and legal documents confirm the identities of fifty-nine. These men were remarkable in two ways. First, by and large they were white (whether foreign- or native-born). Of the forty-eight for whom nativity can be verified, thirty-nine were American-born and white, seven were northern European or Canadian in origin, one was African American, and one was eastern European. Records are somewhat less conclusive about the others: one may have been black, but the others were white and all probably American-born.

Second, they were overwhelmingly "middle class," according to the categories set forth in Alfred Kinsey's class analysis of homosexuality presented in his monumental 1948 study *Sexual Behavior in the Human*

Male: nearly 80 percent of the men implicated in the 1912 scandal had occupations associated with Kinsey's lower and upper white-collar and professional groups. It is especially noteworthy that more than two-thirds of those implicated in 1912 had lower white-collar occupations. Like H. L. Rowe, they were primarily clerks, bookkeepers, and office workers. In Portland's 1928 same-sex vice crackdown, ten of the thirteen men arrested also fell within Kinsey's lower-middle-class occupational groups: they were salesmen, clerks, teachers, and owners of small shops.[3] That middle-class men, and specifically white-collar workers, should have made up the core of Portland's early homosexual community as exposed in the 1912 scandal correlates closely with Kinsey's findings regarding homosexuality in the United States as a whole for the first half of the twentieth century. Kinsey discovered that those most likely to engage in same-sex activities *and* most likely to spend a significant portion of their lives exclusively homosexual in behavior were men from the lower white-collar socio-occupational group.[4]

The question of why homosexuals were largely middle class remains open. Possibly, the location of white-collar jobs in the quickly growing urban centers played a role. Although scholars disagree slightly as to the exact connections between homosexuality, gay community, and urban life, they do recognize, as John D'Emilio first pointed out in the early 1980s, that a direct historical relationship exists.[5] Some scholars propose that urban centers, in contrast to small towns, allowed for the high degree of secrecy as well as anonymous social relations that homosexually inclined individuals needed to pursue their desires without risking legal prosecution. Others have demonstrated that "anonymity" is relative and that the term should be applied carefully to encounters of prototypical gays within the urban context. The large city might indeed provide migrants from rural areas—not to mention those already living in the city—freedom to construct their own lives with a certain degree of liberty from their families. Furthermore, the large size of the city made it possible to lead a dual life in which leisure activities could very easily be separated from those of the workplace. But more important, the vast numbers of people with similar sexual feelings congregating in the urban center allowed for the construction of a homosexual subculture that simultaneously enjoyed a certain anonymous relationship to the dominant society and provided a milieu whose participants were hardly unknown to one another. As the historian George Chauncey has remarked, "the complexity of the city's social and spatial organization made it possible for gay men to construct multiple public identities," enabling them to participate visibly in the gay world yet at the same time to keep their personal lives separate and hidden from their straight peers.[6] These analyses echo some explanations put forth in the early twentieth century. After men were arrested in the Rose City in late November, one law enforcement official asserted that they had been "driven out of former haunts, and took refuge in Portland on the supposition that they would escape detection [there]."[7] The emerging social and spatial arrangements of this rapidly growing urban center granted gay men anonymity from the broader public and created the conditions in which they could follow their desires, meet others like themselves, and construct a community.

Of course, the urban environment afforded all inhabitants the same opportunities; thus other factors must be at work in the emergence of the gay community particularly among middle-class men. John D'Emilio has stressed economic developments, pointing out that the newly dominant wage-labor system allowed greater numbers of men and women "to detach themselves from a family-based economy and strike out on their own." This made it "possible for homosexual desire to coalesce into a personal identity—an identity based on the ability to remain outside the heterosexual family and to construct a personal life based on attraction to one's own sex." Accordingly, by the end of the nineteenth century, a number of men and women who lived independently recognized their erotic desires for their own sex and began to form the first modern homosexual communities.[8]

Such an explanation partly accounts for what occurred in Portland. Yet the striking fact that the men involved in the 1912 scandal were primarily white-collar workers challenges us to move beyond an exclusive focus on the wage-labor system. We must examine the era's newly emerging corporate capitalist economy, which created not only myriad alterations in society but also the very occupations of the men implicated in the 1912 scandal—clerks, bookkeepers, auditors, credit men, office assistants, and department managers and salesmen in large stores—positions filled by men who, according to Kinsey, were those most likely to be exclusively homosexual in behavior. The development of the modern corporate economy thus appears to hold one of the keys that can unlock the mystery of how urban gay community and identity emerged in America.

The Corporate Economy and the Emergence of the Middle-Class Homosexual and His Community

At about the midway mark of the nineteenth century, the modern corporation made its appearance. But not until the years between 1890 and

1916, according to the historian Martin J. Sklar, did the corporate re-construction of America take place, as corporate capitalism replaced en-trepreneurial or proprietary capitalism as the dominant economic sys-tem in the country. Entrepreneurial capitalism had depended for its existence on the expansion of the country's boundaries and on technol-ogy, transportation, and markets of limited (albeit advancing) sophisti-cation. Throughout much of the nineteenth century, relatively easy ac-cess to natural resources and land, as well as continuing, though ever-declining, reliance on handcrafts, permitted and even encouraged the decentralization of property and the tools of trade. Because so many could and did own property and the means of production, society was composed of a sizable number of independent yet small businessmen, farmers, and skilled craftsworkers. On their farms and in their shops, the owners usually served as operators. They often worked side by side with family members or a modest number of employees. In shops they trained future generations of entrepreneurs who, initiated into business as clerks or in other lowly positions, were setting out on their own quest for fortune and respectability. In this system, the successful busi-nessman was one who demonstrated, in the words of the historian Kevin White, "self-control, discipline, delayed gratification, and self-sacrifice, ideal qualities in an economy geared towards production" and the accumulation of capital for future ventures.[9] Self-reliant, independ-ent, successful, respectable — the "self-made man" was the central figure of the entrepreneurial-capitalist system.

In the latter half of the nineteenth century, industrialization, the spread of national and international markets, and the large-scale mergers of businesses profoundly altered the commercial structure. One key change was the concentration of property and natural resources. As indi-vidual companies or conglomerates came to control more and more land, resources, production processes, markets, and labor, firms grew to sizes never before seen. Big business — the corporation — had arrived. Fewer individual owners were operating or even controlling firms, as supervision of the huge enterprises was turned over to teams of salaried managers. One of the symbols of the new era was the specialized profes-sional who had spent years in school training for a technical position in management, replacing the self-made man who had worked his way up the rungs of business.[10] At the same time, sprawling business and governmental bureaucracies demanded the employment of an unprece-dented number of lower- and mid-level white-collar workers — sales-people, bookkeepers, accountants, stenographers, clerks, and so on. In America between 1880 and 1920, the number of sales clerks alone increased from 386,000 to 1,540,000. In Portland the number of male clerical workers rose slightly more than 30 percent between 1910 and 1920. In the country as a whole, the proportion of white-collar workers within the middle class doubled between 1870 and 1910: by the latter date, 20 percent of the male labor force, or two-thirds of the middle class, was white collar. Roughly forty years later, clerks, sales employees, managers, and professionals had increased to 37 percent of all U.S. workers.[11]

Emergent corporate capitalism's transformation of work and the workplace also eroded the traditional position that middle-class men had held in the family, workplace, community, and society. Under the older entrepreneurial system, a middle-class man's work had been central to his identity. The measure of his character—that is, his "manliness"—rested largely on his ability to succeed in business through hard work, self-reliance, self-denial, and determination, as he climbed from being entry-level clerk to proprietor of his own small establishment. He aspired to secure personal autonomy in work and support his dependents as respectable members of society. As E. Anthony Rotundo has explained, "The power to create the social position of one's family raised the stakes for the nineteenth-century man. No wonder he identified himself so fully with his work; in a social sense, he was what he achieved—and so were those he loved."[12] Although not all succeeded, these men were generally guided by the model of the self-made man.

But within entrepreneurial capitalism, middle-class manliness—and how one went about securing it—was put into question by a pervasive, exclusive, and somewhat monolithic corporate economy and business structure. According to the historian Gail Bederman, between 1870 and 1910 the proportion of self-employed middle-class men dropped from 67 to 37 percent. Some of them witnessed large firms and chain stores squeeze out their small shops. Others lost their livelihoods during the severe depression of the 1890s. Yet others who had hoped to start up their own businesses found their way increasingly blocked by monopolies. At the same time, the expansion of hierarchical bureaucracies created a need for myriad white-collar workers. In an earlier era, middle-class men had viewed clerical positions as providing an entry into business, but now they were often dead-end jobs. Various scholars have found that fewer and fewer clerical and sales workers were able to climb out of their positions or out of white-collar work altogether in the early twentieth century. Moreover, the men performing such jobs became dependent on men higher up the corporate ladder.[13]

The interconnected phenomena of diminishing opportunities for independent business proprietorship, inability to rise through the ranks, and intensifying dependency on other men have led historians to conclude that the new corporate order undermined nineteenth-century forms of manliness, generated a great deal of anxiety among men of this social stratum, and turned clerical positions into confining and demeaning long-term jobs. Some scholars have claimed that the result was a full-blown masculinity crisis: indeed, during this era the meaning of masculinity changed as middle-class men began looking outside their work and family to sustain it.[14] Yet the case of Portland suggests a different interpretation. Because there the core of the male homosexual community came from the corporate white-collar social group, it appears that the new economy and the jobs it produced actually provided greater freedom for some men, especially those who wished to express alternative gender and sexual desires (which the entrepreneurial system generally inhibited). Moreover, other alterations in society caused by the emergent corporate economy also seemed to provide opportunities for homosexual desire to develop. Historians have acknowledged that the new corporate economic and social structure helped emancipate some women, especially those of the middle classes. As their educational and occupational opportunities increased, some women won greater control of their own lives and thus more autonomy from men. For those among them who desired it, this independence afforded the option to form intimate, committed, and even sexual relationships with others like themselves. This "New Woman," in the words of Carroll Smith-Rosenberg, "constituted a revolutionary demographic and political phenomenon."[15] Because this particularly feminist development was one of the threats to middle-class manliness at the turn of the last century, it is all too easy to overlook the possibility that men might experience similar liberation, as they found opportunities outside the relatively rigid and narrowly defined manliness of previous years.

In fact, some or even many middle-class men had been quietly engaged in a revolt of sorts against the demands of the entrepreneurial system since the 1850s. During that decade, the nervous disorder known as neurasthenia first made its appearance. Primarily afflicting middle-class males, this disease usually showed up between the ages of fifteen and fifty. It peaked in near "epidemic" proportions in the 1880s, just before the corporate reconstruction of America took effect. Its symptoms included insomnia, anxiety, depression, and lethargy. Contemporary medical experts pointed to overwork as its cause. Later scholars claim that it also resulted from the pressures felt by middle-class males, young and old alike, as they set about to become self-made men.[16] Because it affected so many and because its treatment demanded extensive rest and relaxation—something antithetical to the demands of nineteenth-century manhood—society often viewed those who suffered from neurasthenia as weak or effeminate. Nonetheless, the afflicted might also be considered as leaders of a rebellion against the entrepreneurial system that expected so much from men in their pursuit of success.

Indeed, some men who suffered neurasthenia also expressed homosexual desires. For example, John Gibson, charged with sodomy in late 1912 in the eastern Washington town of Walla Walla, had suffered the classic signs of neurasthenia early in life. He was born in 1868 in Ohio, where he attended school until age twelve. But in 1880 he suffered his first bout of invalidism. It lasted for ten years, which he spent at home under his parents' care. Gibson was able to muster enough energy, however, to enroll at a commercial college for a four-month shorthand course sometime after he and his parents moved to Des Moines, Iowa, in 1887. Between then and 1893, he found three successive jobs, including one at the local YMCA. But Gibson's illness recurred and he returned to the restful setting of his parents' home for another three-year period. Then he found work for fourteen months as a YMCA secretary in Austin, Texas, until again suffering a breakdown. He went back home for another two years. He next took a position at a St. Paul, Minnesota, YMCA; after nine months, "sickness" again consumed him, forcing him to return home for four more years. In 1910 he headed to Walla Walla. There he engaged in church work and became an editor at a local newspaper. Gibson was arrested in Walla Walla for sexual activities with some young men in late November 1912 as Portland's scandal heightened scrutiny elsewhere in the region. In 1913 J. H. Fellingham, the general secretary of the Des Moines YMCA, wrote confidentially to Washington State Penitentiary officials that his "personal impression" of Gibson "was not very favorable, as he did not seem to evince the strong masculine qualities I like to see in men." The prosecuting attorney and judge in Gibson's trial likewise believed "that his [sexual] acts were in a degree traceable to his nervous condition and general debility."[17]

Obviously, not all men who suffered neurasthenia also had homosexual desires. But for some men like Gibson who apparently did, the ailment provided a means—whether conscious or not—to rebel against the rigid expectations (especially the familial ones) of the middle-class man under the entrepreneurial order. It is telling that neurasthenia almost disappeared in the first few years of the twentieth century, when the corporate reconstruction of America was in full swing. By that time, new liberties and alternatives were appearing for middle-class men, especially for those who had homosexual desires. Those engaged in the new white-collar work, particularly in the lower and mid-level clerical positions, no longer had to dedicate their lives to their careers and relentlessly seek to rise to a higher social level as well as marry and raise a family. By the early twentieth century, more and more middle-class men accepted that their white-collar jobs in the corporate order were indeed becoming permanent. Already in 1905 one survey claimed that only about 50 percent of sales clerks viewed their positions as transitional.[18] Not surprisingly, men looked elsewhere for fulfillment.

The biography of Earl Van Hulen, one of the men implicated in Portland's scandal, illustrates certain elements of this pattern. Born in Kansas in 1888, he, his siblings, and parents relocated to Boise sometime in 1904. There, the elder Van Hulens purchased the Wheeler-Motter dry goods store, advertising it as "Idaho's Leading Cloak and Suit House." All the children worked there, Earl as a clerk. It seems likely that Earl's parents were grooming him to take over the family store, in the typical entrepreneurial scenario of the nineteenth century. But that was not to be. For whatever reason—possibly they were squeezed out by a larger company— the Van Hulens had closed the doors to Wheeler-Motter by 1910. His entry into the entrepreneurial world now effectively blocked, within a year Earl moved to Portland; he first found clerking work in a department store and then employment as an exhibition preparer for the Chamber of Commerce (see map 2). While at the latter establishment he met Harry Wight, who also would be implicated in 1912. Van Hulen and Wight took an apartment together sometime by the end of 1910. Although we know nothing about Van Hulen's sexual history in Boise, he himself said that it was on arrival in Portland that he first began to participate in the homosexual subculture. Van Hulen would subsequently have affairs with several other men.[19] Excused from a small-town family business, newly arrived in the large city, working on his own in clerical positions, and soon meeting and even living with men who had a history of same-sex sexual activities, Van Hulen may very well have typified the early-twentieth-century young urban gay man in the new white-collar stratum of society. In the aftermath of 1912, Van Hulen dropped from city directories. But in later years he reappeared, residing with his sister and clerking for the Oregon-Washington Railroad and Navigation Company. By 1954 Van Hulen had finally moved "up" to investigator for the Union Pacific.[20]

Like Van Hulen, many who surfaced in the 1912 scandal spent their entire adult lives in lower-level white-collar work. Edwin E. Wedemeyer, born in New York in 1877, had by 1900 found employment as a clerk for the railroad in Cleveland. He moved to Portland around 1904 and clerked for a creamery. Within a few years he rose to the level of bookkeeper when he found employment at the Doernbecher sash and door manufacturing company, a position he maintained until just after the 1912 scandal. At that time he returned to Cleveland, where he lived with his sister and brother-in-law and continued keeping books until his death from tuberculosis in 1920 at the age of forty-two.[21] Similarly, as early as 1886, W. H. Allen clerked for Portland's Buffum and Pendleton clothiers. In 1912, at the age of fifty-one, he was still working at that same firm but as a relatively lowly salesman in men's furnishings.[22] Table 2 provides the ages and clerical occupations for a number of the "older" men swept up in the 1912 scandal, indicating that the new corporate world had left them with an unchanging station in life.

In accepting that corporate capitalism's white-collar work was static, many men undoubtedly felt relief at being freed from the obligation to dedicate themselves to climbing ever higher. In addition, preparation for white-collar work was considerably less demanding under the new system than it had been under the entrepreneurial system. Earlier in the nineteenth century, the middle-class male child had been inculcated with the importance of choosing a career that would enable him not only to succeed but to surpass his father's accomplishments. Both his parents set out to teach him from an early age the necessity of developing a manly character and all that went with it—thrift, perseverance, initiative, work ethic, punctuality, and so on. Nevertheless, a great deal of uncertainty surrounded the nineteenth-century boy while he considered his choice of career, formal schooling, and possible apprenticeship. All this the historian Steven Mintz has aptly termed "a prison of expectations."[23] The corporate economy of a later time provided a certain degree of emancipation from this straitjacket. While some training was required for white-collar employment in the new economic system, generally high school would suffice. Of the lower white-collar workers Alfred Kinsey interviewed for his 1948 sex survey, fewer than 44 percent had gone beyond high school.[24]

Besides not having to devote as much energy to careers, to preparation for employment, or to worries about climbing the self-made man's ladder, these middle and lower white-collar workers also did not have to spend as much time on the job. In nonagricultural industries, the

TABLE 2. *Occupations and Ages of Some White-Collar Workers Caught Up in Portland's 1912 Scandal*

Occupation	Age
Clerk/salesman	53
Salesman at Buffum & Pendleton clothing store	51
Collar salesman in department store	43
Clerk in florist shop	43
Mail clerk	42
Bookkeeper in furniture store	39
Clerk at Portland Railway Light & Power Co.	38
Credit man for Marshall-Wells Hardware Co.	38
Bookkeeper at Doernbecher Manufacturing Co.	35

workweek dropped from nearly 59 hours in 1880 to 45.5 in 1920 as white-collar wages increased. Even in the hard times of the 1890s, such workers' pay steadily advanced; during these years, the average white-collar worker's income was about double that of a factory worker.[25] Together, shorter hours and greater affluence afforded these white-collar employees the opportunity to pursue more leisure-time activities. Leisure time for the masses was a creation of the late nineteenth and early twentieth centuries, as capitalists concocted all sorts of popular amusements to cater to those who now had time and money on their hands. The middle-class man who found less of his satisfaction in work turned to movies, vaudeville performances, outdoor recreations, dance halls, and amusement parks for fun and emotional fulfillment. Many of these activities provided opportunities for men with same-sex desires to meet each other. In legal proceedings from 1912 Portland, for example, one witness claimed of another implicated in the affair that he sometimes went to the "moving picture shows" to meet sex partners. "[H]e sat right next to two young men," the witness testified, "and he had got to talking to them about the pictures, and so forth and so on, and he finally...he teased them up, working his hands over their legs, and finally got a little further up and a little further up, and...he finally landed them both."[26]

These leisure activities also helped heighten or perhaps even construct homosexual desire. Historians have noted that turn-of-the-century amusement parks, with their diverse clientele, spontaneity, and sometimes naughty rides, increased heterosexual interests and contacts, and there is evidence that the same was true for homosexuality. The previous chapter noted the potential for working-class same-sex sexual contacts at a variety of amusements in large cities. A similar story, and one that speaks to the notion of the construction of desire, comes from a couple of the young men caught up in Portland's 1912 scandal. In one of the trials, an eighteen-year-old singer maintained that a twenty-year-old drugstore employee took him to the Council Crest amusement park, bought him tickets to the merry-go-round, and showered him with candy and soda. At first the witness claimed he did not know why his friend was being so good to him. Then, as they reposed on the side of the hill, "he put his hand in my pants and unbuttoned them and took out my penis...and went to sucking it." It appears that the younger partner later asked his father what would be the effect of allowing another male to perform such an act, suggesting at the time he had not a full understanding of what he was doing. Although his father strongly warned him against such activities, he apparently enjoyed them, for subsequently he engaged in similar relations with other men.[27]

Higher wages also made it possible for the white-collar worker to live alone and achieve a respectable lifestyle at a relatively young age, something also potentially important for the gay male. The number of individuals living on their own increased at the turn of the last century. Those who maintained their own apartments and rooms in large complexes aside, the percentage of dwellings containing a single person in the United States grew from 3.2 in 1890 to 4.2 in 1900. The latter year's census revealed that proportionally more people (11.7 percent of the population) lived alone in the West than anywhere else in the country.[28] Significantly, a high proportion of the men implicated in Portland's 1912 scandal lived by themselves. The living arrangements of fifty of them can be ascertained. Of the twenty-six who resided alone, nine were between the ages of seventeen and twenty-four and six were between twenty-five and twenty-eight. Others were living or had recently lived together. As already mentioned, Van Hulen shared an apartment with Wight between 1910 and 1911; Claude Bronner, a small restaurant and deli proprietor, and Nathan Healy, a clerk, lived together at about the same time.[29]

The private homes and apartments that these men maintained provided much of the geographical space wherein members of the early gay community socialized and also had sexual relations. After leaving the apartment he shared with Wight, Van Hulen moved into the Burgoyne Hotel. There, late one September evening in 1912, Edwin Wedemeyer and Fred Rodby paid him a visit. At the time their knock came, Van Hulen had just finished taking a bath. He answered the door in his robe

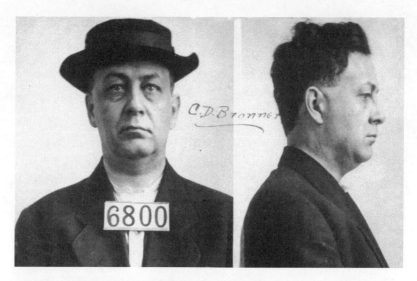

FIGURE 6. Claude Bronner, 1913. Portland authorities arrested Bronner in November 1912 as part of a citywide crackdown on gay men of the middle classes. That year, Bronner lived in an apartment on Washington Street. One newspaper referred to the residence as "a den of corruption so vile as to keep it from being even faintly described." Oregon State Archives, Oregon State Penitentiary, Inmate Files, Photograph 6800.

and soon thereafter sat down on his bed. Wedemeyer allegedly came over, "commenced to love him up...finally got a hold of his penis and placed it in his mouth." Newspapers in late 1912 focused on the apartment that Claude Bronner (figure 6) and Burt Thornton shared, reporting in particularly shocked tones what had presumably gone on there: parties that revolved around sex and female attire.[30]

Other young urban male white-collar workers opted for communal housing, such as that offered at the YMCA. The YMCA began as a nineteenth-century movement designed to supervise and inculcate with wholesome values the large numbers of young single men streaming into the city looking for work in the corporate world. Soon, YMCAs began furnishing their charges with lodgings, and many men in the clerical fields chose to live in them. In 1910 Portland's YMCA (figure 7) housed 160 men, who were employed in fifty-four different occupations. More than 50 percent of them were salesmen, clerks, cashiers, tellers, office workers, stenographers, bookkeepers, accountants, adjusters, real estate agents, or secretaries. Six of the men whose identities came to light as a result of the 1912 homosexual scandal were either then living at the Y or

FIGURE 7. Portland's YMCA in the early twentieth century. Located in the central business district at Sixth and Taylor Streets, the YMCA (larger building on the right) served as home for several lower-middle-class men who participated in the city's early-twentieth-century gay community. The YMCA became the focus of a same-sex sex scandal that erupted in Portland in November 1912. Author's collection.

had lived there within the previous year. Two were clerks, two were salesmen, and two were credit men. In 1911 one of these men had in fact been the assistant physical director at the Y before leaving and taking a position as a credit man for a music store.[31]

Historians have shown that by the early twentieth century, YMCAs across America were acting as a haven for homosexuals. Of course, Portland's Y would take center stage in news headlines during the 1912 scandal. A *Portland News* story is typical, claiming in big bold letters that "CONFESSIONS OF BOYS SHOW THAT THE LOWEST ACTS HUMANITY'S DREGS ARE CAPABLE OF IMAGINING HAVE BEEN REPEATEDLY PERFORMED IN THE ASSOCIATION ROOMS!" Yet trial transcripts from the scandal do not mention the association in any detail, so the veracity of the *News*'s reports is questionable. In fact, the paper's news editor more likely was motivated by political reasons to attack the Y in late 1912, as chapter 5 explains. Nonetheless, other sources support the claim the Rose City's Y was an institution in which same-sex sex could be had or at least learned of. A period letter addressed to the Oregon Social Hygiene Society from a recent Y resident rumored that Harry Baker, another boarder and also a clerk, had a reputation as a "Damn Sissy." On one Sunday and between classes that Baker had invited the letter's writer to attend, the latter explained,

I followed a bunch of fellows out on the side walk there[. T]he speaker started relating the incidents of the night before, which by the way was very interesting to the rest of the fellows, I got so disgusted that I got my hat, and I was leaving, this same fellow had the *crust* to over take me by the hand and say that he was very sorry that I couldn't stay.... My impressions of whole situation is that the majority of the young fellows are growing up with Ideals that are unchristian [*sic*].[32]

It seems more than coincidence that the YMCA attracted homosexuals and same-sex sexual activity and that most of the residents of Portland's Y were lower- and mid-level clerical workers. Scholars have argued that the Y could encourage and even construct same-sex desire within its patrons. The historian John Gustav-Wrathall has explained that the Y's emphasis on physical development helped shape awareness of the male body. Moreover, programs and lectures on sex hygiene introduced the notion that homosexuality existed, even though it was not condoned. These instructional developments, along with the fact that the YMCA buildings were "physically oriented, male-only spaces, largely free of supervision, and safe from police surveillance," promoted and facilitated same-sex sexual desire and expression.[33] The account related above about Harry Baker suggests that such a scenario unfolded at Portland's Y, for the stories that this "Damn Sissy" reportedly told concerning "the night before" had a certain appeal to "a bunch of fellows." Possibly Baker's tales encouraged his young listeners to act on their own incipient desires.

The collapse of the entrepreneurial system and the emergence of corporate capitalism provided middle-class men with various new possibilities as they fashioned their lives. Many men in lower white-collar work elected to remain single. In Portland in 1900, salesmen and clerks in stores, clerks in offices, and bookkeepers were bachelors at a rate (62.3 percent) significantly higher than professionals such as lawyers, physicians, and surgeons (31.8 percent) and even "laborers" (60.7 percent). The latter statistic is particularly significant since, as we saw in chapter 1, the Northwest had a higher proportion of single male laborers than any other part of the country during these years.[34]

Certainly one reason for the high rates of bachelorhood of Portland's white-collar workers was their youthfulness. In 1910 only about 19 percent of male bookkeepers, accountants, cashiers, clerks, and salesmen were over forty-five, whereas close to 36 percent of physicians and 29 percent of laborers fell into that age category. About 74 percent of the clerical workers listed here were between twenty-one and forty-four, and about 12 percent were under twenty-one. In contrast, only 7 percent of laborers and almost no physicians were under twenty-one.[35] Roughly speaking, the older a man became, the more likely he was to marry. It is clear that the men involved in the 1912 scandal were relatively young. Of fifty-four for whom ages could be determined at the time, the oldest was fifty-three and the youngest sixteen. The mean age was thirty, but the median was twenty-seven. I have determined with near certainty that fifty-one of the fifty-nine identified men rounded up in 1912 were either single, divorced, widowers, or separated from their wives. It is worth emphasizing that youthfulness and bachelorhood, or at least singleness, also went along with lower white-collar work *and* the early homosexual community, though there were older and married participants as well. Alfred Kinsey's data support the notion that youth correlated to exclusively homosexual behavior. On the whole, males between the ages of sixteen and thirty were more likely than males of any other age group to live at least a three-year period as exclusively homosexual. For men who went to high school but not beyond, the period of greatest likelihood of exclusive homosexuality extended from ages sixteen to forty.[36]

As revealed in the 1912 scandal, the typical male who participated in Portland's early homosexual subculture was a young, white-collar worker who was single and lived on his own or with others like himself. A number of factors called this individual into existence, but corporate capitalism played a key role. The jobs it created afforded certain liberties to men far beyond those afforded in the nineteenth-century entrepreneurial system. Although formal schooling was important for attaining a position in the new order, this preparation actually required fewer years (at least during the early corporate era) and was more straightforward than that required by the nineteenth-century middle-class youth and adult male attempting to become a self-made man. Because of the new era's rapidly expanding economy, a young man out of high school could with relative ease obtain a position in the corporate world that afforded him a fairly respectable lifestyle, the expectation that his wages would increase, and the ability to support himself away from family at a relatively young age. Such jobs called many of these young men away from the countryside and small towns to the large city, where they found homes of their own or lived for a while communally with others like themselves. In the city, the white-collar worker had ample opportunity to meet a variety of people, not just at work or even where he lived but also in the leisure time that his job made possible. An expanding personal life made it even more likely that such young men could choose to remain bachelors if they so desired. Moreover, the cultural changes that accompanied the development of the corporate economy provided the lower white-collar worker an escape from the rigid expectations that guided the life of the middle-class man of an earlier era. Such a relatively lax atmosphere enabled him to pursue a personal life in which same-sex urges and emotions could be validated and developed. The data from Portland lead to the conclusion that it was indeed among this group that homosexual identity and a homosexual community first emerged. The remainder of this chapter examines more closely various aspects of this same-sex community and identity.

The Contours of Portland's Early-Twentieth-Century Middle-Class Gay Subculture

Portland's 1912 scandal revealed that a number of the men who participated in the city's middle-class homosexual subculture had developed a recognizable community among themselves. Newspapers referred to those rounded up collectively as the "clique," the "band," the "association," and the "brotherhood," giving an air of community to their lives and activities. Such pronouncements in part reflect the tendency of a fearful society to construct a menacing organization of perverts, but some of those involved also referred to themselves as "the fraternity."[37] Dozens of these men knew each other to varying degrees. Many had socialized with each other; several had been acquainted for a number of years. Some had been introduced through cards and personal meetings, and a few had even lived together. When police arrested in Vancouver, British Columbia, a furniture store bookkeeper who was a 1912 suspect, they found in his luggage a number of photographs of Portland's homosexuals.[38]

To be sure, many of the middle-class men who appeared before the law for same-sex offenses in early-twentieth-century Portland did not belong to the specific communities of individuals who came to light in 1912 or again in 1928. But strikingly few members of the working classes who were arrested on similar charges were participants.[39] In the emerging corporate order, sharp lines divided manual from white-collar workers.

The latter, claiming a higher status, felt a sense of superiority. They enjoyed shorter hours, often were given paid sickdays and holidays (and sometimes even vacations), and in many cases had greater job security. Because clerical work required strong English language skills and the ability to follow rules of conduct dictated by an office that was largely white, American, and middle-class, few immigrants other than those from northern Europe and English-speaking Canada could make their way into such positions. Thus racial and ethnic animosities also played a role in white-collar prejudice against laborers. The historian Jürgen Kocka has found that blue-collar bias against white-collar workers, whom laborers increasingly viewed as "stiffs," was also palpable. In a world in which labor unrest was on the increase, factory operatives came to consider the white-collar worker as allied with management. Between about 1900 and the beginning of World War I, Kocka observed, occupational consciousness in the corporate order "took on overtones which divided the clerks from the manual workers, including the skilled crafts[.]" Such consciousness followed workers from their jobs into their personal lives, where different classes seldom mingled socially.[40]

Other factors presumably helped limit the overlap between the working-class and middle-class same-sex sexual subcultures in Portland. Largely confined to the North End and its establishments, transient males had little opportunity for contact with middle-class homosexuals and rarely entered their setting. Furthermore, those from the North End were less likely than those rounded up in the 1912 scandal to have identified themselves as homosexuals. For their part, the men from the middle class probably accepted the dominant notion of working-class males— in particular those of the urban vice district—as poor, drunken, and disorderly, and therefore to be avoided. Likewise, some but not all middle-class men who were concerned with their station in society doubtless abstained from contacts with working-class youths because they understood the risk of being robbed and blackmailed. Finally, as was noted in the previous chapter, Nels Anderson found that mutual animosity existed between homosexual men and transients in the 1920s. Given the abundance of men and youths associated with the migratory culture in Portland's North End, this hostility must have been tangible.[41]

Whether white middle-class men with same-sex desires participated actively in the early homosexual community or avoided it, some occasionally sought out racial minority and working-class males for sex. At least one man and possibly two others arrested in connection with the 1912 scandal were African American. A later example is that of Noel W.,

an American-born white man who apparently grew up in Portland before he moved on to New York City. Noel worked much of his adult life
as a journalist, traveling widely. He returned to the Northwest around
1929 to care for his ailing father. When back at home, Noel recounted
that in the city he had sexual relations with African Americans and Native Americans.[42] As the historian Jeffrey Weeks has pointed out, cross-
class liaisons were a significant theme in middle-class male homosexual
writing at the turn of the twentieth century, when the working-class
man had an aura of particular manliness and therefore became an object
of sexual desire for some men from higher social rankings. This literary
phenomenon at times became sexual reality. In February 1914 George
Struble, a twenty-sex-year-old clerk in the linen department of Portland's
Pullman Company, was arrested with C. E. Shuck, a "laborer," and each
was charged with committing sodomy. In 1910 Virgil St. Clair, a twenty-
year-old clerk; Robert Wolfe, a twenty-two-year-old fireman; and Max
Derrill, a twenty-year-old teamster, were apprehended together for indecent and immoral acts and vagrancy.[43]

Soldiers and sailors were particularly popular fantasy objects among
some middle-class homosexual men in the early twentieth century. Noel
W. recounted that during his 1929 return to the Northwest, he also had
sexual relations with marines and soldiers.[44] One suggestive incident involving lower-middle-class men and sailors occurred on Portland's rain-
dampened streets in 1906. Early one drizzly morning in June, the members of a party composed of five visiting sailors and two singers, W. C.
Deusing and F. N. Irvin, made their way to Paris House, a notorious
North End resort, after meeting up at the Elk's Lodge (see map 2).
Finding no activity of interest there, the seaman then followed the
singers to their hotel in the central business district. Although the reasons that the sailors continued to accompany the performers are unclear,
one possibility is that they had sex on their minds. Law enforcement
officials seem to have had justification for thinking so; when two of
Portland's finest stopped the group for "drunk and disorderly" behavior,
someone hurled at the police the epithet "cocksucker." A melee ensued,
and several in the group were seriously injured by police batons.[45]

Sometimes middle-class men, like their working-class counterparts,
sought out youths for sexual relationships. Frederick Hammerich, a
twenty-five-year-old museum curator in Copenhagen, Denmark, fled his
home country after confessing to sexual relations with a seventeen-year-
old, the admittedly willing and working-class Anders Anderson. While
in Portland for some seven years, Hammerich lived in or near the central

business district and found employment as a clerk for the Pullman Company. Although we know little about his personal life, it is possible that Hammerich participated in the city's nascent homosexual community. In any case, by the time Hammerich arrived in the Rose City his sexual past had parallels to that of some other middle-class men of Portland who had same-sex relations with youths.[46] In 1914 Thomas Ryan, a nurse and sixty-eight-year-old married man from Portland, was arrested in the Oregon coast resort community of Seaside for a sexual relationship with a thirteen-year-old boy who was traveling with him. Four years later, Oscar Hellgreen, a sixty-six-year-old salesman, was arrested for sodomy with a nineteen-year-old laborer.[47] Yet compared to the number of working-class men apprehended in urban centers for relations with youths and boys, relatively few middle-class men came before the law for those offenses. To be sure, it is possible that some men of privilege managed to keep their names out of the records, and reformers and authorities clearly tended to focus on working-class and racial minority males. But middle-class men appear to have been less interested in such relationships. As the furor over the YMCA scandal demonstrates, these men's higher positions in society made it imperative for them to be more discreet in their relationships, regardless of the backgrounds and ages of their partners.

Few males younger than eighteen appear in documents generated during the 1912 scandal, though many newspapers reported on "boys" involved. At the time, *boy* did not mean "teenager"; instead, it referred to a young man between his late teens and late twenties. During the Progressive era, "boy" held a social meaning beyond anything specifically age-related; according to Joe Dubbert, it denoted "opportunity...for the prevention of degenerate and wicked men."[48] Undoubtedly, 1912 officials and news writers employed the term in this way. In truth, news reports and legal documents reveal the identities of only two males under the age of eighteen who can be identified with absolute certainty: one was sixteen, the other seventeen. Neither was a central figure in the scandal, and indeed one seems only tenuously connected to it. Authorities arrested him fifty miles away in Salem, Oregon. Newspapers described him as a valuable witness, since he publicly admitted to having sex with men in Portland, but his name does not appear in the voluminous legal records.[49]

The thirteen young men ages sixteen to twenty who came to light in 1912 all appeared to have willingly participated in sexual relations. Several in this group carried on affairs with each other as well as with older men. Kenneth Hollister, at twenty, had been sexually active for several years by the time of his arrest; he had recently engaged in intimacies with eighteen-year-old Earl Taylor, eighteen-year-old Earl Brown, and nineteen-year-old Benjamin Trout. Trout was indicted for sex with twenty-one-year-old Fred Rodby.[50] Whether youths viewed themselves as homosexual or not, their motives for participating in intergenerational sex with middle-class men could be more complex than the simple fulfillment of sexual desire. The historian Steven Maynard, who has studied intergenerational same-sex relationships in Canada for the first third of the twentieth century, found that whether the relationships were long-term or brief, from these liaisons some boys received much-needed support and often luxuries. Such a description fits the Clarence Brazell–Gordon Franks relationship, which became the most scrutinized case during the 1928 vice crackdown. Brazell was a forty-year-old insurance salesman and Franks a seventeen-year-old truant from Lincoln High School, whose mother and stepfather were comfortably middle-class. Because the Franks experienced a number of difficulties with their willful son, they kicked him out of the house, leaving him to drift. Court documents attested that the Franks were aware of their son's relationship with Brazell for some time before taking action. From his relationship with the older man, Gordon received a place to live, money, cigarettes, access to an automobile, vacation trips, fine clothing, and even the opportunity to canoe with Brazell on Lake Oswego, a summer resort south of town frequented by wealthier Portlanders.[51]

Perhaps the Franks turned a blind eye to Gordon's relationship with Brazell because it kept their troublesome son comfortably out of their hair. Other parents who had little money (like some whom Maynard studied in Ontario) may have accepted their boys' relationships with adult males because they realized that at the least the men would provide for their children. The Portland music teacher Roy Marion Wheeler seems to be one such case. In September 1911 the police arrested him for making "indecent advances" in his studio toward twelve-year-old Oscar Lovegren. As the detectives looked further into the affair, they ascertained that Wheeler "had been in similar trouble about three years ago with his office boy[.]" The authorities were shocked to discover that the same youth not only continued to work for but even resided with the music teacher, "instead of [his] parents, Wheeler providing entirely for him."[52]

Some of the youths who came before the justice system for their sexual relationships with middle-class men had troubled backgrounds. Gordon Franks acknowledged that he stayed out late at night, would not obey his parents, associated with people of dubious reputation, passed bad checks, and engaged in various other criminal acts. He further admitted that his stepfather could not control him and had even committed him to the county jail for a short stay. One young man brought before the courts in 1928 stated that "since age 14 he drank beer, moonshine, [and] wine." Eighteen-year-old Leslie Anderson, involved in the 1912 scandal, had a record of thievery that had landed him on the county rock pile for six months back in 1910. In 1912 he also faced charges of embezzling from a local newspaper.[53]

Although most middle-class men tended to avoid contact with street youths because of the various dangers that such relationships and the boys themselves posed, others, as these cases demonstrate, threw caution to the wind and sometimes found themselves in serious difficulty, especially in the 1920s. In one of the 1928 cases, two teenagers who visited William Armstrong at his downtown hotel waited until he had fallen into a drunken slumber and then "stole into his room and emptied his trousers' pockets of all the money they contained."[54] Youths also attempted to blackmail middle-class men and in some cases readily testified against them to protect their own interests. Apparently to "forestall prosecution of themselves," the two teenagers who robbed Armstrong brought charges against him and another man for sexual relations. In one of the 1912 cases a youth attempted to extort money from a Portland physician in return for keeping quiet. And as noted at the beginning of this chapter, the entire 1912 scandal began when Benjamin Trout, brought in a different charge, apparently attempted to throw suspicion off himself by freely speaking about his sexual relations with various local men and youths.[55]

On various occasions, then, men from the middle class did engage in sexual relations with their working-class counterparts, with men belonging to racial minority groups, and with youths, but liaisons with the last were not as common as they were among the laboring classes. Evidence does suggest that middle-class men in Portland in the late 1920s were more likely than those in the 1910s to have relations with youths, a change that may reflect Portland's shifting demographics. As transient culture faded, street youths may have begun performing sex work among middle-class men, and middle-class men may have become more willing to turn to them. Such youths also altered the roles that they played in sexual affairs with adult males. Two teenagers who engaged in sex work around Portland's downtown bus terminal were arrested in the city's 1928 crackdown. It appears that the two allowed their middle-class client to perform oral sex on them.[56] Possibly these street youths, like some mid- and late-twentieth-century male sex workers, permitted their partner only to fellate them in order to protect their masculinity. The decline of transient culture, which had required youths to perform in the receptive role and had dictated anal and interfemoral intercourse, and the rise of the gay culture, which (as will be explored below) endorsed oral sex, may have enabled "non-homosexual" street youths to dictate the sexual activities that they would engage in. Until we find more evidence from the urban Northwest about the transformation of the early-twentieth-century punk into the mid-twentieth-century hustler, however, this conclusion can only be speculative.

Members of Portland's early middle-class "gay" community also differed from working-class men who engaged in same-sex affairs in their residential patterns. Whereas the latter temporarily or permanently occupied the North End, none of those collared in the 1912 scandal resided there. Though they made their homes in almost every other part of the city, they concentrated in one specific neighborhood. Thus we find in Portland what the historian Marc Stein's careful examination of residential patterns has helped establish for post–World War II Philadelphia: gay men early on clustered in certain urban neighborhoods and not in others.[57] Most of those who surfaced in 1912 lived either in or immediately west of the central business district (see map 2). This early gay neighborhood had various attractions. A reasonably respectable residential area that contained any number of decent apartment and lodging houses as well as some single-family dwellings, in 1910 it had the second-highest percentage of adult male residents in the city. Not surprisingly, given the racial makeup of Portland's gay community, at the time this area was 57 percent white with American-born parents, while the rest of the city was just under 50 percent. It also had the highest rate of adult male literacy in the city, as well as the second-lowest number of families, relative to total population, of any ward in the city.[58] It therefore appealed to young, independent, white-collar, America-born men with same-sex sexual interests.

Naturally, many of the men caught up in the events of 1912 lived near each other; some lived together. This neighborhood is where, on the corner of Eleventh and Columbia, Earl Van Hulen and Harry Wight cohabitated in 1911. Claude Bronner and Nathan Healy occupied an apartment on Morrison between Tenth and West Park from 1909 to 1911. Next door for a short time lived Billy Reames, also implicated in the 1912 scandal. By early 1912, Bronner and Healy had moved to an apartment on Washington Street between Twelfth and Thirteenth. Residing on the same block that year was Earl Van Hulen. Later in 1912, Bronner moved into an apartment on Seventeenth and Taylor with his business partner, Burt Thornton, who also faced indictment that year; they were living there when the scandal broke. Within the same block, but on the Yamhill Street side, could be found yet another man implicated in it, the photographer John Moffit. Also in the central business district, on the northwest corner of Sixth and Taylor, was located the YMCA, where at least six of the men involved in the 1912 scandal roomed sometime during the years 1911 and 1912 (see map 2).[59]

Fully 80 percent of the forty-six men involved in the 1912 scandal whose place of employment can be traced (1911–15) had jobs in the central business district. Several worked in the same firms, and many more worked nearby one another. Between 1906 and 1913, Claude Bronner and Burt Thornton co-owned and operated several delis and restaurants here. Also, Earl Van Hulen and Harry Wight found employment together at the Chamber of Commerce (on Stark, between Third and Fourth Streets). Van Hulen had previously been employed at Olds, Wortman and King, a huge general department store that filled most of the block bounded by Tenth, West Park, Morrison, and Alder. Bruce Stone, another man implicated in the 1912 scandal, also worked there. Both Kenneth Hollister and William Tierney worked at Woodard, Clarke and Company, a drug and medical supply store at Fourth and Washington. Next door stood the Du Fresne Studios, where John Moffit plied his photography trade.[60]

The geographic center of the middle-class male same-sex sexual subculture was located in the central business district and the nearby residential area. This area also provided the city's primary public gay sites: parks, restrooms, and Washington Street. Located in the heart of Portland, these sites were also some of the busiest places in the city, where all types of people gathered, rested, and transacted business. They were hardly the "zones of discard" that some historians and geographers have claimed were the locations of many early gay "spaces" in urban America.[61] Washington Street was among Portland's major business thoroughfares (figure 8). More men of the 1912 affair worked and lived along this one street than on any other in the city. Not surprisingly, it provided a place where men could meet for companionship, sometimes retreating from it for sexual relationships. Louis Burns, a young man from Vancouver, British Columbia, visited Portland in May 1911. He first encountered the attorney E. S. J. McAllister a block away from Washington

FIGURE 8. Corner of Portland's Broadway and Washington Streets, ca. 1910s. Washington Street was the heart of the middle-class gay male world of early-twentieth-century Portland. This view from Washington looking north down Broadway includes a view of the Imperial Hotel (second building on right). The Imperial's basement restrooms served as one of the city's earliest known gay pickup spots. Oregon Historical Society, #OrHi 30016.

Street. Upon invitation, Burns accompanied the lawyer to his residence, which at that time was also located on Washington Street. There, the two undressed and "went to bed." In mid-October 1912, Roy Kadel and Harry Work met up at Sixth and Washington. They proceeded to McAllister's office, where Kadel and the attorney engaged in sex. Also in October 1912, Earl Van Hulen, while making his way down Washington, met up with Fred Rodby. The two went to the physician Harry Start's offices, located just off the thoroughfare. There, Rodby and Start had sex while Van Hulen waited in the lobby.[62] Sometime after leaving Start's offices the two parted company, again on Washington. Near the corner of Broadway, Rodby entered the basement lavatories of the Imperial Hotel, another important gay meeting place (see map 2). For example, Horace Tabb, who himself was indicted for a same-sex crime in 1912, testified at trial that in the fall of 1911 McAllister there propositioned him while he stood at the urinal.[63]

Lownsdale Park (figure 9), located in the central business district on the Plaza Blocks bounded by Salmon, Main, Third, and Fourth, also

FIGURE 9. Portland's Lownsdale Park, ca. 1910. Located in the Plaza Blocks south of the central business district, Lownsdale became an all-male park when Chapman Park, situated in the block directly to the south, became by tradition and then ordinance a retreat for women and children only. Lownsdale was already serving as a popular gay middle-class male meeting place by about 1900. The monument commemorates soldiers who served in the Spanish American War. Oregon Historical Society, #OrHi 74546.

acted as an important pickup venue for middle-class gay men (see map 2). By a tradition dating at least from 1904 (and formally recognized in a 1924 ordinance), Chapman Park, immediately to the south, was designated for the use of women and children only. Therefore Lownsdale emerged as an exclusively male retreat. In his memoir of his early life in Portland, Laurence Pratt told of a visit to Lownsdale in about 1900. While sitting on a park bench there, Pratt recalled,

A young man strolled up and occupied the other end. . . . Soon he began making remarks to me, and moved closer. All I remember of the conversation is that I asked him what his work was, and he said he sold silk. By this time he was near me and put his hand on my knee from time to time. Then he began to squeeze my leg a little above the knee. He moved his hand still higher and squeezed harder. I was very naive, and had never heard of homosexuality, but I felt frightened and jumped up and walked away as rapidly as I could.[64]

The large number of men occupying Lownsdale made it possible for those with same-sex sexual interests to meet each other and at the same time remain almost invisible as they blended in with the downtown crowds.

Gay men referred to Lownsdale simply as "the park," a name that denoted its centrality to their world. New arrivals in town were sometimes first introduced to Portland's gay world there. Harry Work and Roy Kadel originally met in "the park" in about 1909. During one of their first rendezvous there, Kadel pointed out to Work, who at that time was new to the city, other members of the local homosexual community. On another occasion William Homan claimed that as he "came down the street," while "close to the park" he ran into McAllister, who invited him to "stay downtown and have supper with me." Again, that so many men frequented Lownsdale Park undoubtedly made it possible for McAllister, a well-known lawyer and reformer, to be seen there without raising the suspicions of outsiders. From early in the twentieth century, the park was a haunt for men searching for sex partners. By 1953 men had also taken over neighboring Chapman Park. Fifteen years later, city officials expressed concern that its restroom had become a regular meeting place for men interested in same-sex relations.[65]

That sexual partners were met and intimacies shared in places such as lavatories, city parks, and amusement resorts and movie theaters suggests a fairly public side to Portland's early homosexual community. Their meeting places and patterns of behavior are similar to those in working-class same-sex sexual subcultures, described above. Yet a significant geographic as well as social and cultural distinction existed between places such as the Imperial Hotel, Washington Street, and the Plaza Blocks on the one hand and the North End's Globe lodging house, Burnside Street, and the Monte Carlo poolroom on the other. The middle-class homosexual subculture tended to revolve around notions and institutions that had middle-class origins, like the YMCA. But many in this community chose to avoid the Y and other public spaces, preferring instead to retreat into apartment houses, hotels, homes, and professional offices to engage in socializing and sexual relationships.

This propensity to withdraw from the streets was unlike the behavior of men in the transient and working-class community, who admittedly often lacked access to such private quarters. Yet notions of privacy are themselves rooted in class. They can be traced to shifting emphases in daily life as entrepreneurial capitalism gave way in the nineteenth century to the corporate order, industrialization, and immigration. The growth of impersonal cityscapes, the increase in foreigners on city streets, the noise and hubbub that accompanied the rise of factories, the expansion of leisure time, and especially the growing impersonality of jobs in the corporate economy and their lessening connection to broader community needs all encouraged members of the middle class to concentrate on their private rather than public lives. The development of privacy helped the middle class increasingly distinguish itself from the working class.[66] The Portland Vice Commission, which the mayor had appointed in 1911, concluded its work in late 1912 in the midst of the homosexual scandal and unwittingly noted the role played by privacy in the city's gay subculture. "The greater number of...instances wherein two or more men were involved in groups," it reported, "were localized in hotels[.]" Only weeks earlier, the *Oregon Journal* had similarly recounted that "the members of the brotherhood" most often "carried on their acts in...apartment houses, hotels, [and] rooming houses."[67]

During the last years of the nineteenth and first years of the twentieth century, young single men looking for white-collar work crowded into Portland's central business district and the adjacent residential neighborhood. They helped make this area the whitest, the most male, the best educated, and among the least family-oriented in the city. The spatial and social configuration of this part of the city appealed to young middle-class homosexual men. Here they constructed their own community and carried on social lives within private residences and offices. At the same time, because so many others in the district were like themselves—white, male, clerical workers of the corporate world, often living in local hotels or the YMCA—they also blended easily into the district's public spaces; it was thus possible to meet others with same-sex desires in very popular venues while at the same time retaining a level of anonymity. Of course, those desires differentiated them from many other young men in this area. At the same time, the specific nature of their desires and activities also differentiated them from the working-class men who engaged in same-sex affairs in the geographically near but sexually distant North End.

During the most sensational trial of the 1928 vice scandal, one profit-seeking newspaper carried portions of a witness's testimony regarding the drunken "orgies" in which some of the indicted men allegedly participated. His "was a filthy story," the paper trumpeted, "a tale the state's attorneys had difficulty in dragging out." At moments, and apparently because of the scandalous nature of its details, the informant "hesitated a full minute between words."[68] The forced confessions of shocking sexual tidbits simultaneously horrified and titillated the larger citizenry of Portland. They also offered for public scrutiny some of the most intimate and private moments between the men compelled to recount them. These specific sexual details, aired like so much dirty laundry many decades ago, are worth rummaging through again. They disclose much about the meaning of gender and sex acts to the men who participated in the Rose City's early middle-class homosexual community. Moreover, they reveal some of the limits to working-class influences on the changing sexuality and culture of early-twentieth-century America.

In addition to noting the vast economic transformation undergirding the sexual revolution that swept America at the turn of the twentieth century, scholars also have commented on the contributions made to that revolution by the relatively sexually liberated working classes. During the Victorian era, the middle classes had adhered to fairly strict social customs that separated males and females into their respective spheres, limiting their social and thus sexual interaction. In contrast, by the end of the nineteenth century the working classes had developed heterosocial forms of public entertainment, including a broad range of nightlife activities and commercialized amusements. Such activities and amusements often focused on the sexual, facilitating and encouraging attraction and relations. The middle classes were not protected from these developments, whose effects spread quickly; according to John D'Emilio and Estelle B. Freedman, around 1900 "working-class forms of sexual interaction previously beyond the ken of the middle class were projected outward into society." As a result, as the historian Kevin White describes, by the 1920s working-class "patterns of behavior and sexual norms spread to the white middle class."[69] Yet the working class was not alone in influencing America's "first sexual revolution." In fact middle-class practices and attitudes also pushed open the boundaries of sexual experience and expression, as becomes apparent when we examine the nascent homosexual community—particularly the ways in which men of this subculture engaged in sex with each other.

As chapters 1 and 2 have noted, a wide array of sexual acts and partnerships are discernible in the Northwest's working-class same-sex sexual subculture. Nonetheless, the most common form of sex, whether between adult males or between men and youths, was anal and interfemoral penetration. While oral eroticism did occur, working-class men tended to avoid it. Middle-class Noel W. found this to be the case in late 1920s Portland. He asserted that although some of his marine and soldier partners in the city would fellate him, "They were usually not interested in using their mouths."[70] The lower frequency of oral sex among the working classes is confirmed in Alfred Kinsey's research on males of the "lower social levels" during the first half of the twentieth century. Kinsey found that this group generally eschewed oral contacts—whether mouth-genital, mouth-breast, or even kissing—in both homosexual and hetero-sexual encounters.[71]

Some scholars have maintained that working-class men refrained from performing fellation in same-sex encounters because it placed them in the role of receptor—that is, in the traditional "female" posi-tion—and therefore undermined their masculinity.[72] This argument is persuasive, and some data from Portland do support it. Yet it fails to ex-plain why even in heterosexual encounters working-class men also avoided oral eroticism, including kissing. Neither does it acknowledge that within the preferred anal and interfemoral scenarios, the working-class male did take the receptive role, nor why, overall, he used his mouth considerably less often than his legs and anus. Alfred Kinsey rec-ognized that the working-class male was relatively sexually liberated, probably because beginning early in life he had easy access to sexual in-tercourse. Yet this form of sexual abundance also explains certain sexual limitations of the working-class male. That is, Kinsey argued, because he was accustomed to the primary use of his penis in sex, he did not (need to) experiment much beyond it. Generally, the early-twentieth-century man of the lower social level considered oral contacts to be "dirty," "filthy," and a "source of disease," and he dismissed them "with consider-able disgust."[73] Ironically, accompanying relative working-class sexual liberty was also a degree of sexual constraint. Apparently, the influence of this "liberated" class cannot also be credited with the proliferation in the early twentieth century of diverse sexual practices, including oral sex. Not only did some observers of the era judge that both fellation and cunnilingus were on the increase, but they also noted that homosexual men preferred the first to any other form of sex act.[74]

Legal documents from Portland's 1912 scandal support their conclu-sion about homosexual men. Of the crimes identified in the records, more than 84 percent are fellation. None involved anal or interfemoral intercourse. According to Kinsey's findings, oral eroticism, including practices as sedate as kissing, was associated with the middle and upper classes, a fact in keeping with the social class data from 1912 Portland. The middle and upper classes accepted oral stimulation because they had practiced it (often in moderate forms) for years in lieu of inter-course, which social pressures and opportunities proscribed.[75] Contem-porary evidence from elsewhere on the West Coast supports the connec-tion between fellation, gay community, and middle-class sex practices. Not two years after Portland's 1912 affair, a series of official and private investigations uncovered the existence of a thriving gay community in

Long Beach and Los Angeles. This community, like Portland's, was mainly middle- and upper-class; few laborers were involved. Moreover, southern California's gay men referred to oral sex, because of its widespread appeal, as the "twentieth-century way." The historian Sharon Ullman has concluded that in their use of this term, southern California's homosexuals "firmly and knowingly associated themselves with visions of progress and affirmative good." These notions of progress, Ullman rightly notes, pervaded America at the dawn of the new century.[76] I would add further that these were largely middle-class notions.

George Chauncey has argued for the early twentieth century that middle-class men were more apt than working-class men to identify themselves as homosexuals. Middle-class culture more rigidly categorized those men who had sex with other males and those men who had sex with females. Because of these strict divisions, a middle-class man who had sex with another male was likely to possess a full cultural understanding of his actions. Having gone beyond what was acceptable (as well as what was identified as heterosexual), the middle-class man then found it easier to engage in a wide variety of sexual acts, including both the penetrative and receptive roles in fellation. Chauncey writes, "Middle-class men...were more likely to organize sexual practices—and to identify themselves—as 'homosexuals,' who engaged in a variety of sexual relations with men exclusively[.]" In contrast, common laborers found it culturally easier "to alternate between sexual relations with men and relations with women...so long as they played the 'man's part' with both of them." They could have sex with other men without stigma because their sexual culture categorized only one of the men involved as "queer"—the one who played the receptive ("woman's") role.[77]

These findings notwithstanding, Kinsey Institute data reveal that even among early-twentieth-century homosexuals (i.e., just those that Kinsey researchers could identify as homosexuals and not the broader social cross section of men who might have had sex with other males that Chauncey considers), differences remained between working-class and middle-class willingness to perform fellation (see table 3). Working-class homosexual men expressed greater reluctance to perform fellation on their partners than did their middle-class counterparts, probably more because of general working-class inhibitions regarding the use of the mouth in any form of sex than because of any fear of being labeled "queer." For if indeed these men identified as homosexuals, then such fears are moot. Moreover, the sexual practices of the middle-class homosexual were not so much due to the fact that he had already gone beyond

TABLE 3. *Rates of Oral Sex among Homosexual Working-Class and Middle-Class Men Born 1860–1924*

Class and occupation	Never or rarely (1 to 3 times total) performs fellation on partner (%)	Often (in at least 2 out of 3 sexual encounters) performs fellation on partner (%)
Working class: no primary occupation, chronically unemployed, unskilled laborer, semi-skilled laborer, skilled laborer, farmer (*n* = 88)	20.1	59.1
Lower middle class: lower white-collar (*n* = 107)	11.2	75.7
Upper middle class: upper white-collar, professional, executive (*n* = 182)	10.4	74.2

SOURCE: Kinsey Institute for Research in Sex, Gender, and Reproduction, data analysis for author.

the acceptable and therefore could do just about anything, including performing oral sex on his partner. Rather, middle-class males who made up the rank and file of early-twentieth-century gay community brought their middle-class culture's predilection for oral eroticism with them and applied it in the new context. All this, and especially the evidence from 1912 Portland, strongly argues that middle-class sexual practices very much influenced the sexual activities of early-twentieth-century gay men and thereby significantly shaped the overall sexual revolution of the period.

By 1912 fellation predominated among the sexual relations in which the men of Portland's homosexual community engaged. Surviving documents suggest that some men identified those who engaged in oral sex according to the role they performed. Several men indicated that those who received fellation but did not perform it were known as "trade" or, if younger, "chicken." Those who gave fellation they termed "queer," "fruiter," "cocksucker," and "queen"; older men might receive the title "mother."[78] The rigidity of roles, and thus the degree to which the men applied these terms to themselves rather than just to others, is unclear. The men themselves are partly responsible for the uncertainty, for some manipulated terms to avoid prosecution. In fact, those who went to trial were almost exclusively men who performed fellation, often to the consternation of the defense attorneys. For example, the lawyer Charles Page asked of one witness against his client who claimed that he only allowed himself to be "sucked off," "why it is that this man has not been indicted, and that he can go before the grand jury and the district attorney's office and tell all about these things, and yet not be indicted."[79]

Some men scrambled to call themselves trade because they believed that they might receive lighter penalties. Others cast themselves in this role to increase the likelihood of being asked to turn state's evidence. But that they were really telling the truth about themselves is debatable. For example, Harry Allen Work seems to have cut a deal with prosecutors to save himself.[80] While testifying in a proceeding against a prominent local man, Work claimed that he took only the penetrative role in oral sexual encounters and noted that there was "quite a difference...a lot of difference" between one who "sucked cock" and one who permitted it to be done. Nonetheless, it seems that Work was not completely forthcoming on the stand; less than three years after this testimony, he once again came under arrest. This time he faced charges of taking into his mouth "the penis and private parts" of three different young men.[81] Though it is possible that only between 1912 and 1915 did Work expand his sexual practices and begin to perform oral sex, the chronology of events makes this unlikely. In his own testimony of 1912, Work asserted that a man who "is queer [i.e., a cocksucker], they generally give him some nickname some woman's name"; but he himself, one newspaper reported, was also called "Viola."[82]

Clearly, in the minds of some early-twentieth-century Portland homosexuals a division existed between one who "went down" on men and one who permitted another to "go down" on him. Various scholars have examined the class and gender meanings behind these acts, conclusions that need not be recapitulated here. Rather, I wish to point out that the roles in which men within the emerging middle-class homosexual community engaged might actually have their own history. Certain evidence from Portland suggests that the older a man was, the more likely he would be to perform fellation but not receive it. Though the records may be biased and incomplete, it is nonetheless significant that the average age of a man who was indicted for performing fellation (while at the same time no evidence purports that he received it) was almost 36, with the median a fairly high 38. By contrast, those whom records indicate received fellation without in turn performing it had an average age of 22.5 and the median was even lower at 21.

That older men performed oral sex on younger males, rather than the other way around, in the middle-class homosexual subculture of Portland and elsewhere is partially confirmed in some anecdotal evidence. During court proceedings against Portland physician Harry Start, the deputy district attorney attempted to enter into evidence accounts of certain "drag parties" in which a number of local men participated. Such parties were more than occasions for some to dress as women. Rather, as the prosecutor claimed, during these gatherings "young fellows that looked good to them; these young chickens, were just dragged and thrown from one to the other, and when they got to one man they had to go to them all." Two years later in southern California an informant on vice conditions spoke of drag parties and other social functions in which men "resorted to all sorts of unnatural practices with men, especially young men. . . . I have seen men . . . go around on their knees to various other persons present and attempt to 'go down' on them right before the crowd and seemingly they have no shame about it."[83]

Some of the Portland evidence implies that as a man grew older, he would not only be likely to expand his sexual roles to include performing fellation but would also continue to receive it as well. Take for example Kenneth Hollister, a twenty-year-old bill collector at the time of his arrest in 1912. He confessed that while he had allowed other men to go down on him since at least the age of seventeen, only within the months immediately prior to his apprehension had he himself also fellated men. Hollister told about one encounter with Earl Van Hulen when each performed oral sex on the other. Van Hulen corroborated Hollister's statement and also divulged that he had previously permitted men to fellate him.[84] Both young men had begun performing fellation only recently. We also know of several other youthful men caught up in the 1912 scandal who performed both roles in fellation. Their ages were slightly higher than those who apparently only received it and significantly lower than those who only performed it.

This indicates that when a male first began to participate sexually in the turn-of-the-century middle-class gay subculture, he began performing primarily in the role of inserter in oral sexual relations. Within a few years he started taking part in both roles, and at some late point he seemed to confine himself more exclusively to the role of the one who performed fellation. But the biases within the records preclude certainty on these points. In fact, the evidence better indicates that differences between the older and younger members of Portland's homosexual community reflect generational rather than individual life patterns. In this vein we must note that the various men arrested in 1912 who performed both roles in oral sex, and a few of those who only performed it (for example, twenty-two-year-old John Bradley and twenty-four-year-old Horace Tabb), were very young. These men also do not neatly fit into the categories of trade or queen. When Van Hulen took the stand, for instance, he admitted to knowing that a "queen" was a man "that will go down on people." When the defense attorney asked him on five different occasions whether he himself was a queen, he denied it each time. Yet he readily admitted, even when the judge explained to him that he did not have to, that he did indeed perform fellation.[85]

Other young men—such as nineteen-year-old William Homan, twenty-two-year-old Louis Burns, and twenty-one-year-old Fred Rodby—confessed to sexual encounters in which they performed exclusively the penetrative role, in all cases with men considerably older. None referred to himself as "trade" and none seems to have performed the typical trade role, which historically and sociologically is characterized as cold, transactional, and stand-offish—everything that the term implies. Typically trade was a "straight" man who performed sex work. He limited his physical contacts to the penetrative role in oral sex and resisted other forms of intimacies in order to protect his masculinity. If his partner attempted more, he likely responded with a violent reprimand and possibly ended the relationship.[86]

When the various young men arrested in Portland in 1912 performed the same penetrative role that trade would, they nonetheless always permitted other forms of intimacies that trade would simply not allow. These men confessed that their partners kissed them, hugged them, felt them, and "loved" them up. They also at times described rather tender evenings spent with their paramours.[87] Moreover, each of these young men continued encounters with those who hugged, kissed, loved, and went to bed with them, and none suggested that he offered the slightest resistance. It is clear that they, unlike trade, did not find such activities threatening, unacceptable, or indecent.

Several of the men rounded up in 1912 who were in their late teens and twenties performed fellation on other men, particularly their peers. Many other young men claimed only to have received fellation but said that other romantic intimacies made up a considerable part of their encounters. And yet others among the youthful men admitted to performing both penetrative and receptive roles in their oral sexual encounters. Such evidence suggests that while the younger men of Portland's homosexual community recognized terms such as *trade, queen, fruiter,* and so on, these older labels had little relevance to them, their middle-class situation, and their emerging experiences. I would argue that these younger men were in the process of developing an identity broader than that offered by the older, narrower terms. This more capacious, "gay," identity permitted them to participate in a great variety of sexual acts with each other. It was an identity, furthermore, that existed outside or in addition to *trade* and *cocksucker*. Therefore, it did not demand of those who claimed it that they choose one role or label, as these terms no longer applied to their own practices, emotions, and consciousness as gay men.

Portland's early middle-class homosexual subculture exhibited both similarities to and differences from the same-sex sexual subculture that men of the laboring classes constructed inside and outside the city. But the differences appear more significant, especially insofar as they indicate that the middle-class experience first permitted and forged prototypical gay consciousness and community. While some scholars have stressed the role that formative categories of sexuality played in the emergence of homosexual community first among the middle classes, I am proposing that broad economic change, whose direct material consequences were felt in individual lives, permitted middle-class men to form the first homosexual subculture. Furthermore, as younger men began to participate in this emerging subculture and expanded their range of sexual practices, they identified themselves as something different from *trade* and *cocksucker*, terms that did not fit their own feelings and experiences as they willingly engaged in various roles in sexual encounters with each other.

Documentary evidence confirms that emerging homosexual subculture and community first took root in the middle classes. But generally overlooked in the process of examining formative gay identity and community is the role that middle-class sexual practices played. Whereas scholars have largely credited the working classes with shifting the sexual culture of the early twentieth century, it appears that middle-class sexual practices also had an influence. Certainly, the emergence of homosexual community, homosexual identity, and expanding homosexual activities is a significant part of America's first sexual revolution. That such identity, community, and experience derived particularly from middle-class forms confirms the influence that this class had on the convulsive sexual changes pervading the country at the time of Portland's 1912 scandal.

CHAPTER 4

From Oscar Wilde to Portland's 1912 Scandal

Socially Constructing the Homosexual

In the 1880s and 1890s, Northwest newspapers occasionally printed references to local same-sex affairs. In May 1889, for example, Portland's *Evening Telegram* reported that George Morris, awaiting examination for the charge of committing a "crime against nature," had mysteriously disappeared from the dock on the day of his hearing. "Where is George Morris?" the newspaper indignantly asked. The exasperated answer was that he "had made his escape, but when and how nobody could tell[.]"[1] As recounted elsewhere in this volume, other newspapers at the time referred to the Mark Weeks–John Goodock affair; the "crime against nature" that Jack Stafford and Robert Wilkinson allegedly committed; the story of the Fred Jones–Thomas Mosey relationship; and the suspicious saloon scene involving an older and younger man, both of whom were lightly clad. During the period studied here, newspapers were the most widely circulated public source of information. Clearly, Portlanders who did nothing more than pick up a local daily during those years could have learned that same-sex sexual activities were occurring in their city.[2]

Still, such accounts appeared only occasionally, and few were actual "stories." The *Evening Telegram*'s twenty-six-line consideration of the Jones-Mosey affair is the longest report of a local male-male sex case that I have uncovered in Portland newspapers up to the 1912 scandal. Although the relationship between Jones and Mosey was described in the sensational news language of the day, the story garnered no headlines, appearing at the end of a piece covering a variety of local crimes. It is also clear that at this time reports on local affairs, such as the story on Jones and Mosey, remained local.

Oscar Wilde's trials and tribulations of 1895 received the Northwest's first regionwide coverage of male-male sexuality.[3] Though its origins and resolution were in far-off London, newspapers in small towns and large cities throughout this region, as elsewhere in the world, extensively reported on the case. Until Portland's 1912 scandal, the Wilde affair, because of its print coverage, remained the single most important news event to shape the broader public representation of male "homosexuality" in the Northwest. The reason why he received so much attention while early local cases provoked comparatively little public interest has much to do not just with Wilde's international celebrity but also with patterns of news distribution. The urban and small-town papers of the 1880s and 1890s carried important local and state news, but their pages were largely filled with international and national items disseminated over wire services. No doubt, London dispatches carried considerably more weight than did those from Portland—and of course Wilde was a notable public figure. Wilde's class background, specifically his connection to "high society," had scandal value and thus could sell papers. It must also be borne in mind that Wilde was well known in America, where he had toured for several months in the early 1880s. Although he did not travel to the Northwest, he did make his way to the Pacific Coast, sojourning in San Francisco for a short time. Wilde's brief but high-profile association with the United States undoubtedly contributed to America's interest in him in 1895.[4]

Perhaps less obvious than what made Wilde attract newspapers' attention is what limited the newsworthiness of early local same-sex affairs: the parties involved were almost entirely working-class and racial minority males. Members of the dominant society, who wrote the news for their own consumption, accepted that the "lower" classes and races were by *nature* sexually degenerate—a condition that occasioned considerable anxiety and would require action. But that working-class and racial minority males engaged in same-sex sexual activities was hardly "news." In contrast, such actions by a man of Wilde's background, stature, and fame seemed quite unusual to those in the Northwest of the 1890s. Indeed, before 1912 it would have been unconventional to propose that men from their own more "respectable" social classes might enter into same-sex affairs. The example of Wilde certainly forced northwesterners to accept that men other than those from the "lower" classes and races engaged in such practices. At the same time, however, other aspects of Wilde's background as well as the whole historical and cultural context of his story worked to counter the belief that men of the respectable classes in North America might actually perform these same transgressive behaviors. At the time of the Wilde affair, and partly as a result of it, North Americans accepted that sexual degeneracy among the respectable classes was somehow connected to European conditions that had little if any influence on the United States.

In the Northwest, this understanding—when coupled with officials' and reformers' almost exclusive focus on working-class, racial minority, and immigrant males—further worked to blind the broader citizenry to the possibility that local middle- and upper-class men might also engage in same-sex sexual practices, or indeed even create an entire culture around them. In this context we can better understand the sensationalism associated with the 1912 scandal and why this local story would take on regional and even national dimensions. The 1912 scandal forced residents of the Northwest to rethink their older understandings of same-sex sexuality. In doing so, they began socially constructing the "modern" homosexual and located him initially within the middle classes.

This chapter takes a three-part approach to examining these developments. First, I explore the Oscar Wilde scandal, the way newspapers in the Northwest covered it, and the influence it had on the region's understanding of "homosexuality" and the "homosexual" at the turn of the century. Following this, I analyze how Portland's 1912 scandal caused northwesterners to reconceptualize male same-sex sexuality, arguing that the 1912 affair introduced more modern conceptions of homosexuality and homosexual identity while at the same time helping both to promote and to alter older notions that had lurked in social consciousness since at least the time of the Wilde affair. Finally, I examine the ways in which dominant society in the Northwest, around 1912, then began to assign this newer homosexual identity to working-class men who participated in same-sex affairs.

The Wilde Northwest, 1895–1912

The Oscar Wilde scandal began in March 1895 when Wilde, then at the zenith of a brilliant literary career, preferred charges of libel against the marquess of Queensberry. Although gossip had been circulating for some time concerning Wilde's sexual exploits, Queensberry had publicly accused him of being a sodomite—particularly incensed because the writer was carrying on an affair with his wayward son, Lord Alfred Douglas. The damning evidence that came to light against Wilde during

Queensberry's trial forced the writer to withdraw his suit as a lost cause. Immediately thereafter, authorities placed Wilde under arrest for his alleged transgressions. In late April and May he endured two trials; found guilty in the second for gross indecency between males, he went to prison for two years' hard labor. The details from these various trials shook the Western world and also helped create in the popular imagination a male homosexual identity.[5]

The historians Jonathan Ned Katz and Ed Cohen have remarked that during Wilde's trials, newspapers in New York and London remained reticent about the particulars of his exact crime and even the precise charges against him. Just the opposite was true in the Northwest, where newspapers specified "sodomy," "unnatural crimes," and "acts of gross indecency."[6] They also printed the shocking details carried in London dispatches. One such release assailed Wilde's conspirator, Alfred Taylor, as "the keeper of a male brothel" and the "procurer for Wilde." Another described Taylor's well-furnished and "darkened perfumed rooms" in which he dressed "effeminately." Still another contained the testimony of the youthful Charles Parker, one of Wilde's working-class sex partners, who claimed that Taylor had once participated in a marriage ceremony with a young man while dressed in women's attire. After the service, the wedding party reconvened at a nuptial repast and then engaged in a "disgusting org[y]." Of Wilde, papers noted his "intimacies," "indecencies," and "immoral practices" with various males. They also questioned the meaning behind his private and public writings and correspondence, including his description of the "rose red lips" of his young lover Douglas, as well as Douglas's now-famous line concluding a poem, "I am that Love that dare not speak its name." The press also contended that Wilde's celebrated novel *The Picture of Dorian Gray* "upheld [the practice of] sodomy."[7] Clearly, newspapers in the Northwest did not shy from Wilde's infamies, nor from speculating on the hidden evils of his writings.

London transmissions made up the bulk of the articles appearing in papers, but local editors also presented their own observations as well as the thoughts of other American journalists. These reporters and editors tried to explain Wilde's activities by drawing on the popular theory of reverse evolution known as "degeneration." As it happened, an English translation of Max Nordau's attention-grabbing book titled *Degeneration* appeared in America as Wilde's trials were under way. First published in German in 1894, Nordau's study reflected the popular belief that Europe had by the end of the nineteenth century passed its pinnacle of development and was entering into decline. Drawing on the work of thinkers ranging from Jean Lamarck to Charles Darwin to his own mentor Cesare Lombroso, Nordau argued that Europe's decline resulted from a combination of environmental conditions and the dynamics of heredity. Among the former was the unhealthy environment of the large city where people came in contact with air pollution, adulterated and contaminated foods, and alcohol and drugs. Other factors inducing nervous exhaustion were steam power, electricity, and the transportation and communication revolutions. Because the weakened state of an individual's mind and body was passed on to descendants, general social decline was spreading quickly through the West.[8] Signs of decline included high rates of crime, insanity, and sexual immorality, which in turn explained why unrestrained lewdness, greed, lust, and base impulses had become ascendant, how it was that what had previously passed for "mere sensuality" had now become commonplace, and why "elegant titillation" now only began "where normal sexual relations leave off. Priapus has become the symbol of virtue. Vice looks to Sodom and Lesbos,...for its embodiments." Nordau also expressed interest in the manifestation of "degeneracy" in the lives and especially the works of European writers, artists, and philosophers. As he explained, "Degenerates are not always common criminals, prostitutes, anarchists, and pronounced lunatics; they are often authors and artists." Nordau singled out Oscar Wilde for special comment.[9]

Europeans and Americans employed degeneration theory to account for all sorts of social phenomena, including class and racial differences and why some nations in the world seemed better suited to progress while others languished, but it especially helped explain the apparent fading of European civilization. By the 1890s, the pervasiveness of the belief that Western civilization was in decline induced a general anxiety in Europe that gained the French label *fin de siècle malaise,* or "end-of-the-century melancholy." Because *Degeneration* well summarized so many fin de siècle concerns, no other European book of the 1890s, according to the historian John Higham, aroused so much comment in the American press.[10] I would add that part of the popularity of *Degeneration* in the Northwest is attributable to the Wilde trials. The revelations about the life and activities of Wilde provided northwesterners with evidence of a scandalous decadence in European society paralleled only in civilizations that had long since decayed and disappeared. Nordau's study made all this understandable. Therefore, in April and May of 1895 Northwest newspaper editors devoted columns to discussing Nordau's book in order to answer the question "Are We Degenerating?" and to assess how *Degeneration* and "degeneration" could help readers better comprehend Wilde.[11]

Journalists and editors linked Wilde's sexual proclivities to the decline of Western civilization more often than to any other cause. An *Oregonian* commentary, "The Decay of a Race," contended that the true man was devoted to finding a place in the world for himself and a woman. Such a "natural and healthful" pursuit encouraged vigor and the fullest development of mental and physical powers. The problem in the current age was that civilization had reached a point that made it possible for some men to eschew this basic activity. Once they did, then the doors to individual decay and race degeneration were flung wide open. What this editorial termed the "half man," exemplified by Wilde, resulted from "luxury and idleness." He has become soft in manhood and curious about the "exploration of the obscure caverns of unnatural indulgence.... [I]t is only within this generation that the unmanly vices of degenerate Rome and the enfeebled Orient have made their appearance." The *Oregonian* warned that these "certain signs of race decay, or national degeneration.... have preceded the downfall of every great empire from Athens to Bourbon France."[12] Editors throughout the Northwest concurred with these conclusions. One claimed that Wilde was "an abnormal type of which high civilization produced in all ages of the world." Another contended that the very forces that had impelled Wilde into his paths of dishonor and death had "wrecked most, if not all the great nations of antiquity." Yet another offered a more subtle argument, claiming that Wilde had written so often of the "sexual immorality" of England's "aristocratic society" that the thoughts his characters expressed had become planted in his own mind and had "dragged him down."[13]

In placing the blame for Wilde's moral depravity on a declining civilization, editors suggested that he had acquired his sexual desires only after his birth. But a minor strain of argument proposed that Wilde's debauchery resulted directly from heredity. One dispatch, while conceding that none of Wilde's ancestors suffered from the same form of degeneracy as did he, quickly added that the "hereditary problem is far more complex than that. Many forms of nervous disease in parents might produce in the child pathological conditions[.]" The article noted that Wilde's father might have been responsible for his son's depravity, for the elder Wilde had been generally regarded as eccentric as well as a near genius as an oculist and antiquarian. This congenital explanation for sexual depravity emanated from a branch of degeneration theory that held that any form of social corruption, such as alcoholism and environmental pollution or even overstimulation of mental capacities, could have tainted an ancestor; that taint might then manifest itself as any number of mental and physical deficiencies in a future generation. Thus one could acquire degeneracy both biologically and socially.[14]

Whether they theorized that Wilde's sexual proclivities had resulted from higher civilization's luxuries and indolence, were imparted by some process of mental osmosis through the subjects about whom he wrote, or had developed as just one possible outcome of hereditary taint, the editors and journalists who promoted such notions accepted and communicated to readers that same-sex sexual interest—that is, sexual inversion—was an acquired degeneracy. During the last quarter of the nineteenth century, the influential German sexual psychologist Richard von Krafft-Ebing emerged as the greatest champion of this belief. Krafft-Ebing's best-known work, *Psychopathia Sexualis* (1888), was originally written for fellow physicians. It employed technical terms and Latin to keep its readership small. Nonetheless, this book reached a wide audience, and its influence spread through the Western intellectual world. Individuals like Nordau helped convey Krafft-Ebing's conclusions to lay readers.[15]

In the minds of experts of the period like Krafft-Ebing, a male's degeneration to sexual inversion meant, among other things, his "decline" into femininity. Press releases, not surprisingly, described Wilde in these terms. The *Oregonian* reprinted a New York journalist's depiction of Wilde from an encounter of the previous year. The New Yorker avowed that Wilde's "assumed femininity...aroused ridicule if not disgust." While "humped up in a chair, with his eyes turned upward and his voice pitched like a woman's," the writer "twisted his rings nervously, and occasionally pressed a handkerchief with a narrow lace border to his lips as he talked."[16] Americans for some time had viewed Wilde as a "fragrant pansy." But once the positively scandalous news about him spread across the Atlantic, newspapers quickly turned him into more than just an effeminate male: they transformed him into a repulsive monster. In doing so, journalists communicated the popular assumption that degeneration could be detected in an individual's physical appearance. In the New York piece carried by the *Oregonian,* the reporter related Wilde's "unwieldy bulk and general ungainliness"; his teeth were discolored, and fat hung in heavy masses over his jawbones. Furthermore, his temperament could be deduced from his choice of ensemble; he wore thick, cork-soled boots of a cumbersome make, a grease-stained frock so ill-fitting that it might have been fashioned by an obscure "Newark" tailor, and flapping trousers that bagged at the knees. In a word, his whole appearance was "repellant."[17]

Editors also rushed to censure Wilde's novels and plays, fearing their possible adverse influence on the public. When theater managers threatened to withdraw his dramas or, at the very least, erase his name from the playbills, Portland's *Evening Telegram* felt that such actions fell short of what was needed. Wilde's "erotic" literature and theatrical offerings, the paper declared, catered only to the prurient interests of his audience, thereby debauching the young and thoughtless—those on the threshold of maturity who are unable to counter the effects of low and vicious ideas about life, and among whom Wilde's work necessarily encouraged vice. To protect society from such acquired degeneracy, and to guard against Wilde's profiting from the "grossest sensuality," his works merited absolute condemnation. Some newspapers advocated their removal from libraries and the stage; others specified that they should be burned. Upon Wilde's death in 1900, the *Oregonian* reflected on the fate of the writer and his cultural effects, declaring that the "displeasure [recently] visited upon his works" was "salutary." "Society's instinct of preservation," the paper remarked, "rises up at such times and vows that no quarter shall be shown to the moral wretch who defies its canons. The race refuses to view the handiwork separate from the man."[18] The Northwest press also rejoiced at the expected effects of Wilde's punishment. The *Seattle Press-Times* expressed hope that it would be "the beginning of a wide reform; that it means the restoration of the clean and wholesome to their proper place in literature, upon the stage and in every day life." It further concluded that Wilde's incarceration would "do much to stay the rising tide of indecency which threatens to overwhelm...our great cities." As for the young men who had followed Wilde "onto any field where he chose to lead them" and there "tasted almost every flower of sensual pleasure even before their capacity for enjoyment had half developed," they would likely behave as "sheep without a shepherd and will stray back into the fold."[19]

Curiously, while commentators in the Northwest recognized that doing away with Wilde and his literary outpourings would benefit society, they, like other American journalists, also claimed that Wilde and what he represented actually had little connection to or impact on culture and society on the western side of the Atlantic. Middle-class Americans generally accepted Nordau's maxim that their civilization was largely beyond the influence that had affected Wilde. "Why should Americans degenerate?" asked Nordau. "They have a new country, new opportunities, a boundless future, a restless...activity; their eyes are fixed upward, their impulses are toward better and higher things, their ambition is healthier.

How can Americans be degenerate?"[20] Although some disagreement existed, Americans for the most part concurred with Nordau. Thus, when the *Seattle-Press Times*'s editor looked forward to the day when Wilde's unmasking and punishment would finally reverse the tide then apparently menacing "our great cities," he was referring to the great cities of Europe and not those of the United States—and certainly not to the relatively small towns of the 1890s Northwest. Many of the region's newspapers echoed these very sentiments. In one piece a journalist concluded that the country's Puritan strain had largely kept American society free from the "putrid scandals which have latterly disgraced English society." Another reporter maintained that the rottenness of London soil had no parallel in the United States and, in fact, the American people could "hardly comprehend" what the Wilde scandal entailed. He also concluded that the "American mind cannot get down to the point at which the London mind revels."[21]

Even though Northwest newspapers generally feared that Wilde's novels and plays might infect those who came into contact with them, they also endorsed the notion that Americans' innocence had immunized them against such contaminants. The *Evening Telegram* asserted that in the United States, "most theatergoers are plain, decent persons, who live respectable and not extraordinarily eventful lives and are not tired of living them. The men in the average American audience are not all men of debauchery.... The appetites of the majority are not jaded, but fresh, healthy, and undefiled." Yet their relative simplicity and remoteness from Paris and London made it impossible for Americans to critically assess the information with which they were presented. "It is safe to say," the *Evening Telegram* charged, "that nine-tenths of the American men and women who have witnessed the plays written by Wilde...did not really appreciate their motive or the depth of the human depravity they aimed to raise to conventionality. The true inwardness of such dramas is apparent only to the very slim majority [*sic*] of American playgoers over whom the filthy French novel and its crude English imitation have trailed their slime." The newspaper's editor concluded that it is to be hoped that the numbers of these cognoscenti should not increase.[22]

The 1895 Oscar Wilde scandal and trials had an effect on the Northwest. For example, in a bizarre manipulation of London reports, Boise's Hirshland, the "Reliable Clothier and Haberdasher," sponsored a three-week advertising campaign that queried potential customers whether they wished to "be in the swim?" If so, they should call immediately for the current styles: "The Marquis of Queensberry Straw Hat" and "The Lord Douglas Straw Hat," both endowed with four-inch brims.[23]

Of course, the news and editorials about Wilde had a far more profound effect than suggested by these titillating advertisements. First, they helped create a popular image of a male who engaged in same-sex sexual practices. Second, they instructed society on how it should respond to him. Moreover, emerging from the Wilde affair was the belief that the homosexual was, to use the *Oregonian*'s term, only a "half man": that is, a degenerate. His condition resulted from a mental illness attributable to any number of causes, including unhealthful living conditions, a corrupt ancestor, luxuries and idleness, and his own consideration of unwholesome literature. His effeminate behavior, activities, and tastes, as well as his overall decadent physical appearance, gave him away. At the same time, and more significantly, Americans in the 1890s and for a while thereafter concluded that the middle- and upper-class sexual "degenerate," or sexual invert, was necessarily the product and sign of civilization's decline at the fin de siècle. For the time being, middle- and upper-class sexual inversion remained an exclusively European problem. This view may very well explain why, in the immediate wake of the Wilde scandal and trials, we detect no significant alterations in how the law in either the United States or in Canada treated same-sex sex crimes. A survey of arrest rolls, penitentiary records, and criminal statutes throughout the Northwest and British Columbia supports the conclusion that prosecutions for same-sex sex crimes did not increase and that laws concerning them were not altered as part of some sort of reaction against Wilde. The philosopher and historian of ideas Michel Foucault maintained that through history, the economically and politically dominant social classes attempting to suppress sexuality first applied the most rigorous techniques of control not to the poorer and laboring classes but to members of their own group.[24] Since middle- and upper-class "homosexuality" was not a "problem" in 1890s North America, there existed no need to act to suppress it.

This is not to say that Americans denied that either "degeneracy" or "sexual degeneracy" existed in the country, for members of the white middle class used degeneration theory to explain class and race differences. They accepted that the "lower" classes and races were by definition degenerate because of the conditions that they lived in as well as their cultural practices, which included same-sex sexual activities. Such sentiments were communicated during Wilde's trials when one newspaper noted that in "sink[ing] so low" in his practices, Wilde became no better than the "commonest prisoner" or "an unknown tramp."[25] Nonetheless, between the 1880s and about 1910, the term *degenerate* or phrases that implied something similar to it did not often appear either in legal records or in newspaper reports regarding same-sex sexual transgressions among working-class and immigrant men in the Northwest. To be sure, as already discussed in this study, working class and immigrant male-male sexual practices did garner attention in the region. But dominant society did not attack the immigrant male because he was a "homosexual." The issues revolved not around *homo*sexuality but rather around transgressive "sexual practices" generally, focusing even more on class and race specifically.

Various historians have shown that at this historical moment, Western society was only beginning to conceive of an individual who engaged in same-sex sexual activities as a homosexual. The tradition that saw such an individual as a criminal or a transgressor of community standards, without the ascription of any particular sexual identity, was still strong.[26] But more lay behind the failure of dominant society in the Northwest to identify immigrant and working-class men in the 1890s as homosexuals. The hubbub surrounding Oscar Wilde suggests that indeed some understanding of "homosexuality" was already present—but as long as the conditions that had created Wilde in Europe did not exist in America, then neither did the specific sexuality that he represented, regardless of what the working and immigrant classes were up to. "Homosexuality" per se would become a focus of concern only after nativeborn, white, middle-class Americans finally conceded that it existed among themselves. The movement in the Northwest toward acknowledging the existence of the "homosexual" was class-based, and it occurred during the first years of the twentieth century. This historical change is well illustrated by events that took place in Portland in late 1912 and 1913. The Rose City therefore offers an excellent case study demonstrating how more modern understandings of homosexuality and its connection to the middle class in particular took root in America on a local level during the first part of the twentieth century.

Concepts of Homosexuality during and after the 1912 Scandal

Benjamin Trout's confession to Portland police on November 8, 1912, about the city's clandestine same-sex vice quickly erupted into one of the most tumultuous public events that the Northwest witnessed during the convulsive Progressive era. The news hit Portland like a torrent. It then spread rapidly throughout the region, striking other cities such as Seattle, Tacoma, and Vancouver, British Columbia. Within days a spin-off scandal had engulfed the small eastern Washington town of Walla Walla. But the ripple effects of Trout's disclosures went beyond even the most remote boundaries of the region. Newspapers soon linked Portland's ignominy to that of other West Coast cities, such as San Francisco, Los Angeles, and San Diego, and urban centers further afield, including Chicago, Philadelphia, Washington, D.C., and even Mystic, Connecticut![27]

Trout's revelations resulted in paroxysms because they revealed that same-sex sexual activities and a homosexual subculture were flourishing among men of the local "respectable" classes. As one newspaper reported on the arraignment hearings, "It was not a [usual] collection of bums or sots or street scourings; it was an orderly, solemn, quite respectable appearing aggregation." Other headlines confirmed these descriptions, announcing that lawyers, doctors, architects, salesmen, bookkeepers, clerks, businessmen, and other professionals were implicated. One account described those arrested as the "pillars of society."[28]

That the suspects had such well-bred appearances and backgrounds escalated matters into a full-blown scandal. This was *news* in every sense of the word, as few people like these had ever faced such charges in Portland before. These circumstances prompted Frank Collier, the deputy district attorney for Multnomah County and the prosecutor during the scandal, to make one of his most startling announcements. In a heated moment during the first trial of the scandal, Collier brazenly declared, "This is the first time that a case of this nature ever came before this Court." Such an assertion is particularly noteworthy in light of the record of Collier's superior, outgoing District Attorney George Cameron, who had prosecuted many working-class and immigrant men for same-sex crimes during his several years in office. Even as early as the 1890s, Cameron had, as court-appointed counsel, defended men charged with similar sexual transgressions.[29] Thus, what Collier meant was that this was the only case of its kind up to that moment in Oregon history to have so obviously involved a "respectable" member of society, in this instance a physician. Moreover, Collier was also implying that this was the first appearance of a "modern" homosexual before the state's justice system. In the Northwest, the modern homosexual emerged with the first widespread public acknowledgment that white American middle-class males participated in same-sex affairs.

But before arriving at that conclusion, many in the Northwest attempted to understand what was happening by drawing from historical knowledge, consciously reaching back to the case of Oscar Wilde. The editor of a Seattle paper remarked, "It is about 25 years or more since a very similar discovery to...Portland['s], was made in London....When London was put to shame, in this way, the criminals were, as are the Portland degenerates, the 'higher ups.'"[30] In newspaper articles, legal records, investigative reports, letters to the editor, and even private papers, officials, journalists, and laypeople used the terms *degenerate* and *degeneracy* more than any others to describe those implicated in the 1912 scandal. In harking back to Wilde, as this Seattle example demonstrates, Northwest residents admitted that degeneracy had finally spread to middle- and upper-class America. They then employed some of the same explanations for it that had been offered in the 1890s. Oregon Supreme Court Justice Thomas McBride, for example, attributed Portland's degeneracy to "the decay of morals, that accompanies [the] increase of wealth and luxury." Multnomah County Circuit Court Judge Calvin Gantenbein observed, in a rather convoluted sentence, that in "early times...when men were men, and had not lost their virility, as frequently occurs in the advance of civilization—it seems that mental perversion is one of the by-products of civilization, and it was so in Sodom, and it was so in ancient Greece, and it appears to be so in more modern countries today."[31] McBride and Gantenbein gave voice to the assumption that the men who had "lost their virility" were those who had partaken of the "increase of wealth and luxury" that modern civilization afforded. In other words, they were the men of the better social classes.

In a rather ironic twist, even individuals within Portland's working-class circles came to similar conclusions. A letter to the editor of the working-class *Portland News* implied that degeneracy is essentially a middle-class phenomenon, stating that the "working class...[is] the necessary class, without whom the degenerates could not exist." Portland's *Labor Press* reminded readers that social "decay seldom sets in where men are struggling for food, shelter and raiment."[32] This latter proposition echoed sentiments contained in the editorial "The Decay of a Race," quoted previously, which the establishment's *Oregonian* had offered in 1895 as a critique of Wilde and the declining civilization that supposedly produced him.

In 1912 residents of the Northwest fell back on degeneration theory to explain and describe the conditions of middle-class same-sex vice and those who participated in them. In its original nineteenth-century usage, the noun *degenerate* had referred not to a sexual identity, nor even to specific sexual conditions, but to people who suffered from any number of mental, physical, and moral conditions deemed abnormal. To explain how an individual could be reduced to a defective state, society employed degeneration theory. But the events of late 1912 and 1913 helped transform such concepts. In particular, as the YMCA scandal progressed, various observers accepted the emergent understanding that a man could have an identity based on his sexual desires. Thus, someone who participated in same-sex affairs, rather than being lumped together with other "abnormal" types as a degenerate, would now increasingly be thought of specifically as a homosexual. Furthermore, these same observers of 1912–13 also transformed some of their ideas about the origins of same-sex sexuality. Rather than concentrating on degeneracy's social causes, which had been the focus during the Oscar Wilde affair, they now emphasized the idea that homosexuality was congenital in nature. In doing so, they still drew from degeneration theory but also considered more modern ideas. Degeneration theory had maintained that it was possible to acquire one's potential to indulge in "immoral" behaviors not only later in life but also in the womb: such a tendency could be biologically inherited as a result of an ancestor's alcoholism, mental illness, debauchery, epilepsy, or even genius. Degeneration theory also implied that those with same-sex interests had other visible signs of degeneracy and could not function "normally" in their nonsexual capacities.

Certain individuals in the Northwest who attempted to understand the men of the 1912 scandal added to and altered some of these beliefs, drawing from a theory about homosexuality that had only recently arisen in the Western world. This theory held that rather than congenital homosexuality stemming from a biological taint handed down by some miscreant predecessor, it was only one of a limited number of psychodynamic possibilities that could occur as the embryo developed. Moreover, this newer theory stressed that such a congenital homosexual would appear physically "normal" and otherwise act in ways deemed perfectly ordinary.[33] Such a notion undoubtedly proved useful when Portlanders tried to account for how homosexuality could surface in middle-class men who looked and behaved like anyone else in the city. Instead of being the usual collection of "bums or sots or street scourings," those implicated appeared as did H. L. Rowe: "refined, almost dandified [in] appearance." Most of all, they "were well dressed, above the average in intelligence, and with no outward signs of degeneracy."[34]

The evolution of older ideas about degeneracy into newer conceptions of homosexuality during the 1912 scandal are evident in the writings of Multnomah County Deputy District Attorney Frank T. Collier (figure 10). In 1913 he penned three successive legal briefs and filed them with the Oregon State Supreme Court, arguing against the appeals made by men convicted of sodomy.[35] These collected writings illustrate the newly emerging social understanding of homosexuality as an identity and the incipient belief that declared it more a congenital condition than a viciousness acquired later in life.

Investigations into Portland's conditions of middle-class same-sex vice in 1912–13 lasted several months. During this time, dozens of men faced the justice system. Limited or inconclusive evidence acquitted some. Others pleaded guilty to sodomy or, more typically, lesser charges in order to avoid the publicity of trials. But in three celebrated cases in which the state felt the evidence substantial enough to secure conviction on the most serious offense of sodomy, and in which those charged decided that they would take their chances before their peers, major trials ensued. One case involved Harry Start, a physician and a married man; another concerned E. S. J. McAllister, an attorney and Progressive reformer well-known throughout the state; and the third centered on an otherwise obscure bookkeeper, E. E. Wedemeyer.

Harry Start's trial commenced on December 12, 1912, and concluded in five days. After less than an hour of deliberation, the jury found him guilty. Two days later the presiding judge, Calvin Gantenbein, sentenced the physician to the requisite penalty of from one to five years in the state penitentiary. That same day Wedemeyer also appeared before Gantenbein. His case proceeded more swiftly to the jury; the very next day his peers found him guilty in less than thirty minutes. Wedemeyer, like Start, also received the mandatory sentence. McAllister's trial, before Judge John Kavanaugh, took place between February 17 and 21, 1913. Upon its conclusion, the jury deliberated some eighteen hours before returning a guilty verdict. McAllister faced the same sentence as the two men who had preceded him.[36]

The attorneys for Start, Wedemeyer, and McAllister appealed their clients' convictions to the Oregon Supreme Court. One of the points on which each defense team petitioned the higher tribunal concerned the trial judges' "improper" admission of evidence. In each of the proceedings, the defense had strenuously objected when the prosecutor, Frank Collier, called a string of men to testify as to their alleged sexual relations with the defendants. In trial, the defense had argued that legal tradition barred testimony regarding other supposed crimes as a means to prove

FIGURE 10. Frank T. Collier, 1910. As deputy district attorney, Collier had the task in 1912 and 1913 of prosecuting
the men arrested for same-sex sexual relations in what
came to be known in Portland as the YMCA Scandal.
Oregon Historical Society, #OrHi 102012.

that the particular transgression at issue actually occurred. Collier responded that in sex crimes specifically, precedent permitted such testimony to be introduced to illustrate the defendant's disposition to commit such an offense. Defense attorneys countered that similar sex acts
were relevant only when those acts occurred with the *same* party; thus in
their appeals they argued that the lower court had erred in permitting
the testimony regarding similar crimes with *other* people. The admission
of such evidence had forced the defendant into the unfair position of
having to answer for any number of possible crimes for which he had

not been indicted and that did not appear directly linked to the charge on which he currently stood before the court.[37]

During Start's trial, and in response to the first objection that the physician's defense made to such "irrelevant" testimony, the prosecutor claimed that he wanted to introduce it only "to show the condition of the defendant's mind, and that he was in such a frame of mind as to cause him to perform these acts[.]" Judge Gantenbein agreed, ruling that

A *normal* man [emphasis mine] could not by any possibility commit a crime of this character. This involves the question of the state of the mind, and it seems to me that evidence of other acts may be admitted, even with other people, for the purpose of showing the state of his mind, as to whether or not it was so perverted that he would be capable of committing this sort of crime.[38]

When Collier employed similar arguments in the subsequent Wedemeyer and McAllister trials, the court applied the same logic and made the same rulings.

It appears that Collier agreed with Gantenbein's interpretation of what a "normal" man could and could not do. His prosecutions all presumed that the men under indictment were homosexuals, as he contended that only such men could commit the crime in question. Collier did not himself have to clarify this position in Start's trial; the judge did it for him. But this contention became the *only* point that he developed over the course of his responses to the three separate appeals. In the Start brief filed March 24, 1913, Collier dedicated fourteen pages to the issue. A week later he submitted his brief on Wedemeyer and expanded his consideration to eighteen pages. When he filed his McAllister brief on September 2, 1913, he gave a full thirty-nine pages to the topic, dropping all other arguments.

In his first brief, which responded to Start's appeal, Collier claimed that the physician was different in essence from other men. First, the prosecutor contended that Start was a "sex invert." Second, this led (in his mind) to Start's crime being exceptional in the history of the Northwest. In part, Collier made these arguments in order to account for the fact that the defendant came from the more respectable classes; Start was not simply some run-of-the-mill transient, laborer, or immigrant who engaged in same-sex sexual activities because he was by definition degenerate.[39] Collier also had juridical motives, discussed below, for invoking the notion of the sex invert as a fixed identity. But it is worth noting first that to make a more persuasive argument on this point, Collier called on the authority of Richard von Krafft-Ebing. As described earlier, in the 1890s editions of his masterpiece *Psychopathia Sexualis* Krafft-Ebing had indeed promoted the idea that sexual inversion was a functional sign of degeneration and a condition that was acquired either through unfortunate influences later in life or (sometimes) congenitally through a tainted ancestor. But by his twelfth and final edition, published in 1902, Krafft-Ebing had modified this position, having accepted the emerging theory that sexual inversion as a congenital condition was not necessarily caused by the influence of heredity or other social taint. Frank Collier cited the twelfth edition of *Psychopathia Sexualis,* first employing it in the Wedemeyer case. "Sexual psychologists" would define the defendant, Collier contended in this brief, "as a sex invert, that is his normal sexual passions and instincts have become inverted, so that he is, as Kraft-Ebbing [*sic*], the great German writer says, 'A male being with a female mind.'" Months later in the McAllister brief, Collier emphasized Krafft-Ebing's more recently formed conclusions that "those who hold that the origin of homo-sexual feelings and instincts is found to be exclusively in defective education and other . . . influences are entirely in error. . . . The *natural* disposition [emphasis mine] is the determining condition[.]"[40]

The absence of any reference to sexologists and sexual psychology in his first brief (the Start brief) and the misspelling of Krafft-Ebing in his second (the Wedemeyer brief) suggest that Collier consulted those works only recently. His insistence that Start's was the first such case to come before the Oregon courts supports the conclusion that previously in his career he had had no need to draw on either Krafft-Ebing or any of the German's contemporaries. But by the time Collier filed his McAllister brief, he not only had read much of Krafft-Ebing but also had digested the work of other sexologists, including the French physician and medicolegal expert Léon-Henri Thoinot. He also used the writings of Henry Havelock Ellis, the central figure in the early-twentieth-century emergence of the modern sexual ethos. In his multivolume *Studies in the Psychology of Sex,* which began publication in 1897, Ellis criticized Krafft-Ebing's earlier work, eschewed the idea of the invert as an individual with a male body and a female brain, argued against the degeneration model, encouraged the dropping of the term *degenerate* because of the stigma attached to it, urged that homosexuals could be "normal" in their nonsexual activities, and favored the emerging notion that homosexuality was a fixed inborn trait and did not come about as the result of a tainted ancestor. Havelock Ellis's work also led to greater usage of the word *homosexual*. And in fact, in his third brief Collier finally came to employ that term. Collier may have noticed some differences of opinion between Krafft-Ebing and Havelock Ellis, but he ultimately reported the most important early-twentieth-century similarity between them, as well as Thoinot. They "have all agreed," Collier wrote, "that the phenomena, which mankind has [previously] laid to the door of viciousness alone, are in truth and in fact the result of an abnormal state of mind, in the majority of cases, present from birth."[41]

That all the defendants in the Portland trials were, to Collier, homosexual in identity, and had been so even since birth, did more than help him account for homosexuality's manifestation among the middle-class men he prosecuted: it also became his sole argument for the unprecedented procedure of admitting into evidence other sex acts with other individuals. Collier strenuously asserted in his briefs that the state had the legal right in every criminal case "to show, in proving that the defendant did a certain thing, that he had a reason, or motive, or force impelling him to the commission of the act." Because of the "unusual" nature of the crime, Collier claimed, allowing additional testimony regarding similar acts with other people became imperative for the state to demonstrate the force that would impel the defendant to such a crime. No "normal" man, but only a homosexual, the deputy district attorney maintained, would wish to engage in intimate relations with another of his own sex. To show this psychological motivation, Collier believed that the state needed to prove that the defendant was indeed a homosexual. The "only way" to prove this was to expose other occasions when the defendant "performed the physical act which can have but one explanation, and that is that [he is] a sexual pervert." Essentially, then, Collier maintained that homosexuals had a specific identity and composed a special class. "When the state charges a man with the crime against nature, or sodomy," Collier declared, "it, in effect, charges that he is a sexual invert...and that he obtains his sexual gratification in that matter."[42] He concluded that such men should rightly have different laws and court procedures applied to them.

Collier's logic proves circular at best, and a majority of Oregon Supreme Court justices rejected the argument on a variety of grounds. In a 3–2 decision issued on May 20, 1913, they overturned Start's and Wedemeyer's convictions. Regarding the issue at hand, Justice George Burnett wrote for the majority: "To admit testimony...making it appear that the accused has the bent of mind adapted to such actions, would cloud the issue and confuse the jury."[43]

Four days after these two reversals, E. S. J. McAllister's attorneys filed their appeal. Over the summer of 1913, Collier worked on his lengthy response. When he submitted it he presented an argument that addressed only the need of the state to admit into evidence the defendant's sexual acts with people other than those named in the charges in order to prove that he was a homosexual and therefore capable of committing the crime of which he stood accused. Collier's sole concentration on this one point in the McAllister brief is significant. Possibly he ignored the other issues because he suspected that the court's decision on them was inevitable; the McAllister case raised many points that were identical to those on which he had both won and lost in the Start and Wedemeyer appeals. Moreover, even if he accepted that Oregon's highest court would rule against him on those other grounds, Collier felt compelled to attempt to persuade the justices to change their minds on the one issue most important to him, which would prove an invaluable legal tool in future similar cases. In his McAllister brief, Collier therefore asserted his lack of desire to "contend the principles of law enunciated" in the Start case. But he pointed out that the majority in Start "neglected to take into consideration the fact that modern medical science has demonstrated that SODOMY GENERALLY, AND ORAL COITIS [*sic*] IN PARTICULAR are never committed except by reasons impelled by a perverted and diseased mind which perversion is ... in the majority of cases, present from birth."[44]

Despite the earlier Start and Wedemeyer reversals, the supreme court's decision in the McAllister case was by no means a certainty. During the spring of 1913, while the court was wrestling with the previous appeals on this issue, the state legislature expanded the number of justices from five to seven. Perhaps the two new members presiding in the fall term could swing the vote to the other side in the McAllister appeal. Though that did not come to pass, the court's decision against Collier, rendered on November 20, 1913, was again by a one-vote margin, 4–3. And again, as in the earlier reversal, the opposing justices composed strongly worded dissents that accepted Collier's argument. These opinions demonstrate that social conceptions about homosexuals and homosexuality were indeed in flux at the time. In the Start and Wedemeyer case, for example, Justice Thomas McBride declared that

the reports of this court covering a period of 60 years do not reveal a single instance of its occurrence up to the present year. It is a crime so unnatural and abhorrent that in the very nature of things it will be committed in secrecy. ... The rules of evidence ... are servants, not the masters, of justice and they change as the necessities of society change. ... So here we have a new method of crime and new conditions, and to apply archaic rules is like trying to fit a square peg into a round hole.

The newly appointed justice Charles McNary opined in the McAllister dissent that "no man would commit this unnatural act unless his motive be to satisfy a perverted sexual passion, and to prove that emotion it was pertinent to show that defendant had revealed its existence by similar offenses with other persons."[45] McBride's and McNary's responses intimated that neither would be bound by legal precedents. But more significantly for our understanding of shifting notions of sexuality, their contention that such a crime had never come before the court before, that it was new, that it was related to a specific "sexual passion," and that it occurred only under novel conditions suggests that they also perceived that the men of Portland's 1912 scandal exemplified a type who had only recently appeared in history.

On the most practical level, to save his cases Collier needed to demonstrate that the accused were homosexuals. But the argument also helped him explain what appeared to be a new phenomenon among the middle classes. We do not know exactly how the deputy district attorney came to his more contemporary understanding of homosexuality, but an analysis of his in-court arguments and his successive briefs suggests that he harbored such a notion, albeit in embryonic form, from the outset. Only when forced to develop more elaborate defenses for his trial-related actions did Collier turn to the most up-to-date medical literature.

Some others in Portland and elsewhere in the region also seemed to have welcomed the more modern understanding of homosexuality; perhaps Collier's elaborate distillation persuaded them to accept its validity. They included such important personages as Multnomah Country Circuit Court Judges Gantenbein and Kavanaugh, Oregon Supreme Court Justice McBride, and his cohorts who sided with him, Robert Eakin and Charles McNary—the last a future U.S. senator and Republican vice presidential candidate. Even those justices who voted with the majority in ruling against Collier did not explicitly discount the ideas he put forth. Less eminent individuals also appear to have held similar views. Duncan Fraser, a resident of Portland, wrote a letter to the editor of the *Oregon Journal* defending those arrested. In language that echoed that of Havelock Ellis, Fraser asserted that homosexuals are "sports of nature, often more to be pitied than hounded like wild beasts." Havelock Ellis had promoted the idea that homosexuals were indeed only variations in nature and he employed the term *sport* in hopes of moving society away from the common assumption that homosexuals were abnormal. And when Fraser, again like Havelock Ellis, contended that "sexual perverts" come "from parents who are themselves quite normal," he joined the sexologist in discounting the belief that debauched ancestors induced homosexuality.[46]

To be sure, the newer view that homosexuality was inborn—whether reflecting tainted genes or a different psychodynamic possibility—never completely took hold among the general populace. "All perversion," one news writer asserted in 1912, "cannot be charged to inborn depravity. Much of it must be due to acquirement and where mere boys are concerned the acquirement is in ignorance of the horrible results that follow such practices."[47] Indeed, one of the most popular and forceful explanations for middle-class homosexuality espoused during the 1912 scandal harked back to the degeneration theory made familiar during the Wilde episode. Many contended that Portland's middle- and upper-class immorality could be attributed to social decadence and the decline of civilization, both of which had finally spread from Europe to the United States. But the firm links made between the sexual immorality of the better classes, the decline of civilization, and degeneration theory that had served in 1895 could not hold up in their pure form in 1912. Few in the Northwest in 1912 believed in the wane of civilization: instead, a strong progressive spirit infused the region. Inhabitants looked around them at the dawn of the new century and witnessed rapidly growing cities, ample resources, and bountiful opportunities. In 1912, moreover, the region's economy was experiencing one of its greatest booms. Shortly before the homosexual scandal, Portland and Seattle each sponsored major international fairs—the Lewis and Clark Exposition in 1905 and the Alaska-Yukon-Pacific Exposition of 1909. Both drew millions of expectant visitors, trumpeted their hosts' Progressive-era optimism, and announced to the world as the century began that these two cities had taken their place among America's premier urban centers.[48] In this atmosphere, degeneration theory as applied in the 1890s to European conditions could not hold sway for long.

Thus older degeneration theory underwent a transmutation in 1912, as a process of change that was already under way accelerated. In 1910 the *Oregonian* ran an article titled "Do We Owe Our Morals to Women? Degeneration, Says Science, Results from Living without the Sphere of the Gentler Sex." This piece was occasioned by a scandalous string of courts-martial that had recently occurred in Germany, which had resulted from the same-sex sexual activities of some high-ranking military officers. The *Oregonian* prefaced its story with the words of a German magistrate who avowed, "The higher the civilization the greater the segregation of the sexes, and the higher the civilization the greater the prevalence of crime, abuse and vice of every description." Although this and other quotations in the article appear to link Germany's degeneration directly to the overdevelopment of civilization, the article argued that this phenomenon contributed only tangentially to degeneracy, putting primary blame instead on certain features of modern life that required men to keep company exclusively with other men. The military, for example, forced men to live, eat, sleep, and bathe together, without respite. Such conditions as these and not luxury and idleness precipitated same-sex vice.[49]

Similar explications appeared in 1912. A Spokane paper contended that while those guilty in the Portland affair "cannot be held blameless, neither can they be utterly condemned. One must seek the reason for such actions. They do not come without a cause." Among the precipitating factors pointed to by the paper were the forced concentration of men and boys in the military, in prisons, and in reformatories. Here, with "no means of gratifying natural desires[, t]hey take to practices that lead to degeneracy."[50] Although this conclusion clung to notions that sex inversion was acquired, it signifies a retreat from older elitist assumptions that advanced civilization's luxuries and idleness induce sexual immorality in middle- and upper-class men. In abandoning this proposition, northwesterners democratized the reasons for same-sex sexuality. In the late nineteenth century, the so-called better classes did in fact view the "lower" classes as degenerate by nature and thus believed that they willingly participated in "perverted" sexual relations. Nevertheless, they resorted to degeneration *theory* only when it was necessary to explain why members of their own social group turned to same-sex sexual practices. But by the early 1910s the accepted notion was that men from any class could degenerate for the *same* reasons.

Frank Collier and others like him went a step further. They advocated the democratization not simply of degeneracy but also of homosexual identity. Collier repeatedly asserted that the "ordinary" man with "normal sexual instincts" is incapable of committing the crime against nature; it is "only performed" by "sexual inverts."[51] This claim opened up the possibility that *any* male who had sex with another would be defined by society as a homosexual. Necessarily, that category included men from the working and immigrant classes.

The Deployment of "Homosexuality":
Laborers, Race, and Same-Sex Crime after 1912

As noted above, the late Michel Foucault theorized that economically privileged and politically dominant groups historically have problematized, medicalized, and attempted rigorously to suppress certain forms of sexuality—first among themselves, with little concern for the lower classes.[52] Such a scenario fits well the events that transpired in Portland in 1912 and 1913. This chapter has considered alterations in middle-class notions of same-sex sexuality and the new employment of the term *homosexual* to signify an identity, developments that both largely result from the social recognition that those involved in "depraved" practices were white middle- and upper-class men.

Foucault also recognized that the lower and working classes had managed "for a long time to escape the [social elite's] deployment of 'sexuality.'"[53] His observation likewise fits the developments in the Northwest. Before the 1912 scandal, when society turned its attention to the same-sex sexual activities of working-class and immigrant males, it did so not because it agonized over "homosexuality" per se but primarily because it feared the general sexual dangers that working-class and immigrant males seemingly posed. In the Northwest in the wake of the Oscar Wilde affair, terms such as *degenerate* or *sex invert* were seldom applied to working-class men apprehended for sodomy and other same-sex sexual crimes. Only one early and isolated exception that links upper-class degeneracy to working-class offense has come to light, from the small eastern Idaho community of Pocatello. In August 1898, the editor of the *Pocatello Tribune* asserted that Peter Steen, a railroad worker accused of attempting sodomy on a boy, was "of the Oscar Wild[e] variety."[54] To compare a working-class man to Wilde was clearly highly unusual.

Only in later years did authorities and reformers begin to apply sexual "identities" to working-class men arrested for same-sex sexual crimes. On October 18, 1911, for example, Portland police detained F. Ebster for vagrancy around the North End's saloons. The two arresting officers claimed that he "is known to us as being a Sexual Pervert." A month later, in roughly the same location, Nick Adon was apprehended "as a sexual pervert." In 1917 a Portland physician concluded that a North End patient who had come to his office to have "an ordinary tumbler" removed from his rectum "was a sexual pervert." In all these instances, not only did observers employ this term as a noun but they also gave it a specific sexual connotation. In the years following the 1912 scandal, "sexual pervert" continued to show up in Portland arrest records and, for the first time in the early 1920s, in Oregon penitentiary reports as well. In another sign of change, in 1917 investigators of the Oregon State Penitentiary, an institution housing primarily working-class convicts, employed only the terms "homo-sexual" and "homo-sexuality" to inmates who engaged in same-sex sexual activities.[55]

This new willingness to identify working-class males by their sexuality was by no means immediately widespread. But it seems clear that by 1912, the middle and upper classes had begun to expand their understanding of homosexuality to account for the same-sex sexual activities that working-class and immigrant males engaged in. That change made it increasingly likely for laborers and males of ethnic and racial minority status to be persecuted not just for their race, class, and national origin but for their "homosexuality" as well. In no way do I mean to suggest that the working classes themselves accepted middle- and upper-class notions about sexuality. And it surely mattered little to those who engaged in same-sex affairs whether their arrests came about because the socially dominant group viewed them as homosexuals or because of nativism and racism. My point here is that in the wake of the 1912 affair, the socially dominant classes increasingly based their response to working-class and immigrant sexuality on ideas forged during that middle-class scandal, confirming Foucault's theory.

A 1917 case illustrates the shift after the 1912 scandal to persecuting immigrant men for their "sexuality"; in it, we also see a public prosecutor reaching back to the earlier scandal for guidance regarding the very issue of homosexuality. The case concerns a thirty-two-year-old laborer, Tom Kapsales. He was an immigrant from Greece who lived in the small Columbia River community of St. Helens, Oregon, located about twenty-five miles downstream from Portland. In the early twentieth century, St. Helens' principal industries were logging and milling, which both attracted a number of Greek male laborers. These men formed their own neighborhood, known locally as "sawdust flats," near the mills along the river. Since at least 1912 considerable tensions existed between St. Helens' native-born white community and its Greek men. In the early spring of that year, hostility erupted amid regional difficulties in the extractive industries, which included a fierce IWW strike in nearby Grays Harbor, Washington. Then, on the night of March 28, the Columbia County Lumber Company's plant and dock in St. Helens mysteriously blew up and burned down. Officials immediately suspected that

Greek men were responsible, and the discovery of seven sticks of dynamite "near" sawdust flats corroborated their suspicions.[56]

Little more than five years after this catastrophe, Tom Kapsales, who had lived in St. Helens since before the labor troubles of 1912, faced charges of committing sodomy on Alfred Martinsen, a local white teenager. According to Martinsen, on the evening of June 23 Kapsales invited him to his shack and there made a sexual assault. Despite this alleged attack, the boy returned twice to Kapsales's shanty and also interacted with him elsewhere countless times that same summer. Although Martinsen claimed that Kapsales had tried subsequently to have sex with him and that he received some money on his visits, the youth also asserted that at no time other than the first did he actually have sex with the defendant. On August 15 Martinsen, the town marshal, and the Columbia County deputy sheriff devised a plan to ensnare Kapsales. Martinsen made his way to the immigrant's shack, and the deputy hid in nearby shrubbery. After observing relatively innocent activities for some time, he finally moved in; though Kapsales was not actually caught in a sex act, the officer arrested him anyway and charged him with sodomy.[57]

During the ensuing trial held in St. Helens, Kapsales's attorney sought to paint his client as the victim of racism. He attempted to demonstrate that Martinsen had a particular grudge against Kapsales. The day before his arrest, Kapsales had acted as an interpreter between Martinsen and a Greek bootblack in town, as the former accused the latter of stealing his dog. According to Kapsales, Martinsen mistakenly believed that he (Kapsales) had encouraged the other Greek man to confiscate the pet. Kapsales was also said to have reneged on a promise to get the boy a job at a local rock quarry. These incidents, the defense contended, had made Martinsen angry at Kapsales: he had been heard to declare publicly, "I will fix you God damned Greeks." The lawyer also tried to get the boy to admit that he "had it in for the Greeks as a class."[58]

But this defense failed miserably. Indeed, the prosecutor turned community racism to his own advantage. District Attorney Glen Metsker undoubtedly realized that the jury in St. Helens would respond to racial tactics, in light of the recent labor difficulties there, the antiforeign sentiment of the World War I years, and especially the general animus toward Greeks that had prevailed in the Northwest for some time. Signs of prejudice abounded in the trial. At one point, when the defense asked for an interpreter for a Greek witness, Metsker inquired to the courthouse audience, "Is there any white man here that can talk Greek?" The defense exploded angrily, "That is unfair. They are allies of ours. They are fighting for liberty and humanity the same as we are.... [Y]ou say 'white man' that is unfair." Once tempers calmed, the judge agreed with the prosecution, claiming he knew no Caucasian qualified for the task; therefore he did not permit an interpreter to be used. In addition, through the trial Martinsen refused to use the defendant's name and exclusively referred to Kapsales as "the Greek" or "this Greek." In the most blatant example of bigotry, the prosecutor turned to the jury and declared,

Greece at one time was the greatest nation in the world, but where is she today? Where is she today? And there is a reason for it. There is a reason for it. This is just a sample of the reasons. Fine race of people. Degenerates, degenerates, through immorality and vice. That is one of the things one of the greatest things and one of the quickest things that will destroy any man, an individual, and what is true of the individual is true of a race.

Metsker further played on the particular fears that might have arisen in members of the jury during the first year of America's participation in the European war. He claimed that although Greece was an ally, as the defense had pointed out, the country had been ineffective in battle (presumably because the Greeks were a race of "degenerates"). The defense was unsuccessful in objecting to these statements and in imploring the court to instruct the jury to disregard them.[59]

Not surprisingly, though without any hard evidence, the jury found Kapsales guilty; virulent racist sentiment in the community undoubtedly contributed to the verdict. Kapsales's conviction in late 1917 matches the historical treatment of immigrant men in the Northwest who faced criminal charges for same-sex sexual activities. But the proceedings against Kapsales also differed significantly from its apparently similar predecessors. In earlier prosecutions of working-class and immigrant men for same-sex crimes, terms associated with sexuality, however rudimentary, never appeared. When the Columbia County district attorney used the term *degenerate* in the Kapsales case, he certainly spoke to race issues and even to the association of the term with the decline of civilization. But he also invoked more modern notions regarding one's actions and mental condition, and therefore sexuality. During the trial, Metsker even cited Frank Collier's 1913 thirty-nine-page treatise on homosexuality, the response to E. S. J. McAllister's appeal. He repeated the charge that Kapsales's actions revealed a disposition: "A man that will do this once will do it a second time"; "I say a man that will do that once will do it twice and I say a man that will do it twice has probably done it...many times, maybe not on a boy like this"; and finally, "Now, I say, it is a reasonable deduction to say that a man that has committed an offense of this kind once has committed before and probably many times[.]"[60]

Certainly Metsker's approach in 1917 was not as graceful as Collier's had been. The earlier prosecutor had been able to call to the witness stand any number of men who testified to sexual encounters with the defendant, enabling him to argue that these repeated acts proved McAllister to be a sex invert. Yet even without the witnesses such as Collier had, Metsker was able to get the same point across. Kapsales, Metsker claimed, had no doubt committed sodomy before; therefore he would do it a second time, and if he did it a second time he would do it many times. Although Metsker never made the point explicitly, it appears that his conclusion was that Kapsales was like McAllister, a man who because of his nature regularly engaged in sodomy.

Faced with long-standing racial animus in St. Helens, a broader history of discrimination in the Northwest, the heightened concern over immigrants during World War I, and a newly emerging social understanding of sexuality drawn directly from the 1912 scandal, Kapsales had little hope for acquittal. Judge James Eakin, a brother of one of the Oregon State Supreme Court justices who had dissented in the 1913 Start, Wedemeyer, and McAllister reversals, sentenced the immigrant laborer to the penitentiary for a term of one to fifteen years. Kapsales died there on December 5, 1918, from influenza.[61]

Portland's 1912 scandal marks a significant watershed in the history of the city, the state of Oregon, and the Pacific Northwest. It revealed for the first time to the broader citizenry that white middle-class men engaged in same-sex affairs and had developed a homosexual subculture in the region's larger cities. Moreover, during the year that passed between Benjamin Trout's confession and the outcome of E. S. J. McAllister's appeal, the city, the state, and the region traveled a considerable distance in social understandings regarding same-sex affairs. During this time newer, more modern notions about homosexuality and the homosexual crystallized. The older and more general term and concept—*degenerate*—survived, but it was modified and recontextualized. It now competed with other expressions and, necessarily, the understandings that they represented. Terms newly introduced during Portland's same-sex vice scandal included *sex invert, homosexual, sex pervert,* and even *uranism*. These referred to sexual actions, desires, even identity, and not to one's relationship to civilization or class. Moreover, the term *homosexual* would in short order become more common than *degenerate*. Already in 1917 a report on same-sex vice conditions issued by the Commission to Investigate the Oregon State Penitentiary dropped the term *degenerate* altogether, exclusively using *homo-sexual* and *homo-sexuality* instead.[62]

The events that transpired in Portland in late 1912–13 are significant in a national context, too. In the years following Portland's homosexual scandal, other American communities—Philadelphia in 1913; Los Angeles and Long Beach in 1914; and Newport, Rhode Island, in 1919—directly confronted similar incidents that acted as defining moments in their histories. During the same years, a proliferation of medical and vice commission reports brought to public attention the existence of thriving homosexual communities in other American locales, including Chicago, New York, St. Louis, and Denver. Together, these disclosures and local scandals worked collectively to transform understandings of homosexuality and of the homosexual at the national level.[63]

PART III

Progressivism
and Same-Sex Affairs

Personality, Politics, and Sex
in Portland and the Northwest

Shortly after newspapers broke the story about native-born middle-class male homosexuals in Portland, many of those implicated fled the city. In time, three were arrested in Vancouver, British Columbia; two in Fresno, California; one in Los Angeles; one in Salem, Oregon; one in Medford, Oregon; one in Vancouver, Washington; and four in Seattle, where some of those involved lived. As they fled, a few of these individuals were spotted in small towns such as Aberdeen, Washington, and Forest Grove, Oregon, as well as in larger cities like San Francisco. Other Northwest and West Coast cities, including Spokane, Tacoma, Walla Walla, and even San Diego, became variously implicated in the affair. Many people up and down the coast quickly found that Portland's sensational affair had connections with their own locales, and those ties were splashed across local and regional headlines.[1]

As these communities discovered even the most tangential links between themselves and the events in Portland, they responded in different ways. For example, Seattle officials announced that they were "contemplating a general cleanup similar to which [Portland] authorities are engaged in."[2] In other towns and cities, individuals and organizations utilized the revelations to further their own political agendas, attack certain prominent social institutions, and seek revenge against some controversial personalities implicated in the scandal. Moreover, in the city of Portland, the state of Oregon, the Northwest region, and ultimately the nation's capital, reformers swung into action, reacting with force to the news of homosexuality.

Part 3 examines these local, regional, and national responses to Portland's 1912 scandal. Chapter 6 considers juridical and reformist responses from the local to the national levels; the current chapter begins by analyzing the influence that the 1912 scandal had on one long-standing political struggle in Portland. This struggle pitted a coalition composed of the working and lower middle classes, who clung to an older republican vision of society, against the upper classes, who espoused a newly emerging corporate ideal. I then consider the ways in which the scandal played out in some other, smaller Northwest towns. These communities, because they were involved only indirectly and tended to be socially less complex than Portland, generally concentrated more on issues of personality than on broader social concerns. This point is illustrated by the biography of E. S. J. McAllister, the most prominent man caught up in accusations of homosexuality, as I examine the response to him in towns outside Portland where he had conducted business and participated in high-profile and divisive political and reform campaigns prior to 1912. The chapter concludes with an assessment of how the 1912 scandal spread to the small eastern Washington town of Walla Walla and there implicated John Gibson, a locally prominent newsman and church worker. In the socially less complex Walla Walla, revelations about local homosexuality did not have the divisive effect seen in Portland, and the response to Gibson bore little resemblance to the treatment of McAllister. In fact, events in Walla Walla took a surprisingly different turn.

Homosexuality and Class Struggle in Portland

Individuals and social forces in Portland quickly turned the news of middle- and upper-class homosexuality to political ends in the ongoing class struggle in the city, a struggle that had little inherently to do with sexuality. In an insightful analysis of Portland's politics during the Progressive era, the historian Robert D. Johnston has exploded the longstanding myth of the city's conservatism, apparent homogeneity, and lack of class-based divisions. Johnston found that from 1890 until about 1930, Portland experienced a fierce and vigorous struggle between an alliance of workers and the lower middle class (small property holders, shopkeepers, artisans, and skilled laborers) on the one side and the upper middle and elite classes on the other. The latter group supported the emerging corporate order and private privilege, while the lower classes championed an age-old republican ideal that espoused private property and direct democracy and sought to eliminate "unearned" wealth.[3]

We can observe the division, recrimination, and acrimony between the contending groups in the labor strikes that took place from the 1890s through the early 1920s. During such strife, the lower middle classes, against the wishes of the commercial elites, generally supported labor even when organizations as radical as the IWW participated and events sometimes turned violent, as happened in a 1922 strike. Lower-middle-class backing remained palpable as the laborers, in Johnston's words, "were shutting down the waterfront, the lifeline for much of the city's commerce." A less colorful example comes from 1916, when skilled workers, small businessmen, and shopkeepers squared off against the elite's chamber of commerce when that organization supported the open shop. In these and a multitude of other defining struggles during the period, Johnston has explained, class conflict occurred "rhetorically [in] the people versus the [moneyed] interests, but concretely [in] the lower middle class and home-owning working class versus the upper middle class and corporate elite."[4]

The 1912 Portland same-sex vice scandal erupted in this volatile political climate. It soon became a tool wielded by the populist *Portland News* in its editor's protracted battle against the local elites. Not surprisingly, as the *News* kept up its attacks, it met with recrimination and backlash, which only further fanned the flames of class hostility. Dana Sleeth, editor of the *News* at the time (figure 11), was born in 1878 in Iowa; he arrived in Portland in 1903. His father had been a prominent Methodist minister in Nebraska and his mother, upon her move to the Rose City, became a supporter of the local chapter of the Women's Christian Temperance Union, to which she was elected president in 1918. Dana, in contrast, was an agnostic and opposed prohibition. He founded his own working-class newspaper, the *People's Press,* on Portland's working- and lower-middle-class eastside in 1905 and two years later went to work for the *News.*[5] That paper was part of Edward Willis Scripps's media empire, the first national newspaper chain. Scripps designed his papers to appeal to the working class. They were inexpensive, filled with short and often sensational stories, and provided plenty of illustrations. Moreover, editorially they championed working-class causes, such as union efforts and public ownership of utilities. The *News,* established in 1906, was the last of four papers—the others being the Spokane *Press,* the Tacoma *Times,* and the Seattle *Star*—that Scripps founded in the Northwest.[6]

The sensationalist 1912 scandal provided perfect copy for the *News.* Its apparently middle- or even upper-class nature also worked to the advantage of the populist Sleeth, who immediately chose to interpret the scandal along class lines. In part he did so because the *News,* by his account,

FIGURE 11. Dana Sleeth, ca. 1912. Sleeth, a friend of the
working classes, edited Edward Scripp's *Portland News*.
In 1912 Sleeth used the middle- and upper-class background of most of the men implicated in the homosexual scandal as one more means of attacking the Portland
establishment. Sleeth Family Papers, courtesy Peter D.
Sleeth.

was the last newspaper to learn of the story. "Every paper but this one
has known of these things," Sleeth complained; "also for two days the
truth has been bottled and money and influence has [*sic*] stood in the
path of justice[.]" The *News* editor had good reason to suspect that
"money and influence" stood in the way of information and "justice" in
Portland. For years corruption and vice had gone hand in hand with the
ruling elite's control of the city. According to a 1911 exposé penned by
McClure's Magazine correspondent Burton Hendrick, the Portland "ma-

chine, by a regular system of monthly fines, had practically licensed gambling and prostitution, and under this system of official encouragement the city had become a popular headquarters for all the vicious characters in the Northwest."[7]

While Hendrick might have exaggerated slightly, "vice" did abound. In 1911 public pressure finally moved Mayor A. G. Rushlight to create the Portland Vice Commission. In its second report, the commission charged that 431 of 547 hotels, apartments, rooming and lodging houses that it investigated in downtown and in the North End were "wholly given up to immorality." More shocking to middle-class residents was that a number of business and political leaders owned the properties on which these dens of vice stood.[8] Thus, liquor, gambling, and prostitution flourished at least in part thanks to the "better" families who controlled the city's economy and politics. Their power also historically discouraged newspapers from reporting on such iniquity. In the 1890s, Harvey W. Scott, the co-owner and editor of the very powerful *Oregonian,* "absolutely declined" to use his newspaper to help enforce vice laws, admitting that "the persons most concerned in the maintenance of these abuses were the principal men of the city—the men of wealth on whose patronage the paper relied & it could not afford to alienate them. It would ruin this paper." Scott forgot to mention that his partner in the *Oregonian,* H. L. Pittock, also maintained saloons on his own properties.[9]

For Sleeth, then, the city's other papers' initial failure to report on the 1912 scandal served as one more instance of what had been going on for some time. It probably came as no surprise to him when the *Oregonian*—the Republican and upper-class mouthpiece—declared on November 16 that it would "not now nor hereafter print the details of this affair except in so far as the necessities of public justice may require." Indeed, the *Oregonian*'s coverage of the story would be considerably less extensive than that of other papers—but the sensation-generated profits that the puritanical *Oregonian* stood to lose would be recouped by the more liberal approach of its sister paper, the *Evening Telegram.* Once the *News* began unfurling banner headlines about the sex-filled scandal, the somewhat less aristocratic *Evening Telegram* began offering some of the most detailed reports on what authorities were busily uncovering.[10]

For his part, Sleeth used the upper-class pedigree of some of those rounded up to great advantage. "[T]he best circles of the town," he wrote, "make out a practice of sinking lower than the beasts that perish."

As more details came to light, Sleeth asserted that the scandal "was reaching higher and higher into the select class of the town." Certainly, a well-known lawyer, two physicians, and a prominent architect came under arrest. But his claim that "no workingmen or plain folks are included" was untrue, however well it played into class antagonisms. Be that as it may, Sleeth focused on the apparently delicate treatment of some of the more prominent men—they either got out on bail or were "set free to do as they pleased, without even a bond placed on them." Believing that still other guilty members of the elite never did face a court of law, Sleeth made one of his most damning accusations: "Pressure has been brought to bear on the public officials to continue these trials indefinitely; rumors are thick and ugly regarding the possibility of convictions in these cases, and a lot of influence is being brought to bear to stop further work on [them]."[11]

From the beginning, Sleeth fingered Portland's YMCA as a principal contributor to conditions recently uncovered. His first story on the affair announced in huge eye-catching letters: "ROTTEN SCANDAL REACHES INTO THE Y.M.C.A." That the *News* should attack the YMCA was in keeping with general working-class antagonism toward the association throughout America. But in Portland the institution provided a particularly tempting target because it was one of the prized institutions of the middle and upper classes. As it turned out—and as other papers, including the establishment's *Oregonian,* confirmed—a few men involved in the scandal did room at the YMCA. Benjamin Brick, a citizen officer with the local police, who claimed to have been the first to uncover vice there, reported that his initial tip came from an elevator boy and it led him directly "into the Y.M.C.A. building."[12] On November 16, Sleeth charged more pointedly that the "Y.M.C.A. was one of the hotbeds of the practices and the confessions of several men and boys shows that this institution has, to put it mildly, been woefully mismanaged." A few days later, he raised the level of invective when he asked the city's "clean mothers of clean boys" if they knew "that the management of the local Y.M.C.A. has a rule, has had a rule for years, FORCING ALL BOYS OVER 14 TO BATHE IN THE ASSOCIATION TANK WITH MEN AND HAS FORCED THEM TO ENTER THE TANK NAKED?"[13] When Sleeth attributed the Y's disgraceful involvement directly to "mismanagement," even suggesting that officials participated in the sexual activities discovered there, he created a stir that became even bigger than the sensational sex revelations themselves.

The Portland YMCA was formed in 1868. During the next five decades it became a significant social institution in the city, providing (among other things) moral uplift, education, youth outreach, inexpensive meals and lodgings, summer encampments, missionary work in the North End, and a gymnasium and a swimming pool. The organization enjoyed solid support from Portland's middle and elite classes. From its beginning, William S. Ladd, founder of the Ladd and Tilton Bank and head of Portland's first family, lent aid; initially he allowed the Y to use several rooms in his own building on First Avenue and Stark Street. His son, William M. Ladd, was serving as board chairman in 1912, a position he had held for many years. Others among Portland's elites had also come to the Y's aid in the past. Henry W. Corbett, for example, whose estate included twenty-seven downtown holdings, left the organization a $35,000 bequest in 1903.[14] Such an illustrious history and tradition of support explains the *Oregonian*'s assessment that the YMCA "represents in a particular sense the conscience and the character of the community." Not unexpectedly, the *News*'s attacks on that institution and its management met with vigorous opposition. Even B. H. Canfield, the editor in chief of the Scripps chain in the Northwest, cautioned Sleeth to tread carefully in this area. "[T]here are a large number of persons," Canfield warned from Spokane on November 18, "who are so muscle bound in their ideas as to resent anything that looks like an attack on such an institution as the Y.M.C.A. Of course it isn't such an attack on our part, but it looks that way, and I think you'll find that it will arouse the opposition, after the first excitement is over."[15] Canfield's admonition and prediction were understatements. As supporters of the YMCA organized and launched their counteroffensive against the *News,* the politics of class in Portland reached yet another climax.

Already on November 16 the YMCA was readying for a showdown with the *News*. Its board met in a special session to consider "a scandalous story published in an evening paper which has attempted to connect the name of the Association therewith." Among those present were Ladd and invited guests, including Multnomah County Circuit Court Judge William N. Gatens (who had taken personal charge of the vice case investigations) and the juvenile court's chief probation officer, Samuel D. White. At the meeting, the directors created a subcommittee headed by the Y's general secretary, Harry W. Stone. Its tasks included ensuring that local and regional papers publish lengthy statements by Gatens and White exonerating the YMCA and its officials. That evening and the next morning, Portland's three leading papers reported the YMCA's denial of its connection with the scandal and Gatens's and White's declarations of the Y's innocence.[16]

Unfortunately for the board of directors, only a few hours after its special session had adjourned, a maid found an older and respected resident of the institution, William H. Allen, near death in his room. He had attempted to take his own life by consuming poison soon after the police had questioned him about his alleged involvement in the same-sex relations. Sleeth jumped on this item, boldly announcing, "Shortly after it had been unanimously decided that there was nothing to it at all, at all, a resident of the Y.M.C.A. caravansary, weighed down by his sins, took poison. The departing brethren, had they lingered, might have met his ambulance that bore away the testimony to their folly."[17]

With this tragic and embarrassing news pressing on them, the Y's directors reconvened two days later, this time to create another committee that would contact the city's clubs and organizations to solicit their support and have them condemn the *News*. Within days the Transportation Club, Commercial Club, Progressive Business Men's Club, Realty Board, Ad Club, Rotary Club, East Side Business Men's Club, North East Side Improvement Association, Association of Credit Men, Chamber of Commerce, Multnomah Amateur Athletic Club's Board of Trustees, and Greater Portland Plans Association met and drafted resolutions of support for the Y and condemnation of the *News*. On November 20 several Rotary Club speakers indignantly commanded that "[s]uch a newspaper should be suppressed by the business interest of the city by whatever means seems best." Rotarians then elected to exclude the *News* from their homes and withdraw advertising from it.[18] Later that afternoon, Sleeth responded aggressively:

Now here are the only people in town who are after this paper; they always have been after it.

The Employers' association.

The leaders in the big corporations who have hated this paper for years because it fought for the people and against special interests.

The venal clique that assumes leadership of the various clubs and associations that exist for the boosting of the frenzied finance game and to skin the public.

All the elements of the town that this paper has opposed for the good of the plain man.

All the agencies that hate common folk, that despise those not of their class, that live as the tick lives by being a parasite instead of a producer.

The News is hated, has been hated, will be hated by those forces in the town that fatten from political office and special privilege. These interests today are joining hands to "get" The News.

These interests are in the peculiar situation of saying to the others of the city: "We don't care about your boys; let the prosecution stop; hush this matter up and don't read The News."[19]

Condemnation of Sleeth and the *News* continued unabated. The Commercial Club canceled its subscription and ordered copies of the "papers for the remainder of the year to be destroyed." Other newspapers ran editorials censuring Sleeth and the *News*. "It is a bad, wicked, vicious influence in this city," the conservative *Spectator* declared. "Without soul, without honor, without veracity, without good intent," the *Oregonian* blustered, "this sycophant and degenerate continues a quest for tainted money regardless of the good it may destroy." The city's ministers and religious organizations, every bit as numerous as its business clubs, also strenuously defended the YMCA and protested against the *News*.[20] To emphasize the seriousness of the matter, more than one hundred representatives "from every commercial organization in the city" met on the afternoon of Sunday, November 24. They appointed a committee of fifteen, which only a week later was enlarged to fifty. Among the committee's tasks were to investigate matters related to Portland's vice and, in particular, "to put a stop to publication of misrepresentations of the situation" by withdrawing patronage from the *News*.[21]

In reality, Portland's business community had little hope of silencing Sleeth by withdrawing advertising and subscriptions: to forestall that very possibility, Scripps's papers avoided dependency on advertising. Probably recognizing that another approach was necessary, members of the Committee of 15 elected to go directly to Scripps himself, who resided in Pasadena, California. F. C. Knapp, president of the Chamber of Commerce and a member of the Committee of 15 and 50, wrote to his business partner and brother-in-law F. P. Brewer, who conveniently lived in Pasadena and asked him "to take some other reputable citizen[s]... and call on Mr. Scripps with a view of ascertaining if the tirades of the News are in line with his ideas of decency and morality." Brewer only went so far as to forward Knapp's letter to the news mogul. Scripps responded directly to Knapp, in a letter that effectively slammed the door in his and the Portland establishment's face as he expressed his unbounded faith in both Sleeth and Canfield. He felt it was unlikely that they had erred; but if they had, he warned, it was not "nearly as great a mistake as some Portland men have [made], who have believed that it is possible to intimidate these men and to scare me by making an attack on my business, by way of influencing advertising patronage." Scripps concluded by stating that he had long fought too many "corrupt business[es] and corrupt snobs in the social world" to be "influenced by any such tactics." Scripps then promptly informed Canfield of the letters he had received from Knapp and others and explained how he summarily dealt with their writers. Canfield wrote Sleeth gleefully, "The boss sent 'em back some mighty fine replies, telling them just where they got off at. Without having seen a copy of the News he sized up the situation accurately simply from the protests made to him.... [H]aving gone through similar experiences I could have told the writers what they'd get."[22]

While some prominent Portlanders attempted behind the scenes to pressure the *News* and its owner, others threatened a lawsuit. J. E. Werlein, a former city treasurer, member of the Ad Club, and lobbyist for Portland Railway Light and Power (PRL&P), offered the YMCA legal assistance in "overcoming the slanders directed against the organization." B. Lee Paget, a banker, prohibitionist, and member of the Men's Methodist Social Union, urged the YMCA to "take prompt steps to obtain a full retraction and to secure adequate redress of punishment for the perpetrators of this gross libel."[23] Their involvement surely convinced Sleeth that special interests were once again endangering the "safety" of the common people. PRL&P had for some time been the bogey man in Portland's class politics. Considered the city's "first bona fide monopoly," it was sold to eastern interests in 1906 by Portland financiers, with the help of the state legislature and city council. By 1910 PRL&P was a $15 million holding company that, according to *American Banker*, was "liable to anti-trust action under the Sherman Act." Two years later, local disenchantment with PRL&P reached an all-time high. In early 1913, with vice scandal trials still under way, certain Portland interests (including those of the lower-middle-class eastside) filed a complaint with the city council and the Oregon State Public Service Commission against the monopoly. They charged, among other things, that it unfairly favored the downtown establishment.[24] In late 1912 Werlein's involvement in the fight against the *News* enabled Sleeth to claim that a "trust," the PRL&P, stood behind both the news cover-up and the attempt to destroy his paper. This charge played marvelously into age-old animosities: "The News has had a 'hunch' for several days...that Big Business was using the Y.M.C.A. as a shield to arouse public sentiment, that this paper's fight for the common man, and against vested piracy, might be hushed."[25]

Within two weeks of the sensational disclosure regarding same-sex vice, Portland's scandal had moved well beyond affairs of sex. It had also gone far beyond the supposed mismanagement of the YMCA. The politically charged atmosphere in the city and Sleeth's penchant for seeing conspiracy, as well as the clumsy actions of other newspapers, YMCA officials, and representatives from the upper middle and elite classes, had quickly turned the scandal into yet one more battle between the "common folk" and the "special interests." In Sleeth's terse though crude summation, there was "The News on one side, and Big Business and 100 perverts on the other."[26]

If Sleeth's aim had been to damage the elite's esteemed YMCA, he had succeeded. YMCA board of directors' minutes from early 1913 reveal that subscription receipts dropped from $8,500 in 1911 to only $5,700 in 1912. Secretary Stone reported that "the attack in the newspaper on the standing of the Association has had up to this date caused a financial loss of about $10,000. There has been a considerable reduction in membership." A year later, the YMCA was still struggling, and Stone begged Mayor H. R. Albee for assistance. "The senior membership receipts," he lamented, "have fallen since the attack fully $6000. The dormitory rentals decreased $4000 and boys' membership $2000. Other items were effected [sic] until we now face a deficit of practically $15,000." As a result, the Y had to curtail a number of its programs.[27]

In the larger context of Progressive-era Portland, the scandal unquestionably helped further divide the citizenry and polarize municipal politics. More than ever before, business and commercial elements in the city came out decisively against the *News*. Portland's three major papers condemned it; (lukewarm) support came only from the *Labor Press,* the official publication of the Central Labor Council, which itself had fought against the city's corporate interests for some years. At the same time, however, Sleeth gleefully published pages of supportive letters to the editor and boasted of a rise in subscriptions. For example, he claimed that in a two-day period in November he had signed up 145 new subscribers while only losing 6 or 7. He announced that on another day his paper had sold ten thousand copies on the street, "more than the combined sales of all other local papers in that day, or any two days." On January 4, 1913, Sleeth crowed that the average daily circulation of the *News* in December had increased 5,743 over the same month in the previous year.[28] Indeed, a desire to increase sales may well have helped drive Sleeth's attacks on the YMCA. Canfield offered him advice as early as November 20 on how best to play the story to keep people wanting more. Then in early December he notified Sleeth, "According to our arrangement you will have more salary coming to you . . . due to circulation increase[.]" Sleeth received a $50.00 bonus and his circulation manager, George S. Teall, a "$20 prize for highest per cent of circulation increase in the northwest league for the month." But prejudice against the accused also clearly played a role in Sleeth's approach to the scandal. On November 19 the editor of the *News*'s sister paper, the Seattle *Star,* wrote to Sleeth, primarily to congratulate him on his circulation; however, the letter concluded with the suggestion that "you w[h]isper the word 'penitentiary sentence' in [Judge] Gaten's [*sic*] ear. Sending this gang to prison will do more real good than all the vice crusades that [Oregon's] Gov. [Oswald] West ever thought of."[29]

These additional perspectives on Sleeth's use of the 1912 scandal do not discount the long-standing animus between the typical reader of the *News* and the Portland establishment. In the fraught Progressive-era atmosphere, which set republicans against the corporate order, the 1912 scandal quickly was translated into yet one more battle between the city's class alliances. Such struggles, utilizing a variety of ammunition, would continue for years. In the meantime, Sleeth's bitter campaign against the Portland elites had helped crystallize at the local level the notion that the homosexual was a middle- and upper-class character, lacking any roots in the working classes.

The Personal as Political: E. S. J. McAllister, Progressive Reform, and Public Outrage in 1912

One man who emerged as a central figure in the Portland scandal was E. S. J. McAllister (figure 12). A lawyer conspicuously active in social causes, McAllister's political background had won him many enemies in the state long before news of his homosexuality came to light. When it did, one Oregon community (Eugene) seized on the tabloidlike revelations as it railed against him for his political activities that had recently harmed the city. The story of McAllister and of the reaction against him in various small Oregon communities like Eugene deserves attention for at least two reasons. First, it reveals the difficulties that a middle-class notable could face in the early twentieth century when exposed as a homosexual and when, for other reason, he already was lacking community support. And second, it illustrates once again how sex and sexuality can be turned to local political uses.

Edward Stonewall Jackson McAllister was born in Laurel, Delaware, on May 25, 1869. Both his parents, William N. and Sarah Frances (Lowe), as their son's name suggests, originated in the South. As a boy, Edward attended Delaware public schools before entering the Wilmington Academy in Dover when he was fifteen. Five years later he registered at Dickinson College in Carlisle, Pennsylvania, and then went on to Syracuse University, graduating with both his bachelor's and master's degrees in 1895. Immediately thereafter he entered Boston University,

FIGURE 12. E. S. J. McAllister, 1910. McAllister's celebrity as an attorney, emerging politician, and notable reformer in Oregon made him the central personality of Portland's 1912 homosexual scandal. Although the Oregon State Supreme Court overturned his sodomy conviction, McAllister's career lay in ruins. After the scandal, he retired to the small community of Myrtle Creek, about 180 miles south of Portland, where he lived out the remainder of his life. Oregon Historical Society, #OrHi 102013.

where he studied until 1897. One year later he seems to have married Margaret W. Wiley, and he matriculated at the University of Virginia; by June 1904 he had earned his law degree.[30] Later that year McAllister was admitted to the bar of the Commonwealth of Virginia; but in October 1904 he moved to Portland, under circumstances that remain unclear. Apparently his wife did not accompany him. In fact, Margaret never appears in any of Oregon's census records or Portland city directories, and in the 1920 census McAllister would list himself as single. We do know, however, that within a month of his arrival in Portland, the Anti-Saloon League's Oregon and Southern Idaho Department hired him as its attorney. He won a temporary license to practice law in Oregon in November 1904, and permanent admission to the bar on July 3, 1905.[31]

Whatever his motives for relocating, it is significant that McAllister immediately became involved in reform politics in Oregon, a state that—though its role is largely forgotten today—was one of the leaders in the Progressive movement then sweeping the nation. For its reform-related activities, Oregon received much national press from magazine's such as *McClure's, Century,* and *American* and from such noted Progressive-era reporters as Lincoln Steffens, Burton J. Hendrick, and Ray Stannard Baker. From the late 1890s through the 1910s, Oregonians introduced the initiative and referendum, the Australian ballot (i.e., official ballots printed by the state that are voted on secretly at polling places), the direct primary, and the direct election of U.S. senators. Other democratic reforms included the removal from the state legislature of the power to amend city charters, a power given instead to the people who actually lived in their cities. In 1912, eight years before the Nineteenth Amendment to the Constitution was adopted, Oregonians approved woman's suffrage, and several Oregon suffragists helped secure the vote even earlier in the neighboring states of Washington and Idaho. In 1916 Oregon embraced statewide prohibition. Moreover, several Progressive-era issues confronting the state had a national impact. In 1908 the U.S. Supreme Court upheld the right of the state to regulate the hours and conditions of women's employment in the landmark case *Muller v. Oregon.* In *Bunting v. Oregon* in 1917, the Court sustained the ten-hour day for both men and women. More infamously, between 1897 and 1910 a scandal over the looting of the public domain in Oregon gained national attention. Several prominent Oregon officials and politicians, including a U.S. senator and a representative, were convicted of corruption and conspiracy. The trials surrounding their fates helped bring to an end some of the worst abuses of public lands and also encouraged Theodore Roosevelt to push aggressively for conservation. In addition, the initiative and referendum, although neither introduced nor accepted first in Oregon, nonetheless became known nationally as the "Oregon System," thanks largely to the work of the reformer William S. U'Ren, who tirelessly used these two tools to secure many other Progressive reforms in the state.[32]

Immediately upon arriving in Oregon at this exhilarating time, McAllister threw his considerable weight (he was 275 pounds and stood six feet tall) behind reformist causes. His first political battle came early in 1905 when he traveled to Salem, the state capital, and lobbied the legislature on behalf of the Anti-Saloon League. The organization desired to prevent state officials from adopting a newly proposed amendment designed to weaken the local option law that the Oregon electorate had approved in 1904. After passing in the house, the bill went on to the senate, where McAllister's political acumen came into play. According to Portland's *Oregon Journal,* McAllister helped lead the reform lobby and deserved "much of the credit for the defeat of the bill." For some time thereafter, McAllister continued his efforts with the Anti-Saloon League. In 1907, for example, he took up his most memorable case, bringing suit to prevent Medford, a small southern Oregon town and the seat of Jackson County, from permitting its saloons to stay open despite the wishes of the rest of the county. Although he was unsuccessful in this instance, the case brought more notoriety to McAllister. Probably because of his other reform interests—which were considerably more radical than the relatively conservative, middle- and upper-class, Protestant temperance cause of the Anti-Saloon League—by 1910 McAllister had disassociated himself from the prohibitionist campaign.[33]

McAllister's interest in those other political causes had already become clear. On May 27, 1906, he became president of the People's Forum, replacing Rabbi Steven Wise, who was leaving for New York. The forum's members included Abigail Scott Duniway, the leading suffragist in the Northwest. McAllister himself had an interest in women's rights. Only a week after taking office in the People's Forum, he shared a local stage with Dr. Anna Howard Shaw, the president of the National American Woman's Suffrage Association, who was then on tour. According to the newspaper, McAllister followed Shaw to the podium and there "cleverly attacked the case of the anti-suffragists."[34]

Perhaps most noteworthy regarding McAllister's feminist causes was his initial role in *Muller v. Oregon,* one of the more significant U.S. Supreme Court decisions of the early twentieth century. Before the laundryman Curt Muller appealed his case in 1906, McAllister represented him in the lower courts. In *Muller v. Oregon,* decided in 1908, Muller lost his ability to require women in his laundry to work longer hours than the maximum set by the state. Many feminists lauded the Court for its apparent pro–woman's rights sympathies in deciding against Muller, and thus it would seem that here, as in the prohibitionist cause, McAllister was taking a relatively conservative position. Yet at the time and since, other feminists have criticized *Muller v. Oregon* for helping to crystallize in federal law inequality between men and women, and therefore have viewed Curt Muller as something of a hero. The argument made on Muller's behalf, framed in part by McAllister and then later by William Fenton, a better-known lawyer who took the case to the federal courts, put the legal equality of women before the protections afforded by labor legislation.[35]

Through these years, McAllister's legal career flourished. On June 1, 1906, he formed a partnership with Robert J. Upton in Portland under the name McAllister and Upton.[36] As a Democrat in a state and city that were decidedly Republican, furthermore, McAllister's legal and political fortunes initially seemed to turn yet brighter when Portland elected Democratic and reform-minded Harry Lane to two terms as mayor, commencing in 1905. For McAllister, a rising personage in the party, Lane's victory provided a golden opportunity to gain a position of power within Oregon's largest municipality. In 1908, when George Cameron relinquished his job as Portland police judge—newly elected to the post of district attorney for Multnomah County—a number of important Portlanders wrote to Mayor Lane recommending McAllister for the vacancy. The businessman V.E. Campbell suggested that the lawyer "would prove eminently satisfactory to the [D]emocratic party as a whole....None better or worthy could be [recommended]. His ability is known to all." The attorney E.H. Cahalin asserted that McAllister would "in all respects discharge the duties of the office honestly and fearlessly. This is in line with the characteristics of your administration[.]" And H.A. Mosher, an agent for the Portland and San Francisco Asiatic Steamship Companies, gushed that McAllister is "the highest class material we can get into the public service[.]" Lane received each of these letters courteously, responding that McAllister has indeed proved himself a "useful citizen" and would receive "due consideration." In the end, however, the mayor appointed someone else.[37]

This disappointment hardly damaged McAllister's career in the law. In March 1911 he won on appeal to the Oregon Supreme Court a decision against an insolvent corporation, the American Hospital Association, for unpaid services. In the spring of 1912 he announced that he was considering throwing his hat into the ring for a local judgeship in Portland. Simultaneously, he beat out a couple of dozen other attorneys in winning from the state the right to defend H.E. "Jack" Roberts. Roberts stood accused of murdering two young Portland men and injuring another, as they and two other youths innocently motored south of the city on the evening of March 29. The case would bring recognition and was therefore a plum assignment. As it turned out, the court found Roberts guilty and sentenced him to death. Governor Oswald West stayed that order until after the November elections, when voters would consider overturning the capital punishment statute. In the end, Oregonians retained the death penalty and Roberts proceeded to the gallows on December 13, less than a month after McAllister began to face his own difficulties as a result of the same-sex vice scandal. Coincidentally, one of the young men who survived the Roberts shooting was H. L. Tabb, a clerk, who later that year was also indicted in the Portland homosexual affair. He testified at McAllister's trial in 1913 that the lawyer had propositioned him during the Roberts trial and then later again in the public lavatories of the Imperial Hotel.[38]

What brought McAllister his greatest recognition—and ultimately, along with his sexual activities, the greatest condemnation from some— was his association in the People's Power League and the Oregon Single Tax League with William S. U'Ren, Oregon's most famous Progressive reformer and the individual who has been dubbed the "Father of the Oregon System." On the state level, the single tax was one of the hottest and most radical political issues of the era. Drawing directly on Henry George's *Progress and Poverty* (1879), single taxers believed that private property ownership would reduce poverty and corruption and they strenuously opposed "unearned" wealth. That is, they felt it unjust for speculators to purchase land and then hold it idle, waiting to cash in only after others had improved their nearby properties and had thereby driven prices upward. As W. G. Eggleston, a promoter of the single tax, queried, "Does the increased value of land, separate from the improvements, belong to the land owners or to the people who create that value?" For the single taxers, it belonged to the public and should be collected as a tax. It, and it alone, would be enough to support government; no other assessments would be necessary. Such a system would also have the benefit of forcing speculators to sell their land, enabling more people to own property.[39]

Because the single taxers in Oregon made little headway in persuading the state legislature to back this radical plan, the initiative was their main hope. In fact, U'Ren pushed to institute the initiative because he aimed to use it to secure the single tax, an issue he had believed in since 1882, long before coming to Oregon. Through the initiative, single taxers hoped that county by county they could eventually win statewide acceptance for their plan.[40] After securing the initiative and referendum in 1902, U'Ren created the People's Power League, which sponsored a number of reforms throughout the state, including an attempt to abolish the state senate. McAllister became a leader in this organization in 1905; and when the Oregon Single Tax League was formed in 1908, he was elected president and U'Ren secretary. The People's Power League and the Oregon Single Tax League counted among their members a host of important personages, including Harry Lane; B. Lee Paget; H. J. Parkinson, a carpenter and onetime editor of the *Portland Labor Press;* and Harry W. Stone, general secretary of the Oregon YMCA, with whom McAllister had already rubbed shoulders when working for the Anti-Saloon League. One of the most eccentric members of both organizations was C. E. S. Wood, a Portland attorney who moved in the city's elite ranks, defended corporations, and at the same time offered counsel to socialists and anarchists, including the likes of Emma Goldman.[41]

McAllister worked vigorously for both the Oregon Single Tax League and the People's Power movement. In 1910 he encouraged the Fels Fund—which Philadelphia entrepreneur Joseph Fels had created the year before to support the single tax movement nationwide—to invest in the Oregon campaign. In September 1911 McAllister spoke on the meaning of the teachings of Henry George at Portland's commemoration of the seventy-second birthday of the initiator of the single tax idea, who had died in 1897. One month later, McAllister and C. E. S. Wood completed the People's Power League's "short charter" proposal for reorganizing Portland's municipal government along the lines of a commission system. The Rose City did finally adopt such a system in 1913. Although its specifics differed from what McAllister and Wood had proposed, Wood's outspoken support for this new form of government during the 1913 election suggests that indirectly McAllister had an influence on the eventual shape of Portland's municipal government.[42]

But it was the 1912 general election that would prove the climax of McAllister's participation in politics. First, through a 1910 initiative single taxers had secured for counties the power of gaining taxation prerogatives from the state. So irate did this make the legislature that it voted to resubmit the law to citizens in 1912, hoping to have the measure overturned. Not only did single taxers like McAllister have to fight against this repeal effort in 1912, but they also were struggling for another ballot initiative, "The Graduated Single Tax and Exemption Amendment."[43] Second, the 1912 election involved McAllister in yet another controversial referendum, which was designed to roll back the state legislature's recent, generous, and long-overdue appropriations to the University of Oregon. The referendum had originated in the small town of Cottage Grove, located about 120 miles south of Portland in Lane County. In 1910 Eugene, the county seat, had thwarted Cottage Grove's plans to separate from Lane and create a new county (Nesmith) with itself as the seat. This defeat so angered the residents of Cottage Grove that in retaliation against Eugene they struck against its lifeline, the University of Oregon. They hired H. J. Parkinson, a political associate of McAllister and U'Ren, to collect signatures for a referendum on the university's appropriations, paying him $3\frac{1}{2}$ cents for each signature he obtained. To find a place on the ballot, the petitioners needed 6,135 names; they submitted a whopping 13,715.[44]

Early in 1912, the Marion County District Attorney John H. McNary (whose brother Charles, soon to be appointed to the state supreme court, would vigorously attack McAllister and homosexuality in 1913) brought suit against the secretary of state to force him to remove Cottage Grove's measure from the ballot, arguing that many of the signatures favoring the referendum were fraudulent. McNary claimed that Parkinson's circulators "devised an easy method of earning their money. They would get together and pass their petitions around, each signing a few names in a disguised hand, thus minimizing the chance of detection." A lower court agreed with the plaintiffs. U'Ren and Wood appealed the decision, offering arguments defending Parkinson, the signatures, and the referendum; U'Ren had even taken the stand during the lower court trial. Behind the scenes, McAllister offered legal advice. Their involvement indicates no animus toward the university; indeed, a few years previously U'Ren had voiced strong support for education in a letter to the *Oregonian,* declaring, "I would rather see appropriations for educational purposes double rather than reduced a dollar." But U'Ren, Wood, and McAllister wished to defend the initiative process against its detractors and thereby preserve the integrity of direct democracy. The same motive was probably at work in McAllister's seemingly conservative earlier championing of the local option through his Anti-Saloon League affiliation. In 1912 the Oregon Supreme Court did nullify a number of the Cottage Grove petition's signatures, but found enough valid to secure a place on the ballot for the university appropriation referendum.[45]

Such divisive referenda and initiatives—measures dealing with capital punishment and women's suffrage were also before the voters—as well as the national contest between Woodrow Wilson, Theodore Roosevelt, and William Howard Taft, made the 1912 election one of the most exciting in

Oregon's history. Supporters of the university and Oregonians searching for ways to cut corners came out in force on opposing sides of the university measure. Single taxers, including McAllister, spoke throughout the state and carried on a forceful letter-writing campaign on behalf of their issues. According to Robert C. Woodward, by the fall of that year "every interested voter had heard the pro and con" and both sides spent liberally, the single taxers relying on the generosity of the Fels Fund; Fels himself even came to Oregon on a lecture tour. The People's Power League met with bitter opposition from the State Grange, the State Tax Commission, the Rational Tax Reform Association, the Equal Taxation League, and especially the *Oregonian,* which objected to the initiative and referendum as putting too much power into the hands of the people.[46]

The results of the election did not bode well for McAllister. Oregon voters overwhelmingly rejected the single tax measure and also overturned the single taxers' 1910 amendment. This was a crushing defeat for McAllister, who was now firmly associated in some minds with faddism, with a lost cause, and with U'Ren, whose popularity had taken a beating. Moreover, Cottage Grove succeeded in taking its revenge on Eugene: Oregonians voted against state funding for the university by a margin of nearly 3 to 1. Eugenians and especially the editor of the city's newspaper, the *Daily Guard,* were furious.[47]

A week or so after the election, the homosexual scandal broke. As the editor of Eugene's *Daily Guard* picked up the pieces following the vote, he soon realized that they were part of a political puzzle that bore a startling relation to the titillating story then emerging. When the paper's editor discovered McAllister's direct implication in "bestial practices" uncovered in Portland, he recalled for his readers the attorney's association with Parkinson, U'Ren, Wood, and the others who "opposed" the university. "Naturally," the *Daily Guard* concluded, "such men would volunteer their services to defend forgery and fraud when reputable attorneys would hesitate to be identified with the proceedings." When the state hanged Jack Roberts, McAllister's former client, two weeks later, C. E. S. Wood publicly proclaimed that to execute a human would be a "blot on the history of Oregon." The *Daily Guard* fiercely responded, "Now if that other highly moral reformer, E. S. J. McAllister, will come forward with his views on the subject, the atmosphere will be very much clarified." When McAllister was convicted of a sodomy charge in February 1913, the *Daily Guard's* story on the attorney's fate was small but prominently placed on the front page. In a related column two days later, the paper's editor rejoiced that even though H. J. Parkinson "is still in the field one other active enemy of the University will be able to render him little assistance this time. E. J. S. [*sic*] McAllister has been convicted of unprintable offenses and must serve time behind the prison bars." In what appeared to be a reference to McAllister in the editorial on U'Ren that directly followed, the *Daily Guard* claimed that the "limit of political absurdity has been reached."[48]

As news of his sexual activities spread, McAllister came under attack from places beyond Eugene. Other newspapers in small Oregon communities where McAllister had appeared on behalf of his controversial political causes were quick to report on the story. They mentioned his past reform endeavors, but spent more space detailing the present mystery and subterfuge, generously supplying sexual innuendo—all designed, no doubt, to sell newspapers. When the scandal broke, McAllister happened to be in Marshfield (later known as Coos Bay) on the southern Oregon coast. Previously he had visited the town to speak in favor of the single tax issue; at the time, he was taking depositions in a legal case. The *Coos Bay Times* immediately reported the news, embellishing it with information regarding McAllister's current presence in the city. In an interview with the paper published on Tuesday, November 19, McAllister "declared that the charge was absolutely false. He said that he could not imagine who would have preferred such a charge against him or dragged him into such a scandal." The paper also added the tidbit that "Mr. McAllister is accompanied [in town] by a young man stenographer named Schwartz."[49]

According to the Portland papers, McAllister planned to return from the coast voluntarily to face the charges, but he soon went missing. According to the *Coos Bay Times,* during the night before his scheduled departure a "special stage had come through...carrying four men. One was described as very large and without a moustache, which fits McAllister. This man failed to register at any hotels along the way or at Drain," the nearest train stop. Instead of catching the train north to Portland, "the four men left...going south on the Southern Pacific." It therefore appeared that McAllister was attempting to escape to California. However, officials in Medford, near the California border, had been warned of his flight; and when the lawyer arrived at the depot there on November 21, they promptly arrested him. At first McAllister denied his identity, but several "friends" in the town recognized him. The Medford police lodged him in the local jail, an act that the lawyer considered "an outrage." At this point Medford's *Mail Tribune,* like its Marshfield counterpart, reminded its readers of McAllister's political activities and in particular his past efforts in the town on behalf of the Oregon Anti-Saloon League. Soon, however, it turned to more intriguing issues. The paper reported, for example, that McAllister vehemently denied connections with the "several boys" who implicated him in "unprintable crimes," claiming that he was the victim of a "frame-up." The *Mail Tribune* also commented on McAllister's "conspicuous" attire: "a vivid green suit." In the early twentieth century, wearing a green suit was one way that a man could announce his homosexuality to others who sympathized and knew the code. So bold was this ensemble, in fact, that one historian has noted that few dared to wear it.[50]

The Portland newspapers addressing McAllister and his role in the 1912 scandal, unlike their small-town counterparts, shied away from delving too deeply into the lawyer's exceptional political career. The *Oregonian* was probably reticent because editorial policy and establishment pressure prevented it generally from reporting too much detail about the scandal, the *Oregon Journal* because as the leading Democratic newspaper in Oregon it had previously reported on and supported most of McAllister's activities. Especially noteworthy is the response of the *News*. While readily reporting on McAllister's involvement in the sex scandal, Sleeth did not mention the accused's important political role in the state during the previous eight years. In all likelihood, he was silent because he and his paper had been ardent supporters of many of the political and social reforms that McAllister, U'Ren, and the People's Power League had advocated. Instead Sleeth used McAllister's relatively high social position as a Portland lawyer as ammunition in his vendetta against the upper classes. This was a way safely to condemn the man and his class without referring to his Progressive, even populist and republican beliefs.

As for McAllister, once he finally returned to Portland he faced several indictments for the crime of sodomy and was required to post a bond of $6,000. Neither U'Ren nor the unconventional Wood came to his defense, suggesting that even Portland's radical Progressives had their limits.[51] McAllister relied on other counsel and, undoubtedly, his own knowledge of the law. In February he endured a sensational and embarrassing trial in which the prosecution brought forth many young men who testified to having affairs with the lawyer and to regularly seeing him hanging about well-known downtown homosexual pickup places. One witness testified that some men on the streets knew the barrister as "mother McAllister" because he was older than most others who participated in the homosexual community. Certainly the evidence presented against McAllister, particularly the testimony of his sex partners, largely accounts for his conviction on sodomy charges. However, the weight of public opinion against him for his role in the single tax movement, for his stand on university appropriations, and for his connection with the Jack Roberts murder trial also played a role. Nor did being a Democrat in a Republican city and state help his cause. The Multnomah County district attorney and special prosecutor who tried McAllister, Walter H. Evans and Frank T. Collier, were both affiliated with the Republican Party. When appealing their client's conviction to the Oregon State Supreme Court, McAllister's defense team charged that he had been the victim of a conspiracy—though one they claimed was orchestrated by the prosecuting witnesses rather than by Evans's office itself.[52]

Although McAllister won his appeal, his political and legal career was over. His partnership dissolved, and the Multnomah County Bar Association dropped him from its membership without a dissenting vote on January 27, 1914. In 1913 he briefly found employment as a clerk and lived for a while with his friend David Meagher, who had also been indicted in the Portland scandal. Shortly thereafter, McAllister purchased a small farm outside of Myrtle Creek, Oregon, a tiny and relatively isolated community about 180 miles south of Portland and far away from the limelight. In a place where apparently few knew much about him, McAllister reconstructed his life. He cultivated many friends there, became active in the Masonic Lodge and a variety of local literary and civic associations, and, according to the newspaper, "was highly respected by all who knew him." Sometime in 1925 or early 1926 he moved into town. He died there on March 20, 1926, following a short illness brought on by a stroke. He was not quite fifty-seven years old. McAllister's relatively lengthy obituary in the *Roseburg News-Review* mentioned neither his connection to the 1912 scandal nor his past political career. Of his mysterious wife, the paper noted only that she was deceased. Many years later, in June 2000, the Multnomah Bar Association reviewed McAllister's case and voted unanimously to reinstate him as a member, a representative from that organization claiming that the attorney had been "expelled due only to the fact that he was gay."[53]

Walla Walla's Parallel 1912 Sex Scandal

As the Rose City's sensational revelations spread outward, sexual politics affected other local personalities in some other Northwest towns and cities. In Walla Walla, Washington, a scandal both paralleling and diverging from that of Portland and E. S. J. McAllister revolved around a locally prominent news editor and church worker. The town, situated 270 miles east of Portland and just north of the Oregon border, was successively an early fur-trading post, mission, military fort, and stopover point on the Oregon Trail. Walla Walla's proximity to an 1860s gold mining district and to the Columbia River made it an ideal marketing outpost for Portland. In 1890 the town, known locally as the "Garden City," had a population of 4,709. By 1910, when it had 19,364 inhabitants, Walla Walla had emerged as a solidly prosperous and mature Northwest community. Along its tree-lined streets one could find stone buildings, farm machinery factories, produce-processing plants, parochial schools, churches, daily newspapers, a board of trade, Whitman College, a business school, a small symphony orchestra, and, as boosters liked to gush, "more fine homes in proportion to size than any city in the state." Walla Walla also served as home to an active and influential YMCA and—conveniently, as it turned out—the Washington State Penitentiary.[54]

Because of Walla Walla's ties to Portland, its newspapers often carried reports about the Rose City. As early as November 17, 1912, the *Bulletin* began printing details of the YMCA scandal, but more local concerns soon took precedence. Apparently the excitement generated in Portland moved a handful of nervous Walla Walla youths, ages fifteen to eighteen, to accuse one of the Garden City's own, John Gibson, of having "carnally" known them. Gibson was no transient laborer passing through town: he was a trustee of the First Congregational Church, the chairman the previous year of the inland Northwest's arm of the national Men in Religion Forward movement, the city editor of the *Bulletin,* and an energetic organizer of several boys' clubs in Oregon and Washington communities east of the Cascade Mountains.[55]

The Walla Walla *Union,* the *Bulletin*'s competitor and a paper that had previously failed to report on the same-sex vice scandal occurring downriver, immediately linked Gibson to the story in Portland. Because of Gibson's prominence in religious and social work in Walla Walla, rumors rapidly spread through the small community and outward across the inland Northwest that Walla Walla's YMCA was connected to "this matter." As in Portland, concerned leaders in the community denied such reports. The *Bulletin*'s general editor, J. G. Kelly; the Y's secretary, Fred Witham; and others issued a statement on November 22, asserting that Gibson "never had any official connection with the association, for more than a year has not been a member and has been there only on occasional visits," yet the rumors persisted. Businessmen met at the Commercial Club on November 23 and drafted their own statement. They claimed that Gibson had never been a boarder at the local Y. The Commercial Club also pledged its support to Walla Walla's YMCA, and a few days later, the Knights of Maccabees, Tent No. 36, added its endorsement.[56]

A careful reading of the various statements issued by these individuals and groups suggests that in reality Gibson had in fact been a member of the local YMCA, as a large segment of the local populace suspected. Indeed, as a local figure of note, his activities before his 1910 arrival in the tight-knit southeastern Washington community were fairly widely known. Gibson had previously served as YMCA membership secretary in Des Moines, Iowa; secretary of the YMCA in Red Oak, Iowa; secretary of the YMCA in Austin, Texas; and membership secretary of the YMCA in St. Paul, Minnesota. The news spreading up the Columbia River from Portland about the connection between same-sex vice and that city's YMCA only increased uncertainties about Gibson's involvement in their local Y.[57] Nonetheless, gossip soon abated in Walla Walla, and news of the scandal ebbed quickly once the *Bulletin* suggested that "all should endeavor to forget this case." Unlike in Portland, relatively little controversy arose in Walla Walla. But the Gibson affair did have an effect, sending a "repulsive shock" through the community. "Public opinion" demanded scrutiny of the local YMCA; and the very evening after Gibson's arrest, Dr. Stephen Penrose, the president of Whitman College, spoke at a hastily convened meeting of the Walla Walla Men's Club on the necessity of teaching sex hygiene to the community's boys. As the *Union* noted, "A blow has been struck. To some little degree the church work and other religious and social work of the city and community have been checked." But the paper also pointed out that such a scandal had beneficial consequences as well. "[H]undreds and thousands of sincere workers," the *Union* declared, "will but work all the harder in the face of the present [e]ffrontery."[58]

A number of factors help explain the relative mildness of this response, which differed so sharply from the reaction to E. S. J. McAllister described above. First, the political atmosphere was fairly calm in Walla Walla, a sedate and somewhat remote farming community that in 1912 was enjoying the greatest prosperity in its history. Second, although the town's two leading newspapers had responded differently to the initial news of Portland's scandal, their reporting of the Gibson affair was quite similar, further suggesting the presence of a strong political consensus in the community. It is likely, too, that Gibson's quick response to the charges of sodomy helped allay much public curiosity and anxiety. On November 22 when Gibson's own minister—the Reverend Raymond C. Brooks of the First Congregational Church, who had been sworn in as a special deputy sheriff—approached him about the charges of sodomy that youths had made, Gibson "promptly admitted his guilt and asked to receive punishment. He made no effort either to deny or to escape the consequences." Within minutes, a local judge sent Gibson the short distance away to the Washington State Penitentiary on a sentence of one to ten years.[59] "Justice" was quickly and decisively served in Walla Walla.

That the Gibson case was isolated is also significant; it did not reveal a thriving homosexual community in Walla Walla similar to that found in Portland. While Gibson, like the men caught in the larger city's scandal, suffered notoriety because of his middle-class status, Walla Walla responded to its own differently than how small communities in Oregon reacted to McAllister. In the Garden City, certain substantial local citizens actually rallied around Gibson precisely because he had engaged in local and regional social work that all could agree promoted goodwill in the city. Although no one would forgive him his crime, many spoke on Gibson's behalf. J. G. Kelly explained in the *Bulletin* that to write of Gibson in "connection with this matter has been one of the most painful duties of my existence. John Gibson was more than an employe. He was a friend in the full meaning of the word. Until two days ago I held him in the highest esteem." The editor further noted his admiration for Gibson's courage in the face of disgrace. Then, only months after Gibson began serving his sentence, the Reverend Mr. Brooks wrote to the Washington State Penitentiary Board of Pardons, declaring that "[a]part from this one crime Mr. Gibson has been regarded as an unusually worthy and capable citizen[;] ... he has given of his time and strength to promote public interests." Brooks further attested that he felt Gibson's penitence was sincere and begged for his pardon, personally asking that the prisoner be released into his custody at his new home in Berkeley, California. Moreover, both Brooks and Kelly expressed the belief that Gibson's crime was a fluke, appealing to the older explanation for "degeneracy" still prevalent in those smaller communities that apparently had little contact with the emerging middle-class homosexual subculture. For Kelly and Brooks, Gibson's transgression had resulted from physical exhaustion or some sort of nervous breakdown. Unlike the men in the big city of Portland, he was not a homosexual. Kelly also was confident that time served in the penitentiary would undoubtedly reform Gibson; he could be changed back into "a useful member of society." Gibson's support from residents of Walla Walla and eventually, as his prison file reveals, from others from around the country who knew him seems to have convinced the Board of Parole. Within eighteen months of entering the penitentiary, the former YMCA secretary was on his way to Seattle to start a new life.[60]

The meanings of sexuality and gender were sharply realigned during the last years of the nineteenth and the first years of the twentieth century. That realignment contributed yet another dimension to the general upheaval of the Progressive era. America at the beginning of the previous century struggled with the turmoil caused by rapid urbanization, industrialization, vast immigration, imperialism, racism, warfare, women's demands for social justice, and class strife. It was in this atmosphere that modern homosexual identity and homosexual subcultures and communities were able to form and make their first appearance. Not surprisingly, in doing so they necessarily became caught up in the broader political currents of the time—as the stories related here of Portland's early-twentieth-century class struggles, the political and legal activities of E. S. J. McAllister, and the relatively limited ramifications of John Gibson's "degeneracy" in Walla Walla all demonstrate. The appearance of "homosexuality" at this time had implications beyond sex, sexuality, and morality. In Portland, homosexuality and homosexuals became one more tool to be employed by local forces engaged in a long-standing conflict between the classes.

E. S. J. McAllister's association with some of the most radical and therefore divisive reform causes of the time increased the enmity shown him once he was exposed for his same-sex sexual activities. For example, by connecting this attorney to the referendum on funding the University of Oregon, the editor of the *Eugene Daily Guard* devised an explanation for the school's political and financial woes that satisfied himself, local residents, and the university community. McAllister's previous celebrity in Oregon and then infamy in the Portland scandal combined to transform him into a lightening rod for local anguish in Eugene. At the same time, in Portland certain forces chose to use McAllister's social prominence against him and the class he represented. In other communities where McAllister had been politically active, he became the target of sexual innuendo.

At first glance, the case of John Gibson appears very different. In a small and less socially and politically complex Northwest community, the discovery of same-sex sexual activities, even at a time when a similar scandal had the region in an uproar, did not generate the response seen in Portland. Moreover, Gibson's immediate repentance and the substantial support he enjoyed from locals shielded him from the kind of public humiliation suffered by McAllister. Nonetheless, the conclusion to be drawn about what happened is largely the same for Walla Walla as for Portland and Eugene: the political and social climate of the community and the reputation of the accused directly affect the community's response to his perceived transgressions.

In different ways, towns and cities as diverse as Portland, Eugene, and even to a lesser extent Walla Walla utilized early-twentieth-century revelations about homosexuals and homosexual subculture to further a variety of political causes that lacked any apparent connection to issues of sex. But Portlanders, Oregonians, and other residents of the Northwest would not simply turn the Rose City's revelations about homosexuality to these tangential political ends. More important for individuals with same-sex desires, in the wake of the Portland's scandal reformers also undertook a vigorous campaign designed specifically to persecute them. The next chapter examines this development.

CHAPTER 6

Reforming Homosexuality in the Northwest

Two weeks into the 1912 scandal, Portland authorities prepared a brief about "newly" uncovered local homosexual conditions for submission to federal officials. They believed their evidence showed that members of the "vice clique" had used a secret "code" to maintain communications with others of "their kind" on the West Coast. In addition, Portland "inverts" reportedly had ties to a house of male prostitution operating in San Francisco. One journalist announced that the brief connected "the local ring [to] a monster 'vice system' in many other parts of the country, corresponding in some ways to the white slave traffic only not so well organized." The same reporter also insisted that federal authorities had already descended on Portland to clean up this "end...of the system."[1]

Drawing on this inflammatory material, and perhaps aware of the U.S. Immigration Commission's recent admonition to federal legislators not to overlook the existence of a "traffic in boys and men for immoral purposes," Oregon's enigmatic U.S. Congressman A. W. Lafferty leaped into action (figure 13). Lafferty, who represented the Portland area, first won office in 1910 and had been reelected only about a week before homosexuality made the headlines. On the morning of November 27, Lafferty pledged that upon his return to Washington he would seek congressional action on what he believed was a nationwide problem. Once back East, Lafferty announced his hopes of establishing a federal commission to investigate and "stamp out infamous crimes," applying the Interstate Act to same-sex sexual transgressors, turning congressional attention to the homosexual problem in the District of Columbia, and using

Justice Department spies to aid state authorities in gathering evidence. Apparently anticipating that immediate action would spring from such rhetoric, Portland's U.S. District Attorney John McCourt called on local residents to come forward if they had evidence that the practices recently uncovered were "interstate" in extent. He also awaited the signal to implement his "machinery" and "get busy" on the local cases.[2] But it never came. Other than rousing the interest of congressmen from some "other states" and consulting with representatives from the Department of Justice and the Public Health and Marine Hospital Service, Lafferty did little; he seems never to have introduced a bill in Congress regarding homosexuality. By mid-December 1912, Lafferty's activities, whatever they may have been, no longer received mention in the columns of Northwest newspapers. Apparently, the Oregon representative had lost interest in this nascent national crusade. This pattern of much bluster and little action is typical of Lafferty's demagogic record as an elected official; his second term proved a disappointment and Lafferty lost in the next election. Ironically, a few years later he became ensnared in his own sex scandal. In 1919 a Portland grand jury indicted him for contributing to the delinquency of a fourteen-year-old-girl. By the time authorities reached his downtown offices to place him under arrest, Lafferty had fled the city for Missouri, the state where he was born.[3]

While Lafferty's actions produced little federal activity, a considerably more concerted and far-reaching reformist campaign against homosexuality took place throughout the Northwest as a result of the 1912 scandal. The immediate response is appropriately understood within the context of more general developments that occurred between 1890 and 1930. Even before the Portland scandal, for instance, citizens and public and private organizations were expressing concern over same-sex sexuality; but it was especially afterward, in various corners of the region, that reformers launched investigations into conditions that might contribute to homosexual vice, redefined and strengthened sodomy laws, worked to limit and shape public discussion of homosexuality, and expanded and harshened the punishments used to deal with same-sex sexual offenders.

These diverse reform endeavors both converged with and diverged from the Progressive era's response to opposite-sex sexual expression and transgressions. To make possible a fuller grasp of the period's social reaction to same-sex sex crimes and offenders, this chapter begins by briefly surveying concomitant reform activities addressing "heterosexual" immorality. I then examine varied legal and reformist responses to

FIGURE 13. A. W. Lafferty, ca. 1910. Lafferty was
U.S. representative from Portland when the 1912
YMCA scandal occurred. He pledged to ignite a
national crusade against homosexuality in Washington, D.C. Although his efforts were short-
lived, they did draw same-sex affairs to the attention of a number of federal authorities and
politicians holding national office. Oregon
Historical Society, #OrHi 27734.

same-sex sexual practices and homosexuality from 1890 to 1930, emphasizing the role of the 1912 scandal in pushing them forward.

Progressive-Era Moral Reform: Monitoring Opposite-Sex Relations in the Northwest

In the late nineteenth century myriad economic, social, and cultural changes, sometimes ambiguously referred to by historians as the "modernization" process, confronted American society with problems seemingly more complex and intractable than ever. In response, citizens from all walks of life, but especially from the middle classes, undertook a campaign of redress popularly referred to as the "Progressive reform movement." Infused with a sense of optimism, altruism, efficiency, and professionalism, Progressives worked for a variety of improvements in society from the local to the national levels. For example, they implemented zoning laws and building codes, constructed city parks, established the commission system of municipal government, created national forests, introduced the initiative and referendum, tackled industrial pollution, professionalized the civil service, regulated monopolies, and amended the U.S. Constitution to permit the direct election of senators and to give women the vote.[4]

Reformers also reacted to moral "problems" caused in part by the era's sexual revolution. At the national level, Congress passed the Mann Act in 1910 to counter white slavery. During World War I the War Department worked with the American Social Hygiene Association to educate recruits about venereal diseases and to police prostitution near military installations. Portland became the first city voluntarily to build a wartime venereal isolation center for women. This project set the standard for the national urban anti-venereal program that Oregon's U.S. Senator George Chamberlain outlined in the Chamberlain-Kahn Act of 1918.[5] However, most moral reformers concentrated their efforts at the local level, placing greater emphasis where they felt they could have maximum impact. In particular, they targeted the quickly growing metropolis, believing that its dance halls, vaudeville and movie theaters, amusement parks, saloons, boardinghouses and hotels, and crowded thoroughfares provided fertile ground for depravity to take root. Dozens of America's larger municipalities sponsored vice commissions. In the Northwest, Portland was the only major city to authorize such an investigative body. Like many other vice commissions, Portland's concentrated on female prostitution.[6]

At both the national and local levels, some reformers felt that immorality could best be combated by breaking "the conspiracy of silence," a central tenet of Victorian-era decency. Victorian morality held that too much publicity about sexual matters might plant unclean thoughts where before none had existed and thereby lead to individual and ultimately social corruption. But beginning in the 1890s, the increasing public discussion of sex could no longer be contained. After the turn of the century the newly emerging social hygiene movement, embraced especially by public health officials and medical doctors, went on the offensive. Its adherents proposed that moral depravity grew not from publicity but rather from ignorance. Consequently, they advocated a new era of progress in which sex education and public enlightenment would squelch vice and disease.[7]

The social hygienists' promotion of the frank discussion of some sexual matters is exemplified in Portland's Progressive endeavors. In 1908 local physicians, the reformist mayor Harry Lane, and then-governor George Chamberlain founded the Social Hygiene Society. In 1911 it reorganized into the Social Hygiene Society of Portland (soon of Oregon) and became affiliated with the American Federation for Sex Hygiene. At the inaugural conference, it flung open its doors to all reformers and concerned citizens and provided them with straightforward discussion and lectures on topics such as masturbation, venereal diseases, and the sexual activities of youths. Soon, the Oregon Social Hygiene Society (OSHS) hit the road with programs, slide shows, and conferences. During the next few years its representatives visited many towns in the state and sometimes traveled to Idaho and Washington. The society also furnished the public with circulars and bibliographies and left placards in public restrooms. All of these candidly addressed various aspects of the sex and vice "problem." Among the pamphlets that the society published were *A Reasonable Sex Life for a Man, Vigorous Manhood,* and *Masturbation.* OSHS also operated a free Portland clinic providing advice for boys and men who wished to learn about "all sexual disorders and diseases," including how to "eradicate bad habits." As an outreach to the denizens of the North End, OSHS even hosted an exhibit there on the social emergency. The display eventually made its way to the state fair. So well-known and lauded had it become that in November 1913 municipal officials in distant Lyons, France, invited OSHS to send the exhibit to its international exposition.[8]

During these years, OSHS's lectures, pamphlets, clinics, and exhibits concentrated on opposite-sex relations. The organization, like the social hygiene movement nationwide, wished to halt the spread of venereal diseases by curtailing female prostitution. It also desired to replace the Victorian double standard, which had turned a blind eye to the indiscretions of young men while it required women to remain chaste until marriage, with a single standard of sexual purity for both males and females. As the national movement worked toward these goals, it naturally experienced backlash from "traditionalists" who remained convinced that any discussion of sex would bring about ruin. Nonetheless, the various activities undertaken by OSHS and other groups did succeed in breaking down Victorian barriers against public discourse on sex, with such success that in 1914 William Trufant Foster, the president of OSHS, confidently announced to a national audience that the "conspiracy of silence...is now broken." The new candor that developed between 1905 and 1914 has been labeled by the historian John C. Burnham the first revolution in American attitudes toward sex. Yet this breaking of the conspiracy of silence did not necessarily mean that all subjects were now fair game. Jeffery P. Moran has pointed out that because social hygiene workers still harbored some of the traditional concerns about the possible corrupting influence of sex information, they closely regulated their "open" treatment, confining themselves to rather scientific (and therefore what proved to be rather boring) discussions of reproduction and relatively few other matters.[9]

Some scholars have emphasized the Progressives' backward-looking sentiments, but the historian Robert H. Wiebe has argued that the reformers who best exemplified the period were those who embraced modern social developments, drawing their inspiration and their course of action from them. Although Wiebe did not consider moral reform in detail, it is clear that vice commissions and social hygiene societies often behaved like the forward-looking reform movements that he had in mind. Not only did they open up, while still regulating, the discussion of sex as well as work to curtail the double standard, but they also embraced the use of the modern interventionist state in order to achieve their goals. The municipality of Portland, for example, created and funded a vice commission and eventually adopted as law some of that organ's recommendations regarding female prostitution. Also thanks to this commission, city authorities overhauled the police department and during World War I established the women's detention home. In 1913 the Oregon legislature, again at the urging of the Portland Vice Commission, enacted a law to abate prostitution and created a morals court for the Rose City.[10] Unlike the vice commissions that municipal governments sponsored, social hygiene societies like the one in Portland usually began as private organizations. But they also pressed for laws regulating public morals. OSHS executed a successful lobbying campaign that culminated in the state legislature's adopting a 1913 bill prohibiting quacks from advertising their "remedies" for sex maladies. Pressure from OSHS also led to better enforcement of the curfew ordinance in Portland.[11]

Together vice commissions and social hygiene societies helped influence a significant development of the era—the proliferation of municipal ordinances, state laws, and federal legislation regulating sex and morality. On the surface this development seems a blatant attempt on the part of social reformers to circumscribe individuals' sex activities and sexuality. A closer look, however, suggests that the approach to opposite-sex relations was somewhat different. Take, for example, the "crackdown" on prostitution. It is true that once the Oregon legislature adopted its abatement statute in 1913, the red-light district in Portland was legally outlawed. A similar scenario played out in towns and cities across the country between 1909 and the end of World War I. This attack on the "social evil" has led some historians to conclude that by 1920 "the red-light district had passed into history; the system of commercialized prostitution that reigned in American cities for almost half a century was destroyed."[12] But despite such abatement laws, various other statutes and ordinances, vice commissions, and periodic reform crusades, prostitution was still flourishing at the conclusion of the Progressive era: it had simply been driven underground. Case studies of various cities across the country, including Portland and Boise in the Northwest, show the same thing happening. Moreover, the powers that be in these municipalities continued to turn a blind eye to the commerce in sex.[13]

Beyond this official hesitancy to extirpate female sex work, the state legislatures that busily expanded the number of laws regulating sex made the laws considerably more specific, thus liberating opposite-sex relations from the broadly worded moral laws of the past. Legislatures also worked subtly to ease penalties on certain adult "heterosexual" sex "crimes," such as adultery, seduction, and pimping. In Washington State in 1891, for example, an individual convicted of adultery might be punished with a penitentiary sentence of not more than three years, or with a fine not exceeding three hundred dollars *and* a stay in the county jail not longer than one year. But by 1917, a convicted adulterer would receive no more than two years in the penitentiary or a fine of not more than one thousand dollars—a considerable reduction in maximum jail time, and the possibility of no imprisonment at all (though the possible fine increased). In another significant change, by 1917 the prosecution of adultery required the complaint of the offended spouse. Under the more broadly worded earlier law, the case could conceivably be initiated by anyone, including the state. The crime of seduction underwent a similar change in treatment. The 1854 territorial law prescribed a sentence of one to ten years in the penitentiary or a fine not to exceed five hundred dollars along with confinement in the county jail for no more than a year. In 1909 the state assembly passed legislation that raised the possible monetary penalty, but decreased the time behind bars; the minimum penitentiary sentence was dropped and the maximum was reduced to five years. And for this crime as well, initiating prosecution was made more difficult: a seduction case could move forward only if it was first determined that the alleged victim had previously maintained a "chaste" character. Finally, a pimp, whether a husband who pressured his wife into selling her body or a man who lived off the earnings of a prostitute, also saw penalties decline over the years. In 1903 the Washington courts would slap such a man with a penitentiary sentence of anywhere between one and five years and a fine of between one thousand and five thousand dollars. By 1909, though the maximum stint in the pen was still five years, the fine was reduced to not more than two thousand dollars.[14]

In some ways, the Washington State legislature made more specific the meaning of and lessened the penalties for the crime of rape. In 1897 the law provided a sentence of up to life for a male who had unforced intercourse with any female who was under eighteen. But by 1909 a man who had unforced intercourse with a female who was between fifteen and eighteen years old would face no more than ten years in the penitentiary or no more than one year in the county jail. Moreover, as was true of seduction, the prosecution would now also have to prove that the alleged victim previously had a "chaste character" before the charge of rape could go forward.[15]

In the Northwest, persistent ambivalence toward female sex work and the gradual easing of restrictions on opposite-sex sexual relations simply exemplified a broader Western trend of the period: the emergence and normalization of the notion of "heterosexuality"—that is, opposite-sex erotic desire—and the expression of it outside the framework of marriage and reproduction. This sexual system came to replace Victorian-era sexual morality, in which scholars have noted a great irony. On the one hand, the Victorians accepted the double standard and tolerated prostitution as a necessary evil; on the other hand, they held that sexual relations should ideally be confined to marriage and engaged in only for procreation. All expressions of sex that did not fit the ideal were tabooed and severely penalized. A host of interrelated social changes at the end of the nineteenth century led to an alteration in this view: opposite-sex relations were associated less with reproduction (and thus less with marriage) than with pleasure. As society accepted this standard, its laws began to reflect the shift, decreasing the penalties for and eventually decriminalizing altogether certain forms of nonmarital, adult, opposite-sex sexual relations.

As Michel Foucault and other historians have shown, this legitimation of heterosexuality led to the greater stigmatization and scrutiny of homosexuality and other sexualities that threatened the new norm. In consequence, as the Northwest illustrates, as laws governing certain aspects of adult heterosexual relations relaxed and the open discussion of such sexuality became more acceptable, society worked to increase regulation of same-sex sexual activities. It likewise attempted to control public discourse on the issue of homosexuality. Indeed, the hope largely seemed to be to silence same-sex affairs. However, as Foucault pointed out with regard to sex in general, attempts to impose a new "conspiracy of silence" on the subject of homosexuality inadvertently increased the discussion of it.[16]

Regulating Public Discourse and Preventing the Spread of Homosexuality to Youths

Attempts to regulate discourse on opposite-sex relations during the Victorian era naturally spilled over into same-sex activities as well. For much of the nineteenth century the legal system's wording for the sexual penetration of one male by another never went beyond the "crime against nature" or the "crime which could not be named." Only once in nineteenth-century Oregon did a legal proceeding even remotely related to sodomy make its way into official publication. In that case, a middle-aged Portland street commissioner, Jacob Shartle, sued W. I. Hutchinson for slander after Hutchinson publicly denounced him as a sodomite. In court documents the Oregon judiciary refused to employ the English language in referencing the offense of which Hutchinson accused Shartle. Instead it preferred the Latin phrase *pecatum illud inter christianos non nominandum*—or, "the sin that must not be named among Christians."[17]

By the end of the nineteenth century judicial records became more specific in their definition of same-sex sex crime, yet a certain degree of vagueness and a reluctance to be explicit persisted. In 1912, for instance, an Oregon court charged a man with having "grossly disturbed the public peace and health and openly outraged public decency and injured public morals" when he committed certain acts that were just "too filthy and unmentionable & obscene to spread upon the records of this court[.]" Four years later the Idaho Supreme Court referred to sodomy periphrastically as "one of the most heinous and unspeakable forms of crime." Such phrasing, whether in Latin or English, endeavored to cover up specifics. But it is also true that despite the reluctance of the courts to name the crime, these legal tribunals also recognized that society was hardly ignorant of such matters. In 1913, when E. S. J. McAllister was indicted for the "crime against nature," the state added that "said crime being too well understood and too disgusting to be herein more fully set forth."[18]

In 1909 the Washington State legislature attempted to limit public discussion of same-sex sexual activities. A new statute made it a misdemeanor for "[e]very person who shall publish, and every proprietor, manager or editor who shall permit to be published, in any book, newspaper, magazine or other printed publication" any detailed account of sodomy, or of a similar sex offense, or of the trial of someone for such a crime.[19] Ironically, in making this law the legislature had to engage the topic of sodomy; it also necessarily published its deliberations on the subject in its session-ending journals and legal compendiums. Even in the absence of such a law, however, the public press in the Northwest seldom reported on same-sex sexuality. When the occasional item appeared, editors ordinarily included few details. The notable exception to this common practice is the Oscar Wilde affair of 1895 — but as discussed in earlier chapters, the historical, upper-class, and European context of that case made it possible for Americans generally to view Wilde's actions as having little relevance to anything happening in the United States. Thus papers could report rather openly on the scandal without worrying about the possible harm to their readers' morals.[20]

Conditions in 1912 were different. At first glance the wide-ranging coverage of Portland's scandal appears to indicate a lack of desire to regulate the public discussion of homosexuality. On closer inspection, we see that a good portion of the scandal and publicity was attached not so much to the vice ostensibly being reported on but rather to the working-class *News*'s use of reports about homosexual conditions to aid its long-standing struggle against local elites. Moreover, when the establishment press reacted to the *News*, it expressly condemned that paper's willingness to report so broadly on same-sex sexual matters, fearing that such stories would popularize "unspeakable practices." Already on November 17, the *Oregon Journal* avowed that the *News*'s coverage was "printed for degenerates to feed on and an effective agency for aiding the spread of degeneracy among youth." The *Journal*'s editor continued:

An army of young boys peddling this scarlet infamy at five cents a copy is seed sown for spread of the unspeakable practice. With curiosity excited, every child and boy in Portland will sooner or later learn the facts, and thereby will be laid the foundation for infection and contamination. In the whole history of Portland, no more damnable influence has been spread broadcast for the contamination of youth than is this scarlet story, told in scarlet headlines.[21]

Of course, when this Rose City paper rebuked another for its free discussion of same-sex affairs, it did so publicly.

Moral reformers purposely broke the Victorian "conspiracy of silence" on a variety of (opposite) sex issues in the early twentieth century in order to eradicate the ignorance that had, they believed, led to physical and moral disease. In this endeavor, however, they also tried to retain rigid control over the subject. In responding to the issue of same-sex sexuality, the same "Progressives," like the *Oregon Journal*'s editor, similarly insisted on controlling that subject, and doing so completely; they demanded its entire exclusion from public discussion, for even its mention would bring about individual and social ruin. Ironically, these demands were often put forth publicly. Thus, the final report of Portland's Vice Commission, completed on the heels of the 1912 scandal, contained more than two hundred pages, but only one-half of one page focused on "sex perversion." The commissioners refused to report more because "it could do no possible good to set out those details which are within its knowledge, and might do irremediable injury."[22] But that some details were in fact put forth seems to have contradicted their stated hopes.

Indeed, much of Portland's reformist reaction to the 1912 scandal concerned the very issues that so worried the Vice Commission. That is, middle-class reformers expressed considerable anxiety over injury that the public discussion of homosexuality might do to society, an anxiety that ultimately focused on the safety of the local youth. The *Oregon Journal* captured this sentiment best when it charged that the *News*'s sensational headlines would no doubt excite the curiosity of every boy who peddled the newspaper—"and thereby will be laid the foundation for infection and contamination." But the *News* also feared, in its own way, for the city's youths, claiming in one horrified statement that "[w]herever boys gather there do degenerates gather to prey on them." Dana Sleeth constantly appealed in his editorials to citizens concerned about the "safety" of the city's boys. For example, he asked the "clean fathers of boys, whether you prefer the policy of The News or of its critics." In another instance, a headline claimed "THE MOTHERS ARE WITH THE NEWS IN THIS FIGHT—READ AND SEE." One "mother" responded, "Perhaps if the mothers and fathers of the boy victims in this case had known of such crimes, and warned their boys, they would have discovered the demon who was wearing the cloak of friendship for boys." Others in the city expressed similar concerns about the dangers that homosexuality presented to youth. The Vice Commission avowed that those who "engaged in homosexual practices... seduce young boys." And Mayor A. G. Rushlight publicly pledged municipal assistance to state officials as part of his duty to advance the "safety of the boys of the city."[23]

Portland's scandal erupted in an atmosphere charged with anxiety over the perceived breakdown of the middle-class family and the threat that working-class, racial minority, immigrant, and transient men seemingly posed to it, especially through their sexual relations with boys. When locals discovered that a few of the middle-class men arrested in 1912 had residential or employment links to the YMCA—a youth-focused organization—the revelation only served to further associate homosexuality with the endangerment of the boy, as the News's headlines demonstrate. As noted in chapter 3, the abundant surviving documents definitively link very few under the age of eighteen to the scandal. Yet as it covered the affair, the News reported on many other local cases of male-male sex crime that had no connection with the middle-class scandal. These arrests of working-class men and youths, which were frequently carried out by the authorities particularly in the North End, normally would have earned little or no space in the paper; but now, as the reports appeared beside columns overtly treating the 1912 scandal, they heightened fears over the role of boys in any type of same-sex sexual underworld, as well as over the pervasiveness of the "problem." Yet the age of many of those arrested in 1912—in their late teens and early twenties, they were still considered boys—probably most influenced the public to conclude that homosexuality and homosexuals (like working-class and racial minority males) imperiled youth. Moreover, the persistence of older ideas of degeneracy—in particular, the notion that it was something contagious—also fed into anxieties about the vulnerability of boys.

Not surprisingly, in the wake of the 1912 scandal many reformers concentrated their efforts on the boy, hoping to save him from homosexuality. Portland's influential Congregational minister Luther Dyott, for instance, urged greater parental supervision. "Want of parental control," he averred at a meeting held conspicuously at the YMCA, "is responsible for the vice conditions that have recently been revealed."[24] In addition, the city's middle-class mothers, like the *Oregon Journal,* grew anxious that the most impressionable of newsboys had become exposed to same-sex immorality as they hawked the *News*'s "lurid" headlines on the city's streets. In the spring of 1913, a number of women's organizations lobbied for a municipal ordinance requiring newsboys to be at least twelve years old. The proposal created quite a stir among working-class households that depended on the income of their boys who sold newspapers. After a considerable political struggle, the city council compromised by setting a minimum age of ten. Although ultimately this reform did not entirely succeed, fears over the supposed corrupting influences of same-sex sexual activities helped set it in motion.[25]

A more concerted response to the "boy problem" came from the Oregon Social Hygiene Society. In November 1912, immediately after the scandal broke, it launched a multifaceted plan that took a novel approach to thwarting the spread of same-sex sexual "vice" to the city's youth. In order to block the possibility that the "seed of abnormality" might be planted as a result of a frank consideration of homosexuality, a fear widespread at the time, OSHS positively and aggressively promoted breaking the conspiracy of silence on matters of opposite-sex sexuality. It thereby intended to stimulate heterosexual thoughts in youths and young men. Budgetary concerns also played an indirect but crucial role in OSHS's response to the 1912 scandal: the organization used anxieties over homosexuality and the vulnerability of youths to push for state funding for its broader reform crusade.[26]

In its first pragmatic move OSHS revamped its Advisory Department. On November 15 the society decreed that its outreach office would henceforth "cater as little as possible to older men and those who are diseased and that its chief function shall be to assist young men and boys by wise council [*sic*]"—in other words, the relatively innocent who still might be safeguarded.[27] Second, OSHS acted to influence the Committee of 15, which quickly expanded into the Committee of 50. Local business and professional men formed the two investigative bodies as a means to silence the *News* and to examine the "vicious conditions alleged to exist in the city." A member of OSHS, Rabbi Jonah Wise, sat on the three-person panel that formulated the committee's goals. He and several others from the society—most prominent among them William Trufant

Foster and its then-president, Dr. Calvin S. White—served in the two organizations. On December 12 the Committee of 50 issued its first report,
which condemned the *News,* contending that its coverage of "degeneracy" brought about "the contamination of innocent minds." It also called
on parents to become more active in monitoring their children's affairs, a
relatively conservative approach. But in a sign of the influence of OSHS
members, the Committee of 50 took the radical step of demanding sex
education in the public school system. OSHS had advocated such a curriculum for some months, battling the social taboos against discussing
sex with children without success; now the "vicious" moral dilemma facing Portland breathed new hope into their cause. Indeed, the Committee
of 50 charged that the city's homosexual conditions required that "campaigns for public education as those conducted by the Social Hygiene
Society" be undertaken. The Committee of 50 implied that this instruction would check the spread of "vile practices" by implanting "wholesome sex" ideas into the ignorant minds of youth.[28]

The Committee of 50, moreover, called on the state legislature to
provide funding to aid OSHS in these endeavors. The timing of that
plea could not have been more opportune. Early in November, the
Oregon Board of Health, which would have a rocky relationship with
the organization for several years, had pledged to block an appropriations bill that OSHS had planned to have introduced in the upcoming
legislative session. As a result, OSHS's budget committee called for re-
trenchment, warning that the organization had no definite source of income and little hope of receiving public funding. But by December the
situation had considerably brightened for OSHS simply because the
moral outlook in Portland appeared so gloomy. In February 1913 the
state assembly complied with the Committee of 50's request and
granted $20,000 to the organization for the next biennium. Thanks
largely to the specter of sex perversion, OSHS's financial troubles were
at least temporarily over.[29]

Already in January 1913, a month before it received its public revenues,
OSHS sponsored a three-night conference in Portland. The composition
of the gathering was particularly telling: whereas the society's founding
meeting in 1911 had been open to all interested, the organizers of the 1913
conference invited only thirty of the city's *male* educators, physicians,
ministers, and social workers. Among the sessions this select body attended was one titled "What are we going to do about the situation in
Portland?" Following this conference, OSHS initiated its third approach
for dealing with same-sex vice: it applied itself seriously to influencing

the debate on sex education in the public school system. Within a year, the society had won the cooperation of the Oregon Conference of Educators, which endorsed the idea that all teachers should "be prepared" to bring about "a right attitude towards sex" in Oregon's youth. The curriculum backed by the educators stressed the role of sex in personal health, and especially in the opposite-sex issues of reproduction, family, community, and industrial life. Moreover, "perversion in the most threatening sex abnormalities...should not be dwelt upon at length and should be relatively unemphasized." In a separate resolution adopted at the conference, OSHS's Committee on Sex Education for High Schools declared that "the basis of sex instruction should be the *normal,* the abnormal and pathological taking its proper subordinate place."[30] Its substantial support from educators notwithstanding, OSHS could not secure this ambitious sex curriculum. Nonetheless its various activities in the days and even years following the 1912 scandal had a significant social impact. The society's influence on the Committee of 50, its sponsorship of conferences, its impact on the state's educators, and its outreach through its advisory department, as well as its invited appearances at schools and other venues where youths and young men gathered, all helped push forward the ideology of heterosexuality by strictly controlling what would be said on matters related to homosexuality.

Such work as this undoubtedly helped make Portland a city that recoiled from the subject of homosexuality for some years, as Emma Goldman, a prominent socialist agitator, discovered on her visit to the Rose City in 1915. That August, Goldman arrived to speak on a number of subjects. Immediately following her announcement that one of her planned addresses was titled "The Intermediate Sex: A Study of Homosexuality," several Portland residents lodged a protest with the mayor. Josephine De Vore Johnson was among those who conveyed her views on the subject: "I am taking it for granted that it will not be permitted...for the matter to be publicly treated of or for the...unspeakable suggestion to be made.... (There are some young boys who attend Miss Goldman's lectures....So it is especially detrimental to permit this propaganda.)." Contradicting herself later in her long missive, Johnson actually advocated permitting the lecture to go forward, but only "for the sake of gathering complete evidence" so that Goldman might be placed under arrest. In any case, in Johnson's opinion, it "certainly ought not to be repeated in this city." In fact, the Portland police did apprehend Goldman and her colleague Dr. Ben Reitman—for distributing literature on birth control. The colorful C. E. S. Wood defended the two; the court fined them each one hundred dollars and Goldman was set free. She then proceeded with her lectures, including the one on homosexuality.[31]

Less than three months after the visit by Goldman and Reitman, George Edwards reflected on his comrades' recent trouble-filled sojourn in Portland. Although Edwards's main concern was the birth control fiasco, he first considered the hullabaloo over homosexuality. In particular, he noted the effect that the 1912 scandal had had on the city. "Portland," Edwards observed, "was [still] evidently sensitive about it, and like the old time 'ladies' who were properly shocked when anybody mentioned their legs, pretended that she had no such members."[32] Edwards thus hinted that more than the scandal itself had created Portland's stifling atmosphere: the conspiracy to regulate public discourse on homosexuality had played a role as well.

Reforming Homosexual Transgressors and Policing Same-Sex Sexual Relations

As they attempted to control public discourse regarding homosexuality and focused on boys, Northwest moral reformers and state governments during the Progressive era worked also to increase the severity of punishment for men convicted of same-sex sex crimes—with a notable, though brief, exception. For a time the state of Washington operated the "Friend Program." It offered early parole and possibly a complete pardon to men convicted of a variety of crimes, including sodomy, if the offenders could find a sponsor in the community who would take charge of them and provide them with work. Through the Friend Program, Alex Polson, the proprietor of the Polson Logging Company and also a Washington state senator, offered employment to "a good many" men from the penitentiary. Polson particularly interested himself in rehabilitating those who had committed crimes while under the influence of alcohol. One such was John Hayes, a thirty-eight-year-old logger who, while reportedly inebriated, had taken a "young boy" into a lodging room in a small western Washington town and there committed sodomy. When Polson wrote to Hayes in late 1912 about the Friend Program, he vowed to the convict that "[i]f you can promise yourself and us that you will never touch the cursed stuff again we will be glad to do anything for you we can." Hayes made the commitment; in April 1913 he left prison and went to work for Polson in Hoquiam. Six months later the lumber magnate happily informed the penitentiary warden that he "could not ask for a better behaved or more conscientious man amongst men [than Hayes]. . . . I have every confidence that none of us will ever again be disappointed in his conduct."[33]

But not everyone in Washington State approved of allowing men like Hayes to participate in the Friend Program. The Chehalis County sheriff, who had arrested the logger, argued that he "should never be set at liberty" because what he had done "was the most revolting [thing] I have heard in court for a long while." The potential parole into the Friend Program of another man succeeded in tearing open one Washington community. Early in 1912 William Boyd, a farmer and six-year resident of Kingston (located on the western shore of Puget Sound), was convicted of attempting the crime of sodomy with a youth whom he employed. Shortly after his penitentiary confinement, seventeen of his friends and supporters petitioned the Board of Pardons for his release and return to his home under the sponsorship of G. R. Wallace, who promised him work cutting shingle bolts. These petitioners maintained that Boyd's past record in the community "was good" and they believed that he had "sufficiently Paid the Penalty for his offense." But others in Kingston had a different opinion, and their opposing petition charged that those who advocated Boyd's release were "an irresponsible and small number of our residents." They further declared Boyd a "vulture" and a "menace to our homes and children and to all we hold dear. Not even can the spirit of charity or sympathy be invoked for the prisoner for he is without family or friends, save the misguided ones who are trying to effect his release." Nearly seventy individuals affixed their signatures to this circular, which was conveyed directly to the governor.[34]

Boyd's supporters and opponents made their pleas just as the six-month minimum sentence for the crime he committed expired. The state's parole board waited another year before it returned the convict to his community under the Friend Program, possibly showing deference to the wishes of the hostile petitioners from Kingston. That the board even brushed aside the recommendation of the judge and the prosecuting attorney in the case, both of whom spoke of Boyd's previous good record and had counseled the prison to parole him as early as possible, suggests that it did take their concerns seriously.[35] But whatever the reason for the delay, the majority feeling running through the coastal community reflected general developments across the region: from the late nineteenth through the early twentieth centuries, society reacted with increasing ferocity against men convicted of same-sex sexual crimes and demanded tougher punishment from them.

Northwest states through the Progressive era made the penalties on same-sex sex offenders harsher as they expanded and strengthened laws against sodomy. Typically, they did so when their statutes regulating same-sex offenses were challenged. Such proved to be the case in Idaho and Montana, which adopted identical sodomy statutes in 1864 and 1865, respectively, prescribing a possible sentence of life imprisonment. In Montana in 1915 and in Idaho in 1916, similar appeals from men convicted under these statutes came before the states' supreme courts. In both instances, the appellants contended that "the infamous crime against nature" was anal penetration solely and thus the oral sex acts that they had committed and had been indicted for fell outside the limits of the law. An important precedents that the lawyers for the appellants cited in their arguments in the Montana case was English common law, which held that *sodomy* meant only "anal penetration." In Idaho, defense attorneys pointed to *Prindle v. Texas,* an 1873 judgment that had reversed a lower court ruling because the Texas sodomy law did not expressly include oral sex. In both the Montana and Idaho appeals, however, the courts rejected these arguments as simply contravening common sense: the justices had no doubt that when the territorial legislatures had used the phrase "against nature," they had included in its meaning the use of the mouth in sex acts. In making its decision, the Montana court even relied on a similar opinion handed down by the Oregon Supreme Court in one of the 1912 Portland cases. In any event, the courts in both states set precedents for the future, interpreting the laws so that they could be applied broadly and without question to cases involving oral sex. These Idaho and Montana decisions mirrored the national trend.[36]

The state of Washington, through both judicial and legislative action, also altered its laws relating to same-sex sex crimes when those who were accused pointed out their inadequacies. The Washington assembly failed before 1893 to draw up a statute that criminalized sodomy, although there was a law on the books that punished the *attempt* to commit "the infamous crime against nature." In 1892 Lewis County authorities arrested H. C. Place after he performed sodomy on a youth. They charged him with the only offense they thought indictable: an attempt to commit the act. After the jury found Place guilty, Place's lawyers, on appeal, cleverly argued to the state's highest tribunal that their client could not have attempted to commit a crime because in fact the legislature had not made the "infamous crime against nature" a "crime." Although the Washington court reversed the lower court's verdict for another reason (the judge had permitted members of the jury to separate and mingle with a crowd before deliberation, and thus their impartiality had been tainted), it rejected this particular argument, declaring that under the 1881 Washington Code the legislature had made *all* common-law crimes indictable. Nevertheless, the Place case persuaded the 1893 Washington assembly finally to adopt a sodomy law. The new statute, furthermore, removed possible confusion over the meaning of "sodomy" and the "crime against nature" (a point typically raised on appeal in such cases at the time) by making the two synonymous. It also punished offenders with imprisonment at hard labor for not less than ten nor more than fourteen years. The assembly approved the law with a single dissenting vote, issued by a legislator who felt the law was "imperfect."[37]

Perhaps this lawmaker anticipated the problems that would eventually lead to the statute's revision. In 1908 Governor Albert Mead appointed a commission of five district attorneys to examine Washington's complete criminal code and suggest modifications to it. Based on their experiences as prosecutors in various parts of the state, the district attorneys recommended augmenting the sodomy statute not only expressly to include penetration of the "anus" (the classic definition of sodomy) but also to cover oral sex, an activity presumably becoming more common. In addition, the panel of lawyers called on the state now to apply the law to the individual who "voluntarily" submitted to sodomy as well as to the one who performed the penetrative role. The assembly made these recommendations law in March 1909. This broadening of the definition of sodomy was in keeping with the era's general practice, but the new law's easing of the penalty—replacing ten to fourteen years of hard labor with a maximum of ten years' imprisonment—was not. Nowhere else in the Pacific Northwest was the punishment for such a crime relaxed during this period (though Canadian national law, which affected British Columbia, in 1886 dropped altogether the minimum penalty for sodomy, while still maintaining the possibility of a life sentence). In Washington the new statute applied to opposite-sex sodomy, too, so perhaps the legislators reduced the penalty as part of another ongoing pattern—the easing of restrictions on various consensual heterosexual acts.[38]

In Oregon the expansion of the sodomy law by both the legislative and judicial branches was a direct result of the 1912 scandal. The statute on the books in 1912 had been adopted by Oregon Territory back in 1853. In keeping with nineteenth-century conventions, the legislature worded the law without many particulars: "Every person who shall commit sodomy, or the crime against nature, either with mankind or any beast, shall, on conviction, be punished[.]" Either because the statute was vague or because it essentially followed common law, some men rounded up in the 1912 scandal believed it pertained only to anal penetration and did not cover oral sex. One young man testified during the trial of Harry Start that the defendant had suggested at the outbreak of the scandal there was no reason to worry, for they had been performing oral sex: "'There isn't anything covering it and they can't do anything with me or you or any of the rest of them.'" When Start took the stand in his own defense, the prosecutor questioned him about whether he had indeed informed this witness, and apparently some other young men as well, that "there was no statute to cover this crime." Naturally, Start denied it. Yet at the commencement of his trial, Start's attorney had made the same argument, citing several cases from other states wherein the courts had ruled that oral sex was not indictable under sodomy statutes similar to Oregon's. The judge in the Start trial, however, ruled against the defense and the trial proceeded. The issue returned again when Start's attorneys appealed their client's conviction.[39]

But months before the Oregon Supreme Court considered the case, the Oregon legislature took action to amend the law. When it became clear as early as December 21, 1912, that Start's appeal would rest partly on this point, the *Oregonian* editor noted that although the Supreme Court would settle the question as to whether the existing sodomy statute was "broad enough to cover the specific offence" of oral sex, the state legislature "will take the proposition up and make the statutes read specifically and definitely along this line." On January 17, 1913, only four days after the session opened, Clifton McArthur, speaker of the house and representative from Portland, introduced House Bill 145 "relating to crimes against nature." In its original form, the bill broadened the 1853 law specifically to include oral sex. When the bill reached the senate, the Committee on Revision of Laws expanded it to include "any act or practice of sexual perversity." Both houses of the legislature passed the revised bill without a dissenting vote. It became law when the governor signed it on January 31.[40]

Meanwhile, the attorneys for Start as well as E. E. Wedemeyer were busily preparing their appeals. Both made the claim that the law under which their clients had been convicted did not apply to oral relations. In late May of 1913, though Oregon's supreme court overturned these men's convictions for other reasons, the justices upheld the notion that the crime against nature necessarily included fellation, offering one of the era's most unusual arguments in doing so. They noted that the mouth and the rectum constitute openings at either end of the alimentary canal.

Food entering one is discharged as waste at the other. The "natural function" of the system is to get nutrition to the body. "It is self evident," the justices opined, "that the use of either opening of the alimentary canal for the purpose of sexual copulation is against the natural design of the human body. In other words, it is an offense against nature."[41]

In the short term, the Oregon legislature's expansion of the sodomy statute was rendered superfluous with the state supreme court's ruling later in the year. However, in 1928 the updated law proved useful to those wishing to convict Clarence Brazell of sodomy for having manually masturbated a teenage boy. Brazell's lawyers appealed his conviction, arguing that the state's sodomy law did not specifically include masturbation. But Oregon's justices immediately dismissed the claim, charging that a man's practicing of masturbation "upon a boy" fell under the "any act of sexual perversity" clause.[42] Thus this latter phrase, which the 1913 Senate Committee on Revision of Laws presciently inserted into the new sodomy statute, became useful to the legal system in the late 1920s and beyond.

But Oregon's 1913 sodomy law had more immediate consequences. The 1853 statute provided a sentence of from one to five years. When McArthur originally introduced his bill to alter the sodomy statute, he suggested increasing both ends of the range. Although the Senate's Committee on Revision of Laws recommended leaving the minimum sentence untouched rather than raising it to three as proposed, they accepted his maximum of fifteen years; thus the final bill tripled the possible time that a man could serve for sodomy or any other act of "sexual perversity." The result was that sentences became longer. Between 1886 and 1906, the fourteen men convicted of sodomy who spent time in Oregon's penitentiary served an average of 18.5 months each; between 1907 and 1916, the twenty-three men convicted of sodomy spent an average of 21.5 months behind bars; and from 1917 to 1926, sixteen men served an average time of 32.7 months in prison.[43]

During the Progressive era, judiciaries in Idaho and Montana ruled that older, broadly worded sodomy laws included oral sex. In Washington the legislature added oral relations to the state's sodomy statute. But Oregon ultimately went further in broadening its definition of sodomy. Not only would that act now include oral relations, but it would also embrace any form of "sexual perversity." This expansion resulted directly from the most upsetting events relating to same-sex sexual activities ever witnessed in the region's history. Yet despite some individual variations, it is clear that over the first two decades of the twentieth century, Idaho,

Montana, and Washington took action similar to Oregon's by expanding the definition of sodomy. In addition, penalties for same-sex sexual activities increased overall in the region. Montana and Idaho and the Canadian law affecting British Columbia retained the possibility of life imprisonment for those convicted of sodomy, and Oregon tripled the maximum sentence to the penitentiary. While it is true that Washington reduced the number of years one might remain behind bars, the state at the same time criminalized sodomy in statute and expanded the definition of that crime. The result was an overall increase in penalty for same-sex sexual expression in that state. During the Progressive era, then, legal systems throughout the Northwest responded to same-sex sexual activities in a way just opposite to how they reacted to heterosexual crimes.

Washington State's Friend Program, the strengthening of sodomy laws, and the increase in prison time for same-sex sex crimes represent only a few of the ways in which some Northwest reformers reacted against homosexual sex and those who engaged in it. In the most draconian of measures, they also advocated and achieved through state-mandated eugenics laws the sterilization of men convicted of sodomy and of men who were homosexuals. In fact, revelations about homosexuality in the Northwest helped sweep aside past concerns that sterilization seriously infringed on the rights of individuals and that it was too cruel and unusual a punishment.

Sterilizing Same-Sex Sex Offenders and Homosexuals

Eugenic ideas evolved in Europe and America during the last third of the nineteenth century. Like so many Western intellectual developments of the period, eugenics is traceable to Social Darwinists' assertions that in modern society there exists a struggle in which the "fit" will survive and the "unfit" will succumb. Eugenists wished to intervene in this process. They were convinced, in the words of the historian Mark H. Haller, that the "continued evolution of man might be assured by preventing the unfit from propagating and encouraging the fit to propagate early and often."[44]

By the early twentieth century, European concerns over social degeneracy and the possibility that Western civilization had entered into decline was influencing some American eugenists. According to one early-twentieth-century observer, these reformers (known as "alarmists") argued that the "nation must defend itself against national degeneration as much as against the external foreign enemy." But this belief never appealed to all eugenists; as discussed in the analysis of America's response to Oscar Wilde and changing notions of degeneracy in chapter 4, this country was thought to be largely immune to such moral decay. Moreover, as Haller contends, the eugenists never could overcome the American notion that the nation's "environment and education would open opportunities so that even the lowliest could rise[.]"[45] Lacking wide appeal, the eugenics crusade was generally engineered and led by specialists, such as physicians, health department officials, superintendents of correctional and mental institutions, and criminologists. These individuals focused on the pragmatic goals of halting the spread of ever-higher rates of crime, reducing the number of inmates in state-operated facilities and thus the tax burden on the public, and preventing the immigration of those deemed not assimilable. Such ends as these, it was believed, would be more attractive to the average American than would grand social theories about the decline of civilization. Thus Bethenia Owens-Adair, one of the Northwest's earliest female physicians and the region's foremost crusader for eugenics, wrote, "I am fully aware that the reduction of taxes is not the highest aim in this matter but feel that it is the appeal that will bring the earliest response."[46]

The formal eugenics movement got under way in the first few years of the twentieth century when a handful of state legislatures legalized involuntary asexualization. Most these new laws prescribed vasectomy and salpingectomy (i.e., surgical removal of the fallopian tubes) for those confined to publicly supported correctional and mental institutions. In Oregon and Washington, Owens-Adair launched the campaign in 1904. Her backers in the legislatures of those two states first introduced her bill in 1907, in both cases without success. Owens-Adair persisted; two years later she returned to Salem and Olympia and won a partial victory: Washington State passed a eugenics law. In its final form, the 1909 statute was punitive in scope, prescribing surgery as a penalty for those guilty of rape or those considered habitual criminals. Although Owens-Adair advocated sterilization as a form of punishment, most eugenists disagreed with her position. For one thing, they felt that the question of punishment complicated their purely eugenic goals. Moreover, they feared that such laws might be declared unconstitutional on the grounds that they mandated cruel and unusual punishment. Nonetheless, in 1912 the Washington State Supreme Court ruled the 1909 law constitutional and it remained on the books in its original form until 1921. While Owens-Adair favored this statute, as the years passed she urged that it be broadened to include more mainstream eugenic and therapeutic objectives.[47]

In her home state of Oregon, Owens-Adair failed yet again to win passage of a eugenics law in 1911. A number of reasons account for her repeated defeats. Some officials thought sterilization a joke, others believed it put too much power in the hands of a few to decide the fate of many, others believed it too harsh a punishment, and yet others raised constitutional issues.[48] Her proposals, submitted in the legislative sessions of 1907, 1909, and 1911, prescribed sterilization for the feebleminded, epileptics, imbeciles, idiots, the insane, prisoners committed for life, confirmed criminals, and rapists. Although technically under these bills a man convicted two or more times of sodomy could be subjected to the knife, at no time during these years did the proposed laws explicitly mention such "criminals." The only sex offenders listed were rapists, and even they were not specifically included in the earliest bills.[49]

The homosexual scandal of 1912 dramatically changed attitudes in Oregon toward a eugenics law. Within days of the staggering revelations, those perceiving a new reason for state-mandated sterilization began to voice their opinions. "It would be far better for Portland and Oregon," the *Oregonian's* editor declared, "if this simple operation were allowable in the case of the perverts who have lately been brought to justice than to shut them up in prison, where they will merely infect all around them with the venom of their disease."[50] The most powerful supporter of the idea that the men involved in the Portland affair should be sterilized was Governor Oswald West (figure 14).

The governor already had an established record on moral reform. For example, in 1912 West had conducted a high-profile statewide crusade against female prostitution. He had also recently spent time with the superintendent of the penitentiary, whose accounts of inmates' same-sex sexual practices had deeply troubled him. West made certain that those convicted for these activities received additional punishment; he ordered the "degenerates" to be kept locked up in the state prison while what he called the "higher type of criminals, such as murderers, highwaymen, bank and train robbers" were permitted greater freedom to work on road crews around the state without the supervision of armed guards.[51] West was thus predisposed to punish same-sex offenders harshly, and after the vice scandal broke he warmly received Owens-Adair's proposal for the upcoming 1913 legislative session. But before incorporating sterilization into his personal package of vice bills, the governor revamped her measure. In particular he insisted that "moral degenerates should be sub-

FIGURE 14. Oswald West, 1910. West was serving as governor of Oregon at the time of Portland's 1912 homosexual scandal. Known for his moral reforms, West pushed the 1913 legislature to adopt its first eugenics law. West called for castration specifically of the men arrested in the scandal and more generally for others who would come before the state's courts for similar sexual transgressions in the future. Oregon Historical Society, #OrHi 6425.

jected to a more drastic surgical operation" than that proposed by the eugenist. In his message to the 1913 legislature, he referred to Portland's offenders as "degenerates who slink, in all their infamy, through every city, contaminating the young, debauching the innocent, cursing the State": for them, "emasculation" was "an effective remedy."[52]

Although mainstream eugenists tended to refrain from arguing for castration, some reformers and physicians in the second decade of the twentieth century increasingly promoted the radical surgery for homosexuals and other men who engaged in same-sex sexual activities. A few medical doctors prescribed and performed it on some male homosexuals in hopes that it would eliminate erotic desires for other men, feelings which their patients reported had cost them their jobs and had harmed their businesses. And reformers such as West and Owens-Adair advocated emasculation as a form of discipline. The latter, for instance, contended that she did "not think . . . that castration, even if it were thought of as a punishment, is a punishment disproportionate to the crimes of rapists and sodomists."[53] To be sure, when enacting eugenics laws it was necessary that state legislatures avoid overtly punitive measures to prevent endless challenges to and possible overturning of the law in court. No doubt such concerns led West to carefully rewrite what became House Bill (HB) 69 in 1913; he in fact contended that Owens-Adair had originally "inartistically drawn" up the measure and it therefore needed reworking.[54] Nevertheless, West's expressed feelings, the actual wording of the law, and also the constellation of events surrounding its passage make clear that the bill allowed castration as a procedure to *punish* homosexuals and other men who engaged in same-sex sexual activities.

At the request of West, Representative L. G. Lewelling of Albany, a former guard at the penitentiary, introduced HB 69 on January 15. It declared "habitual criminals, moral degenerates, and sexual perverts [to be] menaces to the public peace, health and safety." It defined moral degenerates and sexual perverts as "those addicted to the practice of sodomy or the crime against nature, or to other gross, bestial and perverted sexual habits and practices prohibited by statute." Thus, for the first time in the history of eugenics bills in Oregon, the very people whom society increasingly conceptualized as "homosexuals" and who had come to attention in the recent Portland scandal were now singled out and specifically targeted for sterilization. While Oregon's lower legislative chamber considered HB 69, Robert S. Farrell of Portland introduced a similar bill in the senate; but after HB 69 passed the house by a vote of 49–8, the upper chamber voted on and approved the same bill, 16–11. West enthusiastically signed it into law on February 18.[55]

As the vote over the sterilization bill—particularly the closer margin in the senate—suggests, there still existed opposition to eugenics in 1913. In fact, a week after Lewelling introduced the bill, some civic organizations, Oregon's Catholic clergy, and others against sterilization began to mobilize. A number of reformers, including William S. U'Ren and C. E. S. Wood, created the Anti-Sterilization League; after HB 69 became law, it led the campaign to repeal the statute by referendum. In November 1913, Oregon voters overturned the eugenics law by a vote of

53,319 to 41,767.Sentiment against the law focused primarily on the issue of its putting too much power into the hands of a few and on the prescribed treatment, which was seen as simply too cruel a form of punishment. Only one defense of homosexuals during the referendum campaign has come to light. "As to sexual perverts," Duncan Fraser wrote to the *Oregon Journal,* "how often do they propagate themselves? The very nature of their practices makes the likelihood of their having offspring remote."[56] His line of argument makes it clear that Fraser accepted the emergent notion that those who engaged in relations with members of their own sex were by definition homosexuals, who did not engage in procreative acts with the opposite sex, but it also reveals that he misunderstood the purpose of Oregon's sterilization law. Fraser spoke to the mainstream, traditional eugenic idea that asexualization would protect society from unwanted traits' being passed down to subsequent generations, but the law's designers intended that it *punish* those who committed same-sex acts, most notably the homosexual.

The outcome of the 1913 referendum in no way curtailed the eugenics campaign, which had undergone significant change. Because of Portland's scandal, the influence of Governor West, and the wording of the short-lived 1913 law, eugenists in Oregon had added to their arsenal a whole new rationale for sterilization: vengeance against homosexuals. Future eugenics bills would have to couch punitive aims carefully; but from 1913 onward, sterilization measures that the Oregon legislature considered and approved would take aim at same-sex offenders and homosexuals.

Eugenics proponents introduced bills into each chamber in 1917. Some lawmakers argued that they should abide by the wishes of the people, who had repealed the similar 1913 statute. Nonetheless, the legislature passed the house version of the bill, which the supportive Governor James Withycombe signed into law on February 19. It prescribed sterilization for the same groups as the 1913 law. But the 1917 version took pains to answer the most serious concerns of the 1913 critics. For example, it put authority to decide who should be sterilized into the hands of the newly created State Board of Eugenics. This panel would be composed of members of the Board of Health and the superintendents of various penal and mental institutions around the state. The new statute also permitted a more elaborate appeals process for the persons targeted for surgery. To avoid the charge of cruel and unusual punishment, it prescribed emasculation only in the case "that such operation . . . be found necessary to improve the physical, mental, neural or psychic condition of the inmate." Yet the law not only permitted but in some instances prescribed castration.[57]

A report from the Commission to Investigate the Oregon State Penitentiary that appeared in January 1917 likely influenced the legislature's favorable consideration of the eugenics bill, and in particular its continued advocacy of castration of homosexuals. This prison commission examined a variety of conditions at the penitentiary, including "the existence of vice among inmates." The investigators concluded that sodomy occurred in "alarming proportions" and agreed that "for the most part it is the result of the two men to the cell system." The commission urged implementing the "one man to the cell system.... at the earliest possible moment" and also felt it necessary to take additional steps against those inmates who evinced "congenital homo-sexuality." Because, the commission members of the board claimed, isolation would have no correctional value for these men and vasectomy would not obliterate sexual desire, it was necessary to enact a "well guarded law, providing for castration."[58] This disturbing report thus demanded that sterilization be mandated to punish homosexuals in ways that went beyond the 1913 law: the knife would be employed in an attempt to eliminate a state-recognized inborn desire that society deemed simply unacceptable for men to harbor. This prescription for castration ultimately fit well the carefully worded 1917 statute.

In 1919 the legislature approved another eugenics law but did not repeal the 1917 legislation. Both statutes empowered Oregon to conduct a sterilization program and employ various surgical procedures, including castration. By June 1944, 1,750 wards of the state had been sterilized by various means. Only a handful were actual inmates of the penitentiary. None had been involved in the 1912 scandal. By 1917 the only man who had been sent to the penitentiary (although others had served time in the county jail) as a result of the affair had been paroled. Some of the victims of the 1917 and 1919 laws had engaged in sodomy while in prison. From available records it is impossible to ascertain if any of these prisoners or other victims from other state institutions were homosexuals. But we do know that at least early on, men of ethnic and racial minority and working-class background were affected. In the Board of Eugenics' first meeting, which took place on June 30, 1917, the state penitentiary warden reported that "sodomy was rampant" at his institution and he submitted the names of eight men whom he felt needed to be sterilized. By the end of the year, the board had approved sterilization for two—both were new immigrants and emasculation was prescribed in each case. One man was Bram Sing, whom we encountered in chapter 2; he was one of the Indian immigrants who had been found guilty of sodomizing an American youth in a Washington logging town in early 1912. Three years later, Sing was sentenced to the Oregon penitentiary for robbery. While serving his sentence, authorities caught him in the "act of practicing sodomy." Another man for whom the Board of Eugenics also prescribed emasculation was Tony Lagallo, an immigrant from Italy. He had been convicted twice of sodomy during his years in Oregon. The board later rescinded its decision when, on appeal from Lagallo's attorney, the governor urged the penitentiary to release the immigrant, provided he return to Italy and serve in the army.[59] Records suggest that half of the eight inmates whom the Board of Eugenics did ultimately sterilize by 1921 were males who had engaged in same-sex sexual activities. One was a seventeen-year-old youth. Using reasoning that defied even the most hideous logic behind eugenics, officials prescribed his castration as a remedy for "allowing other prisoners to commit sodomy on his person." The postoperative report claimed that the surgery "has had the desired effect, at least we have no further trouble with the boy."[60]

A more complicated case involved James Riley (figure 15), an American-born white man who had a number of aliases. While he was serving time in the penitentiary in 1916 on a different charge, officials discovered him engaging in sodomy with another prisoner. When the Board of Eugenics considered Riley's case in 1917, it contemplated sterilizing him for eugenic and therapeutic purposes. Because he had previously been convicted of five separate crimes, including burglary and assault with a deadly weapon, Riley could be categorized as a "habitual criminal." Yet when the board finally authorized Riley's operation, they did so because of his "[d]egenerative practices."[61]

Soon after the board's recommendation, Riley agreed to permit the Portland attorney and eugenics opponent Tom Garland, who wished to test the constitutionality of the Oregon law, to appeal his case. However, Riley later changed his mind and consented to the surgery. Explaining his decision to Garland, Riley wrote that he had been a criminal for twenty years, fifteen of which he had spent behind bars. Although he had attempted assiduously to reform, he admitted that each time he had fallen harder than before. He further asserted that "the officials are trying to help me so I am going to give them a chance, of course this may not do me any good, but I don[']t see where it can do me much harm." In closing, Riley maintained that "he had not been urged or persuaded, but I have merely made my choice." However, it seems more likely that a good deal of pressure was applied; on the very day Riley wrote this let-

FIGURE 15. James Riley (aka Herbert Merithew), 1916. Under Oregon's 1917–19 statutes providing for the sterilization of men arrested for participation in same-sex sexual activities, surgeons at the Oregon State Penitentiary in Salem castrated Riley in 1921. Oregon State Archives, Oregon State Penitentiary, Inmate Files, Photograph 7507.

ter from the prison in the presence of a notary, and before it could possibly have reached Garland in Portland, the penitentiary surgeon castrated him. As for the "therapeutic" success of his operation, prison authorities claimed that "there has been a marked change in him since [the] operation. He has caused us no trouble[.]" But the record speaks otherwise. During the seventeen years after his 1922 release from the Oregon prison, Riley landed behind bars in California four times for burglary, once for suspicion of burglary, and twice for grand theft.[62]

Tom Garland did eventually succeed in finding another eugenics case to appeal, although it concerned rape rather than sodomy. Owing to the attorney's efforts, on December 13, 1921, after nearly two hundred people in Oregon had already been sterilized, the Marion County Circuit Court declared that the statute denied the plaintiff due process of law, contrary to the Fourteenth Amendment. The 1923 legislature responded by passing a new law in 1923. Although this statute also applied, as had the previous measures, to "moral degenerates and sexual perverts," it was less specific in defining who belonged to those categories. In 1925 Oregon lawmakers amended the 1923 law to clarify that they were people convicted of sodomy or any other "crime against nature." This law remained on the books until its repeal in 1965.[63]

Portland's 1912 homosexual scandal first compelled Oregon's law-makers to target men "addicted to the practice of sodomy or the crime against nature" for sterilization in the 1913 eugenics statute. Between that year and 1925, when the legislature secured its final law, the various bills that it considered or enacted all included, in one form or another, some mention of these men whom society increasingly understood to be homosexuals. Moreover, Oregon's debates and laws had an effect across the region. In 1921 the Washington State assembly substituted for its 1909 statute a broader law based closely on Oregon's 1917 and 1919 legislation. Washington now not only singled out "moral degenerates" and "sexual perverts" for sterilization, but it also defined them exactly as Oregon had in its various bills and laws since 1913. Additionally, it pre-scribed castration just as did the Oregon law. In 1919 the Idaho legisla-ture adopted a bill identical to Oregon's in every respect, including the definition of sexual perverts. The governor vetoed it, but the legislature persisted; in 1925 Idaho enacted its first sterilization statute, which cov-ered moral degenerates and sexual perverts. The *Idaho Daily Statesman* reported that lawmakers "patterned [it] after the Oregon bill." Develop-ments in Oregon and the remainder of the American Pacific Northwest seemed to have only a limited impact on British Columbia. Although as early as the 1910s eugenists north of the border praised American laws on the "sterilization of degenerates," the law adopted by the province in 1933 applied only to the insane and the mentally deficient.[64] But with the exception of British Columbia, by the end of the 1920s—either directly or indirectly because of Portland's 1912 scandal—the Northwest had adopted eugenics decrees aimed against homosexuals. The campaign to secure laws prescribing the sterilization of these men had come to a suc-cessful conclusion roughly a decade after the 1912 scandal erupted.

In the late nineteenth and early twentieth centuries, just as the "modern homosexual" made his appearance, society reacted with force against him and, as a logical extension, others who engaged in same-sex sexual activities. In the Northwest, reformers redefined and strengthened sodomy laws. They led a vigorous campaign to control public discus-sion of homosexuality and actually used it to promote the more open expression of heterosexual erotic desire. They worked to increase pun-ishment of same-sex sexual offenders and homosexuals. Some attempted individual "rehabilitation" of these men through early parole and work programs. One of the "crowning achievements" of Northwest Progres-sives who opposed homosexuals was the securing of state laws that permitted the castration of them as a punishment and as a way to eliminate their desires. But even as it clamped down ever harder on same-sex sexual expression, society generally became more permissive with regard to heterosexuality. These developments were inversely related. Pushing into openness the ideology of heterosexuality required the increased regulation and vilification of homosexuality. In the process, both sexual constructs became increasingly monolithic.

Among scholars studying the history of sex and sexuality, common wisdom maintains that Progressive reformers targeted the working class as they sought to prevent what they perceived to be a decline in traditional moral values.[65] Thus, they attacked working-class institutions such as saloons and vaudeville theaters, dance halls and inexpensive lodging houses, amusement parks and pool halls. The reformers also focused their energies on prostitutes, who typically were working-class women. Although my study has supported such a thesis, I have also argued that this interpretation of early-twentieth-century moral reform needs to be broadened, for reasons made clear by the story of the Progressive response to homosexuality. Certainly, reformers early in the century did express anxiety over same-sex sexual activities to which working-class lodgings, saloons, and poolrooms might contribute. But none of these concerns actually galvanized concerted public or even reformist response. The single most significant event in bringing about the most sweeping reforms in the Northwest regarding same-sex affairs was Portland's 1912 scandal—which was essentially middle class in nature.

Defining, controlling, and eliminating homosexuality in the Northwest also proved to be a middle- and upper-class undertaking. Yet something else needs to be emphasized. As this and previous chapters have either demonstrated or intimated, those who would ultimately feel the reforms' most grievous effects—such as lengthened prison sentences and sterilization through castration—would be men from the working and immigrant classes, not those from higher up the social scale. But in the end, all homosexuals would suffer from the reforms implemented during this era. In time, most (but not all) Northwest states repealed their sodomy and eugenics laws. But various ways in which homosexuals, regardless of class, race, and ethnic background, are socially and legally excluded persist. In addition, homosexuals are still often blamed for endangering children. These are perhaps the most enduring legacies of Progressive-era campaigns against same-sex affairs in the Pacific Northwest.

Epilogue

Same-Sex Affairs in the Pacific Northwest:
1912 and After

Many men implicated in the 1912 scandal quickly departed Portland during the pandemonium that followed Benjamin Trout's confession on November 8, but most eventually did appear before some level of the Oregon judicial system. Not surprisingly, after serving time, most of those who were convicted or who pled guilty to charges abandoned the city once again. For example, George Birdseye, onetime resident of the YMCA and a clerk in a Portland department store, soon found a home and employment in San Francisco. Credit man H. L. Rowe made his way back to his former home, Duluth, Minnesota. Of the forty-five men for whom records are available and who had lived in Portland before the scandal, fewer than 16 percent were still residing and working in the city in 1914.[1]

The subsequent lives of some of these men have been detailed elsewhere in this volume. Among the many tragic stories is that of Dr. Harry A. Start and his wife Mary. Sometime in the spring of 1913, while Start was awaiting the Oregon Supreme Court's decision concerning his appeal for his sodomy conviction, he received an invitation from an old friend, the Chinese nationalist leader Dr. Sun Yat-sen, to come to China and begin life anew. In June 1913, shortly after hearing that Oregon's highest judicial body had overturned the lower court's judgment against him, Start embarked for Hong Kong. When he did so, he promised his wife that once settled in Asia, he would send for her. Mary had stood by her husband throughout the scandal and his trial. She defended him against would-be blackmailers and even endured the intimations of one witness who, during proceedings against Harry, had suggested that she had maintained an extramarital relationship because of her husband's other sexual interests. In the few weeks following Harry's departure for Asia, life became difficult for Mary. Left with limited financial resources, she began selling furniture to pay the bills but could still not meet her obligations. Soon she lost her telephone and electric service. Neighbors complained that Mary spent the nights endlessly moaning, crying, and pacing. Late in the evening of August 21, a strange silence descended over the Starts' residence. The next morning, suspicious neighbors alerted the police. Upon entering Mary's home, authorities found hypodermic needles, cocaine, morphine, and dozens of empty and partially filled whisky and beer bottles strewn about the place, which was also littered with the wreckage of remaining furnishings. But most pathetic of all, at the bottom of the staircase lay Mary's nude, bruised, and lifeless body. Newspapers reported that the postman slipped under the front door that very day a letter Harry sent from Hong Kong, and they speculated that his missive promised a "rosy future," but it "came too late." Mary was about thirty years old.[2]

As for Start himself, not long after landing in Hong Kong he left for the Philippines. Although as a result of the 1912 scandal he lost his Oregon medical license, up through 1941 the *American Medical Directory* listed him as an urologist working principally in Manila. Records are unclear, but it appears that Start may have remained in the Japanese-occupied Philippines until Douglas MacArthur's return, moving to San Francisco shortly thereafter. In 1946 he died at a mental hospital in Stockton, California. Apparently unaware of these developments, the American Medical Association continued to list him through 1958 in the Philippines, but with address and other information simply unknown.[3]

Biographical details such as these help us comprehend, on the level of the individual, certain of the legacies that Portland's 1912 scandal bequeathed to those directly involved. But more significant for understanding broader history are the general themes exposed by an examination of that scandal and its aftermath. Approximately forty years later, during the social bitterness of the early cold war era, there occurred in America the most horrific national attack on gay men and lesbians that the country had yet seen. Historians who have examined this phenomenon, which they closely link to the anti-communist frenzy of the day, explain that it came partly as the result of the widespread and far-reaching changes and disruptions wrought by the Great Depression and World War II on society, family, sexual mores, and gender norms. This anti-homosexual campaign, in the words of John D'Emilio, "represented but one front in the widespread effort to reconstruct patterns of sexuality and gender relations shaken by depression and war." As certain as this conclusion is, others that historians have drawn about the 1950s hysteria appear questionable when set against what happened in the Northwest a generation earlier. D'Emilio has maintained that there had been "no model" for the early cold war anti-homosexual crusade "in America's history." Although Estelle B. Freedman has pointed out that already in the 1930s homosexuals had become identified in broader public consciousness with child molestation, George Chauncey has argued that this belief fully crystallized during the anti-gay fury following World War II. Firmly identified with endangering children, homosexuals were therefore now perceived as a considerable threat to society. "If homosexuals had been relatively invisible before the war," Chauncey asserted, "they had also been considered fairly harmless."[4]

The events in Portland in 1912 shed new light on the 1950s' panic and, more generally, the history of anti-gay and lesbian sentiment in the United States; their analysis therefore leads us to revise some conventional views. First, Portland's scandal does indeed offer a model for the cold war anti-homosexual campaign. While Oregon's local developments only briefly spread to the national level, they nonetheless tapped into serious countrywide xenophobia, concerns about white slavery, and fear that America's men and boys were also at risk. Moreover, Portland's 1912 scandal resulted in a vigorous, tenacious, and concerted multiyear campaign against homosexuals similar to that carried out in the 1950s, despite its smaller scale. In a way, Portland in 1912 foreshadowed the difficult times ahead. Like the cold war homosexual panic that followed, the scandal, too, came during a time in national, regional, and local history of tremendous social disruptions, economic turmoil, high levels of anti-foreign sentiment, and vast alterations in gender norms, sexual mores, and familial relations. Moreover, it brought incalculable ruin and tragedy to a number of individuals.

One apparent difference is in fact an interesting similarity. During the early cold war, society linked communism and membership in the Communist Party with homosexuality and homosexuals; in contrast, in the stridently republican atmosphere of early-twentieth-century Portland, certain working-class forces associated degeneracy and homosexuality with big business, corporate capitalism, and the wealthier elements of society. Yet even though the exact political threats that homosexuality was thought to pose reversed during the intervening forty years, the sexual menace remained a constant. Indeed, the 1912 scandal offers a model for the 1950s panic in that in both cases society associated homosexuality with those political and economic forces that seemed most to threaten traditional social ideals and the status quo.

Even before World War I, society viewed homosexuals and homosexuality as endangering children. In the wake of the 1912 scandal, a certain sector of the middle class wished to silence the public discussion of homosexuality, believing that even its mention might permanently corrupt impressionable boys and youths. But middle-class concern after 1912 went beyond simply the feeling that the idea of homosexuality could be debasing to boys; it also focused on the supposed actions of homosexuals themselves. Portland newspapers in 1912 repeatedly claimed, despite evidence to the contrary, that "boys" had been the "victims" of Portland's homosexuals in 1912.[5]

This social concern over sexual relationships between men and boys arose in a particular context. According to long-standing beliefs, sexual "degeneracy" was akin to a contagious disease and could spread rapidly to the innocent. Moreover, at the turn of the twentieth century family and childhood across the nation were experiencing considerable flux. The result was to heighten suspected connections between social change and sexual danger. More specifically to Portland and the Northwest, by 1912 juvenile court reports, police investigations, sociological research, and arrest records clearly demonstrated that throughout the region sexual associations between men and boys commonly occurred. In and outside the city they permeated transient working-class culture, which had only few commonalities with middle-class same-sex activities. As this study has shown, and despite sensational newspaper articles reporting otherwise, few youths under twenty participated in the middle-class homosexual subculture that came to light in 1912. But the facts mattered little: after the appearance of the "homosexual," society began to view all expressions of same-sex sexuality, including that of the working classes, as homosexuality. In the dominant society's developing view, the seasonally employed jocker who had interfemoral relations with a punk seemed little different from an adult man who clerked in a downtown corporate establishment and who shared an apartment with, and performed mutual oral sex with, another man of his own social standing and age.

Various scholars have described the process by which homosexuality and heterosexuality emerged together. Michel Foucault claimed that as the latter became the established standard, the former came under greater scrutiny. But so too did all other sexualities falling outside the heterosexual norm, including the sexuality of children.[6] Thus as homosexuality and the sexuality of children became simultaneously associated with deviance and endangerment, they also became conflated in broader public representations. The origins of this phenomenon and of the attendant myth that the homosexual is a child molester is dated closer to 1912 than it is to 1950 or even 1930. But in whatever decade it surfaced, the myth of the homosexual child molester spoke to complex social developments in each of these difficult periods.

The significance of Portland's 1912 scandal, of course, goes well beyond its anticipation of the 1950s anti-homosexual campaign. If it were not for the 1912 affair, much of the evidence we have for the existence and nature of Portland's early-twentieth-century homosexual conditions and community would have been lost to history. Myriad sources make it possible to reconstruct the working-class male same-sex sexual subculture that pervaded the late-nineteenth- and early-twentieth-century rural and urban Northwest. But unlike what seems to have happened in North America's megalopolises, early-twentieth-century gay community in the urban Northwest did not take shape in the working-class world. Therefore, the historical materials relating to working-class sexuality inform in only limited ways specific aspects of early gay community in Portland and the region. Nonetheless, these sources do provide us with rich materials for understanding male same-sex sexuality at this time, as well as clues to explain why gay community and culture developed differently in Portland and, likely, many other smaller cities in North America than it did in major cities.

That Portland's early-twentieth-century homosexual community emerged in the middle classes is what made its disclosure so scandalous. The general public was staggered to learn that those involved were doctors, physicians, mailmen, store managers, bookkeepers, office clerks, restaurant and small business proprietors, and teachers—the very people who made up the most respectable and visible part of everyday life in the city. The general shock—and the accompanying desire to forget this distressing episode—is one reason why the early homosexual community in Portland remains rather obscure in historical sources. Another reason is that before 1912 the Rose City's authorities and reformers focused attention on the sexual threat posed by men who were working class, racial minorities, and immigrants and by the North End district that they inhabited. They thus overlooked the activities of middle-class gay men, who, in order to remain relatively anonymous, limited their contacts with the working classes.

In Portland and the Northwest there emerged at least two distinct same-sex sexual subcultures, working-class and middle-class. Fear of public exposure may very well have limited middle-class male desire to fraternize with the working classes. But the conventions of the two cultures also discouraged their mutual participation, as the working-class North End's dominant same-sex sexual system took rather different forms from those of the middle-class gay community. Possible white-collar disdain for the relatively unkempt transient laborer may have contributed to this separation as well. Given that the middle-class homosexual community of Portland was composed principally of men of northern European background, the strong xenophobic feelings that pervaded the Northwest probably also created a barrier between these men and the new immigrant working classes.

In turn-of-the-century Portland, then, separation between working- and middle-class men prevailed. Their same-sex sexual cultures revolved around different centers: for the one, the North End's inexpensive lodging houses, saloons, and poolrooms; for the other, middle-class institutions, social spaces, and notions of privacy. Although there was some overlap between the two, for the most part evidence indicates that middle- and working-class male same-sex sexuality developed separately from each other in these distinctive physical and cultural spaces within the early-twentieth-century Northwest city.

For the Northwest, the year 1912 represents a significant point in the history of these varied same-sex sexual subcultures. The events of that fall helped solidify a public belief that someone might be identified as a homosexual because of his sexual activities and desires. The context in which those events took shape led the dominant society to identify homosexual subculture with the middle classes. Concomitantly, they began the process that eventually conflated several distinct same-sex sexual systems into a monolithic notion of homosexuality. The 1912 scandal also encouraged broader society to develop yet one more weapon in its campaign of discrimination against working-class immigrant males, and to administer harsher social and legal penalties to men who expressed same-sex sexual desires. Not the least of the revelations of 1912 was that homosexuality could be used as a powerful tool for prosecuting local political struggles. Many of these events and developments might sound vaguely familiar even today. Perhaps what is most remarkable about the scandal of 1912 is that in complex and sometimes unfortunate ways, its legacies continue to influence same-sex affairs a century later.

Notes

The following abbreviations are used throughout the notes:

BCAGR British Columbia Attorney General Records
Idaho   *Idaho Reports*
ISHS   Idaho State Historical Society, Boise
ISP   Idaho State Penitentiary
LAR   Legislative Assembly Records
MCARC Multnomah County Archives and Records Center
MCCCC Multnomah County Circuit Court Case (Multnomah County Courthouse, Portland, Ore.)
MCJR   Multnomah County Jail Register
MOC   Mayor's Office Correspondence
OHS   Oregon Historical Society, Portland
OHQ   *Oregon Historical Quarterly*
Or.   *Oregon Reports*
OSA   Oregon State Archives, Salem
OSBH   Oregon State Board of Health
OSCR   Oregon Supreme Court Records
OSHS   Oregon Social Hygiene Society
OSP   Oregon State Penitentiary
P.   *Pacific Reporter*
PABC   Provincial Archives of British Columbia, Victoria
PNQ   *Pacific Northwest Quarterly*

PPAR   Portland Police Arrest Records
PPDDB   Portland Police Detective Day Book
SPARC   Stanley Parr Archives and Records Center, Portland, Ore.
WHQ   *Western Historical Quarterly*
WSAE   Washington State Archives, Ellensburg
WSAO   Washington State Archives, Olympia
WSP   Washington State Penitentiary
WSSCC   Washington State Supreme Court Case

Introduction

1. General histories of Portland are E. Kimbark MacColl, *The Shaping of a City: Business and Politics in Portland, Oregon, 1885–1915* (Portland: Georgian Press, 1976); MacColl, *The Growth of a City: Power and Politics in Portland, Oregon, 1915 to 1950* (Portland: Georgian Press, 1979); and MacColl with Harry Stein, *Merchants, Money and Power: The Portland Establishment, 1843–1913* (Portland: Georgian Press, 1988). More specific studies include Carl Abbott, *Portland: Planning, Politics, and Growth in a Twentieth-Century City* (Lincoln: University of Nebraska Press, 1983); Robert Douglas Johnston, "Middle-Class Political Ideology in a Corporate Society: The Persistence of Small-Propertied Radicalism in Portland, Oregon, 1883–1926" (Ph.D. diss., Rutgers University, 1993); and Gloria E. Myers, *A Municipal Mother: Portland's Lola Greene Baldwin, America's First Policewoman* (Corvallis: Oregon State University Press, 1995).

Population figures come from U.S. Department of Commerce, Bureau of the Census, *Thirteenth Census of the United States, 1910* (Washington, D.C.: Government Printing Office, 1913), 1:94, and U.S. Department of Commerce, Bureau of the Census, *Fifteenth Census of the United States, 1930* (Washington, D.C.: Government Printing Office, 1931), 1:27. The 1890 figure for Portland includes Portland and East Portland, municipalities that merged in 1891.

2. *Portland Evening Telegram*, November 16, 1912, 2. Newspapers did not reveal the identity of the young man who first divulged information to police about homosexuality. However, arrest records suggest that it was Benjamin Trout (PPAR, July 30, 1912, to December 10, 1912, p. 193, SPARC).

3. See John Howard, *Men Like That: A Southern Queer History* (Chicago: University of Chicago Press, 1999), 277; Howard, "The Talk of the County: Revisiting Accusation, Murder, and Mississippi, 1895," in *Where These Memories Grow: History, Memory, and Southern Identity,* ed. W. Fitzhugh Brundage (Chapel Hill: University of North Carolina Press, 2000), 191–218; Lisa Duggan, *Sapphic Slashers: Sex, Violence, and American Modernity* (Durham, N.C.: Duke University Press, 2000); and Neil Bartlett, *Who Was That Man? A Present for Mr Oscar Wilde* (London: Serpent's Tail, 1988). On Mitchell and Wilde, see Duggan, *Sapphic Slashers;* Ed Cohen, *Talk on the Wilde Side: Towards a Genealogy of Discourse*

on Male Sexualities (New York: Routledge, 1993); and Bartlett, *Who Was That Man?*

4. Jennifer Terry, *An American Obsession: Science, Medicine, and Homosexuality in Modern America* (Chicago: University of Chicago Press, 1999), 11, 52–53, 78–79, 89–97, 116; John D'Emilio and Estelle B. Freedman, *Intimate Matters: A History of Sexuality in America* (New York: Harper and Row, 1988), 208–15; Michael Omi and Howard Winant, *Racial Formation in the United States from the 1960s to the 1990s,* 2d ed. (New York: Routledge, 1994), 14–15.

5. See Siobhan B. Somerville, *Queering the Color Line: Race and the Invention of Homosexuality in American Culture* (Durham, N.C.: Duke University Press, 2000); Kevin J. Mumford, *Interzones: Black/White Sex Districts in Chicago and New York in the Early Twentieth Century* (New York: Columbia University Press, 1997), 73–92; and Duggan, *Sapphic Slashers.*

6. Michel Foucault, *The History of Sexuality: An Introduction,* trans. Robert Hurley (New York: Pantheon Books, 1978), 120–23.

7. On the role of medical, religious, and legal and police discourse in socially constructing homosexual identity, see Terry, *An American Obsession;* Lillian Faderman, "The Morbidification of Love between Women by Nineteenth-Century Sexologists," *Journal of Homosexuality* 4, no. 1 (fall 1978): 73–90; Faderman, *Surpassing the Love of Men: Romantic Friendship and Love between Women from the Renaissance to the Present* (New York: William Morrow, 1981); George Chauncey, Jr., "From Sexual Inversion to Homosexuality: Medicine and the Changing Medical Conceptualization of Female Deviance," in *Passion and Power: Sexuality in History,* ed. Kathy Peiss and Christina Simmons with Robert A. Padgug (Philadelphia: Temple University Press, 1989), 87–117; Jeffrey Weeks, *Coming Out: Homosexual Politics in Britain from the Nineteenth Century to the Present,* rev. ed. (London: Quartet Books, 1990); and Steven Maynard, "Through a Hole in the Lavatory Wall: Homosexual Subcultures, Police Surveillance, and the Dialectics of Discovery, Toronto, 1890–1930," *Journal of the History of Sexuality* 5, no. 2 (October 1994): 207–42. For incisive discussions of the role of print culture on popular conceptions of homosexuality, see Marc Stein, *City of Sisterly and Brotherly Loves: Lesbian and Gay Philadelphia, 1945–1972* (Chicago: University of Chicago Press, 2000), esp. 5, 115–76, and Duggan, *Sapphic Slashers.*

8. Because I argue that race played a critical role in the emergence of male homosexuality in the Northwest, I offer here the turn-of-the century racial "identities" of McAllister and Dillige. Later in this study I explore McAllister's biography. His last name suggests Irish ancestry; and only in about the 1880s, according to Noel Ignatiev, did the Irish in America become "white" (see Ignatiev, *How the Irish Became White* [New York: Routledge, 1995]).

9. The paucity of source material on Dillige makes it impossible to trace his itinerant course. But as discussed in more detail later, his immigrant status, his occupation as a "laborer," his arrest in Portland's most prominent transient neighborhood, and his ethnicity all establish him within the region's transient workforce and culture.

10. For example, see George Chauncey, Jr., "Christian Brotherhood or Sexual Perversion? Homosexual Identities and the Construction of Sexual Boundaries in the World War I Era," in *Hidden from History: Reclaiming the Gay and Lesbian Past,* ed. Martin Duberman, Martha Vicinus, and George Chauncey, Jr. (New York: Meridian, 1989), 294–317; Chauncey, *Gay New York: Gender, Urban Culture, and the Making of the Gay Male World, 1890–1940* (New York: Basic-Books, 1994); Elizabeth Lapovsky Kennedy and Madeline Davis, *Boots of Leather, Slippers of Gold: The History of a Lesbian Community* (New York: Routledge, 1993); and Judith Halberstam, *Female Masculinity* (Durham, N.C.: Duke University Press, 1998).

11. On plural sexualities and terminology, see also, for example, Eve Kosofsky Sedgwick, *Epistemology of the Closet* (Berkeley: University of California Press, 1990), 44–48; Valerie Traub, *Desire and Anxiety: Circulations of Sexuality in Shakespearean Drama* (London: Routledge, 1992), 91–116; David L. Eng and Alice Y. Hom, eds., *Q & A: Queer in Asian America* (Philadelphia: Temple University Press, 1998), 1–21; and Lisa Duggan, "Making It Perfectly Queer," *Socialist Review* 22, no. 1 (January–March 1992): 18.

12. See especially Chauncey, *Gay New York.*

13. For example, see John D'Emilio, *Sexual Politics, Sexual Communities: The Making of a Homosexual Minority in the United States, 1940–1970* (Chicago: University of Chicago Press, 1983), and Chauncey, *Gay New York.*

14. Studies of nonurban "gay" subcultures, communities, and lifestyles are beginning to appear. See Howard, *Men Like That;* John Howard, "Place and Movement in Gay American History: A Case from the Post–World War II South," in *Creating a Place for Ourselves: Lesbian, Gay, and Bisexual Community Histories,* ed. Brett Beemyn (New York: Routledge, 1997), 211–25; Howard, ed., *Carryin' On in the Lesbian and Gay South* (New York: New York University Press, 1997); Karen Lee Osborne and William J. Spurlin, eds., *Reclaiming the Heartland: Lesbian and Gay Voices from the Midwest* (Minneapolis: University of Minnesota Press, 1996); Will Fellows, ed., *Farm Boys: Lives of Gay Men from the Rural Midwest* (Madison: University of Wisconsin Press, 1996); and D. Michael Quinn, *Same-Sex Dynamics among Nineteenth-Century Americans: A Mormon Example* (Urbana: University of Illinois Press, 1996).

15. The limited scholarship on regionalism and sexuality includes Howard, *Men Like That* and *Carryin' On;* Osborne and Spurlin, *Reclaiming the Heartland;* Fellows, *Farm Boys;* and Peter Boag, "Sexuality, Gender, and Identity in Great Plains History and Myth," *Great Plains Quarterly* 18, no. 4 (fall 1998): 327–40.

16. State v. Douglas, 118 P. 915 (1912); State of Washington v. Harry Douglas, trial transcripts, WSSCC no. 278, WSAE.

17. On adult-juvenile relationships involving young working-class females, see Mary E. Odem, *Delinquent Daughters: Protecting and Policing Adolescent Female Sexuality in the United States, 1885–1920* (Chapel Hill: University of North Carolina Press, 1995).

Chapter 1. Sex on the Road: Migratory Men and Youths in the Pacific Northwest's Hinterlands

1. Conflicting prison, census, and newspaper reports provide information on Gladden. The account given here is gleaned from Ted Gladden, Inmate 1916, Idaho Territory and State Penitentiary Convict Register, 1884–1916, pp. 206–7, ISHS; Ted Glayton [*sic*], Inmate 7776, OSP Physical Description Records, Volume 1916–1922, OSA; Ted Glayton [*sic*], Inmate 7776, OSP Great Register, 1910–1925, pp. 324–25, OSA; Ted Glayton [*sic*], Inmate 7776, Parole Calendar for November 1918, vol. 5, [n.p.], Oregon State Parole Board Actions, 1915–1938, OSA; State of Idaho v. Ted Gladden, June 8, 1912, Indictment Records for Canyon County, ISHS; U.S. Department of Commerce, Bureau of the Census, Thirteenth Census, 1910, Manuscript Census, Marion County, Oregon, Enumeration District 214, sheet 9B, line 95; U.S. Department of Commerce, Bureau of the Census, Fourteenth Census, 1920, Manuscript Census, Marion County, Oregon, Enumeration District 223, sheet 4B, line 69; *Nampa (Idaho) Leader-Herald*, various stories on hobos and local trouble with hobos, May 1912; and *Albany (Ore.) Daily Democrat*, November 29, 1917, 1, and November 30, 1917, 1.

2. Chris D. Sawyer, "From Whitechapel to Old Town: The Life and Death of the Skid Row District, Portland, Oregon" (Ph.D. diss., Portland State University, 1985), 32.

3. See James Neville Tattersall, "The Economic Development of the Pacific Northwest to 1920" (Ph.D. diss., University of Washington, 1960), 86, 90, 119, 134, 137, 138, 179, 140–41, 200; Dorothy O. Johansen, *Empire of the Columbia: A History of the Pacific Northwest*, 2d ed. (New York: Harper and Row, 1967), 316–17, 372–73; Carlos Arnaldo Schwantes, *The Pacific Northwest: An Interpretive History*, rev. ed. (Lincoln: University of Nebraska Press, 1996), 169–78, 222, 329; Schwantes, *Railroad Signatures across the Pacific Northwest* (Seattle: University of Washington Press, 1993); Richard White, *"It's Your Misfortune and None of My Own": A New History of the American West* (Norman: University of Oklahoma Press, 1991), 257–58, 278–80; Jean Barman, *The West beyond the West: A History of British Columbia* (Toronto: University of Toronto Press, 1991), 108–14; Chuck Davis and Shirley Mooney, *Vancouver: An Illustrated Chronology* (Burlington, Ont.: Windsor, 1986), 26, 33, 40; and James H. Hitchman, *A Maritime History of the Pacific Coast, 1540–1980* (Lanham, Md.: University Press of America, 1990), 42–43.

4. U.S. Department of Commerce, Bureau of the Census, *Fifteenth Census of the United States, 1930* (Washington, D.C.: United States Government Printing Office, 1933), 4:405, 1357, 1691; Canada, *General Report of the Census of Canada, 1880–81* (Ottawa: MacLean, Roger, 1885), 4:2–3; Canada, *Fifth Census of Canada, 1911* (Ottawa: C. H. Parmelee, 1912), 1:520; Canada, Dominion Bureau Statistics, *Seventh Census of Canada, 1931* (Ottawa: J. O. Patenaude, 1933), 2:156.

5. The census definition of *laborer* is somewhat slippery, as it changed throughout this period. The occupational categories included in my analysis are "laborers," farm laborers, lumbermen, raftsmen, woodchoppers, those in the

building and hand trades, saw and planing mill workers, longshoremen and stevedores, sailors and deckhands, fishermen and oystermen, railroad and other transportation labor, lumberyard and coal yard laborers, and warehouse workers. For census definitions and uses of the term *laborer,* see U.S. Department of Commerce, Bureau of the Census, *Thirteenth Census of the United States, 1910* (Washington, D.C.: Government Printing Office, 1914), 4:19–22, 82–88.

Census figures offered in the text come from various census compilations. For the U.S. figures I factored in conjugal status only of men known to census takers, thereby eliminating from calculations those listed as "unknown." U.S. Department of the Interior, Census Office, *Population of the United States, 1890* (Washington, D.C.: Government Printing Office, 1895–97), part 1, 830, 842, 867, 877; part 2, 551, 569, 601, 621.

6. U.S. Department of the Interior, Census Office, *Population of the United States at the Eleventh Census, 1890* (Washington, D.C.: Government Printing Office, 1895), 830, 842, 867, 877; U.S. Department of Commerce, Bureau of the Census, *Fourteenth Census of the United States, 1920* (Washington, D.C.: Government Printing Office, 1922), 2:169.

7. U.S. Department of Commerce, Bureau of the Census, *Thirteenth Census of the United States, 1910* (Washington: Government Printing Office, 1913), 3:523; Nels Anderson, *Men on the Move* (1940; reprint, New York: Da Capo, 1974), 80–82; Nels Anderson, *The Hobo: The Sociology of the Homeless Man* (Chicago: University of Chicago Press, 1923), 150–51. On labor, transience, and racial and ethnic minority groups in the Northwest, see Chris Friday, *Organizing Asian American Labor: The Pacific Coast Canned-Salmon Industry, 1870–1942* (Philadelphia: Temple University Press, 1994); Liping Zhu, *A Chinaman's Chance: The Chinese on the Rocky Mountain Mining Frontier* (Niwot: University Press of Colorado, 1997); Paul George Hummasti, "Finnish Radicalism in Astoria, Oregon, 1904–1940: A Study in Immigrant Socialism" (Ph.D. diss., University of Oregon, 1975); and Erasmo Gamboa, *Mexican Labor and World War II: Braceros in the Pacific Northwest, 1942–1947* (Austin: University of Texas Press, 1990).

8. U.S. Department of Commerce, *Thirteenth Census of the United States, 1910,* 3:993; Zhu, *Chinaman's Chance,* 7–32, 87; U.S. Department of Commerce, *Fourteenth Census of the United States, 1920,* 2:514. On miscegenation laws, especially in Oregon, see Peggy Pascoe, "Race, Gender, and the Privileges of Property: On the Significance of Miscegenation Laws in the U.S. West," in *Over the Edge: Remapping the American West,* ed. Valerie J. Matsumoto and Blake Allmendinger (Berkeley: University of California Press, 1999), 215–30.

The literature on the Chinese in the West is vast; on Portland and the larger Northwest see, besides Zhu, Margaret K. Holden, "Gender and Protest Ideology: Sue Ross Keenan and the Oregon Anti-Chinese Movement," *Western Legal History* 7, no. 2 (summer/fall 1994): 222–43, and Nelson Chia-Chi Ho, *Portland's Chinatown: The History of an Urban Ethnic District* (Portland: Bureau of Planning, City of Portland, 1978).

On Chinese women, Chinese cultural restrictions against their emigration, and U.S. policies against female immigration, see Sucheng Chan, "The Exclusion of Chinese Women, 1870–1943," in *Entry Denied: Exclusion and the Chinese Community in America, 1882–1943,* ed. Sucheng Chan (Philadelphia: Temple University Press, 1991), 94–146, and George Anthony Peffer, "Forbidden Families: Emigration Experiences of Chinese Women under the Page Law, 1875–1882," *Journal of American Ethnic History* 6, no. 1 (fall 1986): 28–46.

On Chinese and South Asian migration and experience in nineteenth- and early-twentieth-century America, see Roger Daniels, *Asian America: Chinese and Japanese in the United States since 1850* (Seattle: University of Washington Press, 1988); Ronald Takaki, *Strangers from a Different Shore: A History of Asian Americans* (Boston: Little, Brown, 1989); and Vijay Prashad, *The Karma of Brown Folk* (Minneapolis: University of Minnesota Press, 2000), 71–72.

On Greek immigration and work in the West, see George A. Kourvetaris, *Studies on Greek Americans* (Boulder, Colo.: Eastern European Monographs, 1997), 17–18; Theodore Saloutos, *The Greeks in the United States* (Cambridge, Mass.: Harvard University Press, 1964), 45, 55, 56, 58–59; and Saloutos, *The Greeks in America: A Students' Guide to Localized History,* Localized History Series, ed. Clifford L. Lord (New York: Teachers College Press, 1967), 3–4.

9. Haralambous Kambouris, "Sojourn in America," edited by Konstantinos H. Kambouris, Haralambous Kambouris collection, MS 2638, n. 4 (n.p.), OHS. See also Kourvetaris, *Studies on Greek Americans,* 27; Saloutos, *Greeks in the United States,* 31, 85; Thomas Doulis, *A Surge to the Sea: The Greeks in Oregon* (Portland: Jack Lockie and Associates, 1977), 29; and Chrysie Mamalakis Costantakos, *The American-Greek Subculture: Processes of Continuity* (New York: Arno, 1980), 259.

10. Stewart H. Holbrook, *Holy Old Mackinaw: A Natural History of the American Lumberjack* (New York: Macmillan, 1938), 247 (quotation), 72, 152–55, 246–47. See also Sawyer, "From Whitechapel to Old Town," 188–89; Carlos Arnaldo Schwantes, *Hard Traveling: A Portrait of Work Life in the New Northwest* (Lincoln: University of Nebraska Press, 1994), 28–31; John C. Schneider, "Tramping Workers, 1890–1920: A Subcultural View," in *Walking to Work: Tramps in America, 1790–1935,* ed. Eric H. Monkkonen (Lincoln: University of Nebraska Press, 1984), 224–25. On changing natural resource–based industries and their relationship to labor, see Anderson, *Hobo,* 62–63, and Anderson, *Men on the Move,* 135–68. On the history of Chinese men on successive gold rushes in various parts of the world, see Zhu, *A Chinaman's Chance.*

11. Schwantes, *Pacific Northwest,* 222; White, *"It's Your Misfortune,"* 258–63, 267–68; Norman H. Clark, *Mill Town: A Social History of Everett, Washington* (Seattle: University of Washington Press, 1970), 67–68.

12. Schwantes, *Hard Traveling,* 28–31; Anderson, *Hobo,* 107–9; Sawyer, "From Whitechapel to Old Town," 187–88, 189; Johansen, *Empire of the Columbia,* 404; Schwantes, *Pacific Northwest,* 329.

13. Schwantes, *Pacific Northwest,* 330. See Anderson, *Men on the Move,* 74–75, for a detailed description of one Pacific Northwest laborer's transience over a period of several years.

14. Schwantes has pointed out that it would be wrong to assume that all of the region's workers at this time had few skills and moved about from one job to another. He argues that two categories of wage workers had emerged by the end of the nineteenth century. One was the group outlined here; the other was composed of "skilled workers who married, raised families, and put down roots in the community" (*Pacific Northwest,* 330). Nonetheless, Schwantes rightly notes that large numbers of men in the Northwest alternated between the two, possibly at rates higher than elsewhere in the country.

15. Nels Anderson, "The Juvenile and the Tramp," *Journal of the American Institute of Criminal Law and Criminology* 14, no. 2 (August 1923): 301; Dean Stiff [pseud. of Nels Anderson], *The Milk and Honey Route: A Handbook for Hobos* (New York: Vanguard, 1931), 201, 207, 209, 216, 217; see also Maury Graham and Robert J. Hemming, *Tales of the Iron Road: My Life as King of the Hobos* (New York: Paragon House, 1990), 38, 62–63. Definitions for different elements of migratory society changed over time. Josiah Flynt, in "Homosexuality among Tramps" (appendix A in Havelock Ellis, *Sexual Inversion,* vol. 4 of *Studies in the Psychology of Sex,* 2d ed. [Philadelphia: F. A. Davis, 1904], 219), claimed that there were "two kinds of tramps in the United States: out-of-works and 'hoboes.' The out-of-works are not genuine vagabonds; they really want work and have no sympathy with hoboes. The latter are the real tramps. They make a business of begging[.]"

16. B. R. Burg, *Sodomy and the Pirate Tradition: English Sea Rovers in the Seventeenth-Century Caribbean* (New York: New York University Press, 1983), 50–51.

17. Anderson, "The Juvenile and the Tramp," 301, 302; Flynt, "Homosexuality among Tramps," 220, 223.

18. Alfred C. Kinsey, Wardell B. Pomeroy, and Clyde E. Martin, *Sexual Behavior in the Human Male* (Philadelphia: W. B. Saunders, 1948), 457, 631; Donald Francis Roy, "Hooverville: A Study of a Community of Homeless Men in Seattle" (M.A. thesis, University of Washington, 1935), 60, 88 (quotation).

19. Carleton H. Parker, *The Casual Laborer and Other Essays* (New York: Russell and Russell, 1920), 73.

20. E. F. Seavey, WSP Inmate File 6027, WSAO; Oregon v. Charles Brown, July 30, 1919, MCCCC 77005; Charles Brown, parole calendar for July 1920, vol. 8, [n.p.], OSP Parole Board Actions, 1915–1938, OSA.

21. James Kennedy, Inmate 7215, parole calendar for May 1916, vol. 3, [n.p.], OSP Parole Board Actions, 1915–1938, OSA; James Kennedy, Inmate 7215, OSP Great Register Convict Record, 1910–1925, pp. 212–13, OSA; Attorney General, Inspector of Gaols, Victoria Gaol Records, 1859–1914, GR 0308, vol. 12, p. 104, entry nos. 64 and 67, and vol. 16, entry nos. 13, 16, 27, and 30 for May 1907, PABC.

22. Flynt, "Homosexuality among Tramps," 220; Anderson, *Hobo,* 144.

23. Judith Butler, *Gender Trouble: Feminism and the Subversion of Identity* (New York: Routledge, 1990), 33; see also 24–25, 134–41.

24. See Ken Plummer, *Telling Sexual Stories: Power, Change, and Social Worlds* (London: Routledge, 1995), 157–58; John Marshall, "Pansies, Perverts, and Macho Men: Changing Conceptions of Male Homosexuality," in *The Making of the Modern Homosexual*, ed. Kenneth Plummer (Totowa, N.J.: Barnes and Noble, 1981), 134–37; E. Anthony Rotundo, *American Manhood: Transformations in Masculinity from the Revolution to the Modern Era* (New York: BasicBooks, 1993), 276–78; A. A. Brill, "The Conception of Homosexuality," *Journal of the American Medical Association* 61, no. 5 (August 2, 1913): 335–40; and Gayle Rubin, "The Traffic in Women: Notes on the 'Political Economy' of Sex," in *Toward an Anthropology of Women*, ed. Rayna R. Reiter (New York: Monthly Review Press, 1975), 157–210.

25. See Michel Foucault, *The History of Sexuality: An Introduction*, trans. Robert Hurley (New York: Pantheon Books, 1978), 38, 101; David M. Halperin, *One Hundred Years of Homosexuality: And Other Essays on Greek Love* (New York: Routledge, 1990), 15–18; George Chauncey, Jr., "From Sexual Inversion to Homosexuality: Medicine and the Changing Conceptualization of Female Deviance," in *Passion and Power: Sexuality in History*, ed. Kathy Peiss and Christine Simmons with Robert A. Padgug (Philadelphia: Temple University Press, 1989), 87–117; and Jonathan Ned Katz, *The Invention of Heterosexuality* (1995; reprint, New York: Plume, 1996).

26. G. Frank Lydston, *The Diseases of Society (The Vice and Crime Problem)* (Philadelphia: J. B. Lippincott, 1904), 375. See also John C. Burnham, "Early References to Homosexual Communities in American Medical Writings," *Medical Aspects of Human Sexuality* 7, no. 8 (August 1973): 40, 41.

27. Flynt, "Homosexuality among Tramps," 222; see also 220, 224.

28. Anderson, *Hobo*, 144.

29. On transgenderism and transsexuality, see Judith Halberstam, *Female Masculinity* (Durham, N.C.: Duke University Press, 1998); Joanne Meyerowitz, "Sex Change and the Popular Press: Historical Notes on Transsexuality in the United States, 1930–1955," *GLQ: A Journal of Lesbian and Gay Studies* 4, no. 2 (1998): 159–87; C. Jacob Hale, "Consuming the Living, Dis(re)membering the Dead in the Butch/Ftm Borderlands," *GLQ: A Journal of Lesbian and Gay Studies* 4, no. 2 (1998): 311–48; Vernon Rosario II, "Trans (Homo) Sexuality? Double Inversion, Psychiatric Confusion, and Hetero-Hegemony," in *Queer Studies: A Lesbian, Gay, Bisexual, and Transgender Anthology*, ed. Brett Beemyn and Mickey Eliason (New York: New York University Press, 1996), 35–51; and Rosario, *The Erotic Imagination: French Histories of Perversity* (New York: Oxford University Press, 1997).

30. See Eve Kosofsky Sedgwick, *Epistemology of the Closet* (Berkeley: University of California Press, 1990), 44–48, and Valerie Traub, *Desire and Anxiety: Circulations of Sexuality in Shakespearean Drama* (London: Routledge, 1992), 91–116.

31. G. Legman, "The Language of Homosexuality: An American Glossary," in *Sex Variants: A Study of Homosexual Patterns*, by George W. Henry (New York: Paul B. Hoeber, 1941), 2:1169, 1179.

32. Thomas Mott Osborne, *Prisons and Common Sense* (Philadelphia: Lippincott, 1924), 89–91. See also Louis Berg, *Revelations of a Prison Doctor* (New York: Minton, Bolch, 1934), 142, and George Chauncey, *Gay New York: Gender, Urban Culture, and the Making of the Gay Male World, 1890–1940* (New York: BasicBooks, 1994), 87, 88. For this specific reading of what Osborne meant by "unnatural" and "natural" vice, I am indebted to John Howard.

33. Stewart Hall Holbrook, *Wildmen, Wobblies, and Punks: Stewart Holbrook's Lowbrow Northwest,* ed. Brian Booth (Corvallis: Oregon State University Press, 1992), 232–36; Flynt, "Homosexuality among Tramps," 220, 221; Anderson, *Hobo,* 145; Stiff, *Milk and Honey Route,* 212; Legman, "Language of Homosexuality," 1168, 1169, 1170, 1174, 1179.

On nineteenth-century sailing vessels, the boy in a relationship with a man was typically referred to as a "chicken" or "chickenship." On these terms and other aspects of the sailor's same-sex sexual culture, see B. R. Burg, *American Seafarer in the Age of Sail: The Erotic Diaries of Philip C. Van Buskirk, 1851–1870* (New Haven: Yale University Press, 1994). Philip C. Van Buskirk, the subject of Burg's study, spent much of the 1890s in and around Snohomish, Washington. He died in Bremerton, Washington, in 1903. On Van Buskirk's life, see also Philip C. Van Buskirk, *Sailor on the Snohomish: Extracts from the Washington Diaries of Philip C. Van Buskirk,* ed. with an introduction by Robert D. Monroe (Seattle, 1957), microform; and Van Buskirk's diaries in the Philip Clayton Van Buskirk (1883–1903) Collection, accession no. 3621, Special Collections, University of Washington Manuscript and University Archives Division, Seattle. While the sexual practices of men on the road and sailors have a number of similarities, this and the next chapter focus on the customs of the former.

34. Sources conflict slightly on the age of the typical punk. See Flynt, "Homosexuality among Tramps," 220; Graham and Hemming, *Tales of the Iron Road,* 35; Anderson, *Hobo,* 137; and Anderson, "The Juvenile and the Tramp," 293.

35. Paul H. Gebhard, John H. Gagnon, Wardell B. Pomeroy, and Cornelia V. Christenson, *Sex Offenders: An Analysis of Types* (New York: Harper and Row, 1965), 273, 295; Anderson, "The Juvenile and the Tramp," 306; Anderson, *Hobo,* 145; Roger A. Bruns, *Knights of the Road: A Hobo History* (New York: Methuen, 1980), 94; Roy, "Hooverville," 86.

36. Chauncey, *Gay New York,* 47. On the "fairy" in transient society, see Anderson, "The Juvenile and the Tramp," 305.

37. Legman, "Language of Homosexuality," 1155; Chauncey, *Gay New York,* 47 (quotation), 47–63. See also Marshall, "Pansies, Perverts, and Macho Men," 136.

38. Ted Glayton [i.e., Gladden], Inmate 7776, parole calendar for November 1918, vol. 5, [n.p.], Oregon State Parole Board Actions, 1915–1938, OSA; Flynt, "Homosexuality among Tramps," 221.

39. Kinsey, Pomeroy, and Martin, *Sexual Behavior,* 347, 351, 355, 363, 367, 369, 370, 375.

40. Flynt, "Homosexuality among Tramps," 224; Graham and Hemming, *Tales of the Iron Road,* 47–48.

41. Flynt, "Homosexuality among Tramps," 223; Anderson, "The Juvenile and the Tramp," 305; Heber DeLong, Inmate 1319, ISP Parole Board Records, ISHS; *Idaho Falls (Idaho) Times,* December 18, 1906, 1.

42. Stiff [Anderson], *Milk and Honey Route,* 161–62.

43. Don Paulson with Roger Simpson, *An Evening at the Garden of Allah: A Gay Cabaret in Seattle* (New York: Columbia University Press, 1996), 26; see also 22, 24.

44. Chapter 2 undertakes a more detailed analysis of male sex work.

45. Lauren Wilde Casaday, "Labor Unrest and the Labor Movement in the Salmon Industry of the Pacific Coast" (Ph.D. diss., University of California, Berkeley, 1937), 213–14; Jack Masson and Donald Guimary, "Asian Labor Contractors in the Alaskan Canned Salmon Industry: 1880–1937," *Labor History* 22, no. 3 (summer 1981): 390–91; Friday, *Organizing Asian American Labor.* I thank Chris Friday for the 1923 reference, which he uncovered in a newspaper clipping in the Alaska Packers Association Scrapbook Collection, Semiahmoo Park, Whatcom County Parks, Bellingham-Blaine Area, Wash.

46. Anderson, "The Juvenile and the Tramp," 300, 301–2; Roy, "Hooverville," 88; see also Gebhard et al., *Sex Offenders,* 272–73; Flynt, "Homosexuality among Tramps," 220; Stiff, *Milk and Honey Route,* 34; and Henning Bech, *When Men Meet: Homosexuality and Modernity,* trans. Teresa Mesquit and Time Davies (Chicago: University of Chicago Press, 1997), 24–25.

47. Bruns, *Knights of the Road,* 94 (quotation), 95; Anderson, *Hobo,* 147; Anderson, "The Juvenile and the Tramp," 301–2, 306, 307–8.

48. Flynt, "Homosexuality among Tramps," 222–23; George McElroy, WSP Inmate File 6206, WSAO.

49. Thomas Minehan, *Boy and Girl Tramps of America* (New York: Gosset and Dunlap, 1934), 143; Anderson, "The Juvenile and the Tramp," 306; Anderson, *Hobo,* 148; Minehan, *Boy and Girl Tramps of America,* 143; see also Gebhard et al., *Sex Offenders,* 289, 316; and Alexander Berkman, *Prison Memoirs of an Anarchist* (New York: Mother Earth Publishing, 1912), 439–40.

50. While an adult and a teenage boy could form a partnership without a sexual component, it was designated a jocker-punk alliance only when sex was involved. According to Stiff [Anderson], by the early 1930s, such sex on the road was so common that "whenever a man travels around with a lad he is apt to be labeled a 'jocker' or a 'wolf,' and the road kid is called his 'punk,' 'prushun,' or 'lamb.' It has become so that it is very difficult for a good hobo to enjoy the services of an apprentice" (*Milk and Honey Route,* 161). From Flynt's description of the jocker-punk relationship ("Homosexuality among Tramps", 220), one can only conclude that it necessarily included sex. In addition, as already noted, the term *jocker* derives from a word meaning "penis" (i.e., *jock*).

51. Kenneth Allsop, *Hard Travellin': The Hobo and His History* (New York: New American Library, 1967), 219; Flynt, "Homosexuality among Tramps," 220; Josiah Flynt, "Children of the Road," *Atlantic Monthly* 77, no. 459 (January 1896): 68; Anderson, *Hobo.*

52. Flynt, "Homosexuality among Tramps," 220; Flynt, "Children of the Road," 68; Bruns, *Knights of the Road,* 94; Graham and Hemming, *Tales of the Iron Road,* 35.

53. Mary E. Odem, *Delinquent Daughters: Protecting and Policing Adolescent Female Sexuality in the United States, 1885–1920* (Chapel Hill: University of North Carolina Press, 1995), 20, 24, 39, 50–51, 53, 54–57.

54. Flynt, "Homosexuality among Tramps," 221 (quotation), 222–23; Anderson, "The Juvenile and the Tramp," 292–97; Josiah Flynt, "How Men Become Tramps: Conclusions from Personal Experience as an Amateur Tramp," *Century Magazine* 50, no. 6 (October 1895): 941–45; Flynt, "Children of the Road," 58–71; Minehan, *Boy and Girl Tramps,* 37–53, 260–61 tables 13, 15, 16.

55. Flynt, "Homosexuality among Tramps," 221, 224; Kinsey, Pomeroy, and Martin, *Sexual Behavior,* 168–71, 383. See also Joseph F. Fishman, *Sex in Prison: Revealing Sex Conditions in American Prisons* (New York: National Library Press, 1934), 69–70; and Chauncey, *Gay New York,* 56.

56. Flynt, "Homosexuality among Tramps," 221; see also Allsop, *Hard Travellin',* 218–19.

57. Roy, "Hooverville," 12, 88; Anderson, *Hobo,* 146; Anderson, "The Juvenile and the Tramp," 307; Charles Smith, WSP Inmate File 6154, WSAO. See also Minehan, *Boy and Girl Tramps,* 143.

58. Anderson, *Hobo,* 146.

59. Bech, *When Men Meet,* 23–25, 18.

60. Parker, *Casual Laborer,* 73; anonymous, quoted in *Flesh: True Homosexual Experiences,* ed. Winston Leyland (San Francisco: Gay Sunshine Press, 1982), 14, as quoted in Walter L. Williams, *The Spirit and the Flesh: Sexual Diversity in American Indian Culture* (Boston: Beacon Press, 1992), 159.

61. Anonymous as quoted in Williams, *Spirit and the Flesh,* 159; Manuel Boyfrank, letter to Roger Austin, December 16, 1974, Manuel Boyfrank Papers, International Gay and Lesbian Archives, West Hollywood, Calif., from notes shared with the author by Walter L. Williams, University of Southern California; E. P. Marsh, "Report on Alaska Cannery Conditions," September 7, 1920, record group 280, file 165–261, United States National Archives, College Park, Md., pp. 5, 7, 8, 12, 14 (I am indebted to Chris Friday for pointing me to this source). See also Masson and Guimary, "Asian Labor Contractors," 389.

62. Masson and Guimary, "Asian Labor Contractors," 391; Casaday, "Labor Unrest," 214; Friday, *Organizing Asian American Laborers,* 54–55, 113–14.

63. Parker, *Casual Laborer,* 73.

64. California v. Thomas Hickey, San Francisco Criminal Case no. 28, In the Supreme Court of the State of California, Transcript on Appeal, April 10, 1895, Los Angeles County Law Library, Los Angeles, Calif.; anonymous quoted in Williams, *Spirit and the Flesh,* 159–60; Anderson, "The Juvenile and the Tramp," 304.

65. Marsh, "Report on Alaska Cannery Conditions," 8, 14.

66. Gus LaMere, WSP Inmate File 5524, WSAO; John Mustard, WSP Inmate File 6593, WSAO; David Gunreth, WSP Inmate File 6607, WSAO.

67. Idaho v. Charles Altwater, Trial Transcripts, Idaho Supreme Court Records, ISHS.

68. Donald H., quoted in Henry, *Sex Variants*, 1:29; see also Laud Humphreys, *Tearoom Trade: Impersonal Sex in Public Places* (Chicago: Aldine, 1970), 108–9.

69. LaMere, WSP Inmate File.

70. Anderson, "The Juvenile and the Tramp," 308.

71. Sedgwick, *Epistemology of the Closet*, 71. See also Chauncey, *Gay New York*, 6–7. In this section I am relying heavily on my reading of Michael P. Brown, *Closet Space: Geographies of Metaphor from the Body to the Globe* (London: Routledge, 2000).

72. Brown, *Closet Space*; Aaron Betsky, *Queer Space: Architecture and Same-Sex Desire* (New York: William Morrow, 1997). Historical treatments devoted at least in part to "queer space" include Marc Stein, *City of Sisterly and Brotherly Loves: Lesbian and Gay Philadelphia, 1945–1972* (Chicago: University of Chicago Press, 2000); John Howard, *Men Like That: A Southern Queer History* (Chicago: University of Chicago Press, 1999); Brett Beemyn, ed., *Creating a Place for Ourselves: Lesbian, Gay, and Bisexual Community Histories* (New York: Routledge, 1997); Chauncey, *Gay New York;* and Elizabeth Lapovsky Kennedy and Madeline D. Davis, *Boots of Leather, Slippers of Gold: The History of a Lesbian Community* (New York: Routledge, 1993).

73. See, for example, John D'Emilio, *Sexual Politics, Sexual Communities: The Making of a Homosexual Minority in the United States, 1940–1970* (Chicago: University of Chicago Press, 1983); and Chauncey, *Gay New York*.

74. Graham and Hemming, *Tales of the Iron Road;* Bruns, *Knights of the Road;* Parker, *Casual Laborer,* 148; Clark C. Spence, "Knights of the Tie and Rail— Tramps and Hoboes in the West," *WHQ* 2, no. 1 (January 1971): 5, 15; Allsop, *Hard Travellin',* 96, 97.

75. Henry, *Sex Variants*, 1:24–31; Donald H. quoted, 29.

76. For a perceptive critique of the urban bias against rural same-sex sexuality, see Howard, *Men Like That,* and John Howard, "Place and Movement in Gay American History: A Case from the Post–World War II South," in Beemyn, ed., *Creating a Place for Ourselves,* 211–25. An example of scholarship focusing on rural western America that laments the lack of homosexual community is Jerry Lee Kramer, "Bachelor Farmers and Spinsters: Gay and Lesbian Identities and Communities in Rural North Dakota," in *Mapping Desire: Geographies of Sexualities,* ed. David Bell and Gill Valentine (London: Routledge, 1995), 200–213.

77. Tim Retzloff, "Cars and Bars: Assembling Gay Men in Postwar Flynt, Michigan," in Beemyn, ed., *Creating a Place for Ourselves,* 229 (quotation), 227–52; Howard, *Men Like That,* 99–115.

78. Schwantes, *Hard Traveling,* 27.

79. Kinsey, Pomeroy, and Martin, *Sexual Behavior,* 457.

80. Flynt, "Homosexuality among Tramps," 222–23. See also Anderson, *Hobo,* 16–26, and Anderson, "The Juvenile and the Tramp," 307.

81. Graham and Hemming, *Tales of the Iron Road,* 19, 35; Legman, "Language of Homosexuality," 1175.

82. Schwantes, *Railroad Signatures,* 104, 17, 26; Schwantes, *Hard Traveling,* 19, 31; Allsop, *Hard Travellin',* 155–61; Graham and Hemming, *Tales of the Iron Road,* 47–48; Smith, WSP Inmate File; Flynt, "Homosexuality among Tramps," 221.

83. Schwantes, *Railroad Signatures,* 29, 244; Henry, *Sex Variants,* 1:29.

84. Marsh, "Report on Alaska Cannery Conditions," 14, 8, 7, 16; Casaday, "Labor Unrest and the Labor Movement," 213.

85. Allan East, "The Genesis and Early Development of a Juvenile Court: A Study of Community Responsibility in Multnomah County, Oregon, for the Period 1841–1920" (M.A. thesis, University of Oregon, 1939), 14; *Nampa (Idaho) Leader-Herald,* various articles from May 7, 14, 17, 21, 24, and 28, 1912.

Chapter 2. Sex in the City: Transient and Working-Class Men and Youths in the Urban Northwest

1. PPDDB, box 9, vol.: Graddock et al., April 1, 1911, to June 13, 1914, pp. 79–80, 81–84, 87 (April 8, 9, 12, 14–16, 19, 21, and May 8), SPARC; PPAR, vol.: April 13, 1913, to August 18, 1913, p. 10, SPARC; James C. Gill, Police Officer, to Mayor Harry Lane, "Partial list of houses of ill fame," April 16, 1909, MOC, box 14, folder 15, SPARC; Oregon v. Andrew Dillige, June 15, 1913, MC-CCC 52505; OSP Great Register, 1910–1925, pp. 142–43, OSA; MCJR, Federal and State Prisoners, 1913–1914, vol. 8, entry for Grover King, April 19, 1913, OSA.

2. I do not include in this figure the several dozen men arrested in late 1912 during the YMCA scandal, who were part of a onetime concerted citywide vice crackdown. Records used here for surveying same-sex sex crime in Portland, 1870–1921, are PPAR, SPARC; PPDDB, SPARC; Portland Municipal Court Register Index, 1895–1907, SPARC; Portland Police Court Docket, State Cases, 1874–1891, SPARC; MCCCC, 1888–1920; OSP Convict Description Book, Physical Description Records, Record/Register, Great Register, OSA; and various newspaper reports. On "indecent exposure" and other vaguely defined crimes as tools for prosecuting men interested in same-sex relationships, see Joseph F. Fishman, *Sex in Prison: Revealing Sex Conditions in American Prisons* (New York: National Library Press, 1934), 60, 64–65; Allan Bérubé, "The History of Gay Bathhouses," in *Policing Public Sex: Queer Politics and the Future of AIDS Activism,* ed. Dangerous Bedfellows (Boston: South End Press, 1996), 189, 194–95, 196; and John Donald Gustav-Wrathall, *Take the Young Stranger by the Hand: Same-Sex Relations and the YMCA* (Chicago: University of Chicago Press, 1998), 161.

3. Henry Russell Talbot et al., *Report of the Portland Vice Commission to the Mayor and City Council of the City of Portland, Oregon* (Portland: Henry Russell Talbot, 1913), 136.

4. Although it is possible to determine Portland's racial/nativity breakdown according to U.S. census categories—American-born white, foreign-born white, Negro, Chinese, Japanese, and other—for the years 1900, 1910, and 1920, the same cannot be done between 1870 and 1890. Thus the figures here are only indicative of the population's makeup for the earlier dates for which arrest records are available. See U.S. Department of Commerce, Bureau of the Census, *Fourteenth Census of the United States, 1920* (Washington, D.C.: Government Printing Office, 1922), 2:57, 730; U.S. Department of Commerce, Bureau of the Census, *Thirteenth Census of the United States, 1910* (Washington, D.C.: Government Printing Office, 1913), 3:523; U.S. Department of Commerce, Bureau of the Census, *Twelfth Census for the United States, 1900* (Washington, D.C.: U.S. Census Office, 1901), 1:901.

5. Roger Daniels, *Not Like Us: Immigrants and Minorities in America, 1890–1924* (Chicago: Ivan R. Dee, 1997); Daniels, *Coming to America: A History of Immigration and Ethnicity in American Life* (New York: HarperCollins, 1990); Leonard Dinnerstein and David M. Reimers, *Ethnic Americans: A History of Immigration,* 4th ed. (New York: Columbia University Press, 1999); Ronald Takaki, *A Different Mirror: A History of Multicultural America* (Boston: Little, Brown, 1993); Takaki, *Strangers from a Different Shore: A History of Asian Americans* (Boston: Little, Brown, 1989); David M. Reimers, *Unwelcome Strangers: American Identity and the Turn against Immigration* (New York: Columbia University Press, 1998); Michael Omi and Howard Winant, *Racial Formation in the United States from the 1960s to the 1990s,* 2d ed. (New York: Routledge, 1994), esp. 12; Matthew Frye Jacobson, *Whiteness of a Different Color: European Immigrants and the Alchemy of Race* (Cambridge, Mass.: Harvard University Press, 1998); David R. Roediger, *The Wages of Whiteness and the Making of the American Working Class,* rev. ed. (London: Verso, 1999).

6. Morton Keller, *Affairs of State: Public Life in Late Nineteenth Century America* (Cambridge, Mass.: Belknap Press, Harvard University Press, 1977), 445–47; John Higham, *Strangers in the Land: Patterns of American Nativism, 1860–1925,* 2d ed. (New Brunswick, N.J.: Rutgers University Press, 1988), 73–74, 109–10, 113, 158, 165–66, 168, 177, 183.

7. See Thomas C. McClintock, "James Saules, Peter Burnett, and the Oregon Black Exclusion Law," *PNQ* 86, no. 3 (summer 1995): 121–30; Quintard Taylor, "Blacks and Asians in a White City: Japanese Americans and African Americans in Seattle, 1890–1940," *WHQ* 22, no. 4 (November 1991): 401–29; Taylor, *The Forging of a Black Community: Seattle's Central District from 1870 through the Civil Rights Era,* with a foreword by Norm Rice (Seattle: University of Washington, 1994); Margaret K. Holden, "Gender and Protest Ideology: Sue Ross Keenan and the Oregon Anti-Chinese Movement," *Western Legal History* 7, no. 2 (summer/fall 1994): 222–43; William Toll, "Permanent Settlement: Japanese Families in Portland in 1920," *WHQ* 28, no. 1 (spring 1997): 19–43; Daniel P. Johnson, "Anti-Japanese Legislation in Oregon, 1917–1923," *OHQ* 97, no. 2 (summer 1996): 176–210; David A. Horowitz, "Social Morality and Personal Revitalization: Oregon's Ku Klux Klan in the 1920s," *OHQ* 90, no. 4 (winter 1989):

365–84; Horowitz, "The Klansman as Outsider: Ethnocultural Solidarity and Antielitism in the Oregon Ku Klux Klan of the 1920s," *PNQ* 80, no. 1 (January 1989): 12–20; Jeff Lalande, "Beneath the Hooded Robe: Newspapermen, Local Politics, and the Ku Klux Klan in Jackson County, Oregon, 1921–1923," *PNQ* 83, no. 2 (April 1992): 43–52; Eckard V. Toy, "The Ku Klux Klan in Oregon," in *Experiences in a Promised Land: Essays in Pacific Northwest History,* ed. G. Thomas Edwards and Carlos A. Schwantes (Seattle: University of Washington Press, 1986), 269–86; Dorothy O. Johansen, *Empire of the Columbia: A History of the Pacific Northwest,* 2d ed. (New York: Harper and Row, 1967), 348–49, 479–83, 487, 494–98; and Gordon B. Dodds, *The American Northwest: A History of Oregon and Washington* (Arlington Heights, Ill.: Forum Press, 1986), 118–24, 128–32.

8. *Portland Evening Telegram* (hereafter, *Evening Telegram*), September 24, 1890, 3; August 12, 1891, 2. See PPAR, vol.: January 1, 1890, to December 31, 1890, p. 202, SPARC.

9. *Portland, Oregon Journal* (hereafter, *Oregon Journal*), November 29, 1912, 10; Portland, Ore., *Mayor's Message and Municipal Reports, 1912* (Portland: Schwab, n.d.), 621.

10. *Portland Oregonian* (hereafter, *Oregonian*), January 23, 1913, 10.

11. *Evening Telegram,* January 23, 1913, 1; *Oregonian,* January 23, 1913, 10; January 25, 1913, 4; May 26, 1914, 4; *Oregon Journal,* January 23, 1913, 6; January 25, 1913, 2; *Portland News,* January 24, 1913, 1; January 25, 1913, 1; January 27, 1913, 6; August 22, 1918, 1; August 30, 1918, 12.

12. Nayan Shah, *Contagious Divides: Epidemics and Race in San Francisco's Chinatown* (Berkeley: University of California Press, 2001), 191, 313 n. 48; Takaki, *Strangers from a Different Shore,* 294–95; Patricia E. Roy, *A White Man's Province: British Columbia Politicians and Chinese and Japanese Immigrants, 1858–1914* (Vancouver: University of British Columbia Press, 1989), 164, 186, 191; Vijay Prashad, *The Karma of Brown Folk* (Minneapolis: University of Minnesota Press, 2000), 71–72.

13. Takaki, *Strangers from a Different Shore,* 294–314; Roy, *White Man's Province,* 164, 186, 191; *Portland News,* July 29, 1913, 2; *Oregonian,* December 9, 1913, 12. On hookworm, see Shah, *Contagious Divides,* 174, 190–91, 195–96, 199–200.

14. Hugh Johnston, *The Voyage of the Komagata Maru: The Sikh Challenge to Canada's Colour Bar* (Delhi: Oxford University Press, 1979), 2, 3, 4–5, 6–7, 8, 15, 35–88; Takaki, *Strangers from a Different Shore,* 300–301; Roy, *White Man's Province,* 164, 186, 191; Alan Morely, *Vancouver: Milltown to Metropolis* (Vancouver: Mitchell, 1991), 167–70.

15. Johnston, *Voyage of the Komagata Maru,* 2, 3, 4–5, 6–7, 8, 15, 35–88; Roy, *White Man's Province,* 164, 186, 191; Morely, *Vancouver,* 167–70.

16. Indiana Matters, "'Unfit for Publication': Notes towards a Lavender History of British Columbia," paper presented at Sex and State Conference, Toronto, July 3–6, 1985, 13–14. I wish to acknowledge my indebtedness to Matters's paper for pointing me to some of these sources at PABC and bringing to my attention the *Komagata Maru* incident. BCAGR, GR [Government Record]

0419, box 134, folder 1909/50; box 143, folder 1910/48, 1910/49, 1910/53; box 187, folder 1914/91, PABC.

17. Rex v. Nar Singh, BCAGR, GR 0419, box 134, folder 1909/50, PABC.

18. BCAGR, box 197, folder 1915/31, PABC.

19. Don Sing, WSP Inmate 6453; Jago Sing, WSP Inmate 6452; and Bram Sing, WSP Inmate 6454, WSAO; P. L. Verma to Secretary, Board of Prison, Walla Walla, Washington, August 4, 1912, in Don Sing, Jago Sing, Bram Sing Inmate Files; Trial Transcripts, Washington v. Sing et al., in Don Sing, Jago Sing, Bram Sing Inmate Files, pp. 1, 2, 3, 8, 9, 20, 29, 37.

20. *Portland News,* November 23, 1912, 6.

21. Materials in Christ Vlassis, WSP Inmate File 6187, WSAO.

22. John D'Emilio and Estelle B. Freedman, *Intimate Matters: A History of Sexuality in America* (New York: Harper and Row, 1988), 85–108; 215–21; Jennifer Terry, *An American Obsession: Science, Medicine, and Homosexuality in Modern Society* (Chicago: University of Chicago Press, 1999), 11, 52–53, 78–79, 89–97, 116; Siobhan B. Somerville, *Queering the Color Line: Race and the Invention of Homosexuality in American Culture* (Durham, N.C.: Duke University Press, 2000), 15–38; Kevin J. Mumford, *Interzones: Black/White Sex Districts in Chicago and New York in the Early Twentieth Century* (New York: Columbia University Press, 1997).

23. Havelock Ellis, *Sexual Inversion,* vol. 4 of *Studies in the Psychology of Sex,* 2d ed. (Philadelphia: F. A. Davis, 1904), 27–28, 27 n. 1; the note refers to Richard F. Burton, *The Book of the Thousand Nights and a Night: A Plain and Literal Translation of the Arabian Nights Entertainments* (London: Burton Club, 1885), 207 (quotation), 206. See also James G. Kiernan, "Sexual Perversion and the Whitechapel Murders," *Medical Standard* 4, no. 6 (December 1888): 172. It appears that Ellis's conclusions about Greece were based at least in part on the common knowledge of homoeroticism in classical times. For a discussion of the myth and reality of same-sex sexuality in ancient Greece and its relationship to the modern era, see Scott Bravmann, *Queer Fictions of the Past: History, Culture, and Difference* (Cambridge: Cambridge University Press, 1997), 47–67.

24. W. Ray Jones, "Two Questions of Justice Relating to Sexual Offenders," *American Journal of Urology and Sexology* 13, no. 7 (July 1917): 325.

25. On the middle class connecting immigrants and racial minorities to prostitution and the white slave panic, as well as on whites as victims, see D'Emilio and Freedman, *Intimate Matters,* 208–15; Mumford, *Interzones,* 37–49; Mary de Young, "Help, I'm Being Held Captive! The White Slave Fairy Tale of the Progressive Era," *Journal of American Culture* 6, no. 1 (spring 1983): 96–98; Frederick K. Grittner, *White Slavery: Myth, Ideology, and American Law* (New York: Garland, 1990), 61, 64, 75; Ruth Rosen, *The Lost Sisterhood: Prostitution in America, 1900–1918* (Baltimore: Johns Hopkins University Press, 1982), 15, 112; and Barbara Meil Hobson, *Uneasy Virtue: The Politics of Prostitution and the American Reform Tradition* (New York: Basic Books, 1987), 142. On the middle class connecting immigrants and racial minorities to sexual diseases and on the social construction of social diseases, see Shah, *Contagious Divides;* Allan M. Brandt,

No Magic Bullet: A Social History of Venereal Disease in the United States Since 1880, expanded ed. (New York: Oxford University Press, 1987); Elizabeth Fee and Daniel M. Fox, eds., *AIDS: The Burdens of History* (Berkeley: University of California Press, 1988); and Douglas Crimp, *AIDS: Cultural Analysis, Cultural Activism* (Cambridge, Mass.: MIT Press, 1988).

26. Alfred J. Zobel, quoted in "Primary Gonorrhea of the Rectum in the Male," *American Journal of Urology* 5, no. 1 (November 1909): 451; U.S. Congress, Senate, *Reports of the Immigration Commission,* 61st Cong., 3d sess., 1911, S. Doc. 753, p. 86.

27. Deepening fears were also related to the era's and region's general desire to police the sexual boundaries of race and sexuality through antimiscegenation laws. See Peggy Pascoe, "Race, Gender, and the Privileges of Property: On the Significance of Miscegenation Law in the U.S. West," in *Over the Edge: Remapping the American West,* ed. Valerie J. Matsumoto and Blake Allmendinger (Berkeley: University of California Press, 1999), 215–30; and Pascoe, "Miscegenation Law, Court Cases, and Ideologies of 'Race' in Twentieth-Century America," *Journal of American History* 83, no. 1 (June 1996): 44–69.

28. Jeffrey P. Moran, *Teaching Sex: The Shaping of Adolescence in the Twentieth Century* (Cambridge, Mass.: Harvard University Press, 2000); Harvey J. Graff, *Conflicting Paths: Growing Up in America* (Cambridge, Mass.: Harvard University Press, 1995); David I. Macleod, *Building Character in the American Boy: The Boy Scouts, YMCA, and Their Forerunners, 1870–1920* (Madison: University of Wisconsin Press, 1983); Steven Mintz and Susan Kellogg, *Domestic Revolutions: A Social History of American Family Life* (New York: Free Press, 1988); Joseph F. Kett, *Rites of Passage: Adolescence in America, 1790 to the Present* (New York: Basic Books, 1977); Kathy Peiss, *Cheap Amusements: Working Women and Leisure in Turn-of-the-Century New York* (Philadelphia: Temple University Press, 1988); E. Anthony Rotundo, *American Manhood: Transformations in Masculinity from the Revolution to the Modern Era* (New York: BasicBooks, 1993); Peter G. Filene, *Him/Her/Self: Sex Roles in Modern America,* 2d ed. (Baltimore: Johns Hopkins University Press, 1986); Robert M. Mennel, *Thorns and Thistles: Juvenile Delinquents in the United States, 1825–1940* (Hanover, N.H.: University Press of New England, 1973); Robert H. Bremner, ed., *Children and Youth in America: A Documentary History,* 3 vols. (Cambridge, Mass.: Harvard University Press, 1970–74).

29. "Report of Committee Appointed by the Mayor," July 12, 1913, p. 13, Council Documents, box 128, folder: Police, 1913, SPARC. See also "YMCA's First 100 Years" (Portland: YMCA of Columbia-Willamette, n.d.); H. W. Stone, "What We Are Doing for the Boy," *Pacific Monthly* 10, no. 3 (September 1903): 139–46; and Allan East, "The Genesis and Early Development of a Juvenile Court: A Study of Community Responsibility in Multnomah County, Oregon, for the Period 1841–1920" (M.A. thesis, University of Oregon, 1939), 16, 35.

30. Moran, *Teaching Sex,* 1, 15, 14–22.

31. Macleod, *Building Character in the American Boy,* 19–27; Kett, *Rites of Passage.*

32. Tony Lagallo, Inmate 7715, Parole Board Calendar for October 1918, vol. 5, [n.p.], OSP Parole Board Actions, 1915–1938, OSA; see also D'Emilio and Freedman, *Intimate Matters,* 90–93, 103–4, 106–7. On the "threat" that Chinese bachelorhood in San Francisco posed to heterosexual marriage, morality, and family life, see Shah, *Contagious Divides,* 12–16, 77–79, 253.

33. *Evening Telegram,* August 28, 1894, 6.

34. BCAGR, GR 0419, box 187, folder 1914/91, PABC.

35. In this section on the social construction of the vice district and the conflation of the vice district and its patrons and residents, I am indebted to Kay J. Anderson, *Vancouver's Chinatown: Racial Discourse in Canada, 1875–1980* (Montreal: McGill-Queen's University Press, 1991); Shah, *Contagious Divides;* and Mumford, *Interzones.*

36. This and the following paragraph are based on information from W. J. Fishman, *East End 1888: Life in a London Borough among the Laboring Poor* (Philadelphia: Temple University, 1988), 209–29; *Oregonian,* December 23, 1885, 1; Heather Lee Miller, "From Moral Suasion to Moral Coercion: Persistence and Transformation in Prostitution Reform, Portland, Oregon, 1888–1917" (M.A. thesis, University of Oregon, 1996), 19–23; Chris D. Sawyer, "From Whitechapel to Old Town: The Life and Death of the Skid Row District, Portland, Oregon" (Ph.D. diss., Portland State University, 1985), 111–15.

37. Portland, Ore., *Mayor's Annual Message and Municipal Report, 1903* (Portland: Schwab Printing, 1904), 187.

38. Other Northwest cities also called their vice districts "Whitechapel." Although the term *Skid Road* would stick to Seattle's tenderloin, back as early as 1891 at least one Seattle newspaper referred to this area as the Whitechapel. In 1896 a Boise paper used the term for that city's red-light district. See Kathryn S. Brandenfels, "Down on the Sawdust: Prostitution and Vice Control in Seattle, 1870–1920" (M.A. thesis, Hampshire College, 1981), 31; and Jo Anne Russell, "A Necessary Evil: Prostitutes, Patriarchs and Profits in Boise City, 1863–1915" (M.A. thesis, Boise State University, 1991), 117.

39. H. W. Scott, ed., *History of Portland, Oregon* (Syracuse, N.Y.: D. Mason, 1890), 436, already used "North End" to designate this area; Portland's police chief still called it "Whitechapel" in 1903 in Portland, Ore., *Mayor's Annual Message, 1903,* 187.

40. *Portland City Directory, 1884* (Portland: J. K. Gill, 1884), 27–28, as quoted in Paul Gilman Merriam, "Portland, Oregon, 1840–1890: A Social and Economic History" (Ph.D. diss., University of Oregon, 1971), 178. See also Stewart Holbrook, "Portland's Greatest Moral Crusade," *Oregonian,* Northwest Magazine section, August 2, 1936, 1; Sawyer, "From Whitechapel to Old Town," 212; E. Kimbark MacColl with Harry Stein, *Merchants, Money, and Power: The Portland Establishment, 1843–1913* (Portland: Georgian Press, 1988), 291; Christopher Joseph Head, "Nights of Heaven: A Social History of Saloon Culture in Portland, 1900–1914" (B.A. thesis, Reed College, 1980), 15; Scott, *History of Portland,* 431; and Laurence Pratt, *I Remember Portland, 1899–1915* (Portland: Binford and Mort, 1956), 24.

41. Portland, Ore., *Mayor's Annual Message, 1903*, 187–88.

42. Nelson Chia-Chi Ho, *Portland's Chinatown: The History of an Urban Ethnic District* (Portland: Bureau of Planning, City of Portland, 1978), 10; Sawyer, "From Whitechapel to Old Town," 203; Pratt, *I Remember Portland*, 16–18; Scott, *History of Portland*, 437–38; U.S. Department of Commerce, Bureau of the Census, *Twelfth Census of the United States, 1900* (Washington, D.C.: United States Census Office, 1901), 1:637; U.S. Department of Commerce, *Thirteenth Census of the United States, 1910*, 3:523.

43. Omi and Winant, *Racial Formation*, 15. See also Roediger, *Wages of Whiteness*, 100, 120–21; and Jacobson, *Whiteness of a Different Color*, 7.

44. *Oregonian*, June 12, 1888, 6; Scott, *History of Portland*, 453; Portland, Ore., *Mayor's Annual Message, 1903*, 187, 188, 190; Talbot et al., *Report of the Portland Vice Commission*, 33 (also 10, 34); Portland, Ore., *Mayor's Message, 1912*, 621.

45. Scott, *History of Portland*, 453.

46. Portland, Ore., *Annual Reports of the Officers of the City of Portland, 1879* (Portland: Niles and Beebe, 1880), 5; A. G. Rushlight, "Annual Message from His Honor the Mayor for 1912," January 3, 1912, Annual Reports—Mayor—Municipal Court, 1855–1913, box 12, folder 7, SPARC; Sawyer, "From Whitechapel to Old Town," 188, 218, 276, 328. See also John C. Schneider, "Tramping Workers, 1890–1920: A Subcultural View," in *Walking to Work: Tramps in America, 1790–1935*, ed. Eric H. Monkkonen (Lincoln: University of Nebraska, 1984), 224–25.

47. U.S. Department of Commerce, *Thirteenth Census of the United States, 1910*, 3:523.

48. Scott, *History of Portland*, 451–55.

49. *Oregonian*, April 28, 1895, 20; see also Sawyer, "From Whitechapel to Old Town," 188–90, 194, 241, 244, 141; Portland, Ore., *Annual Reports, 1879*, 5; and Portland, Ore., *Mayor's Annual Message, 1903*, 189. On the saloon's free lunch, see Madelon Powers, *Faces along the Bar: Lore and Order in the Workingman's Saloon, 1870–1920* (Chicago: University of Chicago Press, 1998), 207–26.

50. Sawyer, "From Whitechapel to Old Town," 253, 254, 279–84, 192, 196, 200, 226–30, 243, 333; U.S. Department of Commerce, *Thirteenth Census of the United States, 1910*, 3:523. See also Paul Groth, *Living Downtown: The History of Residential Hotels in the United States* (Berkeley: University of California Press, 1994), 131–67.

51. BCAGR, GR 0419, box 187, folder 1914/91, PABC; George McElroy, WSP Inmate File 6206, WSAO. See also Talbot et al., *Report of the Portland Vice Commission*, 34–45.

52. "Portland's Cheap Lodging Houses," report by the Sociological Department, Woman's Club, April 14, 1910, MOC, 1910, box 22, folder 3, SPARC. For another investigative report, see *Oregonian*, April 28, 1895, 20.

53. *Oregonian*, November 6, 1907, 7; and November 26, 1907, 12. On the connection between transients and urban vice districts and cheap amusements, see also Nels Anderson, *The Hobo: The Sociology of the Homeless Man* (Chicago: University of Chicago Press, 1923), 140–42, and Anderson, "The Juvenile and the

Tramp," *Journal of the American Institute of Criminal Law and Criminology* 14, no. 2 (August 1923): 292.

54. On amusements and vices and the working classes in general, see Lewis A. Erenberg, *Steppin' Out: New York Nightlife and the Transformation of American Culture, 1890–1930* (Westport, Conn.: Greenwood, 1981); Peiss, *Cheap Amusements;* and Robert Sklar, *Movie-Made America: A Social History of American Movies* (New York: Random House, 1975). On Portland's vices, see Merriam, "Portland, Oregon, 1840–1890," 131–32; Sawyer, "From Whitechapel to Old Town," 143, 144; Stewart H. Holbrook, *Holy Old Mackinaw: A Natural History of the American Lumberjack* (New York: Macmillan, 1938), 198; and Gloria E. Myers, *A Municipal Mother: Portland's Lola Greene Baldwin, America's First Policewomen* (Corvallis: Oregon State University Press, 1995), 193–95. On opium dens, see Portland, Ore., *Annual Reports, 1879,* 15; Head, "Nights of Heaven," 33. On gambling, see, for example, *Oregonian,* June 12, 1888, 6; Scott, *History of Portland,* 452; Portland, Ore., *Mayor's Annual Message, 1903,* 188; and Portland, Ore., *Mayor's Message and Municipal Reports, 1906* (Portland: n.d.), 223. On prize-fighting, see *Oregonian,* September 6, 1893, 8. On dance halls, see *Oregonian,* January 17, 1895, 5. On obscene picture shows, see C. Gritzmacher, chief of police, to Hon. Harry Lane, mayor, March 10, 1908, MOC, box 12, folder 3, SPARC.

55. *Oregonian,* June 12, 1888, 6; see also Kett, *Rites of Passage,* 170; and Anderson, "The Juvenile and the Tramp," 300–301.

56. Portland, Ore., *Mayor's Annual Message, 1903,* 190–91.

57. In New York City, according to George Chauncey, the working-class gay subculture was largely patterned on working-class culture more generally (*Gay New York: Gender, Urban Culture, and the Making of the Gay Male World* [New York: BasicBooks, 1994], 41). And indeed, such seems to have become the case in the Northwest as the twentieth century advanced. Vilma commented that during the years of Prohibition, a number of Seattle's working-class resorts such as pool halls and speakeasies "let the queens in" (Don Paulson with Roger Simpson, *An Evening at the Garden of Allah: A Gay Cabaret in Seattle* [New York: Columbia University Press, 1996], 22). And by 1930 the Casino was designated a place primarily for gays in Seattle. Yet in a slightly earlier era in that city, same-sex sex in the working-class world was an element wholly integrated into transient culture. I do not argue, therefore, for a separate working-class homosexual community that could be found in such social institutions as the saloon and pool hall. Rather, the same-sex affairs that took place there were an integral part of transient culture.

58. Roy Rosenzweig, *Eight Hours for What We Will: Workers and Leisure in an Industrial City, 1870–1920* (Cambridge: Cambridge University Press, 1983), 57, 53–61; Powers, *Faces along the Bar;* Jon M. Kingsdale, "The 'Poor Man's Club': Social Functions of the Urban Working-Class Saloon," in *The American Man,* ed. Elizabeth H. Pleck and Joseph H. Pleck (Englewood Cliffs, N.J.: Prentice-Hall, 1980), 257, 260–62, 264–68; Peiss, *Cheap Amusements,* 15–21; Head, "Nights of Heaven."

59. *Portland Sunday Mercury,* June 29, 1889, 3.

60. Oregon v. George Lifte, March 6, 1913, MCCCC 50958 (court documents refer to Stfe as Lifte and Sitf; possibly he was the George Stfe listed in the 1910 manuscript census, U.S. Department of Commerce, Bureau of the Census, Thirteenth Census, 1910, Manuscript Population Census Returns, Multnomah County, Oregon, Enumeration District 169, sheet 8A, line 1); Archibald W. Frater, "Court Methods, Mothers' Pensions, and Community Dangers," in *Why Children Go Wrong,* Annual Report of the Seattle Juvenile Court for 1913 (Seattle: Seattle Juvenile Court, January 1, 1914), 9–11.

61. Talbot et al., *Report of the Portland Vice Commission,* 127, 128; PPDDB, box 9, vol.: Craddock et al., April 1, 1911, to June 13, 1914, p. 79 (April 8, 1913), SPARC.

62. W. C. Curlburt to [Mayor] Harry Lane, July 21, 1905, MOC, 1905, box 2, folder 2, SPARC; A. DuChamp to Mr. T. G. Greene, August 18, 1908, MOC, 1908, box 12, folder 9, SPARC. See also E. Kimbark MacColl, *The Shaping of a City: Business and Politics in Portland, Oregon, 1885–1915* (Portland: Georgian Press, 1976), 270; and Myers, *Municipal Mother,* 41.

63. William Trufant Foster, *Vaudeville and Motion Picture Shows: A Study of Theaters in Portland, Oregon,* Social Service Series no. 2 (Portland: Reed College, 1914), 6, 15, 16, 17, 28; Talbot et al., *Report of the Portland Vice Commission,* 143, 144. On the role played by commercialized amusements in the sexual transformation of America, see D'Emilio and B. Freedman, *Intimate Matters,* 196, 195–96, 197; Peiss, *Cheap Amusements,* 11–33, 127–29; Lary May, *Screening Out the Past: The Birth of Mass Culture and the Motion Picture Industry* (New York: Oxford University Press, 1980), 17, 18; Myers, *Municipal Mother,* 42; and Sharon R. Ullman, *Sex Seen: The Emergence of Modern Sexuality in America* (Berkeley: University of California Press, 1997), 24, 26.

64. Cases of Juvenile Vice, Juvenile Court of Portland, OSHS, MS 1541, box 1, folder 2, various lists, OHS; Lilburn Merrill, "A Summary of Findings in a Study of Sexualism among a Group of One Hundred Delinquent Boys," *Journal of Delinquency* 3, no. 6 (November 1918): 259. In his studies in Canada, Steven Maynard discovered that in Ontario working-class "boys were crazy for 'the Show'" and therefore readily traded sex for the price of entry; they also engaged in sex while inside the auditorium ("'Horrible Temptations': Sex, Men, and Working-Class Male Youth in Urban Ontario, 1890–1917," *Canadian Historical Review* 78, no. 2 [June 1997]: 207–8).

65. PPDDB, box 8, vol.: Jones & Tichenor & Howell, October 24, 1907, to January 31, 1911, p. 47 (February 4, 1909), SPARC; Harry Smith, Inmate 7375, Parole Calendar for June 1916, vol. 3 [n.p.], OSP Parole Board Actions, 1915–1938, OSA. See also George Jackson, WSP Inmate File 6090, WSAO; Thomas Hogan, WSP Inmate File 6089, WSAO; and Charles McCormack, WSP Inmate File 6091, WSAO.

66. PPDDB, box 14, vol.: Abbot & Goltz, February 4, 1915, to February 29, 1916, p. 9 (February 22, 1915), SPARC; G. Thompson [to Portland City Council], October 9, 1905, MOC, box 2, folder 8, SPARC.

67. PPDDB, box 9, vol.: Craddock et al., April 1, 1911, to June 13, 1914, p. 82 (April 16, 1913), SPARC; Lilburn Merrill, "Physical and Mental Conditions," in *Why Children Go Wrong,* 35; see also Maynard, "'Horrible Temptations'"; Chauncey, *Gay New York,* 140; and George Chauncey, "The Policed: Gay Men's Strategies of Everyday Resistance in Times Square," in *Creating a Place for Ourselves: Lesbian, Gay, and Bisexual Community Histories,* ed. Brett Beemyn (New York: Routledge, 1997), 16.

68. Anderson, "The Juvenile and the Tramp," 300 (quotation), 303–4, 307; see also Anderson, *Hobo,* 146.

69. Merrill, "Physical and Mental Conditions," 41, and Merrill, "Summary of Findings," 261–62; PPDDB, box 9, vol.: Craddock et al., April 1, 1911, to June 13, 1914, p. 83 (April 18, 1913), SPARC; PPDDB, box 9, vol.: Coleman & Snow, February 1, 1911, to September 5, 1911, p. 15 (March 2, 1911), SPARC. On juvenile male prostitution in the urban Northwest and its connection to life on the road in a later period, see also Patrick Gandy, "Hamburger Hustlers," paper presented at the American Anthropology Association meeting, November 29, 1971, p. 5 (a copy is in the collection of the Kinsey Institute for Research in Sex, Gender, and Reproduction, Bloomington, Ind.). For more on late-nineteenth-century transient boys and sex work in western cities, see Thomas Jacob Noel, "Gay Bars and the Emergence of the Denver Homosexual Community," *Social Science Journal* 15, no. 2 (April 1978): 60–61.

Somewhat later in the twentieth century, *punk* had become a term that also referred to a boy who willingly had sex with men in the traditionally female role. However, in the first years of the twentieth century, it seems to have been used only within the transient context. See G. Legman, "The Language of Homosexuality: An American Glossary," in *Sex Variants: A Study of Homosexual Patterns,* by George W. Henry (New York: Paul B. Hoeber, 1941), 2:1174; and Albert J. Reiss, Jr., "The Social Integration of Queers and Peers," *Social Problems* 9, no. 2 (fall 1961): 115.

70. Anderson, "The Juvenile and the Tramp," 301, 307; Sawyer, "From Whitechapel to Old Town," 188–89.

71. Anderson, *Hobo,* 146; see also Anderson, "The Juvenile and the Tramp," 300, 303–4, 307.

72. Tony Lagallo, Inmate 7715, Parole Board Calendar for October 1918, vol. 5 [n.p.], OSP Parole Board Actions, 1915–1938, OSA.

73. *Salem (Ore.) Daily Capital Journal,* November 22, 1912, 5; *Evening Telegram,* November 22, 1912, 8; Frater, "Court Methods," 10.

74. Vlassis, WSP Inmate File.

75. Peter Olsen, WSP Inmate File 6409, WSAO.

76. Peiss, *Cheap Amusements,* 110; see also David K. Johnson, "The Kids of Fairytown: Gay Male Culture on Chicago's Near North Side in the 1930s," in Beemyn, ed., *Creating a Place for Ourselves,* 106.

77. Anderson, "The Juvenile and the Tramp," 307; Idaho v. Henry Bacon, Justice Court Transcripts, Ada County Criminal Cases, 1864–1923, ISHS; Rex v. Pappas, Hearing Transcripts, BCAGR, GR 0419, box 186, folder 1914/82, PABC.

78. Washington v. Ernest O'Grady, Second Information of Crime, WSSCC 12337, WSAE; Thomas Tassus, WSP Inmate File 6775, WSAO. See also Reiss, "Social Integration," 112; William Marlin Butts, "Boy Prostitutes of the Metropolis," *Journal of Clinical Psychopathology* 8, no. 4 (April 1947): 674; and Maynard, "'Horrible Temptations,'" 209–10.

79. PPDDB, box 9, vol.: Craddock et al., April 1, 1911, to June 13, 1914, pp. 157, 164 (November 8 and 19, 1913), SPARC.

80. Ibid., p. 80 (April 12, 1913).

81. PPDDB, box 10, vol.: Day & Hyde, December 11, 1911, to November 1, 1912, p. 108 (June 22, 1912), SPARC.

82. In none of the Northwest cities that I studied nor in any of the region's states was I able to uncover any statute or ordinance criminalizing male prostitution. Only charges such as vagrancy, sodomy, and others discussed earlier in this chapter were leveled at male sex workers. Just one Portland ordinance refers rather vaguely to what appears to be male prostitution—a local code that penalized not the sex worker but the establishment that might permit one on its premises (see Ordinance No. 10904, Council Documents, box 69, folder 1, Licenses and Liquor, 1898, SPARC). Thus, male sex workers in the Northwest were not doubly criminalized for engaging in paid sex and in homosexual sex.

83. PPDDB, box 9, vol.: Craddock et al., April 1, 1911, to June 13, 1914, pp. 60, 61 (December 12, 1913), SPARC.

84. PPDDB, box 10, vol.: J. Maloney & Mallet et al., September 7, 1911, to April 5, 1913, p. 26 (October 25, 1911), SPARC.

85. According to Albert J. Reiss, Jr., the youths he interviewed for a 1961 study "regard[ed] hustling as an acceptable substitute for other delinquent earnings or activity" ("Social Integration of Queers and Peers," 103).

86. Arrests by Hellyer and Maloney on July 1, 1909, in Portland Police Detective Department Report, July 31, 1909, MOC, box 17, folder 11, SPARC; PPDDB, box 9, vol.: Craddock et al., April 1, 1911, to June 13, 1914, p. 82 (April 14, 1913), SPARC. On hustlers and hoodlum hustlers, see George W. Henry and Alfred A. Gross, "Social Factors in the Case Histories of One Hundred Underprivileged Homosexuals," *Mental Hygiene* 22 (1938): 606; H. Lawrence Ross, "The 'Hustler' in Chicago," *Journal of Student Research* 1, no. 1 (fall 1959): 15–16; and Gandy, "Hamburger Hustlers," 3.

87. Merrill, "Summary of Findings," 257, 262, 262–63, 259.

88. Jennifer James, "Entrance into Juvenile Male Prostitution, [Seattle]," prepared for the National Institute of Mental Health, Rockville, Md., November 1982, p. 9; Paulson with Simpson, *Evening at the Garden of Allah,* 22–23. Other scholars have noted differences between homosexual and heterosexual male sex workers. See Butts, "Boy Prostitutes," 674; Ross, "The 'Hustler' in Chicago," 13–19; and Reiss, "Social Integration of Queers and Peers," 102–4.

89. Legman, "Language of Homosexuality," 1169, 1155; Paulson with Simpson, *Evening at the Garden of Allah,* 22–23. See also Chauncey, "The Policed," 16.

90. Paulson with Simpson, *Evening at the Garden of Allah,* 24; Merrill, "Physical and Mental Conditions," 42.

91. Mrs. Lola G. Baldwin, Supervisor, "Text Report for December 1918, Seventh District," p. 8, Lola G. Baldwin Papers, folder: "Lola G. Baldwin's Personal Notes forwarded to WPD in 1951," Portland Police Museum, Portland, Ore. On Lola G. Baldwin, see Myers, *Municipal Mother.*

92. PPDDB, box 9, vol.: Day et al., March 23, 1911, to August 30, 1911, p. 118 (November 3, 1911), SPARC; MCJR 1914–1916, vol. 9, entries for G. H. Graham and E. B. Carter, November 4, 1915. See also *Portland City Directory, 1915* (Portland: R. L. Polk, 1915), 291, 519.

93. *Oregonian,* May 21, 1913, 1. For typical coverage of a female-to-male crossdresser (Nell Pickerell), see *Portland News,* April 10, 1912, 3; *Oregonian,* June 4, 1912, 12; *Oregon Journal,* June 4, 1912, 6; and *Evening Telegram,* June 4, 1912, 8.

94. Dean Stiff [pseud. of Nels Anderson], *The Milk and Honey Route: A Handbook for Hobos* (New York: Vanguard, 1931), 161–62.

95. Reiss, "Social Integration of Queers and Peers," 102–3, 109, 114–15; Butts, "Boy Prostitutes," 674–75; Henry and Gross, "Social Factors," 606–7. On "trade" and "rough trade," see Legman, "Language of Homosexuality," 1175, 1177–78.

96. PPAR, vol.: December 18, 1907, to May 1, 1908, p. 148, SPARC; Oregon v. Tom Conley, May 14, 1908, MCCCC 38769; PPAR, vol.: May 1, 1908, to September 30, 1908, p. 55, SPARC; Oregon v. A. G. Ahmed, September 16, 1908, MCCCC 39282; PPAR, vol.: Coleman & Royale et al., September 1, 1911, to January 2, 1912, p. 57, SPARC.

97. PPAR, vol.: October 1, 1908, to February 23, 1909, p. 36, SPARC; Oregon v. Ed Montgomery, October 31, 1908, MCCCC 39521; PPAR, vol.: March 5, 1920, to September 4, 1920, p. 220, SPARC; Oregon v. Michael Dixon, October 15, 1920, MCCCC 81950; Washington v. H. Gemas, Trial Transcripts, pp. 4, 5, WSSCC 15792, WSAE (court records give "Gemas" as the defendant, but in other documents the defendant's name appears as "Demas"). See also Merrill, "Summary of Findings," 258.

98. Chauncey, *Gay New York,* 41; Paulson with Simpson, *Evening at the Garden of Allah,* 22–23.

99. Anderson, "The Juvenile and the Tramp," 305.

Chapter 3. Gay Identity and Community in Early Portland

1. *Portland Evening Telegram* (hereafter, *Evening Telegram*), November 16, 1912, 2. The identity of the unnamed young man whose confession initiated the 1912 scandal is not certain, but arrest records point to Benjamin Trout. Of all those linked to the scandal, only Trout's name appears in arrest ledgers in days prior to the news about same-sex vice becoming public. The arrest ledger gives his age as twenty-two, but at trial Trout said he was nineteen. PPAR, vol.: July 30, 1912, to December 10, 1912, p. 193, SPARC; Benny Trout testimony, Oregon v. Harry A. Start, Trial Transcript (hereafter, Start Transcript), p. 140, OSCR, file 1478, OSA.

2. *Portland Oregonian* (hereafter, *Oregonian*), November 14, 1912, 12; November 16, 1912, 11; *Evening Telegram,* November 16, 1912, 2; Voter Registration Cards, microfilm roll 25, 1912–13, listing for Harry L. Rowe, MCARC.

3. It is impossible to ascertain the class and occupational backgrounds, let alone the exact number, of all those connected with the specific events of 1912. Complicating matters is that some papers reported as members of the "vice clique" other individuals who happened to be arrested for same-sex crimes during these months but otherwise had no connection to Portland's homosexual community. Information regarding occupations of men involved in the 1912 and 1928 scandals comes from various sources, including local newspapers, directories, and legal documents. Others have casually noted a connection between white-collar workers and homosexuality and gay community. See, for example, David K. Johnson, "The Kids of Fairytown: Gay Male Culture on Chicago's Near North Side in the 1930s," in *Creating a Place for Ourselves: Lesbian, Gay, and Bisexual Community Histories,* ed. Brett Beemyn (New York: Routledge, 1997), 106–9.

For a thorough discussion of Kinsey's class categories, see Alfred C. Kinsey, Wardell B. Pomeroy, and Clyde E. Martin, *Sexual Behavior in the Human Male* (Philadelphia: W. B. Saunders, 1948), 78–79. Because this chapter draws extensively on Kinsey and his findings, I must acknowledge the considerable debate and criticism that have surrounded his data. James H. Jones's controversial biography of Kinsey, *Alfred C. Kinsey: A Public/Private Life* (New York: W. W. Norton, 1997), summarizes the critical reception of *Sexual Behavior in the Human Male* at the time of its publication; Jones also contributed significantly to the more recent debates about the validity of Kinsey's findings. Yet despite some problems with Kinsey's data, his sampling methods, and his interviewing processes (and in spite of Jones's revelations about Kinsey's personal life), historians generally accept the validity of Kinsey's conclusions regarding sexuality. On this issue, see Martin Duberman's review of Jones's book, "Kinsey's Urethra," *Nation,* November 3, 1997, 40, 42–43. On the Kinsey controversy, see also Paul Robinson, *The Modernization of Sex: Havelock Ellis, Alfred Kinsey, William Masters, and Virginia Johnson* (New York: Harper and Row, 1976). Another thoughtful explanation of how Kinsey's work is useful to the historical study specifically of homosexuality is offered by George Chauncey in *Gay New York: Gender, Urban Culture, and the Making of the Gay Male World, 1890–1940* (New York: Basic-Books, 1994), 70–71.

4. Kinsey, Pomeroy, and Martin, *Sexual Behavior,* 361, 357, 358, 378, 328, 359, 384, 641, 653, 654.

5. John D'Emilio, *Sexual Politics, Sexual Communities: The Making of a Homosexual Minority in the United States, 1940–1970* (Chicago: University of Chicago Press, 1983), 10–13, 23–39.

6. Chauncey, *Gay New York,* 133 (quotation), 131–35. See also Marc Stein, *City of Sisterly and Brotherly Loves: Lesbian and Gay Philadelphia, 1945–1972* (Chicago: University of Chicago Press, 2000), 20; David F. Greenberg, *The Construction of Homosexuality* (Chicago: University of Chicago Press, 1988), 346; John

D'Emilio and Estelle B. Freedman, *Intimate Matters: A History of Sexuality in America* (New York: Harper and Row, 1988, 226–27; and E. Anthony Rotundo, *American Manhood: Transformations in Masculinity from the Revolution to the Modern Era* (New York: BasicBooks, 1993), 274–75.

7. *Seattle Star,* November 27, 1912, 6. For period observations about homosexuality and its connection to urban life, see James G. Kiernan, "Sexual Perversion, and the Whitechapel Murders," *Medical Standard* 4, no. 5 (November 1888): 129; William Lee Howard, "Sexual Perversion in America," *American Journal of Dermatology and Genito-Urinary Diseases* 8, no. 1 (January 1904): 9; and Charles H. Hughes, "Homo Sexual Complexion Perverts in St. Louis: Note on a Feature of Sexual Psychopathy," *Alienist and Neurologist* 28, no. 4 (November 1907): 488.

8. D'Emilio and Freedman, *Intimate Matters,* 227; John D'Emilio, "Capitalism and Gay Identity," in *The Lesbian and Gay Studies Reader,* ed. Henry Abelove, Michèle Aina Barale, and David M. Halperin (New York: Routledge, 1993), 470. See also D'Emilio, *Sexual Politics,* 10–13; Kevin White, *The First Sexual Revolution: The Emergence of Male Heterosexuality in Modern America* (New York: New York University Press, 1993); and Kathy Peiss, *Cheap Amusements: Working Women and Leisure in Turn-of-the-Century New York* (Philadelphia: Temple University Press, 1988).

9. Martin J. Sklar, *The Corporate Reconstruction of American Capitalism, 1890–1916: The Market, the Law, and Politics* (Cambridge: Cambridge University Press, 1988), 1, 4; White, *First Sexual Revolution,* 8. See also Stuart M. Blumin, *The Emergence of the Middle Class: Social Experience in the American City, 1760–1900* (Cambridge: Cambridge University Press, 1989).

10. On corporate economy in general, see Glenn Porter, *The Rise of Big Business, 1860–1910,* 2d ed. (Arlington Heights, Ill.: Harlan Davidson, 1992); and Alfred D. Chandler, *The Visible Hand: The Managerial Revolution in American Business* (Cambridge, Mass.: Belknap Press, 1977).

11. Richard Hofstadter, *The Age of Reform* (New York: Vintage, 1955), 217–18; C. Wright Mills, *White Collar: The American Middle Classes* (New York: Oxford University Press, 1951), 68–69; Jürgen Kocka, *White Collar Workers in America, 1890–1940: A Social-Political History in International Perspective,* trans. Maura Kealey (London: Sage, 1989), 44–46, 50, 52, 67, 95; Peter G. Filene, *Him/Her/Self: Sex Roles in Modern America,* 2d ed. (Baltimore: Johns Hopkins University Press, 1986), 73; Olivier Zunz, *Making America Corporate, 1870–1920* (Chicago: University of Chicago Press, 1990), 126; Joseph F. Kett, *Rites of Passage: Adolescence in America, 1790 to the Present* (New York: Basic Books, 1977), 151; William Toll, *The Making of an Ethnic Middle Class: Portland Jewry over Four Generations* (Albany: State University of New York Press, 1982), 145; Blumin, *Emergence of the Middle Class,* 267–68.

12. Rotundo, *American Manhood,* 169 (quotation), 168, 178, 179, 249. On masculinity and the workplace, see also Joe L. Dubbert, *A Man's Place: Masculinity in Transition* (Englewood Cliffs, N.J.: Prentice-Hall, 1979), 26–28; Filene, *Him/Her/Self,* 70–71; and Michael S. Kimmel, "The Contemporary 'Crisis'

of Masculinity in Historical Perspective," in *The Making of Masculinities: The New Men's Studies,* ed. Henry Brod (Boston: Allen and Unwin, 1987), 137–49.

13. Gail Bederman, *Manliness and Civilization: A Cultural History of Gender and Race in the United States, 1880–1917* (Chicago: University of Chicago Press, 1995), 12; Blumin, *Emergence of the Middle Class,* 267, 271, 291, 292–93; Kocka, *White Collar Workers in America,* 44, 87, 185, 186; Dubbert, *Man's Place,* 81.

14. On the "masculinity crisis," see Joe L. Dubbert, "Progressivism and the Masculinity Crisis," in *The American Man,* ed. Elizabeth H. Pleck and Joseph H. Pleck (Englewood Cliffs, N.J.: Prentice-Hall, 1980), 305–20; Bederman, *Manliness and Civilization,* 11–13; Jeffrey P. Hantover, "The Boy Scouts and the Validation of Masculinity," in Pleck and Pleck, eds., *American Man,* 288–92; Rotundo, *American Manhood,* 248–51; Chauncey, *Gay New York,* 111–13; and John Higham, "The Reorientation of American Culture in the 1890s," in *The Origins of Modern Consciousness,* ed. John Weiss (Detroit: Wayne State University, 1965), 43–44. Mills (*White Collar,* 272–73) offers a bleak view of the mid-twentieth-century white-collar work while Sklar's perspective (*Corporate Reconstruction,* 26) is more hopeful.

15. Carroll Smith-Rosenberg, *Disorderly Conduct: Visions of Gender in Victorian America* (New York: Knopf, 1985), 15 (quotation), 245–96. For more on corporate capitalism's effects on women, see Smith-Rosenberg, "Discourse of Sexuality and Subjectivity: The New Woman, 1870–1936," in *Hidden from History: Reclaiming the Gay and Lesbian Past,* ed. Martin Duberman, Martha Vicinus, and George Chauncey, Jr. (New York: Meridian, 1989), 264, 266, 273; Mary P. Ryan, *Womanhood in America: From Colonial Times to the Present,* 3d ed. (New York: Franklin Watts, 1983), 200–208, 228–30; D'Emilio and Freedman, *Intimate Matters,* 201, 189–93, 194–95, 197, 199; Steven Mintz and Susan Kellogg, *Domestic Revolutions: A Social History of American Family Life* (New York: Free Press, 1988), 110–11; and Lillian Faderman, *Surpassing the Love of Men: Romantic Friendship and Love between Women from the Renaissance to the Present* (New York: William Morrow, 1981), 178, 184, 185, 204.

16. On the "epidemic" of neurasthenia, see George M. Beard, *Sexual Neurasthenia,* ed. A.D. Rockwell (New York: E.B. Treat, 1884), 70–71; see also Rotundo, *American Manhood,* 185–93; and Bederman, *Manliness and Civilization,* 84–88.

17. Various materials in John Gibson, WSP Inmate File 6708, WSAO.

18. Mintz and Kellogg, *Domestic Revolutions,* 113–19; Kocka, *White Collar Workers in America,* 87. After comparing these 1905 findings to attitudes among German white-collar workers, Kocka concludes that they reveal a "widespread" notion of upward mobility among American white-collar workers. But from a purely American perspective, it is more significant that about half of the clerks — far more than their nineteenth-century counterparts — saw no chance of upward mobility.

19. U.S. Department of Commerce, Bureau of the Census, Thirteenth Census, 1910, Manuscript Population Census Returns, Ada County, Idaho, Enumeration District 4, sheet 3A, line 8; *Boise City Directory, 1905* (Boise: R. L. Polk,

1905); *Boise City Directory, 1906–1907* (Boise: R. L. Polk, 1906); *Boise City Directory, 1908* (Boise: R. L. Polk, 1908); *Boise City Directory, 1909–1910* (Boise: R. L. Polk, 1909); *Portland City Directory, 1911* (Portland: R. L. Polk, 1911); *Portland City Directory, 1912* (Portland: R. L. Polk, 1912); *Portland City Directory, 1913* (Portland: R. L. Polk, 1913); Earl Van Hulen testimony, Start Transcript, 73.

20. *Portland City Directory, 1952* (Seattle: R. L. Polk, 1952); *Portland City Directory, 1953–1954* (Seattle: R. L. Polk, 1954).

21. U.S. Department of Commerce, Bureau of the Census, Twelfth Census, 1900, Manuscript Population Census Returns, Cuyahoga County, Ohio, Enumeration District 107, sheet 6A, line 6; Fourteenth Census, 1920, Manuscript Population Census Returns, Cuyahoga County, Ohio, Enumeration District 494, sheet 27A, line 17; *Portland City Directory, 1904* (Portland: R. L. Polk, 1904); *Portland City Directory, 1905* (Portland: R. L. Polk, 1905); *Portland City Directory, 1906* (Portland: R. L. Polk, 1906); *Portland City Directory, 1907–1908* (Portland: R. L. Polk, 1907); *Portland City Directory, 1909* (Portland: R. L. Polk, 1909); *Portland City Directory, 1911, 1912,* and *1913;* Edward E. Wedemeyer, death notice, October 25, 1920, necrology file, Cleveland Public Library Main Branch, Cleveland, Ohio; *Evening Telegram,* December 19, 1912, 8.

22. *Portland, Oregon Journal* (hereafter, *Oregon Journal*), November 17, 1912, 1; *Portland City Directory, 1886* (Portland: R. L. Polk, 1886); *Portland City Directory, 1912.*

23. Steven Mintz, *A Prison of Expectations: The Family in Victorian Culture* (New York: New York University Press, 1983), 13, 31. See also Rotundo, *American Manhood,* 58–59, 26–30; Dubbert, *Man's Place,* 142; E. Anthony Rotundo, "Romantic Friendship: Male Intimacy and Middle-Class Youth in the Northern United States, 1800–1900," *Journal of Social History* 23, no. 1 (fall 1989): 1–25; Mark C. Carnes, *Secret Ritual and Manhood in Victorian America* (New Haven: Yale University Press, 1989), 113–14; Kett, *Rites of Passage,* 29, 36, 25; Gail Bederman, "Civilization, the Decline of Middle-Class Manliness, and Ida B. Wells' Anti-Lynching Campaign (1892–94)," in *Gender and American History since 1890,* ed. Barbara Melosh (London: Routledge, 1993), 209–10; Mintz and Kellogg, *Domestic Revolutions,* 45, 53; and Mary P. Ryan, *Cradle of the Middle Class: The Family in Oneida County, New York, 1790–1865* (Cambridge: Cambridge University Press, 1981), 161.

24. Kinsey, Pomeroy, and Martin, *Sexual Behavior,* 328.

25. Sebastian de Grazia, *Of Time, Work, and Leisure* (New York: Twentieth Century Fund, 1962), 441, table 1. Kett (*Rites of Passage,* 144) notes that during the pre-entrepreneurial era, when the economy revolved around home production and consumption, young people long stayed dependent within the family. The development of commercial and industrial opportunities in the nineteenth and early twentieth centuries made it possible for young people to achieve adult economic status earlier in life. By about 1920, however, social changes in family, education, and the economy converged to re-create dependency in childhood. The period from 1880 to 1920 was thus a crucial moment in which young middle-class men with a high school education could achieve financial

independence and move to the city. On corporate wages, see Mills, *White Collar*, 72; Kocka, *White Collar Workers in America*, 97; Blumin, *Emergence of the Middle Class*, 271; Zunz, *Making America Corporate*, 129; and Susan Benson Parker, *Counter Cultures: Saleswomen, Managers, and Customers in American Department Stores, 1890–1940* (Urbana: University of Illinois Press, 1986), 219–20.

26. Fred Rodby testimony, Start Transcript, 19–20. See also Mills, *White Collar*, 236; and D'Emilio and Freedman, *Intimate Matters*, 278.

27. Earl Taylor and W. T. Hume testimony, Start Transcript, 26–27, 308–9. On amusement parks and heterosexuality, see, for example, D'Emilio and Freedman, *Intimate Matters*, 196.

28. U.S. Department of Commerce, Bureau of the Census, *Fourteenth Census of the United States, 1920* (Washington, D.C.: Government Printing Office, 1922), 2:387; U.S. Department of Commerce, Bureau of the Census, *Thirteenth Census of the United States, 1910* (Washington, D.C.: Government Printing Office, 1913), 1:47, 522, 534; U.S. Department of Commerce, Bureau of the Census, *Twelfth Census of the United States, 1900* (Washington, D.C.: Government Printing Office, 1902), 2:clxxvii.

29. *Oregon Journal*, November 17, 1912, 1; *Portland City Directory, 1910* (Portland: R.L. Polk, 1910); *Portland City Directory, 1911* and *1912*; Oregon v. Harry White [Wight], November 30, 1912, MCCCC 53578; U.S. Department of Commerce, Bureau of the Census, Thirteenth Census, 1910, Manuscript Population Census Returns, Multnomah County, Ore., Enumeration District 147, sheet 12B, lines 83 and 85 for Claude Bronner and Nathan Healy. The 1910 census lists Bronner and Healy as residents of the same dwelling, but directories give separate addresses. An excellent study on gay residential patterns in the post–World War II American city is Marc Stein's *City of Sisterly and Brotherly Loves*.

30. Bill of Exceptions, Oregon v. E. E. Wedemeyer, pp. 1–2, OSCR, file 1479, OSA; *Oregon Journal*, November 17, 1912, sec. 1, pp. 1, 6; *Evening Telegram*, November 16, 1912, 2.

31. Ryan, *Cradle of the Middle Class*, 176–77; John Donald Gustav-Wrathall, *Take the Young Stranger by the Hand: Same-Sex Relations and the YMCA* (Chicago: University of Chicago Press, 1998), 10–15; David I. MacLeod, *Building Character in the American Boy: The Boy Scouts, YMCA, and Their Forerunners, 1870–1920* (Madison: University of Wisconsin Press, 1983), 35, 76; "YMCA's First 100 Years" (Portland: YMCA of Columbia-Willamette, n.d.); U.S. Department of Commerce, Manuscript Population Census Returns, Multnomah County, Ore., 1910, Enumeration District 145, sheets 1A, 1B, 2A, 2B; *Portland City Directory, 1911* and *1912*; *Evening Telegram*, November 22, 1912, 8.

32. *Portland News*, November 22, 1912, 1; *Portland City Directory, 1912*; anonymous letter, OSHS collection box 1, file 2: Case Histories, MS 1541, OHS. For histories that look at the YMCA and its relationship to homosexuality in the early twentieth century, see Chauncey, *Gay New York*, 155–57; and especially Gustav-Wrathall, *Take the Young Stranger by the Hand*.

33. Gustav-Wrathall, *Take the Young Stranger by the Hand*, 142, 146. One can also see the YMCA and its programs as a microcosm of broader social patterns in

the United States at the time. Scholars who have studied the so-called masculinity crisis of the era note that as middle-class men looked outside of work for new sources to sustain masculinity, they turned to contact sports, outdoor activities, boxing, and bodybuilding. In a sense, they began to concentrate more on physical "masculinity" rather than on the nineteenth-century ideals of "manliness." This emphasis on physical culture was mirrored in the YMCA movement. Also on the broader level, the development of mass consumerism called on all Americans not to exhibit self-control and delay gratification. Moreover, corporate America began selling products to appeal to people's sexual desires; less directly, the male body was sexualized in advertising. Combined, all these developments served to heighten homosexual desire, just as they were also working to heighten heterosexual urges. On topics such as bodybuilding, the sexualization of the male body, advertising, and the consumer society, see White, *First Sexual Revolution*, 24, 27–28, 31–33, 34; and D'Emilio and Freedman, *Intimate Matters*, 188–89, 278.

34. U.S. Department of Commerce and Labor, Bureau of the Census, *Special Reports: Occupations at the Twelfth Census* (Washington, D.C.: Government Printing Office, 1904), 686. By comparison, in Boston (p. 494), an eastern city (much older than Portland) in which the balance between the sexes was tipped slightly in favor of women in 1900, laborers' rate of bachelorhood, standing at 39.3 percent, was much closer to that of men in the other occupations, while that of the lower white-collar group was still high at 62.6 percent.

35. U.S. Department of Commerce, *Thirteenth Census of the United States, 1910*, 4:592–93.

36. Kinsey, Pomeroy, and Martin, *Sexual Behavior*, 653.

37. On terms applied to the homosexual community, see *Portland News*, November 26, 1912, 1; Oregon v. E.S.J. McAllister, Trial Transcript (hereafter, McAllister Transcript), p. 26, OSCR, file 1696, OSA; *Evening Telegram*, November 16, 1912, 2; *Oregon Journal*, November 17, 1912, sec. 1, p. 1.

The application of the term *fraternity* to the men involved in the 1912 scandal is significant, given that one observer in 1897 described the last third of the nineteenth century as the "Golden Age of Fraternity." As Carnes notes in *Secret Ritual and Manhood in Victorian America* (1–2), "on the eve of the twentieth century between 15 and 40 percent of American men, including a majority of those categorized as middle-class," participated in fraternal orders. Carnes explains their attraction: "In an impersonal and bewildering urban environment, the orders provided cohesive social networks....The order became a source of stability amidst the social chaos of modern life." Although no "formal" fraternity existed among the men of Portland's early homosexual community, the widespread use of the term suggests that their informal association had significant communal aspects for both the dominant society and the men who participated in it.

Another example of early-twentieth-century homosexual men using terms to refer to a community among themselves is provided in George Chauncey, Jr., "Christian Brotherhood or Sexual Perversion? Homosexual Identities and the

Construction of Sexual Boundaries in the World War I Era," in Duberman, Vicinus, and Chauncey, eds., *Hidden from History,* 296, 298–99.

38. On socializing and introductions, see Walter H. Evans, Robert F. Maguire, and Frank T. Collier, "Brief of Plaintiff and Respondent," Oregon v. E. E. Wedemeyer, p. 34, OSCR, file 1479, OSA; Roy Kadel testimony, McAllister Transcript, 14; H. L. Tabb testimony, McAllister Transcript, 42; William Homan testimony, McAllister Transcript, 55; Taylor testimony, Start Transcript, III, 113; and Frank T. Collier examination, Start Transcript, 301. On photographs and letters, see *Evening Telegram,* November 23, 1912, 3, and November 26, 1912, 2. On connections between men in the 1912 scandal and other cities, see *Seattle Star,* November 25, 1912, 1, and November 27, 1912, 6; *Salem (Ore.) Daily Capital Journal,* November 30, 1912, 10. On the "brotherhood" in Seattle, see *Evening Telegram,* December 6, 1912, 8.

39. That early homosexual communities were principally a middle-class phenomenon is also confirmed by reports regarding the 1914 homosexual scandal that occurred in southern California. C. K. McClatchy, the editor of the *Sacramento Bee,* stated at the time: "One thing is noticeable and that is that there was not a laborer in the entire list" of men implicated in the 1914 affair. See Homosexual Issue File, Sacramento Archives and Museum Collection Center, Sacramento, Calif. See also Jeffrey Weeks, "Movements of Affirmation: Sexual Meanings and Homosexual Identities," in *Passion and Power: Sexuality in History,* ed. Kathy Peiss and Christina Simmons, with Robert A. Padgug (Philadelphia: Temple University Press, 1989), 81; Steven Maynard, "Through a Hole in the Lavatory Wall: Homosexual Subcultures, Police Surveillance, and the Dialectics of Discovery, Toronto, 1890–1930," *Journal of the History of Sexuality* 5, no. 2 (October 1994): 220; and Chauncey, *Gay New York.*

40. Kocka, *White Collar Workers in America,* 71, 85, 86, 90 (quotation), 96, 97. See also Zunz, *Making America Corporate,* 127, 134–36; and George W. Henry and Alfred A. Gross, "Social Factors in the Case Histories of One Hundred Underprivileged Homosexuals," *Mental Hygiene* 22 (1938): 602. Stein describes racial differences separating gays from each other in post–World War II Philadelphia (*City of Sisterly and Brotherly Loves,* 75–76).

41. This scenario differs somewhat from that described by historians of homosexuality studying other large American cities, who have demonstrated that homosexuals readily found a place in ghettoes and vice districts. For example, see Kevin J. Mumford, *Interzones: Black/White Sex Districts in Chicago and New York in the Early Twentieth Century* (New York: Columbia University Press, 1997); and Eric Garber, "A Spectacle in Color: The Lesbian and Gay Subculture of Jazz Age Harlem," in Duberman, Vicinus, and Chauncey, eds., *Hidden from History,* 318–31. In *Gay New York,* a highly nuanced study of the country's largest megalopolis, Chauncey considers a variety of middle-class male homosexuals and their varied relations with vice districts and ghettoes. Stein found that while within post–World War II Philadelphia gays and lesbians might find refuge in certain African American clubs (*City of Sisterly and Brotherly Loves,* 10, 33–35,

41–42, 75–76), considerable spatial division could occur between races within the gay subculture itself.

42. George W. Henry, *Sex Variants: A Study of Homosexual Patterns* (New York: Paul B. Hoeber, 1941), 1:268, 276, 278.

43. Weeks, "Movements of Affirmation," 81; Oregon v. C. E. Shuck, March 28, 1914, MCCCC 55940; Oregon v. George Stuble, March 28, 1914, MCCCC 55942; *Portland City Directory, 1913;* PPAR, vol.: August 24, 1910, to November 28, 1910, p. 159, SPARC. On middle-class male fantasies about, and interest in, working-class males, also see Chauncey, *Gay New York,* 107–10.

44. Henry, *Sex Variants,* 1:154, 278; 2:26, 27. On sailors, see also Earl Lind [Ralph Werther, also a pseudonym], *Autobiography of an Androgyne,* ed. Alfred W. Herzog (New York: Medico-Legal Journal, 1918), 8–9; Ralph Werther, *The Female-Impersonators,* ed. (New York: Medico-Legal Journal, 1922), 7–22.

45. Portland City Council Documents, box 89, folder 7, "Police, 1906," SPARC. Havelock Ellis found that artistic, literary, acting, and musical occupations are especially attractive to homosexuals (*Sex Inversion,* vol. 4 of *Studies in the Psychology of Sex* [Philadelphia: F. A. Davis, 1904], 46, 173–74, 175).

46. Jonathan Ned Katz, *Gay/Lesbian Almanac: A New Documentary* (New York: Harper and Row, 1983), 235–39; *Portland City Directory, 1895* (Portland: R. L. Polk, 1895); *Portland City Directory, 1896* (Portland: R. L. Polk, 1896); *Portland City Directory, 1897* (Portland: R. L. Polk, 1897); *Portland City Directory, 1898* (Portland: R. L. Polk, 1898); *Portland City Directory, 1899–1900* (Portland: R. L. Polk, 1899); *Portland City Directory, 1900–1901* (Portland: R. L. Polk, 1900); *Portland City Directory, 1901–1902* (Portland: R. L. Polk, 1902). I wish to acknowledge Jonathan Ned Katz for sharing additional information with me about Hammerich, and Wilhelm von Rosen of Copenhagen for copies of Hammerich's America-based correspondence.

47. Thomas C. Ryan, Inmate 7178, Parole Board Calendar for 1915, vol. 2, [n.p.], OSP Parole Board Actions, 1915–1938, OSA; Thomas C. Ryan, Inmate 7178, OSP Great Register, pp. 204–5, OSA; PPAR, vol.: February 25, 1919, to September 20, 1919, entries for September 4, 1919, SPARC.

48. Dubbert, *Man's Place,* 191.

49. *Evening Telegram,* November 22, 1912, 8; *Salem (Ore.) Daily Capital Journal,* November 22, 1912, 5.

50. Taylor testimony, Start Transcript, 126; Oregon v. Earl Brown, September 27, 1913, MCCCC 53580; Oregon v. Benny Trout, November 24, 1914, MCCCC 58806. The evidence suggests that the youths caught up in the 1928 affair also willingly engaged in relations with adults. Myron Hoag, nineteen, and Max Hockgraef, sixteen, fled Portland for Seattle reportedly because they did not wish to testify against their "friend," forty-year-old Clarence Brazell. Another youth claimed that he "did not resist nor resent the advances of" thirty-seven-year-old Arthur Dark. "Nor," the report continued, "did he reproach" yet another youth for submitting at the same time "to the alleged unnatural attractions" of forty-year-old William Armstrong (*Oregonian,* April 8, 1928, 9; *Portland Telegram* [hereafter, *Telegram*], February 10, 1928, 2).

51. Steven Maynard, "'Horrible Temptations': Sex, Men, and Working-Class Male Youth in Urban Ontario, 1890–1935," *Canadian Historical Review* 78, no. 2 (June 1997): 208, 209, 213–15; Oregon v. Clarence Brazell, Trial Transcript (hereafter, Brazell Transcript), pp. 32, 49–51, 56, 71–72, 78–79, 140, 164, OSCR, file 6199, OSA.

52. PPDDB, vol.: J. Maloney and Mallet for September 7, 1911, to May 21, 1912, 2, SPARC. See Maynard, "'Horrible Temptations,'" 213–15.

53. Gordon Franks testimony, Brazell Transcript, 78–79; *Telegram,* February 10, 1928, 2; Leslie Anderson testimony, Start Transcript, 382, 383;, Oregon v. Leslie Anderson, December 28, 1912, MCCCC 50901.

54. *Telegram,* February 10, 1928, 2.

55. *Telegram,* February 10, 1928, 2, and November 16, 1912, 2; Taylor testimony, Start Transcript, 132–33.

56. *Oregonian,* February 10, 1928, 17; *Telegram,* February 10, 1928, 2.

57. Stein, *City of Sisterly and Brotherly Loves,* 17–48.

58. The statistics are based on an analysis of Ward 4 in U.S. Department of Commerce, *Thirteenth Census of the United States, 1910,* 3:523.

59. *Oregon Journal,* November 17, 1912, sec. 1, pp. 1, 6; December 4, 1912, 6; *Evening Telegram,* November 18, 1912, 8; *Portland City Directory, 1910, 1911, 1912,* and *1913;* U.S. Department of Commerce, Manuscript Population Census Returns, Multnomah County, Ore., 1910, Enumeration District 147, sheet 12B, lines 83 and 85; Oregon v. Fred Clarke, August 20, 1913, MCCCC 52578; YMCA Dormitory Residents' Testimonial, August 10, 1911, Council Documents, box 115, folder 2, Licenses—Misc., 1911, SPARC. The 1910 census lists Bronner and Healy as residents of the same dwelling, but the directories give their addresses as separate.

60. *Portland City Directory, 1906, 1907–1908, 1909, 1910, 1911, 1912,* and *1913,* and *Portland City Directory, 1914* (Portland: R. L. Polk, 1914); Van Hulen testimony, Start Transcript, 63; Oregon v. W. D. Tierney, November 16, 1912, MCCCC 58834; Oregon v. Del V. Meagher, January 16, 1913, MCCCC 52691; *Oregon Journal,* November 20, 1912, 6; Kenneth Hollister testimony, Start Transcript, 148–71; William Homan testimony, McAllister Transcript, 55–61; *Evening Telegram,* November 19, 1912, 8; *Portland News,* December 19, 1912, 1.

61. Gordon Brent Ingram, "'Open' Space as Strategic Queer Sites," in *Queers in Space: Communities, Public Places, Sites of Resistance,* ed. Gordon Brent Ingram, Anne-Marie Bouthillette, and Yolanda Retter (Seattle: Bay Press, 1997), 96. See also Stein, *City of Sisterly and Brotherly Loves,* 84–85; and Aaron Betsky, *Queer Space: Architecture and Same-Sex Desire* (New York: William Morrow, 1997), 141.

62. Kadel testimony, McAllister Transcript, 3, 4, 5; Louis Burns testimony, McAllister Transcript, 52, 53; Rodby testimony, Start Transcript, 6, 7–8, 54; Van Hulen testimony, Start Transcript, 91. On the role of city streets in twentieth-century gay community, see Stein, *City of Sisterly and Brotherly Loves,* 94–101.

63. Rodby testimony, Start Transcript, 6, 7–8, 54; Van Hulen testimony, Start Transcript, 91; Oregon v. H. L. Tabb, June 12, 1913, and November 29, 1912, MCCCC 52589 and 58801; Horace Tabb testimony, McAllister Transcript,

43–44. On the significance of public restrooms to gay male culture and homosexual encounters, see Laud Humphreys, *Tearoom Trade: Impersonal Sex in Public Places* (Chicago: Aldine, 1970); Maynard, "Through a Hole in the Lavatory Wall," 207–42; Chauncey, *Gay New York,* 83, 146, 185, 195–201, 264–66; and Stein, *City of Sisterly and Brotherly Loves,* 101–5.

64. Laurence Pratt, *I Remember Portland, 1899–1915* (Portland: Binford and Mort, 1965), 25. See also Harry B. Buckley, superintendent of parks, to Harold Helfer, July 9, 1953, Parks Historic File, box 12, folder 291, SPARC; Monty K. Anderson, Charles A. Merrill, and John V. A. Neal, "The Way of Life in the Lownsdale Square Area" (Portland: Portland State University Urban Studies Center, 1971), 1; and "Men need female escort of children to enter two city parks," *Sunday Oregonian,* July 23, 1972, 4F, in Parks Historic File. On simultaneous visibility and invisibility in city parks and other setting, see Stein, *City of Sisterly and Brotherly Loves,* 86; and Chauncey, *Gay New York,* 179–205.

65. Harry Work testimony, McAllister Transcript, 21, 29; Homan testimony, McAllister Transcript, 55, 56; Francis J. Ivancie, commissioner of public affairs, to Harry Buckley, superintendent of parts, July 18, 1968, Parks Historic File, box 12, folder 12, SPARC. On public parks, see also Maynard, "Through a Hole in the Lavatory Wall," 211–12.

66. Blumin, *Emergence of the Middle Class,* 284–85; Ryan, *Cradle of the Middle Class,* 148, 149, 152–53; Sam Bass Warner, Jr., *The Private City: Philadelphia in Three Periods of Its Growth* (Philadelphia: University of Pennsylvania Press, 1968), 196–97.

67. Henry Russell Talbot et al., *Report of the Portland Vice Commission to the Mayor and City Council of the City of Portland, Oregon* (Portland: Henry Russell Talbot, 1913), ii–iii, 136; *Oregon Journal,* November 17, 1912, sec. 1, pp. 1, 6.

68. *Telegram,* February 10, 1928, 2.

69. D'Emilio and Freedman, *Intimate Matters,* 172 (quotation), 195–97, 231, 241; White, *First Sexual Revolution,* 84. See also Chauncey, *Gay New York;* and Lewis A. Erenberg, *Steppin' Out: New York Nightlife and the Transformation of American Culture, 1890–1930* (Westport, Conn.: Greenwood, 1981).

70. Noel W., quoted in Henry, *Sex Variants,* 2:278.

71. Kinsey, Pomeroy, and Martin, *Sexual Behavior,* 369–71, 373.

72. For example, see Chauncey, *Gay New York,* 119. Also see the interesting debate on working-class reluctance to engage in oral eroticism in Herbert Marcuse, *Eros and Civilization: A Philosophical Inquiry into Freud,* 2d ed. (New York: Vintage, 1966), 16, 32, 35–36, 37, 41, 44–45; Michel Foucault, *The History of Sexuality: An Introduction,* trans. Robert Hurley (New York: Pantheon Books, 1978), 5–6, 120, 121–22; and Jeffrey Weeks, *Sexuality and Its Discontents: Meanings, Myths, and Modern Sexualities* (London: Routledge and Kegan Paul, 1985), 166–70.

73. Kinsey, Pomeroy, and Martin, *Sexual Behavior,* 369.

74. Douglas C. McMurtrie, "Notes on the Psychology of Sex," *American Journal of Urology* 10, no. 2 (February 1914): 99; L. Thoinot, *Medicolegal Aspects of Moral Offenses,* trans. Arthur W. Weysse (Philadelphia: F. A. Davis, 1923), 20,

305; G. Legman, "The Language of Homosexuality: An American Glossary," in Henry, *Sex Variants,* 2:1155; A. C. Cornsweet and M. F. Hayes, "Conditioned Response to Fellatio," *American Journal of Psychiatry* 103, no. 1 (July 1946): 76–77; Humphreys, *Tearoom Trade,* 75, 101; Thomas S. Weinberg, "On 'Doing' and 'Being' Gay: Sexual Behavior and Homosexual Male Self-Identity," *Journal of Homosexuality* 4, no. 2 (winter 1978): 151; Lind, *Autobiography,* 89, 91, 94–95, 96. Ellis (*Sexual Inversion,* 165–66) and Bernard S. Talmey (*Love: A Treatise on the Science of Sex-Attraction,* 4th ed. [New York: Practitioners Publishing, 1919], 288) both claimed that anal intercourse did occur among homosexuals, and was at times more common than fellation. Chauncey (*Gay New York,* 85–86) and Angus McLaren (*The Trials of Masculinity: Policing Sexual Boundaries, 1870–1930* [Chicago: University of Chicago Press, 1997], 153) note that oral sex was becoming more popular because men believed (falsely) that they would not contract venereal diseases from it.

75. Kinsey, Pomeroy, and Martin, *Sexual Behavior,* 369.

76. Sharon R. Ullman, *Sex Seen: The Emergence of Modern Sexuality in America* (Berkeley: University of California Press, 1997), 66. See also McClatchy notes in Homosexual Issue File.

77. Chauncey, *Gay New York,* 119.

78. On various terms for sexual roles, see McAllister Transcript, 7, 17, 20, 21, 22, 27, 29, 40; Start Transcript, 7, 65, 70, 73, 116,155. On the use of these terms by men engaged in same-sex affairs in the early twentieth century, see Chauncey, "Christian Brotherhood or Sexual Perversion?" 297.

79. McAllister Transcript, 27, 61, and specifically Work testimony (32). Chauncey also found in the early twentieth century that "trade" experienced a certain immunity from the law ("Christian Brotherhood or Sexual Perversion?" 303–4).

80. Work testimony, McAllister Transcript, 27; R. J. Slater and Joseph Page, "Brief of the Appellant," Oregon v. E. S. J. McAllister, May 24, 1913, p. 37, OSCR, file 1696, OSA. See also Chauncey, "Christian Brotherhood or Sexual Perversion?" 295–96.

81. Oregon v. Harry Allen Work, November 16 and 17, 1915, MCCCC 62695, 62987, and 62988.

82. Work testimony, McAllister Transcript, 40; *Oregon Journal,* November 20, 1912, 6. Vilma noted of Seattle in the 1930s that he and the gay men he ran with all had female nicknames for themselves and called themselves queens, but were indeed not drag queens (see Don Paulson with Roger Simpson, *An Evening at the Garden of Allah: A Gay Cabaret in Seattle* [New York: Columbia University Press, 1996], 23). Fairies often used female names in public settings, while middle-class homosexual males often did so in more private surroundings. Popular among these names were those of well-known actresses. Because Harry Work's middle name was Allen (which he sometimes went by), he may have chosen Viola in honor of the actress Viola Allen, perhaps also having in mind her critically acclaimed portrayal of Viola in *Twelfth Night.* On Allen, who began her stage career in the 1880s and remained a popular touring star until her retire-

ment in 1918, see Rita M. Plotnicki, "The Evolution of a Star: The Career of Viola Allen, 1882–1918" (Ph.D. diss., City University of New York, 1979); Gerald
Bordman, *The Oxford Companion to American Theatre* (New York: Oxford University Press, 1984), 20–21; Martin Bunham, *The Cambridge Guide to Theatre,*
new ed. (Cambridge: Cambridge University Press, 1995), 18; and Phyllis
Hartwell, ed., *The Oxford Companion to the Theatre,* 4th ed. (Oxford: Oxford
University Press, 1983), s.v. "Allen, Viola."

83. Start Transcript, 163, 164, 165, 166, 168, 169, 290, 291, 301; L. L. Rollins ad-
missions in McClatchy notes in Homosexual Issue File.

84. Hollister testimony, Start Transcript, 148, 157, 158, 163; Van Hulen testimony, Start Transcript, 63, 77–78; Bill of Exceptions, Oregon v. E. E. Wedemeyer, p. 2.

85. Van Hulen testimony, Start Transcript, 70, 73, 77. See also Oregon v. Earl
Brown; Oregon v. C. D. Bronner, March 11, 1913, MCCCC 51623; *Oregon Jour-
nal,* November 29, 1912, 10; Oregon v. Benny Trout; Benny Trout testimony,
Start Transcript, 140, 141; Oregon v. John Doe Bradley, August 18, 1913,
MCCCC 54198; U.S. Department of Commerce, Manuscript Population Cen-
sus Returns, Multnomah County, Ore., 1910, Enumeration District 208, sheet
2B, line 85; Oregon v. H. L. Tabb; Multnomah County Voter Registration
Records, microfilm 26, 1912–13, card for H. L. Tabb, MCARC.

86. Homan testimony, McAllister Transcript, 55, 59; Burns testimony, McAl-
lister Transcript, 52–55; Rodby testimony, Start Transcript, 4–62, 176–78;
Chauncey, *Gay New York,* 69–70; Albert J. Reiss, Jr., "The Social Integration of
Queers and Peers," *Social Problems* 9, no. 2 (fall 1961): 102–20.

87. Homan testimony, McAllister Transcript, 55–57; Burns testimony, McAllister Transcript, 53–55; Rodby testimony, Start Transcript, 15–16; Hollister testimony, McAllister, Transcript, 48–49; Bill of Exceptions, Oregon v. E. E. Wedemeyer, p. 2.

Chapter 4. From Oscar Wilde to Portland's 1912 Scandal: Socially Constructing the Homosexual

1. *Portland Evening Telegram* (hereafter, *Evening Telegram*), May 9, 1889, 3.

2. *Evening Telegram,* September 24, 1890, 3; August 12, 1891, 2; August 28,
1894, 6; and *Portland Sunday Mercury,* June 29, 1889. For further discussion of
the influence of international, national, and local news print media, and informal news networks on local understandings of same-sex sexuality, see Lisa Duggan, *Sapphic Slashers: Sex, Violence, and American Modernity* (Durham, N.C.:
Duke University Press, 2000); John Howard, "The Talk of the County: Revisiting Accusation, Murder, and Mississippi, 1895," in *Where These Memories Grow:
History, Memory, and Southern Identity,* ed. W. Fitzhugh Brundage (Chapel Hill:
University of North Carolina Press, 2000), 191–218; and Marc Stein, *City of Sisterly and Brotherly Loves: Lesbian and Gay Philadelphia, 1945–1972* (Chicago: University of Chicago Press, 2000).

3. Newspapers in 1892 carried reports on Alice Mitchell, who was involved in a sensational murder case in Tennessee. On Mitchell, see Duggan, *Sapphic Slashers;* and Jonathan Ned Katz, *Gay American History: Lesbians and Gay Men in the U.S.A., A Documentary History,* rev. ed. (New York: Meridian, 1992), 53–58.

4. Neil Bartlett, *Who Was That Man? A Present for Mr Oscar Wilde* (London: Serpent's Tail, 1988), 147–48; Richard Ellmann, *Oscar Wilde* (New York: Knopf, 1988), 155–211. On why some late-nineteenth-century local cases dealing with same-sex sexuality found their way into the newspapers and into public memory while others did not, see Bartlett, *Who Was That Man?;* and Howard, "The Talk of the County."

5. Ed Cohen, "Legislating the Norm: From Sodomy to Gross Indecency," *South Atlantic Quarterly* 88, no. 1 (winter 1989): 181–217; Cohen, *Talk on the Wilde Side: Towards a Genealogy of Discourse on Male Sexualities* (New York: Routledge, 1993); Jeffrey Weeks, "Movements of Affirmation: Sexual Meanings and Homosexual Identities," in *Passion and Power: Sexuality and History,* ed. Kathy Peiss and Christina Simmons, with Robert A. Padgug (Philadelphia: Temple University Press, 1989), 73; Terry L. Chapman, "'An Oscar Wilde Type': 'The Abominable Crime of Buggery' in Western Canada, 1890–1920," *Criminal Justice History* 4 (1983): 99–100, 112–13.

6. Jonathan Ned Katz, *Gay/Lesbian Almanac: A New Documentary* (New York: Harper and Row, 1983), 258–59; Cohen, *Talk on the Wilde Side,* 4. For more evidence, from a different perspective, that Cohen and Katz's observation did not hold for the entire country, see Howard, "The Talk of the County."

7. *Evening Telegram,* April 3, 1895, 1, and April 6, 1895, 1; *Portland Oregonian* (hereafter, *Oregonian*), April 4, 1895, 1, 7; April 7, 1895, 3; May 1, 1895, 2; May 26, 1895, 3; *Boise, Idaho Daily Statesman* (hereafter, *Idaho Daily Statesman*), April 4, 1895, 1; April 27, 1895, 1; May 26, 1895, 1; *Seattle Post-Intelligencer* (hereafter, *Post-Intelligencer*), April 4, 1895, 2; April 5, 1895, 2; April 7, 1895, 2; May 1, 1895, 2; May 26, 1895, 2; *Seattle Press-Times* (hereafter, *Press-Times*), April 19, 1895, 1.

8. Max Simon Nordau, *Degeneration,* trans. of the 2d German ed. (New York: Appleton, 1895), vii, 5, 16, 34–37, 40–43. See also John Higham, "The Reorientation of American Culture in the 1890s," in *The Origins of Modern Consciousness,* ed. John Weiss (Detroit: Wayne State University Press, 1965), 38; R. B. Kershner, Jr., "Degeneration: The Explanatory Nightmare," *Georgia Review* 40, no. 2 (summer 1986): 419–24, 429–30; Frank J. Sulloway, *Freud, Biologist of the Mind: Beyond the Psychoanalytic Legend* (New York: Basic Books, 1979), 284; and Richard Burton, "Degenerates and Geniuses," *Critic,* n.s., 22, no. 651 (August 11, 1894), 85.

9. Nordau, *Degeneration,* vii, 5, 13, 40, 41–45, 317–22.

10. Higham, "Reorientation of American Culture," 38.

11. For examples of consideration of Nordau's *Degeneration* in the regional press, see *Oregonian,* April 23, 1895, 4; April 19, 1895, 4; April 28, 1895, 4, 19; May 12, 1895, 4. An excellent collection of essays examining various ways in which Europeans and Americans applied degeneration theory is J. Edward Chamber-

lain and Sander L. Gilman, eds., *Degeneration: The Dark Side of Progress* (New York: Columbia University Press, 1985).

12. *Oregonian*, April 23, 1895, 4. The *Oregonian* editor, probably Harvey W. Scott, also named a female "hellish twin of Oscar Wilde": England's Sarah Grand, the pen name of Francis Elizabeth McFall (1854–1943). Grand pioneered the idea of the New Woman in her novel *Ideala* (1888). The newspaper editor asserted: "The woman who emancipates herself from the sacred duties of her sex to feed its perverted energies and appetites upon morbid dreams of masculine liberty of conduct, of social relations, or employment of self-indulgence, springs from the same diseased social root[.]" Significantly, Scott opposed woman's suffrage, challenging the work of his older sister, the dedicated suffragist Abigail Scott Duniway, who for some time had also published in Portland her own feminist newspaper, *The New Northwest*. On Abigail Scott Duniway and her brother Harvey, see Ruth Barnes Moynihan, *Rebel for Rights: Abigail Scott Duniway* (New Haven: Yale University Press, 1983). On Sarah Grand, see Gillian Kersley, *Darling Madam: Sarah Grand and Devoted Friend* (London: Virago, 1983).

13. *Press-Times*, April 16, 1895, 2; editorial from the *Walla Walla (Wash.) Union*, reprinted in the *Oregonian*, April 19, 1895, 4; *Evening Telegram*, April 6, 1895, 2.

14. *The Dalles (Ore.) Times Mountaineer*, May 11, 1895, 1; see also *Oregonian*, May 4, 1895, 2; and *Press-Times*, May 3, 1895, 1. On the acquisition of sexual degeneracy, see Sulloway, *Freud*, 284, 288 n. 7; Paul Robinson, *The Modernization of Sex: Havelock Ellis, Alfred Kinsey, William Masters, and Virginia Johnson* (New York: Harper and Row, 1976), 6–7; Sheila Rowbotham and Jeffrey Weeks, *Socialism and the New Life: The Personal and Sexual Politics of Edward Carpenter and Havelock Ellis* (London: Pluto Press, 1977), 150; Richard von Krafft-Ebing, *Psychopathia Sexualis*, trans. Charles G. Chaddock from the 7th German ed. (Philadelphia: F.A. Davis, 1892), 288–89; Havelock Ellis, *Sexual Inversion*, vol. 4 of *Studies in the Psychology of Sex*, 2d ed. (Philadelphia: F.A. Davis, 1904), 36–38, 50.

15. Jeffrey Weeks, *Sexuality and Its Discontents: Meanings, Myths, and Modern Sexualities* (London: Routledge and Kegan Paul, 1985), 76–77; Rowbotham and Weeks, *Socialism and the New Life*, 150; Robinson, *Modernization of Sex*, 4, 5, 6; Sulloway, *Freud*, 284; G. Frank Lydston, *Sex Hygiene for the Male and What to Say to the Boy* (Chicago: Hamming Publishing, 1912), 197–98; George Chauncey, Jr., "From Sexual Inversion to Homosexuality: Medicine and the Changing Conceptualization of Female Deviance," in Peiss and Simmons, with Padgug, eds., *Passion and Power*, 99–100.

16. *Oregonian*, April 7, 1895, 3.

17. Ibid. See also Lionel Brown, "The Queer Career of Oscar Wilde," *Modern Man* 6, no. 3 (September 1956): 17–18, 52.

18. *Evening Telegram*, April 6, 1895, 2; April 11, 1895, 2; *Oregonian*, December 3, 1900, 4. See also Bartlett, *Who Was That Man?*, 157; *Post-Intelligencer*, April 7, 1895, 2; April 14, 1895, 4; April 15, 1895, 4; and *Oregonian*, May 31, 1895, 4.

19. *Press-Times*, April 16, 1895, 2; May 25, 1895, 4.

20. Nordau, quoted in James G. Kiernan, "Are Americans Degenerates? A Critique of Nordau's Recent Change of View," *Alienist and Neurologist* 18, no. 3 (October 1896): 446. Kiernan argued that Nordau's theory can appropriately be applied to the United States.

21. All quoted in *Evening Telegram,* April 22, 1895, 2. See also *Oregonian,* April 23, 1895, 4, in which the *New York Evening Sun* defended American writers, artists, and the public as not degenerates like "foreigners." For a consideration of the emergence of an "American white" identity opposed to the European, and the role that it had in shaping same-sex sexual scandals in the 1890s, see Duggan, *Sapphic Slashers,* esp. 24–27.

22. *Evening Telegram,* April 8, 1895, 2.

23. *Idaho Daily Statesman,* May 12, 1895, 6; May 29, 1895, 6.

24. Michel Foucault, *The History of Sexuality: An Introduction,* trans. Robert Hurley (New York: Pantheon Books, 1978), 120, 123. On the lack of changes in the North American judicial system subsequent to the Wilde trials, see Chapman "'An Oscar Wilde Type,'" 112–13, and D. Michael Quinn, *Same-Sex Dynamics among Nineteenth-Century Americans: A Mormon Example* (Urbana: University of Illinois Press, 1996), 315.

25. *Press-Times,* April 6, 1895, 2. See also Chauncey, "From Sexual Inversion to Homosexuality," 100; Michael Omi and Howard Winant, *Racial Formation in the United States from the 1960s to the 1990s,* 2d ed. (New York: Routledge, 1994), 14–15; and Jennifer Terry, *An American Obsession: Science, Medicine, and Homosexuality in Modern Society* (Chicago: University of Chicago Press, 1999), 11, 52–53, 78–79, 89–97, 116.

26. See, for example, Jonathan Ned Katz, *The Invention of Heterosexuality* (1995; reprint, New York: Plume, 1996); Siobhan B. Somerville, *Queering the Color Line: Race and the Invention of Homosexuality in American Culture* (Durham, N.C.: Duke University Press, 2000), 15–38; Kevin J. Mumford, *Interzones: Black/White Sex Districts in Chicago and New York in the Early Twentieth Century* (New York: Columbia University Press, 1997), 77–86; John D'Emilio and Estelle B. Freedman, *Intimate Matters: A History of Sexuality in America* (New York: Harper and Row, 1988); and Martin Duberman, Martha Vicinus, and George Chauncey, Jr., eds., *Hidden from History: Reclaiming the Gay and Lesbian Past* (New York: Meridian, 1990).

27. *Evening Telegram,* November 16, 1912, 2; December 6, 1912, 8; *Seattle Star,* November 25, 1912, 1, 10; November 27, 1912, 6; *Salem (Ore.) Daily Capital Journal,* November 26, 1912, 1; November 30, 1912, 10; *Portland News,* January 3, 1913, 1; November 26, 1912, 1; *Salem Daily Oregon Statesman,* November 23, 1912, 1. On the Walla Walla scandal, see, for example, *Walla Walla (Wash.) Sunday Morning Bulletin,* November 17, 1912, 1; *Walla Walla (Wash.) Evening Bulletin,* November 18, 1912, 1, 2; and John Gibson, WSP Inmate File 6708, WSAO.

28. *Portland News,* home edition, November 21, 1912, 1 (quotation); November 16, 1912, 7; *Evening Telegram,* November 14, 1912, 8; November 16, 1912, 2; *Spokane Industrial Worker,* November 28, 1912, 1 (quotation).

29. Oregon v. Harry A. Start, Trial Transcript (hereafter, Start Transcript), p. 98, OSCR, File 1478, OSA. For an example of George Cameron as court-appointed counsel, see Oregon v. William King, April 25, 1898, MCCCC 27484.

30. *Seattle Patriarch,* November 23, 1912, 2. A letter to the editor of the *Portland News,* November 25, 1912, 3, asserted that "Wildeism" had clearly been traced into the cities' YMCA. On the tendency of late-nineteenth- and early-twentieth-century newspapers to link isolated same-sex sexual scandals to each other through references such as those considered in this paragraph, see Howard, "The Talk of the County"; and Duggan, *Sapphic Slashers,* esp. 123–55.

31. State v. Start, 132 P. 518 (1913); Start Transcript, 10–11.

32. *Portland News,* November 23, 1912, 6; *Labor Press,* November 25, 1912, 3. See also *Portland News,* November 20, 1912, 1.

33. Ellis, *Sexual Inversion,* 50, 181, 183–84; Mumford, *Interzones,* 77–86; Sulloway, *Freud,* 284, 288 n. 7, 294, 295, 307; Robinson, *Modernization of Sex,* 5, 7, 8, 9; Rowbotham and Weeks, *Socialism and the New Life,* 150.

34. *Portland News,* home edition, November 21, 1912, 1; *Oregonian,* November 14, 1912, 12.

35. Frank Collier lost his job as deputy district attorney when George Cameron, the district attorney, left office on January 6, 1913. However, the new district attorney, Walter H. Evans, retained Collier as a special prosecutor (*Portland News,* December 24, 1912, 1).

36. Oregon v. Harry A. Start, OSCR, File 1478, OSA; Oregon v. E. E. Wedemeyer, OSCR, File 1479, OSA; Oregon v. E. S. J. McAllister, OSCR, File 1696, OSA. See also the coverage in various local papers.

37. Start Transcript, 17, 18, 20, 96–100; Sam M. Johnson and Wilson T. Hume, "Brief of the Defendant and Appellant," Oregon v. Harry A. Start, February 18, 1913, pp. 4, 8–9, 18–27, OSCR, file 1478, OSA; [Alexander] Wilson & [Oscar] Neal and George Roosman, "Appellant's Brief," Oregon v. E. E. Wedemeyer, February 26, 1913, pp. 5, 8–9, 20–25, OSCR, file 1479, OSA; Bill of Exceptions, Oregon v. E. E. Wedemeyer, pp. 6–7, OSCR, file 1479, OSA; R. J. Slater and Joseph Page, "Brief of the Appellant," Oregon v. E. S. J. McAllister, May 24, 1913, pp. 9–12, 27–28, 35–37, OSCR, file 1696, OSA.

38. Start Transcript, 20, 18, 99.

39. Walter H. Evans, Frank T. Collier, and Robert F. Maguire, "Brief of the Plaintiff and Respondent" (hereafter, Evans, Collier, and Maguire, "Start Brief"), Oregon v. Harry A. Start, March 24, 1913, pp. 23–24, OSCR, File 1478, OSA.

40. Walter H. Evans, Robert F. Maguire, and Frank T. Collier, "Brief of Plaintiff and Respondent" (hereafter, Evans, Maguire, and Collier, "Wedemeyer Brief"), Oregon v. E. E. Wedemeyer, March 31, 1913, pp. 19–20, OSCR, file 1479, OSA; Walter H. Evans, Robert F. Maguire, and Frank T. Collier, "Brief of the Respondent" (hereafter, Evans, Maguire, and Collier, "McAllister Brief"), Oregon v. E. S. J. McAllister, September 2, 1913, p. 12, OSCR, file 1696, OSA. See also Jeffrey Weeks, *Coming Out: Homosexual Politics in Britain from the Nineteenth Century to the Present,* rev. ed. (London: Quartet Books, 1990), 26, 62, 64;

Robinson, *Modernization of Sex,* 5; and Rowbotham and Weeks, *Socialism and the New Life,* 157.

41. Evans, Maguire, and Collier, "McAllister Brief," 12, 15–18, 29. See also Ellis, *Sexual Inversion,* 50, 181, 183–84, 188–89; Robinson, *Modernization of Sex,* 2, 3, 4, 6; Weeks, "Movements of Affirmation," 70; Sulloway, *Freud,* 288 n. 7.

Thoinot also believed that perversion was congenital rather than acquired and argued against the theory that linked homosexuality (sex degeneration) to the decline in civilization (L. Thoinot, *Medicolegal Aspects of Moral Offenses,* trans. Arthur W. Weysse [Philadelphia: F. A. Davis, 1923], 275–76, 286; Collier obviously used the first printing, published in 1911). On the congenital nature of sex inversion, see pp. 269, 297–314, 306, 316.

42. Evans, Collier, and Maguire, "Start Brief," 25–26, 24; Evans, Maguire, and Collier, "Wedemeyer Brief," 27–28.

43. State v. Start, 132 P. at 516.

44. Evans, Maguire, and Collier, "McAllister Brief," 15–16.

45. State v. Start, 132 P. at 517–18; State v. McAllister, 136 P. 360 (1914).

46. *Portland, Oregon Journal,* November 3, 1913, 8; Ellis, *Sexual Inversion,* 317.

47. *Pendleton Eastern Oregonian,* November 23, 1912, 4.

48. On the Lewis and Clark and Alaska-Yukon-Pacific Expositions, see Carl Abbott, *The Great Extravaganza: Portland and the Lewis and Clark Exposition* (Portland: Oregon Historical Society, 1981); Robert Rydell, "Visions of Empire: International Expositions in Portland and Seattle, 1905–1909," *Pacific Historical Review* 52, no. 1 (February 1983): 37–66. The fin de siècle malaise that consumed Europe in the 1890s and contributed to the popularity of degeneration theory never had such an extensive impact on America, as numerous historians have observed. Higham notes that Americans resisted pessimism and sweeping theories, instead preferring practical realities and activism—the fundamentals of the Progressive ethos that took hold in the country early in the twentieth century ("Reorientation of American Culture," 38–47).

49. The writer of the article on the German officers also pointed out what other American journalists noted during the Wilde scandal—that the conditions responsible, prevalent in Europe, did not exist in America: "we have rarely an army idle in sufficient numbers and for a sufficient length of time to develop the symptoms of degeneracy which are common abroad." Aware that the Northwest's all-male lumber and mining camps might raise a question for the more thoughtful reader, the author made sure to remark that in these "men work ten hours a day and are too tired at night to do more than feed and roll into their bunks, though there is little grace among the lumber jacks who are cut off from domesticity" (*Oregonian,* July 24, 1910, sec. 6, p. 8). Of course, such statements not only proved self-serving but actually contradicted the premise of the entire article: that is, that degeneration results from the concentration of men together. On the German homosexual scandal, see James D. Steakley, "Iconography of a Scandal: Political Cartoons and the Eulenberg Affair in Wilhelmin Germany," in Duberman, Vicinus, and Chauncey, eds., *Hidden from History,* 233–63.

50. *Spokane Industrial Worker,* November 28, 1912, 1, 8.

51. Evans, Collier, and Maguire, "Start Brief," 23–24.

52. Foucault, *History of Sexuality*, 120.

53. Ibid., 121.

54. *Pocatello (Idaho) Tribune*, August 24, 1898, 1.

55. PPDDB, box 9, vol.: Day et al., March 23, 1911, to August 30, 1911, SPARC; PPDDB, box 12, vol.: Coleman et al., September 1, 1911, to January 2, 1911, pp. 37, 38, SPARC; Ben N. Wade, "Case of Foreign Body in the Rectum," *Medical Sentinel* 25, no. 9 (September 17, 1917): 3689. See also PPDDB, box 14, vol.: Abbot & Goltz, February 4, 1915, to February 29, 1916, SPARC; Oregon, State Board of Control, *Fifth Biennial Report of the Oregon State Board of Control, 1921–22* (Salem: State Printing Department, 1923), 123; George H. Thacher et al., "Report of Committee Appointed by the Mayor on the Advisability of a House of Detention and an Industrial Home," July 12, 1913, p. 13, in Council Documents, 1913, box 128, folder: Police, 1913, SPARC; and L. J. Wentworth, E. E. Brodie, and F. W. Mulkey, *Report of the Commission to Investigate the Oregon State Penitentiary* (Portland, January 26, 1917), 74–76.

56. *Oregonian,* March 30, 1912, 6.

57. *St. Helens (Ore.) Mist,* December 14, 1917, 1; Oregon v. Tom Kapsales, Trial Transcript (hereafter, Kapsales Transcript), pp. 6, 9–10, 12–13, 15–18, 21–22, 27–29, 32, 36–37, 39, 40, 46–47, 53, 62, 63–65, 67, 68, 129–34, 143–47, OSCR, file 3500, OSA.

58. Kapsales Transcript, 6, 63–65, 67–68, 129–34, 143–47.

59. Ibid., pp. 158–60.

60. Ibid., pp. 1–2, 4–6, 158–60.

61. Tom Kapsales, Inmate 7867, OSP Great Register, 1910–1925, pp. 342–43, OSA; Tom Kapsales, Inmate 7867, OSP Physical Description Records, 1887–1922, OSA. Although Kapsales's inmate records give his age as twenty-four, he testified in trial that he was thirty-two, which is the age I use here.

62. Wentworth, Brodie, and Mulkey, *Report of the Commission,* 74–76. "Pervert," "sex pervert," and "perversion" showed up more frequently in 1912 than "sex invert" and "homosexual," but less frequently than "degenerate." They referred to a wide range of sexual "deviations," but specifically to homosexuality. While the older term *degenerate* reflected the understanding of an individual's relationship to civilization, *sex pervert* had a strictly *sexual* connotation. On sexual perversion, see Katz, *The Invention of Heterosexuality,* 19–20, 22, 29. As an example of a source in which "sex pervert" and "perversion" were used in 1912, see *Portland News,* home edition, November 18, 1912, 1. "Sexual inversion," "sex invert," and "homosexual" can be found in Henry Russell Talbot et al., *Report of the Portland Vice Commission to the Mayor and City Council of the City of Portland, Oregon* (Portland: Henry Russell Talbot, 1913), 136. "Uranism" referred to a state of mind and derived from the older German term *Urning,* which Karl Heinrich Ulrichs, himself a homosexual, coined in 1862. Ulrichs conceived of an Urning as a male with an inborn sexual desire for another male; his work influenced Krafft-Ebing. For brief references, see Katz, *The Invention of Homosexuality,* 51; and Steve Hogan and Lee Hudson, *Completely Queer: The Gay and Lesbian Ency-*

clopedia (New York: Henry Holt, 1998), 551–52. "Uranism" appears once during the 1912 scandal, in Evans, Maguire, and Collier, "McAllister Brief," 35.

63. On Newport and Long Beach, see George Chauncey, Jr., "Christian Brotherhood or Sexual Perversion? Homosexual Identities and the Construction of Sexual Boundaries in the World War I Era," in Duberman, Vicinus, and Chauncey, eds., *Hidden from History,* 294–317; and Sharon R. Ullman, *Sex Seen: The Emergence of Modern Sexuality in America* (Berkeley: University of California Press, 1997), 45–71. Examples of turn-of-the-century reports on homosexual communities in America include G. Frank Lydston, *The Diseases of Society (The Vice and Crime Problem)* (Philadelphia: J. B. Lippincott, 1904), 375; Charles H. Hughes, "Homo Sexual Complexion Perverts in St. Louis: Note on a Feature of Sexual Psychopathy," *Alienist and Neurologist* 28, no. 4 (November 1907): 487–88; and Magnus Hirschfeld, *Die Homosexualität des Mannes und des Weibes* (Berlin: Louis Marcus, 1914), 550–54, as noted in Katz, *Gay American History,* 49–53.

Chapter 5. Personality, Politics, and Sex in Portland and the Northwest

This chapter expands my article "Sex and Politics in Progressive-Era Portland and Eugene: The 1912 Same-Sex Vice Scandal," *OHQ* 100, no. 2 (summer 1999): 158–81. I wish to thank Robert D. Johnston for supplying me with many details on E. S. J. McAllister. I also thank Peter D. Sleeth for granting me access to the papers of his grandfather, Dana Sleeth, cited here as Sleeth Family Papers, courtesy Peter D. Sleeth.

1. *Portland Evening Telegram* (hereafter, *Evening Telegram*), November 22, 1912, 8; December 7, 1912, 2; February 15, 1913, 2; December 4, 1912, 1; November 23, 1912, 3; November 19, 1912, 8; *Portland News,* home edition, November 19, 1912, 1; *Portland, Oregon Journal* (hereafter, *Oregon Journal*), December 1, 1912, 4; *Seattle Star,* November 27, 1912, 6, November 25, 1912, 1; *Salem (Ore.) Daily Capital Journal,* November 30, 1912, 10.

2. *Evening Telegram,* December 6, 1912, 8.

3. Robert Douglas Johnston, "Middle-Class Political Ideology in a Corporate Society: The Persistence of Small-Propertied Radicalism in Portland, Oregon, 1883–1926" (Ph.D. diss., Rutgers University, 1993); Johnston, "The Myth of the Harmonious City: Will Daly, Lora Little, and the Hidden Face of Progressive-Era Portland," *OHQ* 99, no. 3 (fall 1998): 248–97.

4. Johnston, "Middle-Class Political Ideology," 207–8, 413–27, 131–34, 166–67.

5. Peter D. Sleeth, "Biographical Sketch of Dana P. Sleeth," in author's possession.

6. Gerald J. Baldasty, "Newspapers for 'the Wage Earning Class': E. W. Scripps and the Pacific Northwest," *PNQ* 90, no. 4 (fall 1999): 171–75.

7. Portland News, extra, November 16, 1912, 1; Burton J. Hendrick, "'Statement No. 1,'" *McClure's* 37, no. 5 (September 1911): 506.

8. E. Kimbark MacColl, *The Shaping of a City: Business and Politics in Portland, Oregon, 1885–1915* (Portland: Georgian Press, 1976), 185–99, 228, 258, 327–28, 402–12. A private Portland group organized a vice commission in the 1890s; it had little power. John D'Emilio and Estelle B. Freedman (*Intimate Matters: A History of Sexuality in America* [New York: Harper and Row, 1988], 172) consider the issue of American entrepreneurs profiting from "vice."

9. H. V. Rominger and H. G. Wallace, "Committee Report on gambling houses, saloons, etc. [1891–93]," 9, 13–14, MS 1286, OHS.

10. *Portland Oregonian* (hereafter, *Oregonian*), November 16, 1912, 11. See also Joseph Gaston, *Portland, Oregon: Its History and Builders* (Chicago: S. J. Clarke, 1911), 1:503, 507; and Laurence Pratt, *I Remember Portland, 1899–1915* (Portland: Binford and Mort, 1965), 51–52.

11. *Portland News*, extra, November 15, 1912, 1; *Portland News*, home edition, November 29, 1912, 1; December 10, 1912, 1. Sleeth also accused the Portland elites of protecting their own. None of the men whose names have come to light in association with the 1912 scandal were sons of Portland's entrenched families. Sleeth may have been right; Elizabeth Lapovsky Kennedy has found that during the first part of the twentieth century some elite families in Deadwood, S.D., effectively shielded their lesbian daughters from local recrimination ("'But we would never talk about it': The Structures of Lesbian Discretion in South Dakota, 1928–1933," in *Inventing Lesbian Cultures in America,* ed. Ellen Lewin [Boston: Beacon Press, 1996], 15–39). Moreover, in the course of my research I encountered one glaring gap in the legal records that may be attributable to certain powers wishing to keep names out of documents. The men arrested during the 1912 scandal were processed not through the Portland Police Department but through the Multnomah County Jail, part of the state system. The Multnomah County Jail register in which the Portland scandal arrests are recorded is complete except for one page that is curiously missing, and with it the names of fifty men processed through the jail between November 20 and November 25— at the height of the 1912 arrests.

12. *Portland News*, extra, November 15, 1912, 1; *Portland News*, home edition, November 18, 1912, 1; November 19, 1912, 1 (quotation); *Oregonian*, November 17, 1912, sec. 2, p. 8; *Spokane Industrial Worker*, November 28, 1912, 1, 8. Brick claimed that he initiated his investigation a couple of weeks before the news got out but did not "break" the story before the election because he "thought people would say I was doing it for publicity as I was a candidate." When Brick started talking, he seemed to do so only to the *News,* possibly because like Brick, Dana Sleeth also carried a star as a "special police officer" of Portland. The relationship between these two men and the timing of the revelations only add to the mystery of who knew what and when. *Portland News,* home edition, November 19, 1912, 1; John Clark, chief of police, to Hon. H. R. Albee, mayor, July 17, 1913, MOC, box 55, folder 55, SPARC. On the YMCA, see David I. Macleod, *Building Character in the American Boy: The Boys Scouts, YMCA, and Their Forerunners, 1870–1920* (Madison: University of Wisconsin Press, 1983), 214, 216, 217, 223–24;

John Donald Gustav-Wrathall, *Take the Young Stranger by the Hand: Same-Sex Relations and the YMCA* (Chicago: University of Chicago Press, 1998), 53, 54–55;

13. *Portland News,* home edition, November 16, 1912, 7; November 23, 1912, 1.

14. On various aspects of Portland's YMCA history, see *Oregon Journal,* April 7, 1912, sec. 2, p. 4; December 7, 1913, sec. 5, p. 12; *Oregonian,* March 27, 1907, 10; April 1, 1878, 3; November 26, 1911, sec. 1, p. 11; "YMCA's First 100 Years" (Portland: YMCA of Columbia-Willamette, n.d.), 1–10; E. Kimbark MacColl with Harry Stein, *Merchants, Money, and Power: The Portland Establishment, 1843–1913* (Portland: Georgian Press, 1988), 360. More generally, see Nina Mjagki and Margaret Spratt, eds., *Men and Women Adrift: The YMCA and the YWCA in the City* (New York: New York University Press, 1997).

15. *Oregonian,* November 17, 1912, sec. 3, p. 6; BHC [B. H. Canfield] to D. Sleeth and Bensyl Smythe, November 18, 1912, Sleeth Family Papers, courtesy Peter D. Sleeth.

16. Minutes of the Young Men's Christian Association of Portland, Oregon (hereafter, YMCA Minutes), November 16, 1912, YMCA of the Columbia-Willamette, Portland; *Evening Telegram,* November 16, 1912, 1; *Oregon Journal,* November 17, 1912, sec. 1, p. 6; *Oregonian,* November 17, 1912, sec. 2, p. 8.

17. *Portland News,* home edition, November 18, 1912, 1. See also *Oregon Journal,* November 17, 1912, sec. 1, p. 1, and *Evening Telegram,* November 18, 1912, 1.

18. YMCA Minutes, November 18, 1912; *Oregonian,* November 20, 1912, 13.

19. *Portland News,* home edition, November 20, 1912, 1.

20. Portland Commercial Club Minutes, Portland Chamber of Commerce Collection, vol. 6, November 26, 1912, MS 686–2, OHS; *Portland Spectator,* December 21, 1912, 1; *Oregonian,* November 25, 1912, 6. See also *Evening Telegram,* November 18, 1912, 7, and *Oregon Journal,* November 25, 1912, 5.

21. *Oregonian,* November 25, 1912, 14. See also *Oregon Journal,* November 24, 1912, 5; November 25, 1912, 5; *Oregonian,* November 24, 1912, sec. 1, p. 1; *Evening Telegram,* November 25, 1912, 8; December 2, 1912, 3.

22. F. C. Knapp to F. P. Brewer, November 26, 1912; E. W. Scripps to F. V. [*sic*] Knapp, December 7, 1912; and BHC [B. H. Canfield] to [Dana] Sleeth, December 10 [1912]: all Sleeth Family Papers, courtesy Peter D. Sleeth. See also Baldasty, "Newspapers for 'the Wage Earning Class,'" 171.

23. *Oregonian,* November 21, 1912, 16; November 22, 1912, 14. See also *Portland News,* home edition, November 25, 1912, 1; John E. Caswell, "The Prohibition Movement in Oregon: II. 1904–1915," *OHQ* 40, no. 1 (March 1939): 65.

24. MacColl, *Shaping of a City,* 10, 159–61, 413–16.

25. *Portland News,* home edition, November 25, 1912, 1.

26. *Portland News,* home edition, November 20, 1912, 1.

27. YMCA Minutes, January 14, 1912; Harry Stone to Hon. H. R. Albee, January 9, 1914, MOC, box 30, folder 7, SPARC.

28. *Portland News,* home edition, November 19, 1912, 4; November 20, 1912, 1; November 25, 1912, 1, 6; January 4, 1913, 1. See also *Portland Labor Press,* November 25, 1912, 4.

29. BHC [B.H. Canfield] to [Dana] Sleeth, November 20 [1912]; BHC [B.H. Canfield] to D. Sleeth, December 2, 1912; and B.H. Canfield to Geo. S. Teall, December 3, 1912, carbon copy; "Sawyer" to Dana Sleeth and Bensyl Smythe, November 19, 1912: all Sleeth Family Papers, courtesy Peter D. Sleeth.

30. *Roseburg (Ore.) News-Review,* March 22, 1926, 2; *History of the Bench and Bar of Oregon* (Portland: Historical Publishing, 1910), 175; U.S. Department of Commerce, Bureau of the Census, Fourteenth Census, 1920, Manuscript Population Census Returns, Douglas County, Ore., Enumeration District 139, sheet 13B, line 90; application of E.S.J. McAllister for admission as an attorney, Oregon Supreme Court Offices, Salem, Ore. According to *History of the Bench* (175), McAllister earned his degree in Virginia in 1903; however, in his application for admission to the Oregon bar McAllister writes that he completed his studies at the University of Virginia on June 15, 1904.

31. *Roseburg (Ore.) News-Review,* March 22, 1926, 2; *History of the Bench,* 175; Manuscript Population Census Returns, Douglas County, Ore., 1920, Enumeration District 139, sheet 13B, line 90; *Oregon Journal,* February 15, 1905, 24; application of E.S.J. McAllister for admission as an attorney.

32. MacColl, *Shaping of a City,* 187, 191, 204, 221–22, 224, 227, 289, 297, 395–96; Gordon B. Dodds, *Oregon: A Bicentennial History* (New York: W.W. Norton; Nashville: American Association for State and Local History, 1977), 161–84; Lincoln Steffens, "The Taming of the West," *American* 64 (October 1907): 585–602; Steffens, *Upbuilders* (New York: Doubleday, Page, 1909); Burton J. Hendrick, "The Initiative and Referendum and How Oregon Got Them," *McClure's* 37, no. 3 (July 1911): 235–48; Hendrick, "Law Making by the Voters," *McClure's* 37, no. 4 (August 1911): 435–50; Hendrick, "'Statement No. 1,'" 505–19; Ray Stannard Baker, "The Great Northwest," *Century* 65, no. 5 (March 1903): 647–67; Dorothy O. Johansen, *Empire of the Columbia: A History of the Pacific Northwest,* 2d ed. (New York: Harper and Row, 1967), 447–63; Russell G. Hendricks, "Election of Senator Chamberlain, the People's Choice," *OHQ* 53, no. 2 (June 1952): 63–88; C.B. Galbreath, comp., *Initiative and Referendum* (Columbus, Ohio: F.J. Heer Printing, 1911), 51–52, 58–63; Ruth Barnes Moynihan, *Rebel for Rights: Abigail Scott Duniway* (New Haven: Yale University Press, 1983); John Messing, "Public Lands, Politics, and Progressives: The Oregon Land Fraud Trials, 1903–1910," *Pacific Historical Review* 35 (1966): 35–66; Robert C. Woodward, "William Simon U'Ren: In an Age of Protest" (M.A. thesis, University of Oregon, 1956); Johnston, "Middle-Class Political Ideology."

33. *Medford (Ore.) Mail Tribune,* November 22, 1912, 3; Caswell, "Prohibition Movement," 69; Tony Howard Evans, "Oregon Progressive Reform, 1902–1914" (Ph.D. diss., University of California, Berkeley, 1966), 104–6; *Oregon Journal,* February 19, 1905, 24; November 1, 1910, 9.

E.S.J. McAllister explained to the *Oregon Journal* (November 1, 1910, 9) that he daily received "big bunches" of angry letters from both sides of the prohibitionist issue, as some people confused him with Harry C. McAllister, secretary of the Home Rule Association, an anti-prohibitionist organization. "[I]n desperation," the *Oregon Journal* reported, he "has turned to the newspapers for relief," declaring that "he has not taken any stand, one way or the other, in the wet and dry fight in the state." Although this statement seems disingenuous, there may have been some truth to it. Probably McAllister's early work for the Anti-Saloon League did not reflect his ideological views on liquor; he may have worked for the organization simply because he needed a job after relocating to Oregon in haste. It is even more likely that his other political stands compelled him to support the league's fight to retain the integrity of the local option law in 1905. During this struggle McAllister became closely associated with William S. U'Ren, the architect of Oregon's use of the initiative and referendum. In 1904 Oregonians had adopted the local option through the initiative process, and U'Ren's efforts on the floor of the legislature in 1905 seem to have been largely motivated by his desire to defend the people's ability to make laws, not his personal feelings about alcohol. McAllister's close and lengthy association with U'Ren suggests that he likely held many of the same political beliefs about the initiative, leading him eventually to leave behind the Anti-Saloon League. On other occasions, both U'Ren and McAllister defended initiatives as the people's work even when they did not favor the issue. See Dodds, *Oregon,* 180; Peter H. Odegard, *Pressure Politics: The Story of the Anti-Saloon League* (New York: Columbia University Press, 1928), 121–22; Woodward, "William Simon U'Ren," 150; Thomas C. McClintock, "Seth Lewelling, William S. U'Ren, and the Birth of the Oregon Progressive Movement," *OHQ* 68, no. 3 (September 1967): 197–220.

34. *Oregonian,* May 28, 1906, 8; June 4, 1906, 8 (quotation).

35. My summary of *Muller* is based on Robert Johnston's work in progress on class politics in early Portland. For a good summary of *Muller* and its complexities, see Nancy Woloch, *Muller v. Oregon: A Brief History with Documents* (New York: Bedford, 1996).

36. *History of the Bench,* 175, 238; Robert J. Upton testimony, Oregon v. E. S. J. McAllister, Trial Transcript (hereafter, McAllister Transcript), pp. 66–67, OSCR, file 1696, OSA.

37. V. E Campbell to Hon. H. Lane, June 15, 1908, and Mayor [Harry Lane] to Mr. V. Campbell [carbon copy], June 17, 1908, MOC, 1908, box 9, folder 4, SPARC; H. A. Mosher to Hon. Harry Lane, June 23, 1908, and Mayor [Harry Lane] to H. A. Mosher [carbon copy], June 25, 1908, MOC, 1908, box 12, folder 7, SPARC; E. H. Cahalin to Hon. Harry Lane, June 19, 1908, and Mayor [Harry Lane] to Mr. E. H. Cahalin [carbon copy], June 23, 1908, MOC, 1908, box 9, folder 4, SPARC. See also Johnston, "Middle-Class Political Ideology,"163–77, and MacColl, *Shaping of a City,* 316–47.

38. McAllister v. American Hospital Association, 62 Or. 530–39 (1913); *Oregon Journal,* April 25, 1912, 6; *Oregonian,* April 9, 1912, 9; 10 April 1912, 14; April 12, 1912, 18; August 24, 1912, 5; *Evening Telegram,* December 13, 1912, 1; Stewart H. Holbrook, "Whitehouse Mystery," *Oregonian,* Magazine section, May 16, 1937, 12, 16; Horace Tabb testimony, McAllister Transcript, 40–44.

39. Eggleston, letter to the editor, *Oregon Journal,* October 30, 1912, 8, as quoted in Robert C. Woodward, "W. S. U'Ren and the Single Tax in Oregon,"

OHQ 61, no. 1 (March 1960): 49; Dodds, *Oregon,* 180. On the single tax in Oregon, see Woodward, "W. S. U'Ren," 46–63; Johnston, "Middle-Class Political Ideology," 355–99; and James H. Gilbert, "Single-Tax Movement in Oregon," *Political Science Quarterly* 31, no. 1 (March 1916): 25–52.

40. Gilbert, "Single-Tax Movement," 49; Dodds, *Oregon,* 162.

41. Woodward, "W. S. U'Ren," 49–52; MacColl with Stein, *Merchants, Money, and Power,* 346; Johnston, "Middle-Class Political Ideology," 225–29, 355–99; Dodds, *Oregon,* 169–71; *Oregonian,* February 16, 1908, 9. On C. E. S. Wood, see Robert Hamburger, *Two Rooms: The Life of Charles Erskine Scott Wood* (Lincoln: University of Nebraska Press, 1998).

42. *Single Tax Conference Held in New York City, November 19 and 20, 1910* (Cincinnati: Joseph Fels Fund Commission, 1911), 28; Woodward, "W. S. U'Ren," 52; *Portland Labor Press,* September 7, 1911, 2; October 19, 1911, 8; Johnston, "Middle-Class Political Ideology," 228; MacColl, *Shaping of a City,* 441–45.

43. Woodward, "W. S. U'Ren," 55.

44. *Eugene (Ore.) Daily Guard,* November 4, 1912, 4; *Oregon Journal,* October 26, 1910, 10; Paul Thomas Culbertson, "A History of the Initiative and Referendum in Oregon" (Ph.D. diss., University of Oregon, 1941), 135–36; State ex rel. v. Olcott, 62 Or. 284–85 (1913); I. H. Van Winkle, W. S. U'Ren, and C. E. S. Wood, "Appellant's Abstract of Record," Oregon v. Ben W. Olcott, pp. 10–11, OSCR, file 1256, OSA.

45. Culbertson, "History of the Initiative," 135–36; State ex rel. v. Olcott, 62 Or. at 284–85; Van Winkle, U'Ren, and Wood, "Appellant's Abstract of Record," 10–11; W. S. U'Ren, letter to *Oregonian,* March 22, 1907, 8.

46. Woodward, "W. S. U'Ren," 46, 52–59, 58; *Oregonian,* February 23, 1914, 1, 3. See also *Marshfield (Ore.) Coos Bay Times,* November 19, 1912, 2; and Johnston, "Middle-Class Political Ideology," 370–82.

47. *Eugene Daily Guard,* November 11, 1912, 6; November 27, 1912, 3.

48. *Eugene Daily Guard,* November 19, 1912, 6; November 20, 1912, 4; December 12, 1913, 1; February 22, 1913, 1; February 24, 1913, 4.

49. *Marshfield (Ore.) Coos Bay Times,* November 19, 1912, 2.

50. Ibid.; *Medford (Ore.) Mail Tribune,* November 22, 1912, 3; *Oregonian,* November 22, 1912, 7; George Chauncey, *Gay New York: Gender, Urban Culture, and the Making of the Gay Male World, 1890–1940* (New York: BasicBooks, 1994), 52.

51. *Evening Telegram,* December 21, 1912, 1; Woodward, "W. S. U'Ren," 60.

52. Harry Work testimony, McAllister Transcript, 29, 40; R. J. Slater and Joseph Page, "Brief of the Appellant," State of Oregon v. E. S. J. McAllister, May 24, 1913, p. 37, OSCR, file 1696, OSA.

53. Upton testimony, McAllister Transcripts, 66, 67; *Oregon Journal,* January 28, 1914, 7; *Evening Telegram,* January 28, 1914, 9; *Portland City Directory, 1913* (Portland: R. L. Polk, 1913); *Portland City Directory, 1915* (Portland: R. L. Polk, 1915); *Roseburg (Ore.) News-Review,* March 22, 1926, 2; Pat Young, "Case Closed: The Multnomah Bar Association Rights an 88-Year-Old Wrong," *Just Out,* September 1, 2000, 9.

54. U.S. Department of Commerce, Bureau of the Census, *Thirteenth Census of the United States, 1910* (Washington, D.C.: United States Government Printing Office, 1914), 4:97; Katherine G. Morrissey, *Mental Territories: Mapping the Inland Empire* (Ithaca, N.Y.: Cornell University Press, 1997), 26, 27; D. W. Meinig, *The Great Columbia Plain: A Historical Geography, 1805–1910* (Seattle: University of Washington Press, 1968), 62, 127, 164, 165, 212, 217, 219, 223, 231–32, 233, 324–26, 355, 453–54, 510; booster quotation, 453.

55. *Walla Walla (Wash.) Sunday Morning Bulletin,* November 17, 1912, 1; *Walla Walla (Wash.) Evening Bulletin,* November 18, 1912, 1, 2; *Oregon Journal,* November 22, 1912, 12; *Walla Walla (Wash.) Union,* November 23, 1912, 2; materials in John Gibson, WSP Inmate File 6708, WSAO.

56. *Walla Walla (Wash.) Union,* November 23, 1912, 2; *Spokane (Wash.) Spokesman-Review,* November 24, 1912, 11; *Walla Walla (Wash.) Evening Bulletin,* November 23, 192, 4, and November 28, 1912, 8; *Walla Walla (Wash.) Sunday Morning Bulletin,* November 24, 1912, 6.

57. Material in Gibson, WSP Inmate File.

58. *Walla Walla (Wash.) Evening Bulletin,* November 25, 1912, 6; *Walla Walla (Wash.) Union,* November 24, 1912, 4.

59. Raymond C. Brooks, Berkeley, Calif., to Board of Pardons, State Penitentiary, Washington, Walla Walla, Wash., September 29, 1913, in Gibson, WSP Inmate File; *Spokane (Wash.) Spokesman-Review,* November 23, 1912, 3.

60. *Walla Walla (Wash.) Evening Bulletin,* November 23, 1912, 4; Brooks to Board of Pardons, September 29, 1913, in Gibson, WSP Inmate File.

Chapter 6. Reforming Homosexuality in the Northwest

1. *Salem (Ore.) Daily Capital Journal,* November 26, 1912, 1. See also *Seattle Star,* November 25, 1912, 1; November 27, 1912, 6; November 30, 1912, 6; *Portland News,* home edition, November 26, 1912, 1.

2. *Seattle Star,* November 28, 1912, 3; November 30, 1912, 6; December 3, 1912, 1; *Portland News,* home edition, November 26, 1912, 1; November 27, 1912, 1; December 3, 1912, 1; *Portland News,* city edition, November 30, 1912, 1; *Salem (Ore.) Daily Capital Journal,* November 26, 1912, 1; *Astoria (Ore.) Daily Budget,* November 27, 1912, 1; *Pendleton Eastern Oregonian,* November 27, 1912, 1; *Corvallis (Ore.) Weekly Gazette,* November 29, 1912, 1; December 7, 1912, 7; *Medford (Ore.) Mail Tribune,* December 3, 1912, 1. See also *Seattle Star,* November 25, 1912, 1; November 27, 1912, 6.

3. Lafferty returned to Portland in 1946 and resumed work as a lawyer. He ran for a seat in the U.S. House of Representatives in 1950, 1952, 1954, and 1956, and for the U.S. Senate in 1962. Lafferty spent several months in the Oregon State Hospital in 1955. He died in 1964. See *Portland Oregonian* (hereafter, *Oregonian*), January 16, 1964, 1, 11; December 30, 1951, Magazine section, 8; January 31, 1919, 13; February 2, 1919, sec. 1, p. 7; *History of the Bench and Bar of Oregon* (Portland: Historical Publishing, 1910), 167; *Portland, Oregon Journal* (hereafter,

Oregon Journal), November 4, 1910, 2; *Portland News,* January 31, 1919, 1; February 1, 1919, 3.

4. The literature on Progressivism is extensive. For an introduction, see Arthur S. Link and Richard L. McCormick, *Progressivism* (Wheeling, Ill.: Harlan Davidson, 1983).

5. John D'Emilio and Estelle B. Freedman, *Intimate Matters: A History of Sexuality in America* (New York: Harper and Row, 1988), 202, 211–12; Gloria E. Myers, *A Municipal Mother: Portland's Lola Greene Baldwin, America's First Policewoman* (Corvallis: Oregon State University Press, 1995), 127–43; Ruth Rosen, *The Lost Sisterhood: Prostitution in America, 1900–1918* (Baltimore: Johns Hopkins University Press, 1982), 19, 33–36; Allan M. Brandt, *No Magic Bullet: A Social History of Venereal Disease in the United States since 1880,* expanded ed. (New York: Oxford University Press, 1987), 52–121.

6. Mary de Young, "Help, I'm Being Held Captive! The White Slave Fairy Tale of the Progressive Era," *Journal of American Culture* 6, no. 1 (spring 1983): 97; Brandt, *No Magic Bullet,* 32, 33; Rosen, *Lost Sisterhood,* 14, 15; Henry Russell Talbot et al., *Report of the Portland Vice Commission to the Mayor and City Council of the City of Portland, Oregon, January 1913* (Portland: Henry Russell Talbot, 1913), ii–iv, 216; City of Portland, Council Proceedings, September 27, 1911, in Council Proceedings, 36:749, SPARC; E. Kimbark MacColl, *The Shaping of a City: Business and Politics in Portland, Oregon, 1885–1915* (Portland: Georgian Press, 1976), 202–10; Heather Lee Miller, "From Moral Suasion to Moral Coercion: Persistence and Transformation in Prostitution Reform, Portland, Oregon, 1888–1917" (M.A. thesis, University of Oregon, 1996), 98–114.

7. D'Emilio and Freeman, *Intimate Matters,* 60–61, 159–61; Jeffrey P. Moran, *Teaching Sex: The Shaping of Adolescence in the Twentieth Century* (Cambridge, Mass.: Harvard University Press, 2000), 27–67; Peter T. Cominos, "Late-Victorian Sexual Respectability and the Social System," *International Review of Social History* 8 (1963): 46–48; John C. Burnham, *Paths into American Culture: Psychology, Medicine, and Morals* (Philadelphia: Temple University Press, 1988), 152–59, 162, 165, 199–201; John C. Burnham, "The Progressive Revolution in American Attitudes toward Sex," *Journal of American History* 59, no. 4 (March 1973): 885–908; Brandt, *No Magic Bullet,* 37–38, 46.

8. Walter W. R. May, "Some Highlights in the History of the Oregon Social Hygiene Society," University of Oregon Leaflet Series 15, no. 3 (March 1930); OSHS, *The State-Wide Work of the Oregon Social Hygiene Society,* pamphlet no. 25 (Portland: OSHS, 1917); OSHS, *Progress: The Second Annual Report* (Portland: OSHS, 1913); Social Hygiene Society of Portland, Oregon, *A Social Emergency: The First Annual Report* (Portland: Social Hygiene Society of Portland, Oregon, 1912); William T. Foster, "State-Wide Education in Social Hygiene," *Social Hygiene* 2, no. 3 (July 1916): 309–29; *Boise Evening Capital News,* November 22, 1912, 6; *Boise Idaho Daily Statesman,* November 22, 1912, 3; OSHS, *Vigorous Manhood,* pamphlet no. 8 (Portland: OSHS, 1917); OSHS, *A Reasonable Sex Life for a Man,* pamphlet no. 23 (Portland: OSHS, 1917); OSHS, *Masturbation,* pamphlet no. 22 (Portland: OSHS, 1917); MS 1541, the OSHS Collection, OHS;

Myers, *Municipal Mother,* 7, 91–92. Lack of funds ultimately prevented OSHS from sending its display to France.

9. William Trufant Foster, "The Social Emergency," in *The Social Emergency: Studies in Sex Hygiene and Morals,* ed. William Trufant Foster (Boston: Houghton Mifflin, 1914), 5 (quotation), 5–12; Burnham, *Paths into American Culture,* 161; Moran, *Teaching Sex,* 45–49. OSHS also had difficulty persuading the public to accept sex education in schools. Occasionally, organizational minutes reveal other uncertainties. For example, in the winter of 1911–12, OSHS's Committee on Exhibits presented to the organization its newly developed slide show, which included a segment on sex organs and their diseases. After viewing the program, a couple of members objected that "much evil may result from such skin pictures as shown [here]." One of those protesting against certain slides also favored omitting from an OSHS bibliography the fairly lurid Chicago and Minneapolis vice commission reports as well as a book by Clifford G. Roe titled *Panders and Their White Slaves* (1910). But despite some internal squabbles, overall OSHS pushed back the boundaries of public discussion on sex issues in Oregon. See OSHS Minutes, January 26, 1912, box 3, folder 2, OSHS Collection. Examples of local concern over public school instruction in matters of sex include sentiments expressed by Dr. Henry Waldo Coe of Portland, who wrote "Halt in Sexual Instruction," *Medical Sentinel* 21, no. 4 (April 1913): 853–54.

10. Robert H. Wiebe, *The Search for Order, 1877–1920* (New York: Hill and Wang, 1967), 165, 132; Burnham, *Paths into American Culture,* 219–21; Myers, *Municipal Mother,* 105, 106, 120–21; Miller, "From Moral Suasion to Moral Coercion," 114–23.

11. OSHS, *State-Wide Work,* 1–2; Oregon, *General Laws, 1913* (Salem: State Printer, 1913), 323–24; Oregon, *General Laws, 1915* (Salem: State Printing Department, 1915), 458–59; Oregon, *General Laws, 1917* (Salem: State Printing Department, 1917), 637–38; OSHS Minutes, September 20 and October 27, 1911.

12. D'Emilio and Freedman, *Intimate Matters,* 211, 213 (quotation). See also Myers, *Municipal Mother,* 105; Joseph Mayer, "The Passing of the Red Light District—Vice Investigations and Results," *Social Hygiene* 4, no. 2 (April 1918): 197–209; Kevin J. Mumford, *Interzones: Black/White Sex Districts in Chicago and New York in the Early Twentieth Century* (New York: Columbia University Press, 1997), 19–35; Miller, "From Moral Suasion to Moral Coercion."

13. Jo Anne Russell, "A Necessary Evil: Prostitutes, Patriarchs, and Profits in Boise City, 1863–1915" (M.A. thesis, Boise State University, 1991); "Commercialized Prostitution Survey, Portland, Oregon, Dec. 4–6, 1932," in box 1, folder 18, OSHS Collection.

14. Washington State, *General Statutes and Codes, 1891* (San Francisco: Bancroft-Whitney, 1891), 2:705; Washington State, *Session Laws, 1917* (Olympia: Frank M. Lamborn, 1917), 341–42, chap. 98; Washington Territory, *Statutes, 1854* (Olympia: George B. Goudy, 1855), 95–96; Washington State, *Remington and Ballinger's Annotated Codes and Statutes of Washington,* by Arthur Remington and Richard A. Ballinger (Seattle: Bancroft-Whitney, 1910), 1:1152; Washington State, *Session Laws, 1903* (Tacoma: Allen and Lamborn, 1903), 231.

15. Washington State, *Session Laws, 1897* (Olympia: O. C. White, 1897), 19–20; Washington State, *Remington and Ballinger's,* 1:1151. Michel Foucault also notes that both adultery and rape were "condemned less and less" over the years (*The History of Sexuality: An Introduction,* trans. Robert Hurley [New York: Pantheon Books, 1978], 39).

16. Foucault, *History of Sexuality,* 8, 17, 38. While Foucault argues that there has been a "discursive explosion" about sex since the end of the sixteenth century, he does point out that discussion was controlled for certain ends (27). Different perspectives on the emergence of heterosexuality and homosexuality, and their respective normalization and stigmatization, are offered by Foucault, *History of Sexuality,* 36–49; Jonathan Ned Katz, *The Invention of Heterosexuality* (1995; reprint, New York: Plume, 1996); and Kevin White, *The First Sexual Revolution: The Emergence of Male Heterosexuality in Modern America* (New York: New York University Press, 1993).

17. Jacob Shartle v. W. I. Hutchinson, 3 Or. 337–39 (1911). See also Vern L. Bullough and Martha Voght, "Homosexuality and Its Confusion with the 'Secret Sin' in Pre-Freudian America," in *The Other Americans: Sexual Variance in the National Past,* ed. Charles O. Jackson (Westport, Conn.: Praeger, 1996), 82, and Mrs. Harry I. Hiday, *United States Census of the City of Portland, Oregon, 1870* (Portland: Genealogical Forum of Portland, 1972), 121 (listing for Jacob Shartle, household 629).

18. Oregon v. Dell [*sic*] V. Meagher, June 15, 1913, MCCCC 52736; State v. Altwatter [*sic*], 29 Idaho 110 (1917); State v. McAllister, 136 P. 355 (1914).

19. Washington State, *Session Laws, 1909* (Olympia: E. L. Boardman, 1909), 952. This law also forbade the public reporting of some (but certainly not all) "heterosexual" crimes involving rape, seduction, and adultery.

20. On local newspapers' careful use of language, their assumptions about public knowledge of same-sex sexual practices and criminals, and their linkage of the "known" to the "unknown" in reports in the 1890s, see John Howard, "The Talk of the County: Revisiting Accusation, Murder, and Mississippi, 1895," in *Where These Memories Grow: History, Memory, and Southern Identity,* ed. W. Fitzhugh Brundage (Chapel Hill: University of North Carolina Press, 2000), and Lisa Duggan, *Sapphic Slashers: Sex, Violence, and American Modernity* (Durham, N.C.: Duke University, 2000).

21. *Oregon Journal,* November 17, 1912, sec. 2, p. 4.

22. Talbot et al., *Report of the Portland Vice Commission,* 136.

23. *Portland News,* home edition, November 26, 1912, 1; November 21, 1912, 1 (which quotes Mayor Rushlight); November 18, 1912, 1; November 25, 1912, 3; Talbot et al., *Report of the Portland Vice Commission,* 136.

24. Dyott, quoted in *Oregonian,* December 3, 1912, 10.

25. *Portland News,* March 25, 1913, 1; April 22, 1913, 1; *Oregon Journal,* May 14, 1913.

26. For more on the broader connection between sex education and newly emerging understandings of youths and the problems that the middle class faced in the early twentieth century, see Moran, *Teaching Sex.*

When OSHS formed in September 1911, it did so in close connection with Portland's YMCA, the organization that put forth the call for the meeting at which it was founded and that provided space for more than a year for the society's weekly meetings. OSHS's constitution made the treasurer of the YMCA its treasurer, and it included as ex-officio members of the Executive Committee the YMCA's general secretary and its physical director. But on November 15, 1912, just when the same-sex vice scandal began to make banner headlines, OSHS completely severed its ties to its parent organization. Although OSHS records are unclear on this point, it seems that this move resulted directly from the homosexual scandal. The directorship of OSHS first contemplated breaking with the YMCA on the evening of November 8, shortly after the arrest of Benjamin Trout, whose confession brought middle-class same-sex vice to the attention of police. A prominent member and onetime vice president of OSHS, W. N. Gatens, was a Multnomah County circuit and juvenile court judge and took personal charge of the vice cases. Authorities immediately sent Trout to the juvenile court after his arrest, and it is likely that Gatens forewarned the YMCA and OSHS before the upsetting news became public knowledge.

When OSHS broke with the YMCA, it attempted to affiliate with the Oregon State Board of Health, but the desire to change affiliation is more likely a result than a cause of the move. The two organizations were not always allies, as explained a little later in the text. Taken together, its uneasy relationship with the Board of Health and its very uncertain future suggest that OSHS left the YMCA in an effort at damage control (OSHS scrapbook, "A Synopsis of the Work of the Oregon Social Hygiene Society," box 2, folder no. 17, OSHS Collection; OSHS minutes, September 20, 1911, November 15, 1912, November 8, 1912, OSHS Collection; *Portland Evening Telegram* [hereafter, *Evening Telegram*], November 16, 1912, 1; November 16, 1912, 1; OSBH minutes, November 8, 1912, OSA).

27. OSHS minutes, November 15, 1912, OSHS Collection.

28. *Oregonian,* November 25, 1912, 14; November 23, 1912, 13; December 14, 1912, 9 (quotation); *Evening Telegram,* December 2, 1912, 3; November 25, 1912, 8; December 13, 1912, 2 (quotation); *Seattle Star,* December 14, 1912, 3.

29. OSBH minutes, November 8, 1912, OSA; OSHS minutes, November 15, 1912, OSHS Collection; Oregon, *House Journal, 1913* (Eugene: Guard Printing, 1913), 126, 1027, 1045, 1145.

30. Committee on School Co-Operation Report, December 13, 1912, in OSHS minutes, November 1, 1912 to November 5, 1913, OSHS Collection; Minutes of the Conference of Educators in Schools and Colleges, April 3 and 4, 1914, in OSHS minutes, September 1, 1913 to October 9, 1914, OSHS Collection.

31. Josephine De Vore Johnson to Mr. William Warren, August 5, 1915, MOC, 1915, box 33, folder J, envelope 18, SPARC; Emma Goldman, *Living My Life* (1931; reprint, Garden City, N.Y.: Garden City Publishing, 1934), 555–56; *Oregonian,* August 7, 1915, 12; August 8, 1915, 11; August 14, 1915, 9; *Evening Telegram,* August 7, 1915, 2; *Portland News,* August 7, 1915, 1; August 9, 1915, 1; August 13,

1915, 1; *Oregon Journal,* August 7, 1915, 1, 8; August 8, 1915, sec. 1, p. 11; August 13, 1915, 1; August 14, 1915, sec. 1, p. 4.

32. George Edwards, "A Portrait of Portland," *Mother Earth* 10, no. 9 (November 1915): 312, 313.

33. Materials in John Hayes, WSP Inmate File 5888, WSAO.

34. Ibid.; materials in William Boyd, WSP Inmate File 6467, WSAO.

35. Materials in Boyd, WSP Inmate File.

36. Idaho Territory, *Laws of the Territory of Idaho, 1864* (Lewiston: Territorial Printer, 1864), 444; Montana Territory, *Acts, Resolutions and Memorials, 1866* (Virginia City: D. W. Tilton, 1866), 24; State v. Guerin, 152 P. 747–49 (1916); State v. Altwatter [*sic*], 29 Idaho at 107–12; Lawrence W. Murphy, "Defining the Crime against Nature: Sodomy in the United States Appeals Courts, 1810–1940," *Journal of Homosexuality* 19, no. 1 (1990): 55, 56, 57–58. On the history of sodomy laws in the United States, see Murphy, "Defining the Crime against Nature," 49–66, and George E. Campbell, "Criminal Law—Sodomy—The Crime and the Penalty," *Arkansas Law Review* 8, no. 4 (fall 1954): 497–500.

37. State v. Place, 32 P. 736–37 (1893); State of Washington v. H. C. Place, Trial Transcript, WSSCC no. 741, WSAE; *Chehalis (Wash.) Nugget,* February 24, 1893, 1, 4; *Seattle Post-Intelligencer,* February 19, 1893, 2; Washington State, *Session Laws, 1893* (Olympia: O. C. White, 1893), 470–71; *Olympia, Washington Standard,* March 3, 1892, 2.

38. Washington State, *Third Message of Gov. Albert E. Mead to the Legislature of 1909* (Olympia: C. W. Gorham, 1909), 14; Washington State, *Session Laws, 1909,* 950; *Seattle Post-Intelligencer,* March 7, 1909, sec. 2, p. 5; Terry L. Chapman, "'An Oscar Wilde Type': 'The Abominable Crime of Buggery' in Western Canada, 1890–1920," *Criminal Justice History* 4 (1983): 106.

39. Oregon Territory, *Statutes of Oregon, 1855* (Salem: Asahel Bush, 1855), 233, 281; Campbell, "Criminal Law—Sodomy," 497; Oregon v. Harry A. Start, Trial Transcripts, 262, 296, 319, 7–12, File No. 1478, OSCR, OSA; State v. Start, 132 P. 512–13 (1913).

40. *Oregonian,* December 21, 1912, 11; February 1, 1913, 5; Oregon, *House Journal, 1913,* 3, 4, 5, 6, 88, 89, 144–45, 288, 296; Oregon, *Senate Journal, 1913* (n.p., 1913), 2, 4, 237, 248–49; Oregon, *General Laws, 1913,* 56.

41. State v. Start, 132 P. at 512–13. See also Sam M. Johnson and Wilson T. Hume, "Brief of the Defendant and Appellant," Oregon v. Harry A. Start, February 18, 1913, pp. 9–16, OSCR, file 1478, OSA; [Alexander] Wilson & [Oscar] Neal and George Roosman, "Appellant's Brief," Oregon v. E. E. Wedemeyer, February 26, 1913, pp. 10–20, OSCR, file 1479, OSA.

42. State v. Clarence Brazell, 126 Or. 580 (1929).

43. Oregon, *Senate Journal, 1913,* 237. The figures given in the text are lower than the total number of men incarcerated in the Oregon State Penitentiary for sodomy, because those who died while in prison are not included; the statistics come from OSP Great Registers, OSA.

44. Mark H. Haller, *Eugenics: Hereditarian Attitudes in American Thought* (New Brunswick, N.J.: Rutgers University Press, 1984), 4 (quotation), 3–4, 5, 6;

Philip R. Reilly, *The Surgical Solution: A History of Involuntary Sterilization in the United States* (Baltimore: John Hopkins University Press, 1991), 2.

45. J. H. Landman, *Human Sterilization: The History of the Sexual Sterilization Movement* (New York: Macmillan, 1932), 5 (quotation), 4; Haller, *Eugenics,* 6

46. B. A. Owens-Adair, *Human Sterilization: Its Social and Legislative Aspects* (n.p.: B. A. Owens-Adair, 1922), 17; see also Haller, *Eugenics,* 124, 52–54, 46, 132; Reilly, *Surgical Solution,* 39, 12–17, 18, 22–24; Daniel J. Kevles, *In the Name of Eugenics: Genetics and the Uses of Human Heredity* (New York: Knopf, 1985), 73–76, 96–97; and B. Owens-Adair, *Human Sterilization* (n.p., [1909]), 1, 3, 8, 9, 20, 25, 39, 47, 48.

47. Haller, *Eugenics,* 6, 48, 132, 133; Reilly, *Surgical Solution,* 29; Owens-Adair, *Human Sterilization* (1922), 45–48, 55–63; Owens-Adair, *Human Sterilization* (1909), 1, 7, 36, 52–53, 54–55, 56; Landman, *Human Sterilization,* 56; Harry Hamilton Laughlin, *Eugenical Sterilization in the United States* (Chicago: Municipal Court of Chicago, 1922), 6.

48. Owens-Adair, *Human Sterilization* (1922), 56, 63; Oregon, *House Journal, 1907* (Salem: Willis S. Duniway, 1907), 745; Oregon, *House Journal, 1909* (Salem: Willis S. Duniway, 1909), 618; Oregon, *Senate Journal, 1909* (Salem: Willis S. Duniway, 1909), 245; Oregon, *Senate Journal, 1911* (Salem: Willis S. Duniway, 1911), 25.

49. Twenty-Fourth [1907] Regular Session, Oregon Legislature, House Bill No. 395, LAR, box 6, folder HB267–445, OSA; Twenty-Fifth [1909] Regular Session, Oregon Legislature, Senate Bill 68, LAR, box 7, folder SB1–125, OSA; Twenty-Sixth [1911] Regular Session, Oregon Legislature, Senate Bill 90, LAR, box 8, folder SB1–100, OSA.

50. *Oregonian,* November 24, 1912, sec. 3, p. 6.

51. MacColl, *Shaping of a City,* 402–4; Oregon, *Messages and Documents, 1913* (Salem: Willis S. Duniway, 1913), 1:18; Oswald West, "The Battle of Life … By 'Os' West," *Sunday Oregonian,* November 7, 1937, in Oswald West Biography File, OHS.

52. Oregon, *Messages and Documents, 1913,* 1:18–19. See also West, "The Battle of Life"; Fred Lockley, "Oswald West Outlines His Services in Oregon," *Oregon Journal,* July 16, 1950, clipping in Oswald West Collection, MS 589, folder: "Misc. Articles on Oregon State Affairs by West," OHS; Owens-Adair, *Human Sterilization* (1922), 65–66.

53. Owens-Adair, *Human Sterilization* (1922), 20. See also Reilly, *Surgical Solution,* 29; Charles H. Hughes, "An Emasculated Homosexual: His Antecedent and Post-Operative Life," *Alienist and Neurologist* 35, no. 3 (August 1914): 277–80; A. A. Brill, "The Conception of Homosexuality," *Journal of the American Medical Association* 61, no. 5 (August 2, 1913): 337; and Jeffrey Weeks, *Coming Out: Homosexual Politics in Britain from the Nineteenth Century to the Present,* rev. ed. (London: Quartet Books, 1990), 31.

54. West, "The Battle of Life."

55. *Oregon Journal,* January 23, 1913, 2; Oregon, *House Journal, 1913,* 55, 318; Oregon, *General Laws, 1913,* 99–100; Oregon, *Senate Journal, 1913,* 47, 395;

Twenty-Seventh [1913] Regular Session, Oregon Legislature, Senate Bill No. 40, LAR, box 10, folder SB1–150, OSA.

56. *Oregon Journal,* November 3, 1913, 8. See also *Oregon Journal,* January 21, 1913, 15; January 24, 1913, 6; March 11, 1913, 5; April 18, 1913, 3; *Salem, Oregon Statesman,* January 24, 1913, 2; *Portland News,* March 1, 1913, 6; October 22, 1913, 4; Laughlin, *Eugenical Sterilization,* 43; Oregon, *Measures with Arguments Respecting the Same to be Submitted to the Electors of the Oregon at the Special Election on Tuesday, November 4, 1913,* by Ben W. Olcott (n.p., n.d.), 2, 13–14; Robert Douglas Johnston, "Middle-Class Political Ideology in a Corporate Society: The Persistence of Small-Propertied Radicalism in Portland, Oregon, 1883–1926" (Ph.D. diss., Rutgers University, 1993), 284–87.

57. Oregon, *General Laws, 1917,* 518–21; Twenty-Ninth [1917; Oregon] Legislative Assembly, Regular Session, Senate Bill No. 73, LAR, box 14, folder SB1–100, OSA; Oregon, *Senate and House Journals, 1917* (Salem: State Printing Department, 1917), 135. See also Owens-Adair, *Human Sterilization* (1922), 73–76, and Landman, *Human Sterilization,* appendix D, pp. 300–301.

58. L. J. Wentworth, E. E. Brodie, and F. W. Mulkey, *Report of the Commission to Investigate the Oregon State Penitentiary* (Portland, January 26, 1917), 74–75. The prevalence of same-sex sexual activities — engaged in not by inmates alone — caused the Oregon State Penitentiary official embarrassment for some time. For example, on April 30, 1913, an inmate accused William Quartier, the prison pharmacist, of "degenerate practices." As a reporter melodramatically related, "the accusation was made under dramatic circumstances and he was led away a crushed and broken man" (*Portland News,* April 30, 1913, 3). For general references to earlier homosexual conditions at the prison, see Joseph (Bunko) Kelley, *Thirteen Years in the Oregon Penitentiary* (Portland, 1908), 13.

59. Oregon, *General Laws, 1919* (Salem: State Printing Department, 1919), 387, 415–18; OSBH, *Twenty-First Biennial Report* (Salem: State Printing Department [1945]), 84; OSBH minutes, June 30, 1917, December 21, 1917, and September 20, 1918, OSA; Braham Singh [Bram Sing], Inmate 7440, Parole Board Calendar for November 1919, vol. 7 [n.p.], OSP Parole Board Actions, 1915–1938, OSA; Tony Lagallo, Inmate 7715, Parole Board Calendar for October 1918, vol. 5 [n.p.], OSP Parole Board Actions, 1915–1938, OSA.

60. As quoted in Owens-Adair, *Human Sterilization* (1922), 145. See also Owens-Adair, *Human Sterilization* (1922), 144–45; OSBH, *Thirteenth Biennial Report* (Salem: State Printing Department, 1928), 81.

61. Information on Merithew is contained in Herbert Merithew, OSP Inmate File 8090, OSA; Herbert Merithew and James Curtis, OSP Inmate Files 7507 and 7146, OSP Great Register, 1910–1925, pp. 270–71, OSA; James Riley, Inmate File 8090, OSP Great Register, 1910–1925, pp. 386–87, OSA; OSBH minutes, December 21, 1917, OSA. While the Board of Eugenics minutes for December 21, 1917, recommended Merithew (Riley) for sterilization because he was an habitual criminal, the "Record of an Individual Case of Sterilization of Any Type" filed with the Eugenics Record Office in Cold Spring Harbor, New York,

states the reason for sterilization as "Degenerative practices." Although Merithew was recommended for a vasectomy, he was castrated.

62. Various materials in Merithew, OSP Inmate File; Riley, OSP Great Register, 1910–1925, pp. 386–87. See also Owens-Adair, *Human Sterilization* (1922), 78–79, 145.

63. Owens-Adair, *Human Sterilization* (1922), 79–82; Laughlin, *Eugenical Sterilization*, 271–89; Oregon, *General Laws, 1923* (Salem: State Printing Department, 1923), 280–84; OSBH, *Thirteenth Biennial Report*, 81; Landman, *Human Sterilization*, 75–77; Oregon, *Oregon Laws, 1965* (Salem: State Printing, 1965), 524.

64. Washington State, *Session Laws, 1921* (Olympia: Frank M. Lamborn, 1921), 161–66; Laughlin, *Eugenical Sterilization*, 48–49; State of Idaho, *General Laws, 1925* (Boise: Syms-York, 1925), 358–62; *Boise, Idaho Daily Statesman*, January 12, 1925, 5; Angus McLaren, "Sex Radicalism in the Canadian Pacific Northwest, 1890–1920," *Journal of the History of Sexuality* 2, no. 4 (April 1992): 543, 544 n. 83; Angus McLaren, "The Creation of a Haven for 'Human Thoroughbreds': The Sterilization of the Feeble-Minded and the Mentally Ill in British Columbia," *Canadian Historical Review* 67, no. 2 (June 1986): 129; British Columbia, *Statutes of the Province of British Columbia, 1933,* by J.W. Fordham Johnson (Victoria: Charles F. Banfield, 1933), 199–201.

65. D'Emilio and Freedman, *Intimate Matters*, 203.

Epilogue. Same-Sex Affairs in the Pacific Northwest: 1912 and After

1. *Portland Evening Telegram* (hereafter, *Evening Telegram*), November 21, 1912, 8; *Medford (Ore.) Mail Tribune*, November 21, 1912, 1; *San Francisco City Directory, 1920* (San Francisco: H.S. Crocker, 1920), 379; *Portland Oregonian* (hereafter, *Oregonian*), January 13, 1913, 14; and various Portland city directories.

2. *Evening Telegram*, June 12, 1913, 8; Earl Van Hulen testimony, Oregon v. Harry A. Start, Trial Transcripts, p. 67, OSCR, file 1478, OSA; *Portland, Oregon Journal*, August 22, 1913, 1; *Oregonian*, August 23, 1913, 7.

3. *American Medical Directory, 1925,* 9th ed. (Chicago: American Medical Association, 1925), 2360; *American Medical Directory, 1942,* 17th ed. (Chicago: American Medical Association, 1942), 2003; *American Medical Directory, 1958,* 20th ed. (Chicago: American Medical Association, 1958), I-469; Harry A. Start, Medical License no. MD00863, granted on April 20, 1905, and revoked on February 18, 1913, author's personal conversation with the Oregon Medical Board of Examiners on June 22, 1998; Henry [*sic*] Start Death Certificate no. 46 016214, State of California Vital Records, Sacramento.

4. John D'Emilio, "The Homosexual Menace: The Politics of Sexuality in Cold War America," in *Passion and Power: Sexuality in History,* ed. Kathy Peiss and Christina Simmons, with Robert A. Padgug (Philadelphia: Temple University Press, 1989), 232, 233, 236; Estelle B. Freedman, "'Uncontrolled Desires': The Response to the Sexual Psychopath, 1920–1960," in ibid., 199–225; George

Chauncey, Jr., "The Postwar Sex Crime Panic," in *True Stories from the American Past,* ed. William Graebner (New York: McGraw-Hill, 1993), 172 (quotation), 175–76, 177. For a different perspective on the reasons for the post–World War II/cold war anti-gay panic, see John Howard, "The Library, the Park, and the Pervert: Public Space and Homosexual Encounter in Post–World War II Atlanta," in *Carryin' On in the Lesbian and Gay South,* ed. John Howard (New York: New York University Press, 1997), 107–31.

5. *Portland News,* home edition, November 26, 1912, 1; November 21, 1912, 1; Henry Russell Talbot et al., *Report of the Portland Vice Commission to the Mayor and City Council of the City of Portland, Oregon, January 1913* (Portland: Henry Russell Talbot, 1913), 136.

6. Michel Foucault, *The History of Sexuality: An Introduction,* trans. Robert Hurley (New York: Pantheon Books, 1978), 38–39.

Bibliography

Primary Sources: Unpublished

Alaska Packers Association Scrapbook Collection. Semiahmoo Park. Whatcom County Parks. Bellingham-Blaine Area, Wash.

Baldwin, Lola G. Lola G. Baldwin Papers. Portland Police Museum, Portland, Ore.

Boyfrank, Manuel. Manuel Boyfrank Papers. International Gay and Lesbian Archives, West Hollywood, Calif.

British Columbia. Attorney General Records. Provincial Archives of British Columbia, Victoria.

California. Henry Start Death Certificate no. 46 016214. State of California Vital Records. Sacramento.

———. Supreme Court Records. Los Angeles County Law Library, Los Angeles.

Evans, Walter H., Frank T. Collier, and Robert F. Maguire. "Brief of the Plaintiff and Respondent." Oregon v. Harry A. Start. File 1478. Oregon Supreme Court Records. Oregon State Archives, Salem.

Evans, Walter H., Robert F. Maguire, and Frank T. Collier. "Brief of the Plaintiff and Respondent." Oregon v. E. E. Wedemeyer. File 1479. Oregon Supreme Court Records. Oregon State Archives, Salem.

———. "Brief of the Respondent." Oregon v. E. S. J. McAllister. File 1696. Oregon Supreme Court Records. Oregon State Archives, Salem.

Idaho. Idaho Supreme Court Records. Idaho State Historical Society, Boise.

———. Justice Court Records. Various Counties. Idaho State Historical Society, Boise.

———. Parole Board Records. Idaho State Historical Society, Boise.

———. State Indictment Records. Idaho State Historical Society, Boise.

———. State Penitentiary Description of Convict Records. Idaho State Historical Society, Boise.

———. Territory and State Penitentiary Convict Register. Idaho State Historical Society, Boise.

Johnson, Sam M., and Wilson T. Hume. "Brief of the Defendant and Appellant." Oregon v. Harry A. Start, February 18, 1913. File 1478. Oregon Supreme Court Records. Oregon State Archives, Salem.

Kambouris, Haralambous. "Sojourn in America." Edited by Konstantinos H. Kambouris. Haralambous Kambouris Collection. MS 2638. Oregon Historical Society, Portland.

Marsh, E. P. "Report on Alaska Cannery Conditions." Washington, D.C.: Department of Labor, Federal Mediation and Conciliation Service, September 7, 1920. 56:28:2/Box 13, National Archives II. College Park, Md.

McAllister, E. S. J. Application for Admission as an Attorney. Oregon Supreme Court Offices, Salem.

McClatchy, C. K. Notes. Homosexual Issues File. Sacramento Archives and Museum Collection Center, Sacramento, Calif.

Necrology File. Cleveland Public Library Main Branch, Cleveland, Ohio.

Oregon. Legislative Assembly Records. Oregon State Archives, Salem.

——. Multnomah County Circuit Court Case Files. Multnomah County Courthouse. File Room, Portland.

——. Multnomah County Jail Registers. Oregon State Archives, Salem.

——. Multnomah County Voter Registration Cards. Multnomah County Records and Archives Center, Portland.

——. State Parole Board Actions. Parole Board Calendars. Oregon State Archives, Salem.

——. State Penitentiary Convict Description Book. Oregon State Archives, Salem.

——. State Penitentiary Great Registers. Oregon State Archives, Salem.

——. State Penitentiary Physical Description Records. Oregon State Archives, Salem.

——. State Penitentiary Record/Register. Oregon State Archives, Salem.

——. State Supreme Court Records. Oregon State Archives, Salem.

Oregon Social Hygiene Society Collection. MS 1541. Oregon Historical Society, Portland.

Oregon State Board of Health. Minutes. Oregon State Archives, Salem.

Portland, Ore. Annual Reports. Stanley Parr Archives and Records Center, Portland.

——. Council Documents. Stanley Parr Archives and Records Center, Portland.

——. Council Proceedings. Stanley Parr Archives and Records Center, Portland.

——. Mayor's Office Correspondence. Stanley Parr Archives and Records Center, Portland.

——. Parks Historic File. Stanley Parr Archives and Records Center, Portland.

——. Police Arrest Records. Stanley Parr Archives and Records Center, Portland.

——. Police Court Docket, State Cases. Stanley Parr Archives and Records Center. Portland.

——. Police Detective Day Books. Stanley Parr Archives and Records Center, Portland.

Portland Commercial Club. Minutes. Portland Chamber of Commerce Collection. MS 686–2. Oregon Historical Society, Portland.

Rominger, H. V., and H. G. Wallace. "Committee Report on gambling houses, saloons, etc. [1891–93]." MS 1286. Oregon Historical Society, Portland.

Slater, R. J., and Joseph Page. "Brief of the Appellant." Oregon v. E. S. J. McAllister, May 24, 1913. File 1696. Oregon Supreme Court Records. Oregon State Archives, Salem.

Sleeth, Dana. Dana Sleeth Family Papers. Courtesy of Peter D. Sleeth. Lake Oswego, Ore.

Sleeth, Peter D. "Biographical Sketch of Dana P. Sleeth." In author's possession.

U.S. Department of Commerce. Bureau of the Census. Fourteenth Census, 1920. Manuscript Census, Cuyahoga County, Ohio.

——. Bureau of the Census. Fourteenth Census, 1920. Manuscript Census, Douglas County, Ore.

——. Bureau of the Census. Fourteenth Census, 1920. Manuscript Census, Marion County, Ore.

——. Bureau of the Census. Thirteenth Census, 1910. Manuscript Census, Ada County, Idaho.

——. Bureau of the Census. Thirteenth Census, 1910. Manuscript Census, Marion County, Ore.

——. Bureau of the Census. Thirteenth Census, 1910. Manuscript Census, Multnomah County, Ore.

——. Bureau of the Census. Twelfth Census, 1900. Manuscript Census, Cuyahoga County, Ohio.

Van Buskirk, Philip. Philip Clayton Van Buskirk Collection. Accession no. 3621. Special Collections, University of Washington Manuscript and University Archives Division, Seattle.

Van Winkle, I. H., W. S. U'Ren, and C. E. S. Wood. "Appellant's Abstract of Record." Oregon v. Ben W. Olcott. File 1256. Oregon Supreme Court Records. Oregon State Archives, Salem.

Washington State. State Penitentiary Inmate Files. Washington State Archives, Olympia.

——. Supreme Court Records. Washington State Archives, Ellensburg.

West, Oswald. Biography File. Oregon Historical Society, Portland.

——. Oswald West Collection. MS 589. Oregon Historical Society, Portland.

Wilson, [Alexander], [Oscar] Neal, and George Roosman. "Appellant's Brief." Oregon v. E. E. Wedemeyer, February 26, 1913. File 1479. Oregon Supreme Court Records. Oregon State Archives, Salem.

Young Men's Christian Association of Portland, Ore. Minutes. YMCA of the Columbia-Willamette, Portland.

Primary Sources: Published Works

American Medical Directory, 1925. 9th ed. Chicago: American Medical Association, 1925.

American Medical Directory, 1942. 17th ed. Chicago: American Medical Association, 1942.

American Medical Directory, 1958. 20th ed. Chicago: American Medical Association, 1958.

Berkman, Alexander. *Prison Memoirs of an Anarchist.* New York: Mother Earth Publishing, 1912.

Boise City Directory, 1905. Boise: R. L. Polk, 1905.

Boise City Directory, 1906–1907. Boise: R. L. Polk, 1906.

Boise City Directory, 1908. Boise: R. L. Polk, 1908.

Boise City Directory, 1909–1910. Boise: R. L. Polk, 1909.

British Columbia. *Statutes of the Province of British Columbia, 1933,* by J. W. Fordham Johnson. Victoria: Charles F. Banfield, 1933.

Burg, B. R. *An American Seafarer in the Age of Sail: The Erotic Diaries of Philip C. Van Buskirk, 1851–1870.* New Haven: Yale University Press, 1994.

Canada. Dominion Bureau Statistics. *Fifth Census of Canada, 1911.* Vol. 1. Ottawa: C. H. Parmelee, 1912.

———. *General Report of the Census of Canada, 1880–81.* Vol. 4. Ottawa: MacLean, Roger, 1885.

———. *Seventh Census of Canada, 1931.* Vol. 2. Ottawa: J. O. Patenaude, 1933.

Goldman, Emma. *Living My Life.* 1931. Reprint, Garden City, N.Y.: Garden City Publishing, 1934.

Graham, Maury, and Robert J. Hemming, *Tales of the Iron Road: My Life as King of the Hobos.* New York: Paragon House, 1990.

Hiday, Mrs. Harry I. *United States Census of the City of Portland, Oregon, 1870.* Portland: Genealogical Forum of Portland, 1972.

Idaho. *General Laws, 1925.* Boise: Syms-York, 1925.

Idaho Territory. *Laws of the Territory of Idaho, 1864.* Lewiston: Territorial Printer, 1864.

Insurance Map of Portland, Oregon. New York: Sanborn-Perris, 1901.

Kelley, Joseph (Bunko). *Thirteen Years in the Oregon State Penitentiary.* Portland, Ore.: n.p., 1908.

Lind, Earl [pseud.; *see* Ralph Werther]. *Autobiography of an Androgyne.* Edited with an introduction by Alfred W. Herzog. New York: Medico-Legal Journal, 1918.

Montana Territory. *Acts, Resolutions, and Memorials, 1866.* Virginia City: D. W. Tilton, 1866.

Oregon. *General Laws, 1913.* Salem: State Printer, 1913.

———. *General Laws, 1915.* Salem: State Printing Department, 1915.

———. *General Laws, 1917.* Salem: State Printing Department, 1917.

———. *General Laws, 1919.* Salem: State Printing Department, 1919.

———. *General Laws, 1923.* Salem: State Printing Department, 1923.

———. *House Journal, 1907.* Salem: Willis S. Duniway, 1907.

———. *House Journal, 1909.* Salem: Willis S. Duniway, 1909.

———. *House Journal, 1913.* Eugene: Guard Printing, 1913.

———. *Measures with Arguments Respecting the Same to Be Submitted to the Electors of the State of Oregon at the Special Election on Tuesday, November 4, 1913.* By Ben W. Olcott. N.p.: n.d.

——. *Messages and Documents, 1913.* Vol. 1. Salem: Willis S. Duniway, 1913.

——. *Oregon Laws, 1965.* Salem: State Printing, 1965.

——. *Senate and House Journals, 1917.* Salem: State Printing Department, 1917.

——. *Senate Journal, 1909.* Salem: Willis S. Duniway, 1909.

——. *Senate Journal, 1911.* Salem: Willis S. Duniway, 1911.

——. *Senate Journal, 1913.* N.p., 1913

Oregon State Board of Control. *Fifth Biennial Report of the Oregon State Board of Control, 1921–22.* Salem: State Printing Department, 1923.

Oregon State Board of Health. *Thirteenth Biennial Report.* Salem: State Printing Department, 1928.

——. *Twenty-First Biennial Report.* Salem: State Printing Department, [1945].

Oregon Territory. *Statutes of Oregon, 1855.* Oregon: Asahel Bush, 1855.

Portland, Ore. *Annual Reports of the Officers of the City of Portland, 1879.* Portland: Niles and Beebe, 1880.

——. *Mayor's Annual Message and Municipal Report, 1903.* Portland: Schwab, 1904.

——. *Mayor's Message and Municipal Reports, 1906.* Portland, n.d.

——. *Mayor's Message and Municipal Reports, 1912.* Portland: Schwab, n.d.

Portland City Directory, 1886. Portland: R. L. Polk, 1886.

Portland City Directory, 1895. Portland: R. L. Polk, 1895.

Portland City Directory, 1896. Portland: R. L. Polk, 1896.

Portland City Directory, 1897. Portland: R. L. Polk, 1897.

Portland City Directory, 1898. Portland: R. L. Polk, 1898.

Portland City Directory, 1899–1900. Portland: R. L. Polk, 1899.

Portland City Directory, 1900–1901. Portland: R. L. Polk, 1900.

Portland City Directory, 1901–1902. Portland: R. L. Polk, 1902.

Portland City Directory, 1904. Portland: R. L. Polk, 1904.

Portland City Directory, 1905. Portland: R. L. Polk, 1905.

Portland City Directory, 1906. Portland: R. L. Polk, 1906.

Portland City Directory, 1907–1908. Portland: R. L. Polk, 1907.

Portland City Directory, 1909. Portland: R. L. Polk, 1909.

Portland City Directory, 1910. Portland: R. L. Polk, 1910.

Portland City Directory, 1911. Portland: R. L. Polk, 1911.

Portland City Directory, 1912. Portland: R. L. Polk, 1912.

Portland City Directory, 1913. Portland: R. L. Polk, 1913.

Portland City Directory, 1914. Portland: R. L. Polk, 1914.

Portland City Directory, 1915. Portland: R. L. Polk, 1915.

Portland City Directory, 1952. Seattle: R. L. Polk, 1952.

Portland City Directory, 1953–1954. Seattle: R. L. Polk, 1954.

Pratt, Laurence. *I Remember Portland, 1899–1915.* Portland: Binford and Mort, 1965.

San Francisco City Directory, 1920. San Francisco: H. S. Crocker, 1920.

Talbot, Henry Russell, et al. *Report of the Portland Vice Commission to the Mayor and City Council of the City of Portland, Oregon.* Portland: Henry Russell Talbot, 1913.

U.S. Congress. Senate. *Reports of the Immigration Commission.* 61st Cong., 3d sess., 1911. S. Doc. 753.

U.S. Department of Commerce. Bureau of the Census. *Fifteenth Census of the United States, 1930.* Vols. 1, 2. Washington, D.C.: Government Printing Office, 1931–33.

——. Bureau of the Census. *Fourteenth Census of the United States, 1920.* Vol. 2. Washington, D.C.: Government Printing Office, 1922.

——. Bureau of the Census. *Special Reports: Occupations at the Twelfth Census.* Washington, D.C.: Government Printing Office, 1904.

——. Bureau of the Census. *Thirteenth Census of the United States, 1910.* Vols. 1, 3, 4. Washington, D.C.: Government Printing Office, 1913–14.

——. Bureau of the Census. *Twelfth Census of the United States, 1900.* Vols. 1, 2. Washington, D.C.: United States Census Office, 1901–02.

——. Census Office. *Population of the United States, 1890.* Parts 1, 2. Washington, D.C.: Government Printing Office, 1895–97.

——. Census Office. *Population of the United States at the Eleventh Census, 1890.* Washington, D.C.: Government Printing Office, 1895.

Van Buskirk, Philip C. *Sailor on the Snohomish: Extracts from the Washington Diaries of Philip C. Van Buskirk.* Edited with an introduction by Robert D. Munroe. Seattle, 1957. Microform.

Washington State. *General Statutes and Codes, 1891.* 2 vols. San Francisco: Bancroft-Whitney, 1891.

——. *Remington and Ballinger's Annotated Codes and Statutes of Washington,* by Arthur Remington and Richard A. Ballinger. Vol. 1. Seattle: Bancroft-Whitney, 1910.

——. *Session Laws, 1893.* Olympia: O.C. White, 1893.

——. *Session Laws, 1897.* Olympia: O.C. White, 1897.

——. *Session Laws, 1903.* Tacoma: Allen and Lamborn, 1903.

——. *Session Laws, 1909.* Olympia: E.L. Boardman, 1909.

——. *Session Laws, 1917.* Olympia: Frank M. Lamborn, 1917.

——. *Session Laws, 1921.* Olympia: Frank M. Lamborn, 1921.

——. *Third Message of Gov. Alert E. Mead to the Legislature of 1909.* Olympia: C.W. Gorham, 1909.

Washington Territory. *Statutes, 1854.* Olympia: George B. Goudy, 1855.

Wentworth, L.J., E.E. Brodie, and F.W. Mulkey. *Report of the Commission to Investigate the Oregon State Penitentiary.* Portland, January 26, 1917.

Werther, Ralph [pseud.]. *The Female-Impersonators.* Edited with an introduction by Alfred W. Herzog. New York: Medico-Legal Journal, 1922.

Newspapers

Albany (Ore.) Daily Democrat
Astoria (Ore.) Daily Budget
Boise Evening Capital News

Boise, Idaho Daily Statesman
Chehalis (Wash.) Nugget
Corvallis (Ore.) Weekly Gazette
The Dalles (Ore.) Times Mountaineer
Eugene (Ore.) Daily Guard
Idaho Falls (Idaho) Times
Marshfield (Ore.) Coos Bay Times
Medford (Ore.) Mail Tribune
Nampa (Idaho) Leader-Herald
Olympia, Washington Standard
Pendleton Eastern Oregonian
Pocatello (Idaho) Tribune
Portland Evening Telegram
Portland Labor Press
Portland News
Portland Oregonian
Portland Oregon Journal
Portland (Ore.) Spectator
Portland Sunday Mercury
Portland Telegram
Roseburg (Ore.) News-Review
Salem (Ore.) Daily Capital Journal
Salem Daily Oregon Statesman
Salem, Oregon Statesman
Seattle Patriarch
Seattle Post-Intelligencer
Seattle Press Times
Seattle Star
Spokane (Wash.) Industrial Worker
Spokane (Wash.) Spokesman Review
St. Helens (Ore.) Mist
Walla Walla (Wash.) Bulletin
Walla Walla (Wash.) Sunday Morning Bulletin
Walla Walla (Wash.) Union

Secondary Sources

Abbott, Carl. *The Great Extravaganza: Portland and the Lewis and Clark Exposition.* Portland: Oregon Historical Society, 1981.
———. *Portland: Planning, Politics, and Growth in a Twentieth-Century City.* Lincoln: University of Nebraska Press, 1983.
Abelove, Henry, Michèle Aina Barale, and David M. Halperin, eds. *The Lesbian and Gay Studies Reader.* New York: Routledge, 1993.

Allsop, Kenneth. *Hard Travellin': The Hobo and His History.* New York: New American Library, 1967.

Anderson, Kay J. *Vancouver's Chinatown: Racial Discourse in Canada, 1875–1980.* Montreal: McGill-Queen's University Press, 1991.

Anderson, Monty K., Charles A. Merrill, and John V. A. Neal. *The Way of Life in the Lownsdale Square Area.* Portland: Portland State University Urban Studies Center, 1971.

Anderson, Nels. *The Hobo: The Sociology of the Homeless Man.* Chicago: University of Chicago Press, 1923.

———. "The Juvenile and the Tramp." *Journal of the American Institute of Criminal Law and Criminology* 14, no. 2 (August 1923): 290–312.

———. *Men on the Move.* 1940. Reprint, New York: Da Capo, 1974.

Baker, Ray Stannard. "The Great Northwest." *Century* 65, no. 5 (March 1903): 647–67.

Baldasty, Gerald J. "Newspapers for 'the Wage Earning Class': E. W. Scripps and the Pacific Northwest." *Pacific Northwest Quarterly* 90, no. 4 (fall 1999): 171–81.

Barman, Jean. *The West beyond the West: A History of British Columbia.* Toronto: University of Toronto Press, 1991.

Bartlett, Neil. *Who Was That Man? A Present for Mr Oscar Wilde.* London: Serpent's Tail, 1988.

Beard, George M. *Sexual Neurasthenia.* Edited by A. D. Rockwell. New York: E. B. Treat, 1884.

Bech, Henning. *When Men Meet: Homosexuality and Modernity.* Translated by Teresa Mesquit and Time Davies. Chicago: University of Chicago Press, 1997.

Bederman, Gail. "Civilization, the Decline of Middle-Class Manliness, and Ida B. Wells' Anti-Lynching Campaign (1892–94)." In *Gender and American History since 1890,* edited by Barbara Melosh, 207–39. London: Routledge, 1993.

———. *Manliness and Civilization: A Cultural History of Gender and Race in the United States, 1880–1917.* Chicago: University of Chicago Press, 1995.

Beemyn, Brett, ed. *Creating a Place for Ourselves: Lesbian, Gay, and Bisexual Community Histories.* New York: Routledge, 1997.

Bell, David, and Gill Valentine, eds. *Mapping Desire: Geographies of Sexualities.* London: Routledge, 1995.

Berg, Louis. *Revelations of a Prison Doctor.* New York: Minton, Bolch, 1934.

Bérubé, Allan. "The History of Gay Bathhouses." In *Policing Public Sex: Queer Politics and the Future of AIDS Activism,* edited by Dangerous Bedfellows, 187–220. Boston: South End Press, 1996.

Betsky, Aaron. *Queer Space: Architecture and Same-Sex Desire.* New York: William Morrow, 1997.

Blumin, Stuart M. *The Emergence of the Middle Class: Social Experience in the American City, 1760–1900.* Cambridge: Cambridge University Press, 1989.

Boag, Peter. "Sex and Politics in Progressive-Era Portland and Eugene: The 1912 Same-Sex Vice Scandal." *Oregon Historical Quarterly* 100, no. 2 (summer 1999): 158–81.

———. "Sexuality, Gender, and Identity in Great Plains History and Myth." *Great Plains Quarterly* 18, no. 4 (fall 1998): 327–40.

Bordman, Gerald. *The Oxford Companion to American Theatre.* New York: Oxford University Press, 1984.

Brandenfels, Kathryn S. "Down on the Sawdust: Prostitution and Vice Control in Seattle, 1870–1920." M.A. thesis, Hampshire College, 1981.

Brandt, Allan M. *No Magic Bullet: A Social History of Venereal Disease in the United States since 1880.* Expanded ed. New York: Oxford University Press, 1987.

Bravmann, Scott. *Queer Fictions of the Past: History, Culture, and Difference.* Cambridge: Cambridge University Press, 1997.

Bremner, Robert H., ed. *Children and Youth in America: A Documentary History.* 3 vols. Cambridge, Mass.: Harvard University Press, 1970–74.

Brill, A. A. "The Conception of Homosexuality." *Journal of the American Medical Association* 61, no. 5 (August 2, 1913): 335–40.

Brod, Henry, ed. *The Making of Masculinities: The New Men's Studies.* Boston: Allen and Unwin, 1987.

Brown, Lionel. "The Queer Career of Oscar Wilde." *Modern Man* 6, no. 3 (September 1956): 15–18, 52–53.

Brown, Michael P. *Closet Space: Geographies of Metaphor from the Body to the Globe.* London: Routledge, 2000.

Bruns, Roger A. *Knights of the Road: A Hobo History.* New York: Methuen, 1980.

Bullough, Vern L., and Martha Voght. "Homosexuality and Its Confusion with the 'Secret Sin' in Pre-Freudian America." In *The Other Americans: Sexual Variance in the National Past,* edited by Charles O. Jackson, 82–92. Westport, Conn.: Praeger, 1996.

Bunham, Martin, ed. *The Cambridge Guide to Theatre.* New ed. Cambridge: Cambridge University Press, 1995.

Burg, B. R. *Sodomy and the Pirate Tradition: English Sea Rovers in the Seventeenth-Century Caribbean.* New York: New York University Press, 1983.

Burnham, John C. "Early References to Homosexual Communities in American Medical Writings." *Medical Aspects of Human Sexuality* 7, no. 8 (August 1973): 34, 40–41, 46–49.

———. *Paths into American Culture: Psychology, Medicine, and Morals.* Philadelphia: Temple University Press, 1988.

———. "The Progressive Revolution in American Attitudes toward Sex." *Journal of American History* 59, no. 4 (March 1973): 885–908

Burton, Richard. "Degenerates and Geniuses." *Critic,* n.s., 22, no. 651 (August 11, 1894): 85–86.

Burton, Richard F. *The Book of the Thousand Nights and a Night: A Plain and Literal Translation of the Arabian Nights Entertainments.* London: Burton Club, 1885.

Butler, Judith. *Gender Trouble: Feminism and the Subversion of Identity.* New York: Routledge, 1990.

Butts, William Marlin. "Boy Prostitutes of the Metropolis." *Journal of Clinical Psychopathology* 8, no. 4 (April 1947): 673–81.

Campbell, George E. "Criminal Law—Sodomy—The Crime and the Penalty." *Arkansas Law Review* 8, no. 4 (fall 1954): 497–500.

Carnes, Mark C. *Secret Ritual and Manhood in Victorian America.* New Haven: Yale University Press, 1989.

Casaday, Lauren Wilde. "Labor Unrest and the Labor Movement in the Salmon Industry of the Pacific Northwest." Ph.D. diss., University of California, Berkeley, 1937.

Caswell, John E. "The Prohibition Movement in Oregon: II. 1904–1915." *Oregon Historical Quarterly* 40, no. 1 (March 1939): 64–82.

Chamberlain, J. Edward, and Sander L. Gilman, eds. *Degeneration: The Dark Side of Progress.* New York: Columbia University Press, 1985.

Chan, Sucheng, ed. *Entry Denied: Exclusion and the Chinese Community in America, 1882–1943.* Philadelphia: Temple University Press, 1991.

Chandler, Alfred D. *The Visible Hand: The Managerial Revolution in American Business.* Cambridge, Mass.: Belknap, 1977.

Chapman, Terry L. "'An Oscar Wilde Type': 'The Abominable Crime of Buggery' in Western Canada, 1890–1920." *Criminal Justice History* 4 (1983): 97–118.

Chauncey, George, Jr. "Christian Brotherhood or Sexual Perversion? Homosexual Identities and the Construction of Sexual Boundaries in the World War I Era." In *Hidden from History: Reclaiming the Gay and Lesbian Past,* edited by Martin Duberman, Martha Vicinus, and George Chauncey, Jr., 294–317. New York: Meridian, 1989.

———. "From Sexual Inversion to Homosexuality: Medicine and the Changing Conceptualization of Female Deviance." In *Passion and Power: Sexuality in History,* ed. Kathy Peiss and Christina Simmons with Robert A. Padgug, 87–117. Philadelphia: Temple University, 1989.

———. *Gay New York: Gender, Urban Culture, and the Making of the Gay Male World, 1890–1940.* New York: BasicBooks, 1994.

———. "The Policed: Gay Men's Strategies of Everyday Resistance in Times Square." In *Creating a Place for Ourselves: Lesbian, Gay, and Bisexual Community Histories,* edited by Brett Beemyn, 9–25. New York: Routledge, 1997.

———. "The Postwar Sex Crime Panic." In *True Stories from the American Past,* edited by William Graebner, 167–78. New York: McGraw-Hill, 1993.

Clark, Norman H. *Mill Town: A Social History of Everett, Washington.* Seattle: University of Washington Press, 1970.

Coe, Henry Waldo. "Halt in Sexual Instruction." *Medical Sentinel* 21, no. 4 (April 1913): 853–54.

Cohen, Ed. "Legislating the Norm: From Sodomy to Gross Indecency." *South Atlantic Quarterly* 88, no. 1 (winter 1989): 181–217.

———. *Talk on the Wilde Side: Towards a Genealogy of Discourse on Male Sexualities.* New York: Routledge, 1993.

Cominos, Peter T. "Late-Victorian Sexual Respectability and the Social System." *International Review of Social History* 8 (1963): 18–48, 216–50.

Cornsweet, A. C., and M. F. Hayes. "Conditioned Response to Fellatio." *American Journal of Psychiatry* 103, no. 1 (July 1946): 76–78.

Costantakos, Chrysie Mamalakis. *The American-Greek Subculture: Processes of Continuity.* New York: Arno, 1980.

Crimp, Douglas. *AIDS: Cultural Analysis, Cultural Activism.* Cambridge, Mass.: MIT Press, 1988.

Culbertson, Paul Thomas. "A History of the Initiative and Referendum in Oregon." Ph.D. diss., University of Oregon, 1941.

Daniels, Roger. *Asian America: Chinese and Japanese in the United States since 1850.* Seattle: University of Washington, 1988.

——. *Coming to America: A History of Immigration and Ethnicity in American Life.* New York: HarperCollins, 1990.

——. *Not Like Us: Immigrants and Minorities in America, 1890–1924.* Chicago: Ivan R. Dee, 1997.

Davis, Chuck, and Shirley Mooney, *Vancouver: An Illustrated Chronology.* Burlington, Ont.: Windsor, 1986.

de Grazia, Sebastian. *Of Time, Work, and Leisure.* New York: Twentieth Century Fund, 1962.

D'Emilio, John. "Capitalism and Gay Identity." In *The Lesbian and Gay Studies Reader,* edited by Henry Abelove, Michèle Aina Barale, and David M. Halperin, 467–76. New York: Routledge, 1993.

——. "The Homosexual Menace: The Politics of Sexuality in Cold War America." In *Passion and Power: Sexuality in History,* edited by Kathy Peiss and Christina Simmons, with Robert A. Padgug, 226–40. Philadelphia: Temple University Press, 1989.

——. *Sexual Politics, Sexual Communities: The Making of a Homosexual Minority in the United States, 1940–1970.* Chicago: University of Chicago Press, 1983.

D'Emilio, John, and Estelle B. Freedman. *Intimate Matters: A History of Sexuality in America.* New York: Harper and Row, 1988.

de Young, Mary. "Help, I'm Being Held Captive! The White Slave Fairy Tale of the Progressive Era." *Journal of American Culture* 6, no. 1 (spring 1983): 96–98.

Dinnerstein, Leonard, and David M. Reimers. *Ethnic Americas: A History of Immigration.* 4th ed. New York: Columbia University Press, 1999.

Dodds, Gordon B. *The American Northwest: A History of Oregon and Washington.* Arlington Heights, Ill.: Forum Press, 1986.

——. *Oregon: A Bicentennial History.* New York: W. W. Norton; Nashville: American Association for State and Local History, 1977.

Doulis, Thomas. *A Surge to the Sea: The Greeks in Oregon.* Portland: Jack Lockie and Associates, 1977.

Dubbert, Joe L. *A Man's Place: Masculinity in Transition.* Englewood Cliffs, N.J.: Prentice-Hall, 1979.

——. "Progressivism and the Masculinity Crisis." In *The American Man,* edited by Elizabeth H. Pleck and Joseph H. Pleck, 305–20. Englewood Cliffs, N.J.: Prentice-Hall, 1980.

Duberman, Martin. "Kinsey's Urethra." Review of *Alfred C. Kinsey: A Public/Private Life,* by James H. Jones. *Nation,* November 3, 1997, 40, 42–43.

Duberman, Martin, Martha Vicinus, and George Chauncey, Jr., eds. *Hidden from History: Reclaiming the Gay and Lesbian Past.* New York: Meridian, 1990.

Duggan, Lisa. "Making It Perfectly Queer." *Socialist Review* 22, no. 1 (January–March 1992): 11–31.

——. *Sapphic Slashers: Sex, Violence, and American Modernity.* Durham, N.C.: Duke University Press, 2000.

East, Alan. "The Genesis and Early Development of a Juvenile Court: A Study of Community Responsibility in Multnomah County, Oregon, for the Period 1841–1920." M.A. thesis, University of Oregon, 1939.

Edwards, G. Thomas, and Carlos A. Schwantes, eds. *Experiences in a Promised Land: Essays in Pacific Northwest History.* Seattle: University of Washington Press, 1986.

Edwards, George. "A Portrait of Portland." *Mother Earth* 10, no. 9 (November 1915): 311–14.

Ellis, Henry Havelock. *Sex Inversion.* Vol. 4 of *Studies in the Psychology of Sex.* 2d ed. Philadelphia: F. A. Davis, 1904.

Ellmann, Richard. *Oscar Wilde.* New York: Knopf, 1988.

Eng, David L., and Alice Y. Hom, eds. *Q & A: Queer in Asian America.* Philadelphia: Temple University Press, 1998.

Erenberg, Lewis A. *Steppin' Out: New York Nightlife and the Transformation of American Culture, 1890–1930.* Westport, Conn.: Greenwood, 1981.

Evans, Tony Howard. "Oregon Progressive Reform, 1902–1914." Ph.D. diss., University of California, Berkeley, 1966.

Faderman, Lillian. "The Morbidification of Love between Women by Nineteenth-Century Sexologists." *Journal of Homosexuality* 4, no. 1 (fall 1978): 73–90.

——. *Surpassing the Love of Men: Romantic Friendship and Love between Women from the Renaissance to the Present.* New York: William Morrow, 1981.

Fee, Elizabeth, and Daniel M. Fox, eds. *AIDS: The Burdens of History.* Berkeley: University of California Press, 1988.

Fellows, Will, ed. *Farm Boys: Lives of Gay Men from the Rural Midwest.* Madison: University of Wisconsin Press, 1996.

Filene, Peter G. *Him/Her/Self: Sex Roles in Modern America.* 2d ed. Baltimore: Johns Hopkins University Press, 1986.

Fishman, Joseph F. *Sex in Prison: Revealing Sex Conditions in American Prisons.* New York: National Library Press, 1934.

Fishman, W. J. *East End, 1888: Life in a London Borough among the Laboring Poor.* Philadelphia: Temple University Press, 1988.

Flynt, Josiah. "Children of the Road." *Atlantic Monthly* 77, no. 459 (January 1896): 58–71.

———. "Homosexuality among Tramps." Appendix A in *Sexual Inversion,* by Havelock Ellis, 219–24. Vol. 4 of *Studies in the Psychology of Sex.* 2d ed. Philadelphia: F. A. Davis, 1904.

———. "How Men Become Tramps: Conclusions from Personal Experience as an Amateur Tramp." *Century* 50, no. 6 (October 1895): 941–45.

Foster, William T. "The Social Emergency." In *The Social Emergency: Studies in Sex Hygiene and Morals,* ed. William T. Foster, 5–12. Boston: Houghton Mifflin, 1914.

———. "State-Wide Education in Social Hygiene." *Social Hygiene* 2, no. 3 (July 1916): 309–29.

———. *Vaudeville and Motion Picture Shows: A Study of Theaters in Portland, Oregon.* Social Service Series no. 2. Portland: Reed College, 1914.

Foucault, Michel. *The History of Sexuality: An Introduction.* Translated by Robert Hurley. New York: Pantheon Books, 1978.

Frater, Archibald W. "Court Methods, Mothers' Pensions, and Community Dangers." In *Why Children Go Wrong,* 3–18. Annual Report of the Seattle Juvenile Court for 1913. Seattle: Seattle Juvenile Court, January 1, 1914.

Freedman, Estelle B. "'Uncontrolled Desires': The Response to the Sexual Psychopath, 1920–1960." In *Passion and Power: Sexuality in History,* edited by Kathy Peiss and Christina Simmons, with Robert A. Padgug, 199–225. Philadelphia: Temple University Press, 1989.

Friday, Chris. *Organizing Asian American Labor: The Pacific Coast Canned-Salmon Industry, 1870–1942.* Philadelphia: Temple University Press, 1994.

Galbreath, C. B., comp. *Initiative and Referendum.* Columbus, Ohio: F. J. Heer Printing, 1911.

Gamboa, Erasmo. *Mexican Labor and World War II: Braceros in the Pacific Northwest, 1942–1947.* Austin: University of Texas Press, 1990.

Gandy, Patrick. "Hamburger Hustlers." Paper presented at the American Anthropology Association Meeting, November 29, 1971. A copy is in the collection of the Kinsey Institute for Research in Sex, Gender, and Reproduction, Bloomington, Ind.

Garber, Eric. "A Spectacle in Color: The Lesbian and Gay Subculture of Jazz Age Harlem." In *Hidden from History: Reclaiming the Gay and Lesbian Past,* edited by Martin Duberman, Martha Vicinus, and George Chauncey, Jr., 318–31. New York: Meridian, 1989.

Gaston, Joseph. *Portland, Oregon: Its History and Builders.* Chicago: S. J. Clarke, 1911.

Gebhard, Paul H., John H. Gagnon, Wardell B. Pomeroy, and Cornelia V. Christenson. *Sex Offenders: An Analysis of Types.* New York: Harper and Row, 1965.

Gilbert, James H. "Single-Tax Movement in Oregon." *Political Science Quarterly* 31, no. 1 (March 1916): 25–52.

Graebner, William, ed. *True Stories from the American Past.* New York: McGraw-Hill, 1993.

Graff, Harvey J. *Conflicting Paths: Growing Up in America*. Cambridge, Mass.: Harvard University Press, 1995.

Greenberg, David F. *The Construction of Homosexuality*. Chicago: University of Chicago Press, 1988.

Grittner, Frederick K. *White Slavery: Myth, Ideology, and American Law*. New York: Garland, 1990.

Groth, Paul. *Living Downtown: The History of Residential Hotels in the United States*. Berkeley: University of California Press, 1994.

Gustav-Wrathall, John Donald. *Take the Young Stranger by the Hand: Same-Sex Relations and the YMCA*. Chicago: University of Chicago Press, 1998.

Halberstam, Judith. *Female Masculinity*. Durham, N.C.: Duke University Press, 1998.

Hale, C. Jacob. "Consuming the Living, Dis(re)membering the Dead in the Butch/Ftm Borderlands." *GLQ: A Journal of Lesbian and Gay Studies* 4, no. 2 (1998): 311–48.

Haller, Mark H. *Eugenics: Hereditarian Attitudes in American Thought*. New Brunswick, N.J.: Rutgers University Press, 1984.

Halperin, David M. *One Hundred Years of Homosexuality: And Other Essays on Greek Love*. New York: Routledge, 1990.

Hamburger, Robert. *Two Rooms: The Life of Charles Erskine Scott Wood*. Lincoln: University of Nebraska Press, 1998.

Hantover, Jeffrey P. "The Boy Scouts and the Validation of Masculinity." In *The American Man*, edited by Elizabeth H. Pleck and Joseph H. Pleck, 287–301. Englewood Cliffs, N.J.: Prentice-Hall, 1980.

Hartwell, Phyllis, ed. *The Oxford Companion to the Theatre*. 4th ed. Oxford: Oxford University Press, 1983.

Head, Christopher Joseph. "Nights of Heaven: A Social History of Saloon Culture in Portland, 1900–1914." B.A. thesis, Reed College, 1980.

Hendrick, Burton J. "The Initiative and Referendum and How Oregon Got Them." *McClure's* 37, no. 3 (July 1911): 235–48.

———. "Law Making by the Voters." *McClure's* 37, no. 4 (August 1911): 435–50.

———. "'Statement No. 1.'" *McClure's* 37, no. 5 (September 1911): 505–19.

Hendricks, Russell G. "Election of Senator Chamberlain, the People's Choice." *Oregon Historical Quarterly* 53, no. 2 (June 1952): 63–88.

Henry, George W. *Sex Variants: A Study of Homosexual Patterns*. 2 vols. New York: Paul B. Hoeber, 1941.

Henry, George W., and Alfred A. Gross. "Social Factors in the Case Histories of One Hundred Underprivileged Homosexuals." *Mental Hygiene* 22 (1938): 591–611.

Higham, John. "The Reorientation of American Culture in the 1890s." In *The Origins of Modern Consciousness*, edited by John Weiss, 25–48. Detroit: Wayne State University Press, 1965.

———. *Strangers in the Land: Patterns of American Nativism, 1860–1925*. 2d ed. New Brunswick, N.J.: Rutgers University Press, 1988.

History of the Bench and Bar of Oregon. Portland: Historical Publishing, 1910.

Hitchman, James H. *A Maritime History of the Pacific Coast, 1540–1980*. Lanham, Md.: University Press of America, 1990.

Ho, Nelson Chia-Chi. *Portland's Chinatown: The History of an Urban Ethnic District*. Portland: Bureau of City Planning, City of Portland, 1978.

Hobson, Barbara Meil. *Uneasy Virtue: The Politics of Prostitution and the American Reform Tradition*. New York: Basic Books, 1987.

Hofstadter, Richard. *The Age of Reform*. New York: Vintage, 1955.

Hogan, Steven, and Lee Hudson. *Completely Queer: The Gay and Lesbian Encyclopedia*. New York: Henry Holt, 1998.

Holbrook, Stewart H. *Holy Old Mackinaw: A Natural History of the American Lumberjack*. New York: Macmillan, 1938.

———. "Portland's Greatest Moral Crusade." 3 parts. *Portland Oregonian*, Northwest Magazine section, August 2, 1936, 1, 12; August 9, 1936, 6; August 16, 1936, 15.

———. "Whitehouse Mystery." *Oregonian*, Magazine section, May 16, 1937, 12, 16.

———. *Wildmen, Wobblies, and Punks: Stewart Holbrook's Lowbrow Northwest*. Edited with an introduction by Brian Booth. Corvallis: Oregon State University Press, 1992.

Holden, Margaret K. "Gender and Protest Ideology: Sue Ross Keenan and the Oregon Anti-Chinese Movement." *Western Legal History* 7, no. 2 (summer/fall 1994): 222–43.

Horowitz, David A. "The Klansmen as Outsider: Ethnocultural Solidarity and Antielitism in the Oregon Ku Klux Klan of the 1920s." *Pacific Northwest Quarterly* 80, no. 1 (January 1989): 12–20.

———. "Social Morality and Personal Revitalization: Oregon's Ku Klux Klan in the 1920s." *Oregon Historical Quarterly* 90, no. 4 (winter 1989): 365–84.

Howard, John. "The Library, the Park, and the Pervert: Public Space and Homosexual Encounter in Post–World War II Atlanta." In *Carryin' On in the Lesbian and Gay South,* edited by John Howard, 107–31. New York: New York University Press, 1997.

———. *Men Like That: A Southern Queer History*. Chicago: University of Chicago Press, 1999.

———. "Place and Movement in Gay American History: A Case from the Post–World War II South." In *Creating a Place for Ourselves: Lesbian, Gay, and Bisexual Community Histories,* edited by Brett Beemyn, 211–25. New York: Routledge, 1997.

———. "The Talk of the County: Revisiting Accusation, Murder, and Mississippi, 1895." In *Where These Memories Grow: History, Memory, and Southern Identity,* edited by W. Fitzhugh Brundage, 191–218. Chapel Hill: University of North Carolina Press, 2000.

———, ed. *Carryin' On in the Lesbian and Gay South*. New York: New York University Press, 1997.

Howard, William Lee. "Sexual Perversion in America." *American Journal of Dermatology and Genito-Urinary Diseases* 8, no. 1 (January 1904): 9–14.

Hughes, Charles H. "An Emasculated Homosexual: His Antecedent and Post-Operative Life." *Alienist and Neurologist* 35, no. 3 (August 1914): 277–80.

——. "Homo Sexual Complexion Perverts in St. Louis: Note on a Feature of Sexual Psychopathy." *Alienist and Neurologist* 28, no. 4 (November 1907): 487–88.

Hummasti, Paul George. "Finnish Radicalism in Astoria, Oregon, 1904–1940: A Study in Immigrant Socialism." Ph.D. diss., University of Oregon, 1975.

Humphreys, Laud. *Tearoom Trade: Impersonal Sex in Public Places.* Chicago: Aldine, 1970.

Ignatiev, Noel. *How the Irish Became White.* New York: Routledge, 1995.

Ingram, Gordon Brent. "'Open' Space as Strategic Queer Sites." In *Queers in Space: Communities, Public Places, Sites of Resistance,* edited by Gordon Brent Ingram, Anne-Marie Bouthillette, and Yolanda Retter, 95–125. Seattle: Bay Press, 1997.

Ingram, Gordon Brent, Anne-Marie Bouthillette, and Yolanda Retter, eds. *Queers in Space: Communities, Public Places, Sites of Resistance.* Seattle: Bay Press, 1997.

Jackson, Charles O., ed. *The Other Americans: Sexual Variance in the National Past.* Westport, Conn.: Praeger, 1996.

Jacobson, Matthew Frye. *Whiteness of a Different Color: European Immigrants and the Alchemy of Race.* Cambridge, Mass.: Harvard University Press, 1998.

James, Jennifer. "Entrance into Juvenile Male Prostitution [Seattle, Wa.]." Prepared for the National Institute of Mental Health, Rockville, Md., 1982.

Johansen, Dorothy O. *Empire of the Columbia: A History of the Pacific Northwest.* 2d ed. New York: Harper and Row, 1967.

Johnson, Daniel P. "Anti-Japanese Legislation in Oregon, 1917–1923." *Oregon Historical Quarterly* 97, no. 2 (summer 1996): 176–210.

Johnson, David K. "The Kids of Fairytown: Gay Male Culture on Chicago's Near North Side in the 1930s." In *Creating a Place for Ourselves: Lesbian, Gay, and Bisexual Community Histories,* edited by Brett Beemyn, 97–118. New York: Routledge, 1997.

Johnston, Hugh. *The Voyage of the Komagata Maru: The Sikh Challenge to Canada's Colour Bar.* Delhi: Oxford University Press, 1979.

Johnston, Robert Douglas. "Middle-Class Political Ideology in a Corporate Society: The Persistence of Small-Propertied Radicalism in Portland, Oregon, 1883–1926." Ph.D. diss., Rutgers University, 1993.

——. "The Myth of the Harmonious City: Will Daly, Lora Little, and the Hidden Face of Progressive-Era Portland." *Oregon Historical Quarterly* 99, no. 3 (fall 1998): 248–97.

Jones, James H. *Alfred C. Kinsey: A Public/Private Life.* New York: W. W. Norton, 1997.

Jones, W. Ray. "Two Questions of Justice Relating to Sexual Offenders." *American Journal of Urology and Sexology* 13, no. 7 (July 1917): 325–26.

Katz, Jonathan Ned. *Gay American History: Lesbians and Gay Men in the U.S.A., A Documentary History.* Rev. ed. New York: Meridian, 1992.

——. *Gay/Lesbian Almanac: A New Documentary.* New York: Harper and Row, 1983.

——. *The Invention of Heterosexuality.* Foreword by Gore Vidal. Afterword by Lisa Duggan. 1995. Reprint, New York: Plume, 1996.

Keller, Morton. *Affairs of State: Public Life in Late Nineteenth Century America.* Cambridge, Mass.: Belknap Press, Harvard University Press, 1977.

Kennedy, Elizabeth Lapovsky. "'But we would never talk about it': The Structures of Lesbian Discretion in South Dakota, 1928–1933." In *Inventing Lesbian Cultures in America,* edited by Ellen Lewin, 15–39. Boston: Beacon Press, 1996.

Kennedy, Elizabeth Lapovsky, and Madeline D. Davis. *Boots of Leather, Slippers of Gold: The History of a Lesbian Community.* New York: Routledge, 1993.

Kershner, R. B., Jr. "Degeneration: The Explanatory Nightmare." *Georgia Review* 40, no. 2 (summer 1986): 416–44.

Kersley, Gillian. *Darling Madam: Sarah Grand and Devoted Friend.* London: Virago, 1983.

Kett, Joseph F. *Rites of Passage: Adolescence in America, 1790 to the Present.* New York: Basic Books, 1977.

Kevles, Daniel J. *In the Name of Eugenics: Genetics and the Uses of Human Heredity.* New York: Knopf, 1985.

Kiernan, James G. "Are Americans Degenerates? A Critique of Nordau's Recent Change of View." *Alienist and Neurologist* 18, no. 3 (October 1896): 446–58.

——. "Sexual Perversion and the Whitechapel Murders." 2 parts. *Medical Standard* 4, no. 5 (November 1888): 129–30; 4, no. 6 (December 1888): 170–72.

Kimmel, Michael S. "The Contemporary 'Crisis' of Masculinity in Historical Perspective." In *The Making of Masculinities: The New Men's Studies,* edited by Henry Brod, 121–53. Boston: Allen and Unwin, 1987.

Kingsdale, Jon M. "The 'Poor Man's Club': Social Functions of the Urban Working-Class Saloon." In *The American Man,* edited by Elizabeth H. Pleck and Joseph H. Pleck, 257–83. Englewood Cliffs, N.J.: Prentice-Hall, 1980.

Kinsey, Alfred C., Wardell B. Pomeroy, and Clyde E. Martin. *Sexual Behavior in the Human Male.* Philadelphia: W. B. Saunders, 1948.

Kocka, Jürgen. *White Collar Workers in America, 1890–1940: A Social-Political History in International Perspective.* Translated by Maura Kealey. London: Sage, 1989.

Kourvetaris, George A. *Studies on Greek Americans.* Boulder, Colo.: Eastern European Monographs, 1997.

Krafft-Ebing, Richard von. *Psychopathia Sexualis.* Translated by Charles G. Chaddock from the 7th German ed. Philadelphia: F. A. Davis, 1892.

Kramer, Jerry Lee. "Bachelor Farmers and Spinsters: Gay and Lesbian Identities and Communities in Rural North Dakota." In *Mapping Desire: Geographies of Sexualities,* edited by David Bell and Gill Valentine, 200–213. London: Routledge, 1995.

Lalande, Jeff. "Beneath the Hooded Robe: Newspapermen, Local Politics, and the Ku Klux Klan in Jackson County, Oregon, 1921–1923." *Pacific Northwest Quarterly* 83, no. 2 (April 1992): 43–52.

Landman, J. H. *Human Sterilization: The History of the Sexual Sterilization Movement.* New York: Macmillan, 1932.

Laughlin, Harry Hamilton. *Eugenical Sterilization in the United States.* Chicago: Municipal Court of Chicago, 1922.

Legman, G. "The Language of Homosexuality: An American Glossary." In *Sex Variants: A Study of Homosexual Patterns,* by George W. Henry, 2:1149–79. New York: Paul B. Hoeber, 1941.

Lewin, Ellen, ed. *Inventing Lesbian Cultures in America.* Boston: Beacon Press, 1996.

Link, Arthur S., and Richard L. McCormick. *Progressivism.* Wheeling, Ill.: Harlan Davidson, 1983.

Lydston, G. Frank. *The Diseases of Society (The Vice and Crime Problem).* Philadelphia: J. B. Lippincott, 1904.

———. *Sex Hygiene for the Male and What to Say to the Boy.* Chicago: Hamming Publishing, 1912.

MacColl, E. Kimbark. *The Growth of a City: Power and Politics in Portland, Oregon, 1915–1950.* Portland: Georgian Press, 1979.

———. *The Shaping of a City: Business and Politics in Portland, Oregon, 1885–1915.* Portland: Georgian Press, 1976.

MacColl, E. Kimbark, with Harry Stein. *Merchants, Money, and Power: The Portland Establishment, 1843–1913.* Portland: Georgian Press, 1988.

MacLeod, David I. *Building Character in the American Boy: The Boy Scouts, YMCA, and Their Forerunners, 1870–1920.* Madison: University of Wisconsin Press, 1983.

Marcuse, Herbert. *Eros and Civilization: A Philosophical Inquiry into Freud.* 2d ed. New York: Vintage, 1966.

Marshall, John. "Pansies, Perverts, and Macho Men: Changing Conceptions of Male Homosexuality." In *The Making of the Modern Homosexual,* edited by Kenneth Plummer, 133–54. Totowa, N.J.: Barnes and Noble, 1981.

Masson, Jack, and Donald Guimary. "Asian Labor Contractors in the Alaskan Canned Salmon Industry: 1880–1937." *Labor History* 22, no. 3 (summer 1981): 377–97.

Matsumoto, Valerie J., and Blake Allmendinger, eds. *Over the Edge: Remapping the American West.* Berkeley: University of California Press, 1999.

Matters, Indiana. "'Unfit for Publication': Notes towards a Lavender History of British Columbia." Paper presented at Sex and State Conference, Toronto, July 3–6, 1985.

May, Lary. *Screening Out the Past: The Birth of Mass Culture and the Motion Picture Industry.* New York: Oxford University Press, 1980.

May, Walter W. R. "Some Highlights in the History of the Oregon Social Hygiene Society." University of Oregon Leaflet Series 15, no. 3, March 1930.

Mayer, Joseph. "The Passing of the Red Light District—Vice Investigations and Results." *Social Hygiene* 4, no. 2 (April 1918): 197–209.

Maynard, Steven. "'Horrible Temptations': Sex, Men, and Working-Class Male Youth in Urban Ontario, 1890–1917." *Canadian Historical Review* 78, no. 2 (June 1997): 191–235.

——. "Through a Hole in the Lavatory Wall: Homosexual Subcultures, Police Surveillance, and the Dialectics of Discovery in Toronto, 1890–1930." *Journal of the History of Sexuality* 5, no. 2 (October 1994): 207–42.

McClintock, Thomas C. "James Saules, Peter Burnett, and the Oregon Black Exclusion Law." *Pacific Northwest Quarterly* 86, no. 3 (summer 1995): 121–30.

——. "Seth Lewelling, William S. U'Ren, and the Birth of the Oregon Progressive Movement." *Oregon Historical Quarterly* 68, no. 3 (September 1967): 197–220.

McLaren, Angus. "The Creation of a Haven for 'Human Thoroughbreds': The Sterilization of the Feeble-Minded and the Mentally Ill in British Columbia." *Canadian Historical Review* 67, no. 2 (June 1986): 127–50.

——. "Sex Radicalism in the Canadian Pacific Northwest, 1890–1920." *Journal of the History of Sexuality* 2, no. 4 (April 1992): 527–46.

——. *The Trials of Masculinity: Policing Sexual Boundaries, 1870–1930.* Chicago: University of Chicago Press, 1997.

McMurtrie, Douglas C. "Notes on the Psychology of Sex." *American Journal of Urology* 10, no. 2 (February 1914): 91–100.

Meinig, D. W. *The Great Columbia Plain: A Historical Geography, 1805–1910.* Seattle: University of Washington Press, 1968.

Melosh, Barbara, ed. *Gender and American History since 1890.* London: Routledge, 1993.

Mennel, Robert M. *Thorns and Thistles: Juvenile Delinquents in the United States, 1825–1940.* Hanover, N.H.: University Press of New England, 1973.

Merriam, Paul Gilman. "Portland, Oregon, 1840–1890: A Social and Economic History." Ph.D. diss., University of Oregon, 1971.

Merrill, Lilburn. "Physical and Mental Conditions." In *Why Children Go Wrong,* 30–43. Annual Report of the Seattle Juvenile Court for 1913. Seattle: Seattle Juvenile Court, January 1, 1914.

——. "A Summary of Findings in a Study of Sexualism among a Group of One Hundred Delinquent Boys." *Journal of Delinquency* 3, no. 6 (November 1918): 255–69.

Messing, John. "Public Lands, Politics, and Progressives: The Oregon Land Fraud Trials, 1903–1910." *Pacific Historical Review* 35 (1966): 35–66.

Meyerowitz, Joanne. "Sex Change and the Popular Press: Historical Notes on Transsexuality in the United States, 1930–1955." *GLQ: A Journal of Lesbian and Gay Studies* 4, no. 2 (1998): 159–87.

Miller, Heather Lee. "From Moral Suasion to Moral Coercion: Persistence and Transformation in Prostitution Reform, Portland, Oregon, 1888–1917." M.A. thesis, University of Oregon, 1996.

Mills, C. Wright. *White Collar: The American Middle Classes.* New York: Oxford University Press, 1951.

Minehan, Thomas. *Boy and Girl Tramps of America*. New York: Gosset and Dunlap, 1934.

Mintz, Steven. *A Prison of Expectations: The Family in Victorian Culture*. New York: New York University Press, 1983.

Mintz, Steven, and Susan Kellogg. *Domestic Revolutions: A Social History of American Family Life*. New York: Free Press, 1988.

Mjagki, Nina, and Margaret Spratt, eds. *Men and Women Adrift: The YMCA and the YWCA in the City*. New York: New York University Press, 1997.

Monkkonen, Eric H., ed. *Walking to Work: Tramps in America, 1790–1935*. Lincoln: University of Nebraska Press, 1984.

Moran, Jeffrey P. *Teaching Sex: The Shaping of Adolescence in the Twentieth Century*. Cambridge, Mass.: Harvard University Press, 2000.

Morley, Alan. *Vancouver: Milltown to Metropolis*. Vancouver: Mitchell, 1991.

Morrissey, Katherine G. *Mental Territories: Mapping the Inland Empire*. Ithaca, N.Y.: Cornell University Press, 1997.

Moynihan, Ruth Barnes. *Rebel for Rights: Abigail Scott Duniway*. New Haven: Yale University Press, 1983.

Mumford, Kevin J. *Interzones: Black/White Sex Districts in Chicago and New York in the Early Twentieth Century*. New York: Columbia University Press, 1997.

Murphy, Lawrence P. "Defining the Crime against Nature: Sodomy in the United States Appeals Courts, 1810–1940." *Journal of Homosexuality* 19, no. 1 (1990): 49–66.

Myers, Gloria E. *A Municipal Mother: Portland's Lola Greene Baldwin, America's First Policewoman*. Corvallis: Oregon State University Press, 1995.

Noel, Thomas Jacob. "Gay Bars and the Emergence of the Denver Homosexual Community." *Social Science Journal* 15, no. 2 (April 1978): 59–74.

Nordau, Max Simon. *Degeneration*. Translation of the 2d German ed. New York: Appleton, 1895.

Odegard, Peter H. *Pressure Politics: The Story of the Anti-Saloon League*. New York: Columbia University Press, 1928.

Odem, Mary E. *Delinquent Daughters: Protecting and Policing Adolescent Female Sexuality in the United States, 1885–1920*. Chapel Hill: University of North Carolina Press, 1995.

Omi, Michael, and Howard Winant. *Racial Formation in the United States from the 1960s to the 1990s*. 2d ed. New York: Routledge, 1994.

Oregon Social Hygiene Society. *Masturbation*. Pamphlet no. 22. Portland: Oregon Social Hygiene Society, 1917.

——. *Progress: The Second Annual Report*. Portland: Oregon Social Hygiene Society, 1913.

——. *A Reasonable Sex Life for a Man*. Pamphlet no. 23. Portland: Oregon Social Hygiene Society, 1917.

——. *The State-Wide Work of the Oregon Social Hygiene Society*. Pamphlet no. 25. Portland: Oregon Social Hygiene Society, 1917

——. *Vigorous Manhood*. Pamphlet no. 8. Portland: Oregon Social Hygiene Society, 1917.

Osborne, Karen Lee, and William J. Spurlin, eds. *Reclaiming the Heartland: Lesbian and Gay Voices from the Midwest.* Minneapolis: University of Minnesota Press, 1996.

Osborne, Thomas Mott. *Prisons and Common Sense.* Philadelphia: Lippincott, 1924.

Owens-Adair, B. *Human Sterilization.* N.p., [1909].

——. *Human Sterilization: Its Social and Legislative Aspects.* N.p.: B.A. Owens-Adair, 1922.

Parker, Carleton H. *The Casual Laborer and Other Essays.* With an introduction by Cornelia Stratton Parker. New York: Russell and Russell, 1920.

Parker, Susan Benson. *Counter Cultures: Saleswomen, Managers, and Customers in American Department Stores, 1890–1940.* Urbana: University of Illinois Press, 1986.

Pascoe, Peggy. "Miscegenation Law, Court Cases, and Ideologies of 'Race' in Twentieth-Century America." *Journal of American History* 83, no. 1 (June 1996): 44–69.

——. "Race, Gender, and the Privileges of Property: On the Significance of Miscegenation Laws in the U.S. West." In *Over the Edge: Remapping the American West,* edited by Valerie J. Matsumoto and Blake Allmendinger, 215–30. Berkeley: University of California Press, 1999.

Paulson, Don, with Roger Simpson. *An Evening at the Garden of Allah: A Gay Cabaret in Seattle.* Between Men ~ Between Women Series, edited by Lillian Faderman and Larry Gross. New York: Columbia University Press, 1996.

Peffer, George Anthony. "Forbidden Families: Emigration Experiences of Chinese Women under the Page Law, 1875–1882." *Journal of American Ethnic History* 6, no. 1 (fall 1986): 28–46.

Peiss, Kathy. *Cheap Amusements: Working Women and Leisure in Turn-of-the-Century New York.* Philadelphia: Temple University Press, 1988.

Peiss, Kathy, Christina Simmons, with Robert A. Padgug, eds. *Passion and Power: Sexuality in History.* Philadelphia: Temple University Press, 1989.

Pleck, Elizabeth H., and Joseph H. Pleck, eds. *The American Man.* Englewood Cliffs, N.J.: Prentice-Hall, 1980.

Plotnicki, Rita M. "The Evolution of a Star: The Career of Viola Allen, 1882–1918." Ph.D. diss., City University of New York, 1979.

Plummer, Ken. *Telling Sexual Stories: Power, Change, and Social Worlds.* London: Routledge, 1995.

Porter, Glenn. *The Rise of Big Business, 1860–1910.* 2d ed. Arlington Heights, Ill.: Harlan Davidson, 1992.

Powers, Madelon. *Faces along the Bar: Lore and Order in the Workingman's Saloon, 1870–1920.* Chicago: University of Chicago Press, 1998.

Prashad, Vijay. *The Karma of Brown Folk.* Minneapolis: University of Minnesota Press, 2000.

"Primary Gonorrhea of the Rectum in the Male." *American Journal of Urology* 5, no. 11 (November 1909): 451.

Quinn, D. Michael. *Same-Sex Dynamics among Nineteenth-Century Americans: A Mormon Example.* Urbana: University of Illinois Press, 1996.

Reilly, Philip R. *The Surgical Solution: A History of Involuntary Sterilization in the United States.* Baltimore: John Hopkins University Press, 1991.

Reimers, David M. *Unwelcome Strangers: American Identity and the Turn against Immigration.* New York: Columbia University Press, 1998.

Reiss, Albert J., Jr. "The Social Integration of Queers and Peers." *Social Problems* 9, no. 2 (fall 1961): 102–20.

Retzloff, Tim. "Cars and Bars: Assembling Gay Men in Postwar Flynt, Michigan." In *Creating a Place for Ourselves: Lesbian, Gay, and Bisexual Community Histories,* edited by Brett Beemyn, 227–52. New York: Routledge, 1997.

Robinson, Paul. *The Modernization of Sex: Havelock Ellis, Alfred Kinsey, William Masters, and Virginia Johnson.* New York: Harper and Row, 1976.

Roediger, David R. *The Wages of Whiteness and the Making of the American Working Class.* Rev. ed. London: Verso, 1999.

Rosario, Vernon A. *The Erotic Imagination: French Histories of Perversity.* New York: Oxford University Press, 1997.

———. "Trans(Homo) Sexuality? Double Inversion, Psychiatric Confusion, and Hetero-Hegemony." In *Queer Studies: A Lesbian, Gay, Bisexual, and Transgender Anthology,* edited by Brett Beemyn and Mickey Eliason, 35–51. New York: New York University Press, 1996.

Rosen, Ruth. *The Lost Sisterhood: Prostitution in America, 1900–1918.* Baltimore: Johns Hopkins University Press, 1982.

Rosenzweig, Roy. *Eight Hours for What We Will: Workers and Leisure in an Industrial City, 1870–1920.* Cambridge: Cambridge University Press, 1983.

Ross, H. Lawrence. "The 'Hustler' in Chicago." *Journal of Student Research* 1, no. 1 (fall 1959): 13–19.

Rotundo, E. Anthony. *American Manhood: Transformations in Masculinity from the Revolution to the Modern Era.* New York: BasicBooks, 1993.

———. "Romantic Friendship: Male Intimacy and Middle-Class Youth in the Northern United States, 1800–1900." *Journal of Social History* 23, no. 1 (fall 1989): 1–25.

Rowbotham, Sheila, and Jeffrey Weeks. *Socialism and the New Life: The Personal and Sexual Politics of Edward Carpenter and Havelock Ellis.* London: Pluto Press, 1977.

Roy, Donald Francis. "Hooverville: A Study of a Community of Homeless Men in Seattle." M.A. thesis, University of Washington, 1935.

Roy, Patricia E. *A White Man's Province: British Columbia Politicians and Chinese and Japanese Immigrants, 1858–1914.* Vancouver: University of British Columbia Press, 1989.

Rubin, Gayle. "The Traffic in Women: Notes on the 'Political Economy' of Sex." In *Toward an Anthropology of Women,* edited by Rayna R. Reiter, 157–210. New York: Monthly Review Press, 1975.

Russell, Jo Anne. "A Necessary Evil: Prostitutes, Patriarchs, and Profits in Boise City, 1863–1915." M.A. thesis, Boise State University, 1991.

Ryan, Mary P. *Cradle of the Middle Class: The Family in Oneida County, New York, 1790–1865.* Cambridge: Cambridge University Press, 1981.

——. *Womanhood in America: From Colonial Times to the Present.* 3d ed. New York: Franklin Watts, 1983.

Rydell, Robert. "Visions of Empire: International Expositions in Portland and Seattle, 1905–1909." *Pacific Historical Review* 52, no. 1 (February 1983): 37–66.

Saloutos, Theodore. *The Greeks in America: A Students' Guide to Localized History.* Localized History Series, edited by Clifford L. Lord. New York: Teachers College, 1967.

——. *The Greeks in the United States.* Cambridge, Mass.: Harvard University Press, 1964.

Sawyer, Chris D. "From Whitechapel to Old Town: The Life and Death of the Skid Row District, Portland, Oregon." Ph.D. diss., Portland State University, 1985.

Schneider, John C. "Tramping Workers, 1890–1920: A Subcultural View." In *Walking to Work: Tramps in America, 1790–1935,* edited by Eric H. Monkkonen, 212–34. Lincoln: University of Nebraska Press, 1984.

Schwantes, Carlos Arnaldo. *Hard Traveling: A Portrait of Work Life in the New Northwest.* Lincoln: University of Nebraska Press, 1994.

——. *The Pacific Northwest: An Interpretive History.* Rev. ed. Lincoln: University of Nebraska Press, 1996.

——. *Railroad Signatures across the Pacific Northwest.* Seattle: University of Washington Press, 1993.

Scott, H. W., ed. *History of Portland, Oregon.* Syracuse, N.Y.: D. Mason, 1890.

Sedgwick, Eve Kosofsky. *Epistemology of the Closet.* Berkeley: University of California Press, 1990.

Shah, Nayan. *Contagious Divides: Epidemics and Race in San Francisco's Chinatown.* Berkeley: University of California Press, 2001.

Single Tax Conference Held in New York City, November 19 and 20, 1910. Cincinnati: Joseph Fels Fund Commission, 1911.

Sklar, Martin J. *The Corporate Reconstruction of American Capitalism, 1890–1916: The Market, the Law, and Politics.* Cambridge: Cambridge University Press, 1988.

Sklar, Robert. *Movie-Made America: A Social History of American Movies.* New York: Random House, 1975.

Smith-Rosenberg, Carroll. "Discourse of Sexuality and Subjectivity: The New Woman, 1870–1936." In *Hidden from History: Reclaiming the Gay and Lesbian Past,* edited by Martin Duberman, Martha Vicinus, and George Chauncey, Jr., 264–80. New York: Meridian, 1989.

——. *Disorderly Conduct: Visions of Gender in Victorian America.* New York: Knopf, 1985.

Social Hygiene Society of Portland, Oregon. *A Social Emergency: The First Annual Report.* Portland: Social Hygiene Society of Portland, Oregon, 1912.

Somerville, Siobhan B. *Queering the Color Line: Race and the Invention of Homosexuality in American Culture.* Durham, N.C.: Duke University Press, 2000.

Spence, Clark C. "Knights of the Tie and Rail—Tramps and Hoboes in the West." *Western Historical Quarterly* 2, no. 1 (January 1971): 5–19.

Steakley, James D. "Iconography of a Scandal: Political Cartoons and the Eulen-berg Affair in Wilhelmin Germany." In *Hidden from History: Reclaiming the Gay and Lesbian Past,* edited by Martin Duberman, Martha Vicinus, and George Chauncey, Jr., 233–63. New York: Meridian, 1989.

Steffens, Lincoln. "The Taming of the West." *American* 64 (October 1907): 585–602.

——. *Upbuilders.* New York: Doubleday, Page, 1909.

Stein, Marc. *City of Sisterly and Brotherly Loves: Lesbian and Gay Philadelphia, 1945–1972.* Chicago: University of Chicago Press, 2000.

Stiff, Dean [pseud. of Nels Anderson]. *The Milk and Honey Route: A Handbook for Hobos.* New York: Vanguard, 1931.

Stone, H. W. "What We Are Doing for the Boy." *Pacific Monthly* 10, no. 3 (September 1903): 139–46.

Sulloway, Frank J. *Freud, Biologist of the Mind: Beyond the Psychoanalytic Legend.* New York: Basic Books, 1979.

Takaki, Ronald. *A Different Mirror: A History of Multicultural America.* Boston: Little, Brown, 1993.

——. *Strangers from a Different Shore: A History of Asian Americans.* Boston: Little, Brown, 1989.

Talmey, Bernard S. *Love: A Treatise on the Science of Sex-Attraction.* 4th ed. New York: Practitioners Publishing, 1919.

Tattersall, James Neville. "The Economic Development of the Pacific Northwest to 1920." Ph.D. diss., University of Washington, 1960.

Taylor, Quintard. "Blacks and Asians in a White City: Japanese Americans and African Americans in Seattle, 1890–1940." *Western Historical Quarterly* 22, no. 4 (November 1991): 401–29.

——. *The Forging of a Black Community: Seattle's Central District from 1870 through the Civil Rights Era.* With a foreword by Norm Rice. Emil and Kathleen Sick Lecture-Book Series in Western History and Biography. Seattle: University of Washington Press, 1994.

Terry, Jennifer. *An American Obsession: Science, Medicine, and Homosexuality in Modern Society.* Chicago: University of Chicago Press, 1999.

Thoinot, L. *Medicolegal Aspects of Moral Offenses.* Translated by Arthur W. Weysse. Philadelphia: F. A. Davis, 1923.

Toll, William. *The Making of an Ethnic Middle Class: Portland Jews over Four Generations.* Albany: State University of New York Press, 1982.

——. "Permanent Settlement: Japanese Families in Portland in 1920." *Western Historical Quarterly* 28, no. 1 (spring 1997): 19–43.

Toy, Eckard V. "The Ku Klux Klan in Oregon." In *Experiences in a Promised Land: Essays in Pacific Northwest History,* edited by G. Thomas Edwards and Carlos A. Schwantes, 269–86. Seattle: University of Washington Press, 1986.

Traub, Valerie. *Desire and Anxiety: Circulations of Sexuality in Shakespearean Drama.* London: Routledge, 1992.

Ullman, Sharon R. *Sex Seen: The Emergence of Modern Sexuality in America.* Berkeley: University of California Press, 1997.

Wade, Ben N. "Case of Foreign Body in the Rectum." *Medical Sentinel* 25, no. 9 (September 17, 1917): 3689.

Warner, Sam Bass, Jr. *The Private City: Philadelphia in Three Periods of Its Growth.* Philadelphia: University of Pennsylvania Press, 1968.

Weeks, Jeffrey. *Coming Out: Homosexual Politics in Britain from the Nineteenth Century to the Present.* Rev. ed. London: Quartet Books, 1990.

——. "Movements of Affirmation: Sexual Meanings and Homosexual Identities." In *Passion and Power: Sexuality in History,* edited by Kathy Peiss and Christina Simmons, with Robert A. Padgug, 70–86. Philadelphia: Temple University Press, 1989.

——. *Sexuality and Its Discontents: Meanings, Myths, and Modern Sexualities.* London: Routledge and Kegan Paul, 1985.

Weinberg, Thomas S. "On 'Doing' and 'Being' Gay: Sexual Behavior and Homosexual Male Self-Identity." *Journal of Homosexuality* 4, no. 2 (winter 1978): 143–56.

Weiss, John, ed., *The Origins of Modern Consciousness.* Detroit: Wayne State University Press, 1965.

White, Kevin. *The First Sexual Revolution: The Emergence of Male Heterosexuality in Modern America.* New York: New York University Press, 1993.

White, Richard. *"It's Your Misfortune and None of My Own": A New History of the American West.* Norman: University of Oklahoma Press, 1991.

Wiebe, Robert H. *The Search for Order, 1877–1920.* New York: Hill and Wang, 1967.

Williams, Walter L. *The Spirit and the Flesh: Sexual Diversity in American Indian Culture.* Boston: Beacon Press, 1992.

Woloch, Nancy. *Muller v. Oregon: A Brief History with Documents.* New York: Bedford, 1996.

Woodward, Robert C. "William Simon U'Ren: In an Age of Protest." M.A. thesis, University of Oregon, 1956.

——. "W. S. U'Ren and the Single Tax in Oregon." *Oregon Historical Quarterly* 61, no. 1 (March 1960): 46–63.

"YMCA's First 100 Years." Portland: YMCA of Columbia-Willamette, n.d.

Young, Pat. "Case Closed: The Multnomah Bar Association Rights an 88-Year-Old Wrong." *Just Out,* September 1, 2000, 9.

Zhu, Liping. *A Chinaman's Chance: The Chinese on the Rocky Mountain Mining Frontier.* Niwot: University Press of Colorado, 1997.

Zunz, Olivier. *Making America Corporate, 1870–1920.* Chicago: University of Chicago Press, 1990.

Index

Aberdeen, Wash., 157
Adon, Nick, 81, 148
Ahmed, S. G., 84
Alaska, 7, 43, 77, 81; salmon canneries, 30–31, 36, 37, 44, 81
Alaska Gold Rush, 81
Alaska-Yukon Pacific Exposition, 146
Albany, Ore., 16, 28, 210
Albee, H. R., 167
Allen, William H., 98, 164
Altwater, Charles, 37, 38
Ambrose, Albert, 75, 83
American Banker, 166
American Hospital Association, 172
American Magazine, 170
American Social Hygiene Association, 8, 188, 189
Anderson, Anders, 107
Anderson, John, 79
Anderson, Leslie, 110
Anderson, Nels, 21, 22–23, 25, 27, 29, 30, 32, 34, 36, 38, 39, 75, 77, 86, 106
Anti-Saloon League (Oregon and Southern Idaho Department), 170, 171, 174, 175, 178
Arabian Nights, 58
Armstrong, William, 110
Austin, Tex., 96, 181
automobiles and homosexuality, 41, 43

bachelor culture: of Asian Indians, 18–19; of Chinese, 18–19; of Greeks, 18–19

Bacon, Henry, 77, 83
Baker, Alice, 82
Baker, Harry, 102–3
Baker, James Arthur, 82
Baker, Ray Stannard, 170
Baldwin, Lola, 81
Baruh, B. H., 52–53
Bederman, Gail, 94
Belanger, Narcisse, 84
Bellingham, Wash., 53
Birdseye, George, 217
Blair, Harry, 36
Blazier's Saloon (Portland), 68
Bliss, Albert, 79
Boise, Ida., 16, 97, 133; prostitution (female) in, 191; prostitution (male) in, 77; vice district in, 241n38
Boston University, 168
Boyd, Reuben, 37, 38
Boyd, William, 201
Boyfrank, Manuel, 36
Bradley, John, 122
Brazell, Clarence, 109, 205
Brewer, F. P., 165
Brick, Benjamin, 162, 267n12
British Columbia, 7, 18, 20, 134. *See also* Vancouver, B.C.; Victoria, B.C.
British Columbia eugenics movement, 215
Bronner, Caude 100, 111–12; photograph of, 101
Brooks, Raymond C., 182
Brooks, Richard, 84

Brown, Charles, 22
Brown, Earl, 109
Buffum and Pendleton (Portland), 98
bum: defined, 21; sexual views of, 29–30
Bunting v. Oregon (1917), 170
Burg, B. R., 21
Burgoyne Hotel (Portland), 100
Burke, Ida., 37
Burnett, George, 143
Burnham, John C., 190
Burnside Street (Portland), 45, 63, 78, 81, 84, 115; photograph of, 64
Burns, Louis, 112–13, 123
Burton, Sir Richard, 58
Butler, Judith, 23

Cahalin, E. H., 172
Caldwell, Ida., 16
California, 7, 20, 22, 33, 35, 36, 38, 82, 122, 177. *See also individual cities*
California Gold Rush, 19
Cameron, George, 136, 172
Caminetti, Anthony, 53
Campbell, V. E., 172
Canadian sodomy laws, 203, 206
Canfield, B. H., 163, 165, 167
Carlisle, Penn., 168
Carter, Ernest B., 81
Cascade Mountains, 180
Case H, 74
Case U, 74
Case Y, 81
Casino (Seattle), 80, 85
Central Park (Vancouver, B.C.), 55
Century Magazine, 170
Chamberlain, George, 188, 189
Chamberlain-Kahn Act (1918), 188
Chapman Park (Portland), 114; as gay site, 115
"charity boys," 76–77
Chauncey, George, 27, 28, 85, 91–92, 119, 219
Chehalis County, Wash., 201
Chicago, Ill., 67, 136, 153
Church, Roy, 32, 67
Chinatown (Portland), 65
Clear Lake, Wash., 37, 38
Cleveland, Ohio, 98
closet: as metaphor, 39–40; as rural geographical space, 40; as urban geographical space, 40, 41
Cohen, Ed, 128

cold war, 218; anti-homosexual hysteria during, 218–19, 220
Colfax, Wash., 37
Collier, Frank, Collier, Frank, 136, 139, 141–142, 143, 144, 147, 151, 152, 179; photograph of, 140
Columbia County Lumber Company, 149
Columbia River, 66, 149, 180, 181
Commercial Club (Walla Walla, Wash.), 181
Commission on Training Camp Activities (Pacific Coast and Arizona division), 81
Commission to Investigate the Oregon State Penitentiary, 153; eugenical sterilization and, 212
Committee of 15 (Portland), 165, 197
Committee of 50 (Portland), 165, 197, 198, 199
congenital homosexuality, 138, 142
Conley, Tom, 84
conspiracy of silence, 189, 190; homosexuality and, 193–94, 195–200
Coos Bay Times's (Marshfield, Ore.): response to E. S. J. McAllister, 177
Copenhagen, Denmark, 107
Corbett, Henry W., 163
corporate capitalism: development of, 92, 93–94; homosexuality and, 10, 97–105; manliness and, 94, 95; masculinity crisis and, 95; privacy and, 115–16; white-collar work and, 94–95; women and, 95
Cottage Grove, Ore., 175, 176
Council Crest (Portland), 71, 100
cowboys and ranchers and homosexuality, 22, 36, 42
Craddock, R. H., 45, 79
crime against nature, 193. *See also* sodomy laws

Darwin, Charles, 129
degeneracy/degenerate, 128–32, 134–35, 137–39, 142, 148, 151, 152, 153, 220
Degeneration (1894), 128–30
degeneration (theory of), 129, 130–32, 137, 138; middle classes and, 137, 147; 1912 scandal and, 137, 138, 146; Pacific Northwest newspapers on, 129–33, 134, 137, 147
Demas, H., 84–85
d'Emilio, John, 91, 92, 117, 218–19

Delaware, 168
De Long, Heber, 29
Denver, Colo., 153
Derrill, Max, 107
Des Moines, Iowa, 96, 181
Deusing, W. C., 107
Dickinson College, 168
Dill, C. C., 57
Dillige, Andrew, 5, 6, 7, 11, 45, 48, 49, 50, 52, 53, 69, 84, 225n9; photograph of, 47
District of Columbia and homosexuality, 185
Dixon, Michael, 84
Doernbecher (Portland), 98
Douglas, Lord Alfred, 127, 134
Dover, Delaware, 168
Drain, Ore., 177
Draper, Milton, 84–85
Dubbert, Joe, 108
Du Fresne Studios (Portland), 112
Duluth, Minn., 217
Duniway, Abigail Scott, 171, 261n12
Dyott, Luther, 197

Eakin, James, 152
Ebster, F., 148
Edwards, George, 200
Eggleston, W. G., 173
Egypt, 58
Ellis, Henry Havelock, 24, 25, 58, 142–43, 145–46
England, 21
Enneking, Raymond, 75–76
entrepreneurial capitalism: development of, 93; manliness and, 94; masculinity crisis and, 95; neurasthenia and, 95–96
Erickson's Saloon (Portland), 67, 68
Eugene Daily Guard, attacks on E. S. J. McAllister, 176–77, 183
Eugene, Ore., 168, 175, 176, 177, 183, 184
eugenics, development of, 206–7. *See also* British Columbia eugenics movement; Idaho eugenics movement; Oregon eugenics movement; Washington state eugenics movement
Evans, Walter H., 179
Evening Telegram (Portland), editorial policy on 1912 scandal, 161
Exclusion Act (1882), 51

Fairmount Hotel (Portland), 5, 45, 72
fairy: characteristics of, 27–28; compared to punk, 27–29, 31, 32; limited presence in Pacific Northwest cities, 48, 85–86; sexual forms of, 28; transient society and, 29–31; working class views on, 29, 31, 32
farmhands, and homosexuality, 42
Farrell, Robert S., 210
Fellingham, J. H., 96
Fels Fund, 174, 176
Fels, Joseph, 174, 176
Ferris, Charles, 79
First Congregational Church of Walla Walla, Wash., 180, 182
first sexual revolution: middle-class contributions to, 10, 117, 118, 120, 124; working class contributions to, 117–18
Flint, Mich., 41
Flynt, Josiah, 22–23, 24, 25, 26, 29, 32, 33, 34, 42, 43
Foot, George, 78
Forest Grove, Ore., 157
Forest, Isaac, 78
Foster, William Trufant, 190, 197–98
Foucault, Michel, 4, 134, 148, 149, 220–21
France, 58
Franks, Gordon, 109
Fraser, Duncan, 145, 146, 211
Frater, Archibald, 70–71
Freedman, Estelle B., 117, 219
Fresno, Calif., 157
Freud, Sigmund, 24
Friend Program, 200–201, 206
Fritz's Saloon (Portland), 68

Gantenbein, Calvin, 137, 139, 141, 145
Garland, Tom, 213
Gatens, William N., 71–72, 163, 168, 276n26
Gate, Wash., 55
George, Henry, 173
George, Nick, 77, 83
Germany, homosexual scandal in, 146–47
Gibson, John, 96, 158; local support for, 182–83, 184; neurasthenia and, 96; 1912 scandal and, 180, 181–83; professional activities of, 180; Young Men's Christian Association and, 181
Gibson, Ray, 78
Girls' and Boys' Aid Society of Oregon, 60
Gladden, Ted, 15–16, 17, 18, 21, 22, 25, 28, 44, 227n1; photograph of, 16
Globe Hotel (Portland), 72, 115

Goldman, Emma, 174; 1915 visit to Portland of, 199–200
Goltz, John, 45, 79
Goodock, John, 52, 125
Graham, George H., 81
Graham, Maury, 29, 33, 42, 43
Grand, Sarah, 261n12
Grays Harbor, Wash., 149
Great Depression, 30, 80, 85, 218
Great Northern Hotel (Vancouver, B.C.), 54
Greater Portland Plans Association, 164
Greece, 19, 58, 137, 151, 239n23
Greek scandal, 3, 4, 45, 52, 53, 71, 74, 89
Gunreth, David, 37

H., Donald, 38, 40–41, 43
Hall, G. Stanley, 60
Haller, Mark H., 206, 207
Hammerich, Frederick, 107–8
Hanna Banna, 80–81
Hastings Street vice district (Vancouver, B.C.), 85
Hayes, John, 200–201
Healy, Nathan, 100, 111–12
Hellgreen, Oscar, 108
Hendrick, Burton J., 160–61, 170
heterosexuality: and stigmatization of homosexuality, 192–93; construction of, 252–53n33; normalization of, 191–93, 197
Hickey, Thomas, 36
Higham, John, 129
Hirshland (Boise), 133–34
Hindoo, as a term, 53
historical sources, problems with, 8–10, 48, 49, 221
hobo, 21, 230n15
Holbrook, Stewart, 20
Hollenbeck, Ernest, 84
Hollister, Kenneth, 109, 112, 122
Homan, William, 115, 123
homosexual (term), 142–43, 152, 153
homosexuality: automobiles and, 41, 43; corporate capitalism and, 10, 97–105; cowboys and ranchers and, 22, 36, 42; deployment among working classes, 148–52; endangerment of youths and, 59–61, 70–73, 74, 195–200, 216, 219, 220–21; eugenics and, 206–16; farmhands and, 42; gender and, 23–24; increasing penalties for, 200,

201, 202–6; legal charges for, 48, 49; loggers and, 22, 35–36, 42, 55–56, 200; as middle-class phenomenon, 3, 4, 5, 6, 7–8, 90–92, 96–97, 99–100, 101–2, 103, 104–5, 124, 251n25, 254n39; miners and, 22, 36, 40, 42; and normalization of heterosexuality, 192–93; public discussion of regulated, 193–94, 195–200; racist campaigns and, 46–47, 50, 52–58, 73, 152; railroads and, 42–44; regionalism and, 4, 6–8, 226n15; rural areas and, 40–44; sailing vessels and, 30–31, 36–37, 43, 232n33; sailors and, 22, 107, 232n33; salmon cannery workers and, 30–31
homosexuality, construction of, 6, 8, 24, 25, 99–100, 103, 220, 222, 225n7, 252–53n33; race and, 4; role of Oscar Wilde in, 126–27, 132–33, 134, 138, 148; role of working classes in, 135; role of middle classes in, 135, 136, 137, 138, 141, 145, 148; role of 1912 scandal in, 4–5, 8, 127, 136–139, 141–47, 148, 152–53
Hong Kong, China, 217
Hoquiam, Wash., 200
Howard, John, 41
hustler, 79–80, 83, 84, 111
Hutchinson, W. I., 193

Iberian Peninsula, 58
Idaho, 7, 8, 16, 18, 29, 32, 42, 44, 45; sodomy laws, 202, 205. *See also individual cities and counties*
Idaho eugenics movement: and 1919 bill, 215; and 1925 law, 215; Oregon's influence on, 215
Imperial Hotel (Portland), 115, 173; restrooms of as gay site, 113
India, 56, 58
Industrial Workers of the World (IWW), 50, 51, 149, 159
Iowa, 159
Irvin, F. N., 107
Italy, 58, 213

Jackson County, Ore., 171
Jack the Ripper, 62, 63
James, Jennifer, 79
jocker, 220; defined, 25; sexuality of, 25–26
jocker–punk relationship: coercion and, 31, 32–33, 34–35; gender and, 27; influence on urban male sex roles, 83–84,

85; nonsexual aspects of, 31–33, 34; sex and, 233n50; sexual forms in, 28, 85; sexuality and, 26; sexual roles in, 83–84; in urban areas, 74–75

Jones, Fred, 61, 125

Jones, W. Ray, 58

Johnson, Josephine De Vore, 199

Johnston, Robert D., 158

jungles, 42

Kadel, Roy, 113, 115

Kallas, Tom, 78, 79

Kamagata Maru, 54, 55

Kambouris, Haralambous (Harry), 19

Kansas, 97

Kapsales, Tom, 149, 150, 151, 152

Katz, Jonathan Ned, 128

Kavanaugh, John P., 61, 139, 145

Keller, Albert, 84

Kelly, J. G., 180, 182–83

Kennewick, Wash., 34

King, Grover, 45, 47, 48, 49, 50, 69, 74, 83

Kingston, Wash., 201

Kinsey, Alfred, 22, 28, 34, 42, 90–91, 98, 104, 117–18, 248n3

Kinsey Institute, 119

Knapp, F. C., 165

Knights of Macabees, Tent No. 36, (Walla Walla, Wash.), 181

Kocka, Jürgen, 106

Krafft-Ebing, Richard von, 131, 142, 143

Ku Klux Klan, 51

laborer, defined, 227–28n5

Ladd and Tilton Bank (Portland), 163

Ladd, William M., 163

Ladd, William S., 163

Lafferty, A. W., 185–86, 272n3; photograph, 187

Lagallo, Tony, 61, 75, 84, 213

Lake Oswego, Oreg., 109

Lamarck, Jean, 129

lamb (term), 25, 26

LaMere, Gus, 37, 38

Lane County, Ore., 175

Lane, Harry, 172, 174, 189

Legmon, Gershon, 26, 28, 80

lesbians, 6, 9

Lewelling, L. G., 210

Lewis and Clark Exposition, 146

Lewis County, Wash., 202

Lincoln High School (Portland), 109

loggers and homosexuality, 22, 35–36, 42, 55–56, 200

Lombroso, Cesare, 129

Long Beach, Calif., 119, 153

Los Angeles, Calif., 1, 119, 136, 153, 157

Lovegren, Oscar, 109

Lownsdale Park (Portland): as gay site, 113–15; photograph of, 114

Lydston, G. Frank, 24

Lyons, France, 189

MacArthur, Douglas, 218

Maine, 37

Manila, Philippines, 218

Mann Act (1910), 188

Marshfield, Ore., 177

Martinsen, Alfred, 150, 151

masculinity crisis, 95, 252–53n33

Massi, Louis, 77

Matters, Indiana, 54

Mawvais, Tom, 78, 79

Maynard, Stephen, 109

McAllister, E. S. J., 5, 11, 112–13, 115, 151, 158, 180, 181, 184, 194; appeal of, 139–41, 144, 152, 179; attempted escape by, 177; biography of, 168–70; *Coos Bay Times* (Marshfield, Ore.) response to, 177; death of, 179; election of 1912 and, 174–76; *Eugene Daily Guard*'s response to, 176–77, 183; green suit of, 178; influence on Portland's municipal government, 174; legal practice of, 172–73, 179; life after the 1912 scandal, 179; *Medford Mail Tribune*'s response to, 177–78; *Muller v. Oregon* (1908) and, 171–72; Multnomah County Bar Association and, 179; *Oregonian*'s response to, 178; *Oregon Journal*'s response to, 178; photograph of, 169; physical description of, 171; political party affiliation of, 172; *Portland News*'s response to, 178; Progressive reforms and, 170, 171, 173–76, 269–70n33; small communities view of, 176–78, 183; trial of, 139–41, 178–79; wife of, 169–70, 179

McAllister, Sarah Frances (Lowe), 168

McAllister, William N., 168

McArthur, Clifton, 204, 205

McArthy, Joseph, 37

McBride, Thomas, 137, 144, 145

McClure's Magazine, 170; reports on Portland vice, 160–61

McCourt, John, 186
McDonald, John, 74
McDonald, N., 54
McElroy, George, 32, 67
McGraw, Andrew, 67
McNary, Charles, 145, 175
McNary, John, 175
Mead, Albert, 203
Meagher, David, 179
Medford, Ore., 157, 171, 177–78
Medford Mail Tribune, response to E. S. J.
    McAllister, 177–78
Men in Religion Forward Movement, 180
Merlotin, Emma, 63
Merrill, Lilburn, 72, 74, 79, 80, 81, 84; 1918
    study on homosexuality in Seattle, 79,
    84
Metsker, Glen, 150, 151, 152
middle class: concerns for youths of, 59–61,
    69, 70–73, 74; construction of homo-
    sexuality and, 135, 136, 137, 138, 141,
    145, 148; first sexual revolution and,
    10, 117, 118, 120, 124; homosexuality
    and, 91–124; oral sex and, 118; Victo-
    rian sexuality and, 117; views on racial-
    minority males, 3, 4, 46–47, 52–53,
    57–59, 59–62, 65, 67, 70–73; views on
    vice districts, 47, 62–73; views on
    working-class males, 3, 4, 47, 57–58,
    59–62, 64, 65–68, 70–73, 105–6, 126, 135
middle-class homosexual subculture (Port-
    land), 105; connection to working-
    class culture, 243n57, 254n41; cross
    dressing and, 82–83, 122; drag parties
    and, 122; emergence of, 3, 6, 91–105,
    251n25; entertainments and, 99–100,
    115; gay identity and, 123–24; gay sites
    of, 112–15; geographic center of,
    112–13; marital status of participants
    in, 103–4; mobility of participants in,
    7–8, 97; occupations of participants,
    90–91, 92; oral sex, 5, 110–11, 118–24;
    privacy and, 115–16; public parks and,
    113–115; public restrooms and, 113, 115;
    race of participants in, 90, 111; racial
    minority men and, 106–7, 110; role of
    youths in, 5, 108–11, 220, 255n50;
    terms for community in, 105, 253n37;
    working class men and, 105–7, 110;
    workplaces of participants in, 112;
    Young Men's Christian Association
    and, 101–3, 115, 116

Minehan, Thomas, 32
miners and homosexuality, 22, 36, 40, 42
Mintz, Stephen, 98
Missouri, 186
Mitchell, Alice, 2
Moffit, John, 112
Montana, 7, 42, 43; sodomy law of, 202,
    205, 206
Monte Carlo poolroom (Portland), 45, 52,
    71, 74, 78, 79, 115
Montgomery, Ed, 84
Moran, Jeffrey P., 60, 190
Morocco, 58
Morris, George, 125
Mosey, Thomas, 61, 125
Mosher, H. A., 172
Muller, Curt, 171–72
Muller v. Oregon (1908), 170, 171–72; E. S. J.
    McAllister and, 171–72
Multnomah County Bar Association (and
    E. S. J. McAllister), 179
Murray, Ben, 77, 84
Murray, Clarence, 55, 56
Mustard, John, 37
Myrtle Creek, Ore., 179
Mystic, Conn., 136

1912 (YMCA) Scandal, 1, 2, 3, 8, 49, 97, 98,
    106, 118, 126, 135–36; arrests during,
    157; attempted suicide during, 164;
    beginnings of, 1, 89, 162, 247n11; class
    and racial context of, 196; class poli-
    tics in Portland and, 158, 159–68, 219,
    222; construction of homosexuality
    and, 4–5, 8, 127, 136–39, 141–47, 148,
    152–53; degeneration and, 137, 138,
    146; eugenical sterilization and,
    208–11, 215, 216; *Evening Telegram*
    and, 161; federal involvement in,
    185–86; flight of men during, 1, 8, 157,
    177, 217; future influences of, 151–52,
    218, 219, 222; middle class nature of,
    90–91, 136, 152; ministerial response
    to, 165, 197; as model for 1950s' anti-
    homosexual hysteria, 218–20; national
    dimensions of, 8, 157; *Oregonian* and,
    161; *Portland News* and, 159–64; Port-
    land newsboys ordinance and, 197;
    Portland politics and, 158, 159–68, 219,
    222; *Portland Spectator* and, 165; Pro-
    gressive reforms and, 2, 157, 186,
    197–99, 203–6, 208–11, 215–16; prosti-

tution (male) and, 185, 186; public discourse and, 195–200; regional influences of, 96, 157, 179–80, 186; regulation of homosexuality and, 194–200; revelations of, 1, 2–3, 89, 90, 105, 136, 152, 185; Seattle, Wash., and, 8, 136, 137, 157; sexual forms of those arrested in, 118–24; significance of, 152, 218, 219–21, 222; small communities and, 157, 168, 176–78; sodomy laws and, 202, 203–5; trials of, 139; working-class men and, 105; Vancouver, B.C., and, 1, 8, 105, 136, 157; Young Men's Christian Association of Portland and, 1–2, 89, 102, 162–67; youths in, 108–9

1928 homosexual crackdown (Portland), 10, 90, 105, 109–11, 116; prostitution (male) in, 110–11; youths in, 109–11

1950s anti-homosexual hysteria, 218–19, 220

National Conference of Charities and Corrections, 43–44

nativism, 51

Nebraska, 159

neurasthenia: causes of, 95–96; and homosexuality, 96; male liberation and, 95–97; symptoms of, 95

Newport, Rhode Island, 153

New Woman, 261n12

New York, 98

New York City, 6, 67, 85, 153, 171

Nordau, Max, 128–29, 131, 132

North End/Whitechapel vice district (Portland), 3, 5, 45, 62, 106, 107, 111, 115, 116, 148, 221, 222; arrests for homosexuality in, 48, 68–69, 72–73, 196; boundaries of, 63; Chinatown and, 65; crime and, 63, 64–65, 66, 77–78; employment agencies in, 67; entertainments of, 68; history of, 62–65; homosexuality in, 70–72; lodging houses in, 67–68, 72; as male space, 66; map of, 46; middle class control of vice in, 161; middle-class homosexual subculture and, 111; name, 62–63; Oregon Social Hygiene Society and, 189; police raids on, 69; pool halls, 68, 71; as racialized space, 65, 67–68; saloons, 67, 68, 70–71; social composition of, 65–66; as working-class space, 65–68; youths and, 69–72, 73

Novig, Claus, 72

101 Ranch Real Wild West Show, 37

Oaks Park (Portland), 71

Odem, Mary, 33

Ogden, Utah, 34

O'Grady, Ernest, 77, 84

Ohio, 96

Olds, Wortman and King (Portland), 112

Olympia, Wash., 207

Omi, Michael, 65

Oregon, 5, 7, 8, 11, 16, 18, 38, 40, 42, 43, 51, 56, 152, 168, 185, 186, 188, 219; election of 1912 in, 175–76; Progressive reforms and, 170–72, 173–76, 203–5, 207–215; and regulation of homosexuality, 203–6, 208–15; sodomy laws of, 203–6. *See also individual cities and counties*

Oregon and Southern Idaho Department, Anti-Saloon League, 170, 171, 174, 175, 178

Oregon Anti-Sterilization League, 210

Oregon Equal Taxation League, 176

Oregon eugenics movement: and castration for homosexuals, 209, 212–14; and 1913 law, 208–9, 210; and 1917 law, 211, 212, 215; and 1919 law, 212, 215; history of, 207, 208; homosexuality and, 208–16; influence of Commission to Investigate the Oregon State Penitentiary on, 212; influence on Idaho, 215; influence on Washington state, 207, 215; 1912 scandal and, 208–9, 210, 211, 215; opposition to, 210–11, 213, 214; origins of, 207; Owens-Adair, Bethenia and, 207, 208, 210; referendum on 1913 law, 210–11; West, Oswald and, 208–10

Oregonian (Portland): attacks on *Portland News*, 165; editorial policy on 1912 scandal, 161; response to E. S. J. McAllister, 178

Oregon Journal (Portland): attacks on *Portland News*, 195; response to E. S. J. McAllister, 178

Oregon Rational Tax Reform Association, 176

Oregon Single Tax League, 173, 174

Oregon Social Hygiene Society (OSHS), 102; Advisory Department of, 197; Committee of 15 and, 197; Committee of 50 and, 197–98; Committee on Sex Education, 199; conservatism of,

Oregon Social Hygiene Society (continued)
274n9; conspiracy of silence and, 190;
exhibits, 189; free clinic of, 189; homosexuality and, 197–99; Idaho and,
189; influence on Progressive reforms,
191; 1912 scandal and, 197–99; North
End and, 189; opposite-sex relations
and, 189–90; Oregon Board of Health
and, 198, 276n26; Oregon State appropriations to, 198; origins of, 189;
programs, 189; publications, 189; response to prostitution, 189–90; response to venereal diseases, 189–90;
sex education and, 198–99; Washington State and, 189; Young Men's
Christian Association of Portland
and, 276n26
Oregon State Board of Eugenics, 211, 212,
213
Oregon State Board of Health: eugenics
and, 211; Oregon Social Hygiene Society and, 198, 276n26
Oregon State Grange, 176
Oregon State Penitentiary, 205, 214; Commission to Investigate, 153, 212; homosexuality and, 153, 212–13, 279n58
Oregon State Public Service Commission,
166
Oregon State Tax Commission, 176
Oregon System, 170, 173
Oregon-Washington Railroad and Naviga-
tion Company, 97
Osborne, Thomas Mott, 26
Owens-Adair, Bethenia, 207, 208, 210

Pacific Northwest: economy of, 7, 17–18,
20–21; history of, 17–18; logging, 17,
20; map of, 7; nativist campaigns, 51;
population of (1880 and 1930), 18;
Progressivism and, 3, 158–84, 186–216;
racist campaigns and homosexuality
in, 46–47, 50, 52–59; railroad construction in, 17, 42–43; social characteristics of, 18–19; transient laborers
and, 7, 15–18, 19–22
Page, Charles, 120–21
Paget, B. Lee, 166, 174
Panama Canal, 52
Panama Hotel (Vancouver, B.C.), 55
Pappas, Thomas, 77
Paris House (Portland), 107

Parker, Charles, 128
Parkinson, H. J., 174, 175, 176–77
Pasadena, Calif., 165
Peiss, Kathy, 76
Penrose, Stephen, 181
People's Power League (Oregon), 173, 174,
176, 178
The Picture of Dorian Gray, 128
Philadelphia, Penn., 111, 136, 153
Philippines, 218
Pioneer Square (Seattle), 77, 85
Pittock, H. L., 161
Place, H. C., 202–3
Plaza Blocks (Portland), 113, 115
Pocatello, Ida., 148
police entrapment for homosexuality, 54,
55, 150
Polson, Alex, 200–201
Polson Logging Company, 200
Portland Ad Club, 164, 166
Portland and San Francisco Asiatic
Steamship Companies, 172
Portland Association of Credit Men, 164
Portland Central Business District: map
of, 46; middle-class homosexual sub-
culture and, 111, 112–15, 116
Portland Central Labor Council, 167
Portland Chamber of Commerce, 97, 112,
159, 164, 165
Portland Commercial Club, 164
Portland Eastside Business Men's Club,
164
Portland Elk's Lodge, 107
Portland Heights, 64
Portland Labor Press, 174; 1912 scandal and,
167
Portland Men's Methodist Social Union,
166
Portland Multnomah Amateur Athletic
Club, 164
Portland News: 1912 scandal and, 159–68;
response to E. S. J. McAllister, 178;
use of degeneration theory by, 137
Portland North East Side Improvement
Association, 164
Portland, Oregon: African Americans in,
65, 106, 107; amusement parks in, 71;
Asian Indian community, 56–57;
Blazier's Saloon, 68; Buffum and
Pendleton, 98; Burgoyne Hotel, 100;
Burnside Street, 45, 63, (photograph)

64, 78, 81, 84, 115; Chapman Park, 114, 115; Chinatown, 65; Chinese in, 65, 69; Committee of 15, 165, 197; Committee of 50, 165, 197, 198, 199; concern over boys in vice district of, 69–72; concern over boys and homosexuality in, 60, 61, 70–72, 73; Council Crest, 71, 100; Doernbecher, 98; Du Fresne Studios, 112; Erickson's Saloon, 67, 68; Fairmount Hotel, 5, 45, 72; Fritz's Saloon, 68; Globe Hotel, 72, 115; Greek community in, 53; history of, 1; history of class struggle in, 158–59, 168; homosexual arrests in, 48–49, 68–69, 72–73; Imperial Hotel, 113, 115, 173; juvenile court system in, 60; Ladd and Tilton Bank, 163; Lewis and Clark Exposition (1905), 146; Lincoln High School, 109; Lownsdale Park, 113–15; middle-class homosexual subculture in, 2–3, 5, 7–8, 97–98, 99, 100–124; middle-class views on North End in, 62–73; middle-class views on racial minorities in, 64, 65, 67, 72–73; middle-class views on the working class in, 64, 66, 67–68, 72–73; Monte Carlo poolroom, 45, 52, 71, 74, 78, 79, 115; moving picture shows in, 71; Native Americans in, 107; newsboys ordinance and homosexuality in, 197; Oaks Park, 71; Olds, Wortman and King, 112; Paris House, 107; Plaza Blocks, 113, 115; police, 45, 50, 64–65, 69, 74, 81, 107, 109, 148; Progressivism in, 158–59, 166, 188, 189–91, 195–99; prostitution (female) in, 191; prostitution (male) in, 71–72, 76, 110–11; Pullman Company, 107, 108; racist campaign against Greeks in, 52–53, 57, 65; St. Helens Hotel, 75; St. Vincent Hospital, 78; transgendered males in, 81–82, 83; Uncle Sam Hotel, 112–13, 115; vice in, 160–61; Washington Street, 112–13, 115; Woodard, Clarke and Co., 112; working class/transients in, 65–68. *See also* North End/Whitechapel vice district

Portland Peniel Mission, 82

Portland People's Forum, 171

Portland Progressive Business Men's Club, 164

Portland Railway Light and Power (PRL&P): class politics and, 166; defense of YMCA, 166; history of, 166

Portland Realty Board, 164

Portland Rotary Club, 164

Portland Spectator: attack on *Portland News,* 165

Portland Transportation Club, 164

Portland Vice Commission (1911–1913), 8, 116, 161, 188; discourse on homosexuality and, 195; female prostitution and, 188, 190; Progressive reforms and, 190

Portland Woman's Club, 67–68

Pratt, Laurence, 114

Prindle v. Texas (1873), 202

privacy, and middle-class homosexual subculture, 115–16

Progress and Poverty (1879), 173

Progressivism, 188; attacks on middle class, 216; attacks on working class, 216; moral reforms of, 188–92; 1912 scandal and, 186, 194–200; Oregon and, 170–72, 173–76, 203–5, 207–15; Pacific Northwest and, 3, 158–84, 186–216; Portland and, 158–59, 166, 188, 189–91, 195–99; reforms and heterosexuality in the Pacific Northwest, 186, 191–92; reforms and heterosexuality in the U.S., 191; reforms and homosexuality in the Pacific Northwest, 186, 192–93, 194, 195–200, 202–16

prostitution (male): Alaska salmon canneries, 30–31; and beating partners, 78; and crime, 77–79; "charity boys" and, 76–77; in Portland, 71–72, 75, 76, 110–11; in Seattle, 70, 76, 77, 79–80; in Spokane, 76; and stealing from clients, 77–78, 79; laws against, 246n82; 1912 scandal and, 185, 186; Portland's links to San Francisco and, 185; punk and, 245n69; racial minorities and, 36; sailing vessels, 30–31; sexual roles and, 83; transgendered males and, 81, 83; in urban areas, 47, 70, 71–72, 74–77, 79–80

Prushun, defined, 26

Psychopathia Sexualis 1st edition (1888), 131, 142

Psychopathia Sexualis 1st edition (1902), 142

Pullman Company (Portland), 107, 108

punk, 220; age of, 27, 232n34; anal/inter-femoral sex and, 28; becoming a jocker, 29; compared to fairy, 27, 28, 29–30, 31, 32; gender of, 27, 28, 29; nonsexual roles of, 31–34; oral sex and, 28; prostitution and, 75–77, 245n69; sexual fulfillment of, 34; sexual role of, 28, 31, 35; as term, 26, 245n69; transformed into hustler, 111; urban areas and, 48, 74–76; urban employment of, 75–76; working class views on, 29, 32

queen, 80, 81, 120, 123, 258n82
Queensberry, Marquess of, 127, 128, 134

racial minorities: Asian Indians, 18, 19, 51, 53–57, 62, 65, 67, 84; Asians, 50; African Americans, 18, 50, 51, 52, 61, 65, 67, 77, 106, 107; bachelor culture of, 18–19; Chinese, 18, 19, 50, 51, 52, 53, 65, 228n8; foreign-born whites, 18, 50, 59; Greeks, 3, 18, 19, 45, 51, 52–53, 57, 62, 65, 67, 76, 77, 78, 81, 84–85, 149–51; and homosexual arrests (in Portland), 48, 49, 50; Italians, 61, 65; Japanese, 50, 51, 53, 65, 67; Latin Americans, 18, 50; Native Americans, 18, 72, 107; Pacific Islanders, 18; Turks, 58–59; urban space and, 65–66, 67–68, 69
racism: African Americans and, 52; Asian Indians and, 19; and campaigns against homosexuality, 46–47, 50, 52–58, 73, 152; Chinese and, 19; Greeks and, 3, 19, 149–51; homosexual arrests and, 46, 50, 51, 52, 53–58, 72–73; and miscegenation, 240n27; new immigrants and, 50, 51, 52–58, 61, 6–62
railroads, and homosexuality, 42–43
Reames, Billy, 111
regionalism, homosexuality and, 4, 6–8, 226n15
Reitman, Ben, 199
Retzloff, Tim, 41
Rice, Dorman, 70
Riley, James, 213–14, photograph of, 213
Roberts, H. E. "Jack," 172, 176, 179
Rodby, Fred, 100, 113, 123
Roosevelt, Theodore, 170, 175
Rosenzweig, Roy, 69
Rotundo, E. Anthony, 94
Rowe, H. L, 89, 91, 138, 217

Roy, Donald, 22, 27, 31, 34
rural areas: as closets, 40; homosexuality and, 40–44, 226n14, 235n76
Rushlight, A. G., 66, 161, 196
Russell, George, 84
Ryan, Thomas, 108

sailing vessels, and homosexuality, 30–31, 36–37, 43, 232n33
sailors: as homosexual fantasy, 107; and homosexuality, 22, 232n33
Salem, Ore., 16, 76, 108, 157, 171, 207
salmon cannery workers, and homosexuality, 30–31
San Diego, Calif., 136, 157
San Francisco, Calif., 30, 59, 61, 67, 81, 126, 136, 157, 185, 217; Barbary Coast of, 81; prostitution (male) in, 81
Sawyer, Chris, 66
Scott, David, 54–55
Scott, Harvey, 66, 161, 261n12
Scripps, Edward Willis, 159; defends *Portland News*, 165–66; newspaper policies of, 165; Pacific Northwest newspaper chain of, 159, 163
Seaside, Ore., 108
Seattle, Wash., 58, 59, 74, 75, 79, 80, 81, 83, 84, 85, 146, 183; Alaska-Yukon Exposition, 146; concern for boys and homosexuality in vice district, 70–71; fairies in, 30; homosexuality and amusement parks, 72; Hooverville of, 22, 27, 31, 34; middle-class homosexual subculture of, 7–8; 1912 scandal and, 8, 136, 137, 157; prostitution (male), 70, 76, 77, 79–80; Pioneer Square, 77, 85; Skid Road vice district, 62, 70, 80, 85, 241n38
Seattle Star, 159, 167–68
Seavy, Ernest, 22
Sedgwick, Eve Kosofsky, 39
Selkok, Fred, 79
sex invert (inversion), 23–24, 141, 142, 147, 148, 152
sex pervert, 82, 148, 149, 152
sexual terminology: chicken, 120; cock-sucker, 120, 121, 124; congenital homosexual, 23, 25, 138, 142; degeneracy/degenerate, 128–32, 134–35, 137–39, 142, 148, 151, 152, 153, 220; fairy, 27–31, 32, 48, 85–86; fruiter, 120, 123; homosexual, 24, 25, 142–43, 152,

153; hustler, 79–80, 83, 84, 111; jocker, 25–26; lamb, 25, 26; mother, 120; prushun, 26; punk, 26, 27, 28, 29–30, 31–34, 35, 48, 74–77, 111, 220, 232n34, 245n69; queen, 80, 81, 120, 123, 258n82; queer, 120, 121; railroad queen, 42; sexual invert/inversion, 23–24, 141, 142, 147, 148, 152; sexual pervert, 82, 148, 149, 152; trade, 83, 120, 121, 123, 124; uranism, 152; wolf, 25–26

Shaw, Anna Howard, 171

Shartle, Jacob, 193

Shelley, Ida., 29

Shuck, C. E., 107

Sing, Bram, 55, 57, 212–13; photograph of, 56

Sing, Don, 55, 56, 57

Sing, Jago, 55, 57

Singh, Nar, 54–55

Skid Road vice district (Seattle), 62, 70, 80, 85, 241n38

Sklar, Martin J., 93

Sleeth, Dana, 267n12; attack on Young Men's Christian Association of Portland, 162, 163, 164; biography of, 159; and fear for Portland's boys, 195–96; 1912 Scandal and, 159–60, 161–62, 163, 164–68; photograph of, 160; response to E. S. J. McAllister, 178

Smith, Charles, 34, 43

Smith, Frank, 78

Smith, Harry, 72

Smith-Rosenberg, Carroll, 95

Social Darwinism, 50, 206

social hygiene movement, 189–190; breaking the conspiracy of silence by, 189; Progressivism and, 190; response to prostitution, 189–90; response to venereal diseases, 189–90; traditionalists and, 190

sodomy laws: in British Columbia, 203, 206; effects on working-class men, 205, 216; effects on racial minority men, 205, 216; in Idaho, 202, 205; in Montana, 202, 205, 206; oral sex and, 202, 203, 204–5; in Oregon, 203–6; strengthened during Progressive era, 202–6; in Washington state, 202–3, 205, 206

South (region of the US), 41

Southern Pacific Railroad, 177

Spokane, Wash., 57, 76, 163; 1912 scandal and, 147, 157

Spokane Press, 159

Stafford, Jack, 52, 61, 125

Start, Harry, 113, 121; appeal of, 139–41, 204, 217; conviction of overturned, 143; death of, 218; life after the 1912 scandal, 217–18; trial of, 139–41, 204

Start, Mary, 217–18

St. Clair, Virgil, 107

Steen, Peter, 148

Stein, Marc, 111

sterilization. See British Columbia eugenics movement; eugenics; Idaho eugenics movement; Oregon eugenics movement; Washington state eugenics movement

Steffens, Lincoln, 170

Stfe, George, 70

St. Helens, Oregon, 149–52; Greek immigrants in, 149–51

St. Helens Hotel (Portland), 75

St. Louis, Missouri, 153

Stockton, Calif., 218

Stone, Bruce, 112

Stone, Harry W., 163, 167, 174

St. Paul, Minn., 96, 181

Struble, George, 107

Studies in the Psychology of Sex (1897), 142–43

St. Vincent Hospital (Portland), 78

Sundstrom, William, 63

Syracuse University, 168

Tabb, Horace, 113, 122, 173

Tacoma, Wash., 53; 1912 scandal and, 136, 157

Tacoma Times, 159

Taft, William Howard, 175

Tassus, Thomas, 77

Taylor, Alfred, 128

Taylor, Earl, 109

Teall, George S., 167

Thoinot, Léon-Henri, 142, 143

Thornton, Burt, 101, 112

Tierney, Willian, 112

tramp, defined, 21, 230n15

transgendered females, 9, 82

transgendered males: limited numbers of in Northwest cities, 81–82, 83; on the road, 25, 30–31, 36; prostitution of, 81, 83; urban areas and, 80, 81, 82

transsexual males. on the road, 25, 30–31
Trout, Benjamin, 1, 89, 109, 110, 135, 136, 152, 217
Tucker, Ira, 78, 84
Twentieth-Century Way, 119

Ullman, Sharon, 119
Uncle Sam Hotel (Portland), 81
Union Pacific Railroad, 97
United States Department of Justice, and 1912 scandal, 186
United States government: concerns over homosexuality, 59, 185; 1912 scandal and, 185–86; Progressive moral reforms of, 188
United States Immigration Commission, 59, 185
United States Public Health and Marine Hospital Service, and 1912 scandal, 186
United States War Department, 188
University of Oregon, 175, 176
University of Virginia, 169
Upton, Robert J., 172
uranism, 152
U'Ren, William S., 170, 173, 174, 175, 176, 177, 178, 210

Vancouver, B.C., 51, 55, 67, 75, 77, 85, 112; Central Park, 55; Great Northern Hotel, 54; Hastings Street vice district, 85; middle-class homosexual subculture of, 7–8; 1912 scandal and, 1, 8, 105, 136, 157; Panama Hotel, 55; police entrapment for homosexuality in, 54, 55; prostitution (male) in, 77; racist campaign against Asian Indians in, 53–55, 62
Vancouver, Wash., 157
Van Hulen, Earl, 97, 100–101, 111, 112, 113, 122, 123
Verma, P. L., 55–56, 57
vice commissions, influences on moral laws, 190, 191. See also Portland Vice Commission (1911–1913)
Victoria, British Columbia, 22
Victorian morality, 189: conspiracy of silence, 189, 193, 195; double standard, 190, 192; homosexuality and, 193; replaced by modern sexual ethos, 192–93
Vilma, 30, 80, 85, 86

Virginia, 169
Vlassis, Chirst, 57, 76

W., Noel, 106–7, 117
Wallace, G. R., 201
Walla Walla, Wash., 32, 67, 96, 184; history of, 180; homosexual scandal of, 179–83; 1912 scandal and, 157, 158, 180–81; response to John Gibson, 182–83; Young Men's Christian Association of, 180–81
Walla Walla Bulletin, 180, 181, 182
Walla Walla Union, 180, 181,
Warner, Harold, 37
Washington (state), 7, 8, 18, 31, 42, 43, 44, 56, 194; Friend Program, 200–201, 206; regulation of heterosexuality, 191–92; regulation of discourse on homosexuality, 194; sodomy laws, 203–4, 205, 206. See also individual cities and counties
Washington eugenics movement: and 1909 law, 207, 215; and 1921 law, 215; Oregon's influence on, 207, 215; origins of, 207; Owens-Adair, Bethenia, and, 207
Washington, D.C., 53, 136, 185
Washington Street (Portland), 112–13, 115; photograph of, 113
Wedemeyer, Edwin E., 98, 100–101: appeal of, 139–41, 204; conviction overturned, 143; trial of, 139–41
Weeks, Jeffrey, 107
Weeks, Mark, 52, 125
Wenatchee, Wash., 33
Werlein, J. E., 166
West, Oswald, 168, 173; moral reforms of, 208; 1912 scandal and, 208–10; Oregon eugenics movement and, 208–9, 210; photograph, 209; views on homosexuals, 208–9
Whatcom County, Wash., 22
Wheeler, Roy Marion, 109
Wheeler-Motter (Boise), 97
White, Calvin, 198
White, Samuel D., 163
Whitechapel, as term for Northwest vice districts, 241n38. See also North End/Whitechapel vice district
White, Kevin, 93, 117
white slavery, 52, 59, 188; 1912 scandal and, 185

Whitman College, 180, 181
Wiebe, Robert, 190
Wight, Harry, 97, 100, 111, 112
Wilde, Oscar, 2, 89, 90, 194, 207; con-
    struction of homosexuality and,
    126–27, 132–33, 134, 138, 148; degener-
    ation and, 128–33, 137, 138; 1912 Scan-
    dal and, 137; Pacific Northwest media
    response to, 126, 128, 129–35, 137
Wiley, Margaret W., 169–70, 179
Wilkinson, Robert, 52, 61, 125
Willamette River, 57, 63, 67
Wilmington Academy, 168
Wilson, Woodrow, 175
Winant, Howard, 65
Wise, Jonah, 197
Wise, Steven, 171
Witham, Fred, 180
Withycombe, James, 211
wolf, 32, 33; defined, 25–26; sexuality of,
    25–26, 36
Wolfe, Robert, 107
wolf–lamb relationship, 25, 32
Women's Christian Temperance Union
    (Portland), 159
Wood, C. E. S., 174, 175, 176, 178, 199–200,
    210
Woodard, Clarke and Company (Portland),
    112
Woodward, Robert C., 176
Word, Tom, 52, 53
Work, Harry, 113, 115, 121; Viola as nick-
    name of, 121, 258–59n82
working class: animosities toward middle
    class, 106; characteristics of in Pa-
    cific Northwest, 18–19; entertain-
    ments of, 68; first sexual revolution
    and, 117, 118; lodging houses and,
    67–68; males as homosexual fantasy,
    107; oral sex and, 28, 37, 38, 84–85,
    117–18, 119–20; pervasiveness of ho-
    mosexuality among, 21–22, 40,
    41–42; transience of, 19–21, 41,
    42–43, 229n13, 230n14; urban spaces
    of, 47, 65–68; views on homosexual-
    ity, 24, 38–39

working-class/transient homosexual sub-
    culture, 3, 5–6, 7, 21–23, 24, 25–44,
    48–86; adult male relations in, 35–38;
    amusement parks and, 72; anal/inter-
    femoral sex and, 6, 28, 48, 83, 84, 85,
    117; and arrests (Portland), 48, 49–50,
    68–69; automobiles and, 43; early
    modern England and, 21; fairy and,
    27–28, 29–30, 31; jungles and, 42;
    lodging houses and, 72; mobility
    and, 41–43; modern gay community
    and, 85–86; movie theaters and,
    71–72; oral sex and, 28, 37, 38, 84–85,
    117–18; poolrooms, 69, 71–72; rail-
    roads and, 42–43; role of youths in,
    4, 5, 17, 22, 25–27, 28, 29, 33–34, 35, 47,
    73–85, 220; rural areas and, 5–6, 15–16,
    17, 21–44; sailing vessels and, 30–31,
    36–37, 43; saloons and, 69–71; trans-
    genderism/transexuality and, 25; ur-
    ban areas and, 5, 6, 47–86; visibility
    of, 221
World War I, 17, 50, 51, 81, 106, 150, 151,
    152, 188, 190, 191, 220
World War II, 218, 219

Yat-sen, Sun, 217
yegg: defined, 21; sexual views of, 29–30
Young Men's Christian Association, 101;
    and homosexuality, 102–3
Young Men's Christian Association of
    Portland, 60, 194, 196, 197; construc-
    tion of homosexuality and, 102–3; de-
    fends itself during 1912 scandal, 163,
    164; effects of 1912 scandal on, 167;
    history of, 162–63; location of, 112; as
    male residence, 101–2; pictured, 102;
    Oregon Social Hygiene Society and,
    276n26; role in 1912 scandal, 1–2, 89,
    102, 162–67; support for during 1912
    scandal, 164–66; white-collar workers
    and, 101–2, 103; Young Men's Chris-
    tian Association of Walla Walla,
    Wash., 180–81

Zobel, Alfred J., 59, 61

Compositor: Impressions Book and Journal Services, Inc.
Text: Galliard
Display: Galliard
Printer and binder: Edwards Brothers